Deep Learning for Sustainable Agriculture

Cognitive Data Science in Sustainable Computing

Deep Learning for Sustainable Agriculture

Edited by

Ramesh Chandra Poonia
Department of Computer Science CHRIST (Deemed to be University),
Bangalore, India

Vijander Singh
Department of Computer Science and Engineering, Manipal University
Jaipur, Jaipur, India

Soumya Ranjan Nayak
Amity School of Engineering and Technology, Amity University
Uttar Pradesh, Noida, India

Series Editor

Arun Kumar Sangaiah
School of Computing Science and Engineering, Vellore Institute of
Technology (VIT), Vellore, India

ACADEMIC PRESS
An imprint of Elsevier

ELSEVIER

Academic Press is an imprint of Elsevier
125 London Wall, London EC2Y 5AS, United Kingdom
525 B Street, Suite 1650, San Diego, CA 92101, United States
50 Hampshire Street, 5th Floor, Cambridge, MA 02139, United States
The Boulevard, Langford Lane, Kidlington, Oxford OX5 1GB, United Kingdom

Notices
Knowledge and best practice in this field are constantly changing. As new research and experience broaden our understanding, changes in research methods, professional practices, or medical treatment may become necessary.

Practitioners and researchers must always rely on their own experience and knowledge in evaluating and using any information, methods, compounds, or experiments described herein. In using such information or methods they should be mindful of their own safety and the safety of others, including parties for whom they have a professional responsibility.

To the fullest extent of the law, neither the Publisher nor the authors, contributors, or editors, assume any liability for any injury and/or damage to persons or property as a matter of products liability, negligence or otherwise, or from any use or operation of any methods, products, instructions, or ideas contained in the material herein.

Library of Congress Cataloging-in-Publication Data
A catalog record for this book is available from the Library of Congress

British Library Cataloguing-in-Publication Data
A catalogue record for this book is available from the British Library

ISBN: 978-0-323-85214-2

For information on all Academic Press publications
visit our website at https://www.elsevier.com/books-and-journals

Publisher: Mara Conner
Editorial Project Manager: Michelle Fisher
Production Project Manager: Punithavathy Govindaradjane
Cover Designer: Mark Rogers

Typeset by STRAIVE, India

Working together
to grow libraries in
developing countries

www.elsevier.com • www.bookaid.org

Contents

Contributors   xiii

1. Smart agriculture: Technological advancements on
    agriculture—A systematical review
    Chanki Pandey, Prabira Kumar Sethy,
    Santi Kumari Behera, Jaya Vishwakarma,
    and Vishal Tande

    1   Introduction   1
    2   Methodology   4
    3   Role of image processing in agriculture   5
        3.1   Plant disease identification   5
        3.2   Fruit sorting and classification   6
        3.3   Plant species identification   7
        3.4   Precision farming   7
        3.5   Fruit quality analysis   8
        3.6   Crop and land assessment   8
        3.7   Weed recognition   8
    4   Role of Machine Learning in Agriculture   9
        4.1   Yield prediction   13
        4.2   Disease detection   14
        4.3   Weed recognition   15
        4.4   Crop quality   15
        4.5   Species recognition   15
        4.6   Soil management   16
    5   Role of deep learning in agriculture   16
        5.1   Leaf disease detection   16
        5.2   Plant disease detection   21
        5.3   Land cover classification   22
        5.4   Crop type classification   22
        5.5   Plant recognition   22
        5.6   Segmentation of root and soil   23
        5.7   Crop yield estimation   23
        5.8   Fruit counting   23
        5.9   Obstacle detection   24
        5.10 Identification of weeds   24
        5.11 Prediction of soil moisture   25
        5.12 Cattle race classification   25

6   **Role of IoT in agriculture**   25
   6.1   Climate condition monitoring   30
   6.2   Crop yield   30
   6.3   Soil patter   30
   6.4   Pest and crop disease monitoring   30
   6.5   Irrigation monitoring system   31
   6.6   Optimum time for plant and harvesting   31
   6.7   Tracking and tracing   31
   6.8   Farm management system   32
   6.9   Agricultural drone   32
7   **Role of wireless sensor networks in agriculture**   32
   7.1   Irrigation management   35
   7.2   Soil moisture prediction   35
   7.3   Precision farming   35
   7.4   Climate condition monitoring   36
8   **Role of data mining in agriculture**   36
   8.1   Irrigation management   39
   8.2   Prediction and detection of plant diseases   39
   8.3   Pest monitoring   40
   8.4   Optimum management of inputs (fertilizer and pesticides)   40
   8.5   Crop yield prediction   41
   8.6   Climate condition monitoring   42
9   **Conclusion**   42
   References   47

2.   A systematic review of artificial intelligence in agriculture

Parvinder Singh and Amandeep Kaur

1   **Precision farming**   57
   1.1   Introduction   57
   1.2   Related work using AI   59
   1.3   Objective and design consideration   61
   1.4   Challenges and future scope   63
2   **Plant disease detection**   65
   2.1   Introduction   65
   2.2   Deep learning in image processing   67
   2.3   Review of plant disease detection using image processing and deep learning   69
   2.4   Performance analysis of some state-of-art techniques   70
   2.5   Research gaps and future scope   70
3   **Soil health monitoring using AI**   73
   3.1   Introduction   73
   3.2   Brief history   73

3.3 Opportunity of AI in soil health monitoring   74
3.4 Current status   74
4 Scope and challenges of AI in agriculture   74
5 Conclusions   75
   References   75

3. Introduction to deep learning in precision agriculture: Farm image feature detection using unmanned aerial vehicles through classification and optimization process of machine learning with convolution neural network
Halimatu Sadiyah Abdullahi and Ray E. Sheriff

1 Introduction   81
2 Deep learning overview   84
3 CNN training   87
   3.1 CNN in agricultural applications   87
4 Methodology   88
   4.1 Data collection and processing   88
   4.2 UAV specification   89
   4.3 Image processing and labeling   90
5 Experiment and results   97
   5.1 Binary classification   97
   5.2 Multiclass classification   99
6 Discussion   101
   6.1 Advantages of the developed model   103
7 Conclusion   103
   References   104

4. Design and implementation of a crop recommendation system using nature-inspired intelligence for Rajasthan, India
Lavika Goel, Akshina Jindal, and Shray Mathur

1 Introduction   109
2 Literature survey   110
3 Proposed methodology   111
   3.1 Preprocessing layer   111
   3.2 Feature extraction   111
   3.3 Optimization layer   113
   3.4 Softmax classification layer   121
4 Results   122
5 Conclusion and future work   126
   References   127
   Further reading   127

5. **Artificial intelligent-based water and soil management**
    Ahmed Elbeltagi, Nand Lal Kushwaha, Ankur Srivastava, and Amira Talaat Zoof

    1   Introduction   129
    2   Applications of artificial intelligence in water management   130
        2.1   Evapotranspiration estimation   130
        2.2   Crop water content prediction   132
        2.3   Water footprint modeling   132
        2.4   Groundwater simulation   132
        2.5   Pan evaporation estimation   134
    3   Applications of artificial intelligence in soil management   135
        3.1   Soil water content determination   136
        3.2   Soil temperature monitoring   136
        3.3   Soil fertilizer estimation   137
        3.4   Soil mapping   137
    4   Conclusion and recommendations for water-soil management   138
        References   138

6. **Machine learning for soil moisture assessment**
    Alka Rani, Nirmal Kumar, Jitendra Kumar, Jitendra Kumar, and Nishant K. Sinha

    1   Introduction   143
    2   Overview of machine learning   145
    3   Machine learning algorithms applied in soil moisture research   146
        3.1   Linear regression   146
        3.2   Artificial neural network/deep neural network   147
        3.3   Support vector machine   148
        3.4   Classification and regression tree   149
        3.5   Random forest   150
        3.6   Extremely randomized trees   150
    4   Applications of machine learning for soil moisture assessment   151
        4.1   Pedotransfer functions   151
        4.2   Prediction models for soil moisture estimation/forecasting   152
        4.3   Soil moisture retrieval through remote sensing   153
        4.4   Irrigation scheduling   156
        4.5   Downscaling of satellite-derived soil moisture products   157
    5   Conclusions   159
        Abbreviations   162
        References   163

7. **Automated real-time forecasting of agriculture using chlorophyll content and its impact on climate change**
   K. Sujatha, R.S. Ponmagal, K. Senthil Kumar, Rajeswary Hari, A. Kalaivani, K. Thivya, and M. Anand

1	Introduction	169
2	Current status	172
	2.1 National Status	174
	2.2 International status	175
3	Problem statement	175
4	Objective of the proposed work	176
5	Research highlights	177
6	Scientific significance of the proposed work	177
7	Materials and methods	178
	7.1 Histogram of oriented gradients	178
	7.2 Principal component analysis	179
	7.3 Backpropagation algorithm	179
8	Detailed work plan to achieve the objectives	181
	8.1 Methodology	182
9	Results and discussion	183
10	Conclusion	188
	References	196

8. **Transformations of urban agroecology landscape in territory transition**
   José G. Vargas-Hernández

1	Introduction	199
2	Agroecological landscapes	200
3	Agroecological practices	201
4	Agroecological territorial transformation and transition	207
5	Conclusion	214
	References	215

9. **WeedNet: A deep neural net for weed identification**
   Shashi Prakash Tripathi, Rahul Kumar Yadav, and Harshita Rai

1	Introduction	223
2	Related work	225
3	WeedNet	226
	3.1 Model architecture	226
	3.2 Complexity analysis	228
4	Evaluation strategy	229
	4.1 Performance metrics	229
	4.2 Data set	231

5   Experimental setup   231
6   Experimental evaluation   231
7   Conclusion   231
    References   234

10. Sensors make sense: Functional genomics, deep
    learning, and agriculture
    *Ross McDougal Henderson, Claudia Rossi, and
    Michelle Burgess*

1   Introduction   237
2   Section I. Functional genomics   239
    2.1   The emerging applications of soil microbial
          metabolites   239
    2.2   Agricultural-based metabolites to advance nutraceutical
          production and drug discovery   240
    2.3   Marine microalgae, aquaculture, and the DL toolbox
          Ludwig   244
    2.4   Pollinators, Ludwig combiners, and the carbon-energy
          cycle   255
3   Section II. DAS networks   259
    3.1   Agricultural factors in the plant-silicon cycle: Genomic
          regulation of blight, drought, and invasive species   259
    3.2   Helically wound DAS   260
4   Section III. GRANITE and the agent-based GRANITE Network
    Discovery Tool   267
5   Conclusions   270
    Acknowledgments   270
    References   270

11. Crop management: Wheat yield prediction and
    disease detection using an intelligent predictive
    algorithms and metrological parameters
    Nandini Babbar, Ashish Kumar, and Vivek Kumar Verma

1   Introduction   273
2   Literature review   276
    2.1   Wheat yield prediction   276
    2.2   Wheat diseases detection   285
3   Discussion   290
4   Conclusion and future scope   290
    References   292

Contents **xi**

12. **Sugarcane leaf disease detection through deep learning**
N.K. Hemalatha, R.N. Brunda, G.S. Prakruthi,
B.V. Balaji Prabhu, Arpit Shukla, and
Omkar Subbaram Jois Narasipura

1	Introduction	297
2	Methodology	299
	2.1 Dataset	299
	2.2 Leaf disease detection system architecture	300
	2.3 Leaf disease detection model architecture	301
	2.4 SAFAL-FASAL android application	303
	2.5 Method of evaluation	304
3	Experimentation	305
4	Results and discussion	308
	4.1 Performance evaluation	318
	4.2 SAFAL-FASAL Android application results	318
5	Conclusion	322
	References	322

13. **Prediction of paddy cultivation using deep learning on land cover variation for sustainable agriculture**
D.A. Meedeniya, I. Mahakalanda, D.S. Lenadora, I. Perera,
S.G.S. Hewawalpita, C. Abeysinghe, and Soumya
Ranjan Nayak

1	Introduction	325
2	Applications of geospatial analytics for agriculture	327
	2.1 Importance of remote sensing to estimate paddy area	327
	2.2 Related studies based on satellite imaginary	328
	2.3 Related studies based on the Internet of Things	330
	2.4 Related studies with integrated data	330
	2.5 Dataset associated with land-use land-cover data	331
	2.6 Comparison of related studies with satellite imagery and deep learning	331
3	Material analysis	334
	3.1 Data source	334
	3.2 Analysis of raster data	335
4	System model design and implementation	337
	4.1 Process view	337
	4.2 Data preprocessing and feature selection	337
	4.3 Transfer learning process	340

5 System evaluation   341
   5.1 Model evaluation   341
   5.2 Ground truth measurement   341
   5.3 Model prediction comparison for contextual analysis 343
6 Discussion   348
   6.1 Contribution of the proposed study   348
   6.2 Limitations of the datasets   349
   6.3 Future research directions   350
7 Conclusions   351
   References   352

14. Artificial intelligence-based detection and counting of olive fruit flies: A comprehensive survey

Nariman Mamdouh, Mohamed Wael, and Ahmed Khattab

1 Introduction   357
2 Literature survey of recognition systems   359
   2.1 Manual detection and counting   360
   2.2 Semiautomatic detection and counting   361
   2.3 Automatic detection and counting   363
3 Evaluation and discussions   373
   3.1 Semiautomatic detection   373
   3.2 Image-based automatic detection   374
   3.3 Nonimage-based automatic detection   377
4 Conclusions   378
   Acknowledgments   378
   References   378

Index   381

Contributors

Numbers in parenthesis indicate the pages on which the authors' contributions begin.

Halimatu Sadiyah Abdullahi (81), Faculty of Engineering & Informatics, University of Bradford, Bradford, United Kingdom

C. Abeysinghe (325), University of Moratuwa, Moratuwa, Sri Lanka

M. Anand (169), Department of Electronics and Communication Engineering, Dr. MGR Educational and Research Institute, Chennai, Tamil Nadu, India

Nandini Babbar (273), Department of Computer Science & Engineering, Manipal University Jaipur, Jaipur, Rajasthan, India

Santi Kumari Behera (1), Department of Computer Science and Engineering, VSSUT, Odisha, India

R.N. Brunda (297), Dr. Ambedkar Institute of Technology, Bangalore, Karnataka, India

Michelle Burgess (237), CAREM, LLC, Falls Church, VA, United States

Ahmed Elbeltagi (129), Agricultural Engineering Department, Faculty of Agriculture, Mansoura University, Mansoura, Egypt

Lavika Goel (109), Department of Computer Science and Engineering, Malaviya National Institute of Technology (MNIT), Jaipur, Rajasthan, India

Rajeswary Hari (169), Department of Bio-Technology, Dr. MGR Educational and Research Institute, Chennai, Tamil Nadu, India

N.K. Hemalatha (297), Dr. Ambedkar Institute of Technology, Bangalore, Karnataka, India

Ross McDougal Henderson (237), CAREM, LLC, Falls Church, VA, United States

S.G.S. Hewawalpita (325), University of Moratuwa, Moratuwa, Sri Lanka

Akshina Jindal (109), Department of Computer Science and Information Systems, Birla Institute of Technology and Science, Pilani, Rajasthan, India

A. Kalaivani (169), Department of Computer Science Engineering, Saveetha School of Engineering, Saveetha Institute of Medical and Technical Sciences, Chennai, Tamil Nadu, India

Amandeep Kaur (57), Department of Computer Science and Technology, Central University of Punjab, Bathinda, Punjab, India

Ahmed Khattab (357), Electronics and Electrical Communications Engineering Department, Cairo University, Giza, Egypt

Ashish Kumar (273), Department of Computer Science & Engineering, Manipal University Jaipur, Jaipur, Rajasthan, India

Jitendra Kumar (143), ICAR-Vivekananda Parvatiya Krishi Anusandhan Sansthan, Almora, Uttarakhand, India

Jitendra Kumar (143), ICAR-Indian Institute of Soil Science, Nabibagh, Bhopal, Madhya Pradesh, India

K. Senthil Kumar (169), Department of Electronics and Communication Engineering, Dr. MGR Educational and Research Institute, Chennai, Tamil Nadu, India

Nirmal Kumar (143), ICAR-National Bureau of Soil Survey and Land Use Planning, Nagpur, Maharashtra, India

Nand Lal Kushwaha (129), Division of Agricultural Engineering, ICAR-Indian Agricultural Research Institute, New Delhi, India

D.S. Lenadora (325), University of Moratuwa, Moratuwa, Sri Lanka

I. Mahakalanda (325), University of Moratuwa, Moratuwa, Sri Lanka

Nariman Mamdouh (357), Electronics and Electrical Communications Engineering Department, Cairo University, Giza, Egypt

Shray Mathur (109), Department of Computer Science and Information Systems, Birla Institute of Technology and Science, Pilani, Rajasthan, India

D.A. Meedeniya (325), University of Moratuwa, Moratuwa, Sri Lanka

Omkar Subbaram Jois Narasipura (297), Indian Institute of Science, Bangalore, Karnataka, India

Soumya Ranjan Nayak (325), Amity School of Engineering and Technology, Amity University Uttar Pradesh, Noida, India

Chanki Pandey (1), Department of Electronics and Telecommunication Engineering, Government Engineering College, Jagdalpur, Chhattisgarh, India

I. Perera (325), University of Moratuwa, Moratuwa, Sri Lanka

R.S. Ponmagal (169), Department of Computer Science Engineering, SRM Institute of Science and Technology, Chennai, Tamil Nadu, India

B.V. Balaji Prabhu (297), Malnad College of Engineering, Hassan; Indian Institute of Science, Bangalore, Karnataka, India

G.S. Prakruthi (297), Dr. Ambedkar Institute of Technology, Bangalore, Karnataka, India

Harshita Rai (223), Analytics and Insights Unit, Tata Consultancy Services, Pune, Maharashtra, India

Alka Rani (143), ICAR-Indian Institute of Soil Science, Nabibagh, Bhopal, Madhya Pradesh, India

Claudia Rossi (237), CAREM, LLC, Falls Church, VA, United States

Prabira Kumar Sethy (1), Department of Electronics, Sambalpur University, Odisha, India

Ray E. Sheriff (81), School of Engineering, University of Bolton, Bolton, United Kingdom

Arpit Shukla (297), National Institute of Technology Srinagar, Srinagar, Jammu and Kashmir, India

Parvinder Singh (57), Department of Computer Science and Technology, Central University of Punjab, Bathinda, Punjab, India

Nishant K. Sinha (143), ICAR-Indian Institute of Soil Science, Nabibagh, Bhopal, Madhya Pradesh, India

Ankur Srivastava (129), School of Engineering, The University of Newcastle, Callaghan, NSW, Australia

K. Sujatha (169), Department of Electrical and Electronics Engineering, Dr. MGR Educational and Research Institute, Chennai, Tamil Nadu, India

Vishal Tande (1), Department of Electronics and Telecommunication Engineering, Government Engineering College, Jagdalpur, Chhattisgarh, India

K. Thivya (169), Department of Electronics and Communication Engineering, Dr. MGR Educational and Research Institute, Chennai, Tamil Nadu, India

Shashi Prakash Tripathi (223), Analytics and Insights Unit, Tata Consultancy Services, Pune, Maharashtra, India

José G. Vargas-Hernández (199), University Center for Economic and Managerial Sciences, University of Guadalajara, Zapopan, Jalisco, Mexico

Vivek Kumar Verma (273), Department of Information Technology, Manipal University Jaipur, Jaipur, Rajasthan, India

Jaya Vishwakarma (1), Department of Electronics and Telecommunication Engineering, Government Engineering College, Jagdalpur, Chhattisgarh, India

Mohamed Wael (357), Electronics and Electrical Communications Engineering Department, Cairo University, Giza, Egypt

Rahul Kumar Yadav (223), Analytics and Insights Unit, Tata Consultancy Services, Pune, Maharashtra, India

Amira Talaat Zoof (129), Civil Engineering Department, Faculty of Engineering, Mansoura University, Mansoura, Egypt

Chapter 1

Smart agriculture: Technological advancements on agriculture — A systematical review

Chanki Pandey[a], Prabira Kumar Sethy[b], Santi Kumari Behera[c], Jaya Vishwakarma[a], and Vishal Tande[a]

[a]Department of Electronics and Telecommunication Engineering, Government Engineering College, Jagdalpur, Chhattisgarh, India, [b]Department of Electronics, Sambalpur University, Odisha, India, [c]Department of Computer Science and Engineering, VSSUT, Odisha, India

1 Introduction

Agriculture is an important sector of the world economy and a strong foundation for human life; it is the largest source of food grains and other raw materials. Agriculture plays a dynamic role in the growth of a country's economy. It is the primary source of income and very helpful for the development of the economic condition of the country (Abate et al., 2018). Traditionally, most diseases were not diagnosed by farmers because of lack of knowledge and unavailability of a local expert. The most basic requirements for the advancement in agriculture are integration of internet technologies and future-oriented technologies for use as a smart object (Keller et al., 2014; Lasi et al., 2014; Liao et al., 2017; Maynard, 2015; Pivoto et al., 2018). Further, data-driven agricultural management can be used to meet the production challenges. Data management is required to analyze the data/information for better production. This approach defines how robots will play a vital role in the evolution of farming (Saiz-Rubio & Rovira-Más, 2020). The growth of technologies is an excellent initiative toward the development of the agriculture sector (Kapur, 2018; Lytos et al., 2020; Rehman & Hussain, 2016). Smart farming concepts, such as precision agriculture and land management, scientific data, such as earth observation and climate science, and cutting-edge technologies, such as image processing, geographic information systems (GIS), and unmanned aerial vehicles (UAVs), would improve agricultural production. Digital agriculture using information and communication technologies provide crop and market information to the farmer (Costa et al., 2011). GeoFarmer is a type of monitoring and feedback

Deep Learning for Sustainable Agriculture. https://doi.org/10.1016/B978-0-323-85214-2.00002-1

1

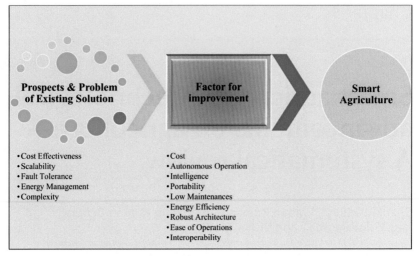

FIG. 1 The transformation from traditional to smart agriculture.

system for agricultural development projects. Farmers can manage their crops and farms better if they can communicate their experiences, both positive and negative, with each other and with experts (Eitzinger et al., 2019). Traditional agricultural farming can be smart agriculture by making suitable improvement in the existing solution, as shown in Fig. 1.

Unluckily farmers still far away from modern technologies and still relying on traditional methods of farming and food supply techniques have low productivity, and countries are producing yields much below their potential (Kumar & Ilango, 2018). To overcome these problems and bring revolution in the agriculture sector, modern technologies can play a vital role and can resolve these problems (Timalsina, 2019). There are various data-driven and data analysis techniques that makes agriculture smart, as illustrated in Fig. 2. The application of these techniques in specific aspects, like data analysis, prediction, estimation, and monitoring, are shown in Fig. 3.

The main objective for preparing the survey discussed in this chapter was to help researchers, farmers, nongovernmental organizations (NGOs), and everyone who associated with the agriculture domain. In this survey, we reviewed about 170 papers that suggested different technological advancements to make agriculture easy, productive, and smart.

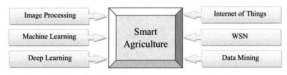

FIG. 2 Technologies used in agriculture.

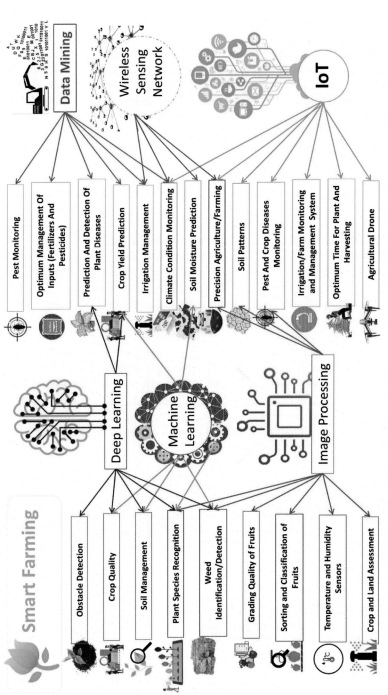

FIG. 3 Application of technologies in agriculture domain.

The chapter begins with a brief description of technological advancements and their applications in the agriculture sector. The chapter then goes on to describe methodology, image processing, machine learning (ML), deep learning (DL), the internet of things (IoT), wireless sensor networks (WSNs), and data mining (DM) application for the advancement of farming and improvements in agriculture. Finally, the chapter presents the conclusions of the survey.

2 Methodology

The literature within the agricultural domain was analyzed in order to develop this chapter. Initially, a keyword-based search forconference papers or journal articles was performed from the scientific databases ScienceDirect and IEEE Xplore and from the scientific indexing services Web of Science and Google Scholar. The methodology used for doing this survey is show in Fig. 4.

The search terms we used to collect the desired research papers and filter out research papers irrelevant to agriculture were: {Image Processing + Agriculture}, {Image Processing + Farming}, {Machine Learning + Agriculture}, {Machine Learning + Farming}, {Deep Learning + Agriculture}, {Deep Learning + Farming}, {IoT + Agriculture}, {IoT + Farming}, {Wireless Sensor Network + Agriculture}, {Wireless Sensor Network + Farming}, {Data Mining + Agriculture}, and {Data Mining + Farming}. Doing so, we downloaded almost 300 papers, including papers from IEEE Xplore, ScienceDirect, Web of Science, and other sources. After downloading the articles, we screened out the duplicates and separated out almost 234 papers for further consideration. For further scanning and filtering, we performed a full text reading and obtained a final set of 170 papers for the articulation of the survey, which involves 19 papers of image processing, 13 of ML, 33 of DL, 14 of WSN, 23 of IoT, 31 of DM, and 37 (papers + Web Source) of agriculture and farming. The statistical information about the technological advancement in agriculture is shown in Fig. 5.

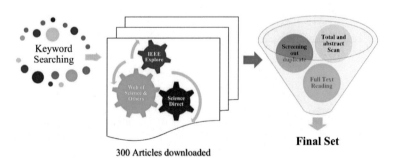

FIG. 4 Flow for obtaining final set for writing review.

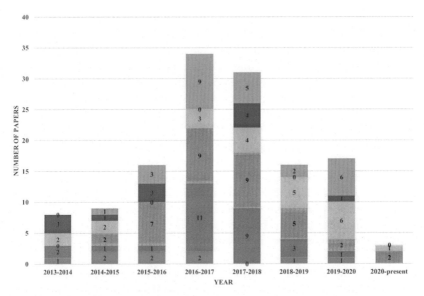

FIG. 5   Number of papers published from 2015 to 2020 on technological advancements in agriculture.

3   Role of image processing in agriculture

Image processing in agriculture is a huge step toward the modernization of agriculture. Image processing is a method used to operate an image to get an enhanced image or extract useful information from it. Image processing is a proven, effective process in the agriculture domain to increase the production rate and sustain agricultural demands throughout the world. Image processing with different spectral measurements, such as infrared and hyperspectral X-ray (Feng et al., 2018) imaging, is helpful in identifying crop diseases, weeds, and land mapping, which can help farmers by decreasing labor cost and time. Identifying crop diseases will help farmers tackle infections and prevent them from spreading to the total yield. Imparting image-processing techniques in modern agriculture will uplift the agricultural production to sustain the market demands and provide timely information to farmers through various automated applications in agriculture. The following subsection describes and analyzes the different specific applications of image processing in agriculture.

3.1   Plant disease identification

Image processing is widely used for the identification of plant diseases in various agriculture crops. Farmers face major threats due to the emergence of various pests and diseases in the crops. Fungi, bacteria, viruses, and nematodes are some of the common reasons for disease infections. Traditionally, most diseases were not diagnosed or suspected by farmers, as they lacked knowledge about crop diseases and required support and suggestions from specialists. However, the diagnosis of infections in their early stages can mitigate crop damage. For identification of plant diseases, image processing plays an important role as the detection and identification of diseases is only done through visual information. A neural network-based methodology is suggested for disease detection and classification (Jhuria et al., 2013). The diagnostic approach is proposed to identify the disease under an intelligent system. The work is carried out on apple and grape plants. The system used two different databases. The authors defined a work on classification and mapping of disease based on color, texture, and morphology. The authors obtained better results, and grading was done. The grade will help farmers determine the requirement of insecticide to be applied. Other researchers (Chahal & Anuradha, 2015) defined a framework for plant disease classification and recognition of plant and leaf disease. The authors also proposed a broad model to perform image processing. The study on some of the effective classification approaches, including support vector machines (SVMs), neural networks, k-means, and principal component analysis (PCA), were also discussed. Some researchers (Tewari et al., 2020) worked on a variable rate chemical spraying system considering the image processing technique. The main motive of the work was to identify diseases on paddy crops. The chromatic aberration-based image segment method was used to detect the diseased region of paddy plants. The author developed a prototype with a diagnostic approach for variable rate application, which uses less chemical. This method is beneficial for the environment and the economy.

3.2 Fruit sorting and classification

Varieties of fruits are distributed in markets for consumption as day-to-day activity increased demand from consumers. These fruits received from the market are sorted out manually, which is a biased, time-consuming, and tiresome process as large quantities of fruits must be sorted out in a short time (Butz et al., 2006). Researchers (Surya & Satheesh, 2014) developed a technology in which image processing combined with other techniques can be used as expert advice to enhance production. The proposed model classifies and illustrates the application of image processing in agriculture and presented an approach for further study in image processing. These methods are supportive in the development of the automation model and in obtaining higher accuracy of information. Automatic sorting and classification of fruits is a postharvest process where the application of image processing is introduced for automation. This method is more advantageous than human labor with more accuracy, reliability, speed, and consistency. The industrial sector is benefited by the automated sorting of fruits and vegetables by applying this nondestructive method of classification (Bogue, 2016). Fruits with different size, color, shape, and texture can be easily identified and separated. Damaged fruits and vegetables can also be easily identified and removed. This automation helps the industries, supermarket stores, and other wholesale fruit stores to sort the fruits in a shorter period with high accuracy.

3.3   Plant species identification

Plant species identification is also an important application useful for botanist, researchers, and even the common man. Content-based image retrieval is used in the species identification from the collection of species images. Plants are identified by their morphological characteristics like texture, size, shape, and color of leaves and flowers. The support of a trained and experienced botanists is needed for species recognition. To conquer this issue, information technology, such as real-time image capturing devices, can be deployed. Feature extraction and image analysis are a vital parts of plant species identification from the collection of species images. Researchers (Farmer & Jain, 2005) suggest that shape analysis on leaves can be done based on the leaf boundary. There are two basic approaches to leaf analysis: region-based and boundary-based. Boundary signatures can be applied over the boundary regions of the leaf to identify the plant species (Femat-Diaz et al., 2011). Other features, such as are color and texture of leaves, are taken into consideration for classification. The accuracy of results can be greater when the color feature is combined along with the shape feature.

3.4   Precision farming

Development in information technology and agriculture science has made it possible to merge these two sectors, leading to the rise of precision farming. This can assist farmers in making better decisions regarding optimal crop production. It involves proper understanding and efficient use of natural resources found within the field. It gives maximum profit and production with minimum input and optimal use of the resource. Farmers need preacquired knowledge about technology and their workings. Proper training is required for farmers to acquire information about precision agriculture. The global positioning system (GPS) and GIS are the technologies used in agriculture equipment in precision agriculture. GIS is used to identify all available data, and GPS supports in identifying the object position on the globe using satellite signals. Remotely acquired images through satellites can be accessed and analyzed in their digital form. The advancement in image processing techniques has made remote sensing, along with GIS, progress independently. For better precision farming, an integrated system is used that consists of combining the remote sensing devices and image processing software package.

3.5   Fruit quality analysis

Consumer awareness and demand for qualitative products in the market has demanded the development of an automation system for quality assessment. This insists on the inspection of fruit quality to have qualitative fruits in the market. Fruit quality is analyzed by characteristics like color, shape, flavor, texture, and size (Freixenet et al., 2002). This computer vision task involves activities like image acquisition, processing, and interpretation for analysis. Extracting the fruit region became a necessary step for analyzing the major characteristics to determine the fruit quality from the background. The fruits are graded into different categories based on quality. Different patterns and classifiers are used for grading. Color, size, texture, and shape are considered some of the important features for grading (Mendoza & Aguilera, 2004). Manual inspection is time-consuming, biased, and prone to errors. To overcome these issues, a nondestructive quality assessment method developed, in contrast to certain destructive assessment methods, could determine the fruit quality with higher accuracy and speed. Nowadays, in many industries, these computer vision-based automated quality assessment tools replace traditional manual inspection (Gao et al., 2010). Classifiers like neural network, SVMs, Bayesian decision theory, k-nearest neighbors (KNN), and PCA are used to grade the quality of fruits (Mans et al., 2010). Decisions of the automated system in the quality assessment are proved to be effective and supportive for numerous food industries. For quality estimation, color, shape, and size are the primary parameters to be considered (Moreda et al., 2012; Prabha & Kumar, 2013). Some research (DePalma et al., 2019) offers essential knowledge and a way of producing pea-based, tofu-free soybeans.

3.6   Crop and land assessment

Remote sensing is one of the important data sources used in GIS for accessing data acquired through satellites. The factor considered important in remote sensing is reflectance of visible light energy from an external source. The external source of energy for passive systems is the sun. Information gathered through satellites has been increased through the use of image sensors. Remotely acquired images through satellites can be accessed and analyzed in their digital form. Advancement in image processing techniques like image enhancement, restoration, and analysis have made remote sensing progress independently in advance of GIS. The main aim of remote sensing is to monitor the Earth's surface and thereby measure geographical, biological, and physical variables to identify the materials on the land cover for further analysis.

3.7   Weed recognition

Weeds are a threat to farmers in that they reduce crop production and quality. Hence, more attention is needed to monitor weeds. The use of herbicide is one of the standard method used to control the growth of weeds. With the latest innovations, weed recognition is automated such that the system automatically distinguishes weeds from crops. The automated system monitors weed growth regularly and decides the time of weed control. Classifiers, along with image-processing methods, make it an easier job to identify weeds and destroy them in their earlier stages (Lamb & Brown, 2001). Researchers (Vibhute & Bodhe, 2012) proposed image processing for analyzing agricultural parameters and describing how image processing on different spectrums, such as infrared and hyperspectral X-ray, can be useful in determining the vegetation indices, canopy measurement, irrigated land mapping, and more. The authors define a work on image porosity with algorithms that can be used for surveying and weed classification. The classification accuracy can be obtained up to 96% with correct imaging techniques and algorithms. Researchers (Poojith et al., 2014) considered image processing to identify weeds in the field. In the proposed model, the images are captured and processed using MATLAB to identify the weed areas in the field. A defined algorithm approach can also identify and spray weedicide on the weeds. For two different types of weeds, the threshold value should be selected carefully.

By adopting this methodology, the usage of weedicides can be reduced, thus saving the environment. The wide-ranging variety of applications on the subject of counting objects in digital images makes it difficult for someone to prospect all possible useful ideas. One article (Pandurng, 2015) defined a work surveying the application of image processing in the agriculture field, such as imaging techniques for crop management. Researchers (Prakash et al., 2017) implemented image processing using MATLAB to detect the weed areas in images that are taken from the fields, which can cause potential solutions for problematic issues to be missed. Again, for the detection and classification of crops and weeds, one study (Bosilj et al., 2018) suggested a method based on SVM with the support of morphology of attributes that classify the detected regions into three classes, namely weed, crop, and mixed. The study's result showed effective and completive classification rates. The proposed method was implemented and evaluated on sugar beets and onions.

Table 1 shows the most popular methods and models based on image processing in smart agriculture.

4   Role of Machine Learning in Agriculture

ML is a promising technology in modern farming. With the help of robots, ML can be used for spraying pesticides, fertilizers, and other chemicals in agricultural fields. The combination of ML and IoT makes it possible to monitor the status of a farm and estimate the exact damage severity. This would decrease the use of fertilizers by 70% by targeting only the effective areas. That will be beneficial for the economy and the environment. These applications of ML would decrease agricultural waste by 60%, which will help reduce the carbon footprint

TABLE 1 Summary of role of image processing in agriculture.

Application goals and scenarios	Author and year	Method adopted	Results obtained	Advantages and disadvantages
Classification and mapping of disease on fruits	Jhuria et al. (2013)	Neural network-based work implemented using MATLAB	Obtained better results and grading has been done.	The grade help farmers determine the required insecticide to be applied
Plant disease classification and recognition	Chahal and Anuradha (2015)	The recognition model with a broader view	An excellent result was achieved	Ability to work in a variety of crops and environments
Identification of diseased crop	Tewari et al. (2020)	Chromatic aberration-based image segment method	The field testing results showed a minimum 33.88% reduction in applied chemicals	This is beneficial for the environment and the economy
Supportive in the development of the automation model	Surya and Satheesh (2014)	Image enhancement and image segmentation method are inevitable methods in varied applications.	Higher accuracy in the higher-level process for decision-making	Higher accuracy of information
Automatic sorting and classification	Bogue (2016)	Nondestructive method of classification	More accuracy, reliability, speed, and consistency	Sorting of the fruits in a shorter time with high accuracy
The detection and classification of crops and weeds	Bosilj et al. (2018)	SVM with the support of morphology of attributes	The results showed effective and completive classification rates	Implemented and evaluated on sugar beets and onions
To identify the plant species	Farmer and Jain (2005)	Region-based and boundary-based approaches for shape analysis	An excellent result was achieved	This approach can be applied over the boundary regions of the leaf

Accuracy of result can be higher when the color feature is combined with the shape feature.	Femat-Diaz et al. (2011)	Same as above, and color and texture features of the leaves were considered.	Accuracy of result can be greater when the color feature is combined along with the shape feature	Better analysis is possible
An automation system for quality assessment	Freixenet et al. (2002)	Image process-based method	Better results obtained	Consumer awareness and demand for qualitative products in the market is possible
For fruit grading	Mendoza and Aguilera (2004)	Model based on image processing with support of computer vision	High classification accuracy	Helps in fruit quality assessment
To determine fruit quality	Gao et al. (2010)	Nondestructive quality assessment method	Higher accuracy and speed	Cost-effective
Automated fruit quality assessment	Mans et al. (2010)	SVM, Bayesian decision theory, KNN	Effective and supportive	Reduce error of manual inspection
Improve fruit quality assessment tools	Moreda et al. (2012), Prabha and Kumar (2013)	Fourier descriptors, shape signatures, and skeleton operator from the morphological operation	Better results were obtained	Increased the efficiency of the existing method for fruit quality assessment
To monitor the weeds	Lamb and Brown (2001)	Classifiers along with image processing methods	Gain more satisfactory results	This approach identifies weeds and destroys them in their earlier stage of growth
Surveying and weed classification	Vibhute and Bodhe (2012)	Image processing on different spectrums, such as infrared and hyperspectral X-ray	Vegetation indices, canopy measurement, and irrigated land mapping were obtained	This approach helps save the environment and reduce cost

Continued

TABLE 1 Summary of role of image processing in agriculture—cont'd

Application goals and scenarios	Author and year	Method adopted	Results obtained	Advantages and disadvantages
Identification of weeds in the fields	Poojith et al. (2014)	Image processing with supports of MATLAB	Acceptable accuracy	We can reduce the usage of weedicides, thus saving the environment.
Weed identification, plant pest identification, machine vision, navigation	Prakash et al. (2017)	Text sym4 function series and bior3.7 wavelet are adopted.	Gain more satisfactory results	Agricultural image denoizing, enhancement processing, and image compression

and protect the environment. This provides farmers with cost-effective and targeted solutions on their farm. ML with its huge applications can be used to perform an activity like crop prediction, crop management, and disease identification. ML models have been applied in multiple applications, such as crop management, yield prediction, and disease detection (Liakos et al., 2018). The following subsection describes and analyzes the different specific applications of ML in agriculture.

4.1 Yield prediction

Yield prediction is one of the most significant research areas in precision agriculture. To increase productivity, there is the high importance of yield estimation, yield mapping, matching of crops supply with the demand, and crop management. One study (Sengupta & Suk, 2013) developed an early yield mapping system that identifies the immature green citrus in a citrus grove under open-air environmental conditions. This study also helps farmers optimize their orchard in terms of profits and increased yields. Another study (Amatya et al., 2015) proposed a methodology strategy and developed a machine vision system that automatically shakes and catches cherries during harvesting. The framework separates and identifies blocked cherry branches with foliage in any situation, even when these are unnoticeable. The objective of the framework was to reduce labor requirements. Another study (Senthilnath et al., 2015) uses expectation maximization (EM) and remote sensors to develop a framework that detects tomatoes. The proposed system senses Red Green Blue (RGB) images, which were captured by a UAV. Based on artificial neural networks (ANNs) and multitemporal remote sensing data, the study (Ali et al., 2016) proposed a model that estimates the grassland's biomass (in kg dry matter/ha/day). In another study, researchers (Pantazi et al., 2016) introduced a technique based on satellite imagery. The proposed method is specifically for wheat yield prediction. The system receives crop growth characteristics fused with soil data, which enhances the system performances and makes the forecast more accurate.

A generalized method was introduced in one study (Kung et al., 2016) for agriculture yield predictions. The method is based on extension neural network (ENN) application on long-period generated agronomical data (1997–2014). The study was a regional prediction, specifically in Taiwan. The study supports farmers in maintaining the market supply, demand, and crop quality. Another study (Ramos et al., 2017) presented an efficient, nondestructive, cost-effective method that automatically counts fruits, in this case, coffee on a branch. The proposed method classifies the coffee fruits into three categories: nonharvestable, harvestable, and fruits with a disregarded maturation stage. This work helps coffee growers plan their work and optimize economic benefits. Other researchers (Ying-xue et al., 2017) provided a model based on SVM and basic geographical data collected from a weather station in China for the rice development stage prediction. Another study (Chlingaryan et al., 2018) defined the

ML approach for crop yield prediction and nitrogen status estimation. A proposed method is about combining ML with other technology to get a hybrid system for cost-effective and compressive solutions for farming. At last, rapid advances in sensing, techniques, and ML will provide cost-effective and compressive solutions for better crop and environmental state estimation. One study (Murugesan et al., 2019) defined work on ML in three platforms: Python, R, and Seaborn for soil management. A prototype of unmanned ground vehicle (UGV) (Aravind et al., 2017; Ribeiro, 2016; Roldán et al., 2017) was also developed to take soil parameters and predict crop yield.

One study (Gonzalez Viejo et al., 2018) adopted a novel approach to food research utilizing computer modeling approaches that could allow a major contribution to accelerated screening of food and brewing items for the food industry and to the application of artificial intelligence (AI). The usage of RoboBEER to evaluate beer content has proven to be an effective, impartial, precise, and time-saving tool for forecasting sensory descriptors relative to professional sensory panels. This approach may also be useful as a fast screening technique for determining the consistency of beer at the end of the manufacturing line for industrial applications.

4.2 Disease detection

The most broadly utilized practice in irritation and disease control is to shower pesticides over the cropping area consistently. This practice, albeit powerful, has a high financial and significant ecological expense. ML is a coordinated piece of precision agriculture management, where agro-synthetic compound input is focused as far as time and spot. One study (Moshou et al., 2004) proposed a methodology strategy for the detection of healthy wheat and yellow rust-infected wheat through the support of an ANN model and spectral reflectance features. A real-time remote sensing model proposed (Moshou et al., 2005) detects yellow rust-infected or healthy wheat based on a selforganizing map (SOM) neural network and data fusion of hyperspectral reflection and multispectral fluorescence imaging. Researchers (Moshou et al., 2013) proposed a system that automatically discriminates between healthy and infected winter wheat canopies in terms of water-stressed Septoria trici. The recommended is based on least square (LS)-SVM classifier along with multisensory optical fusion. Another study (Chung et al., 2016) suggested a methodology for detecting and screening of Bakanae disease in rice seeding. The main motive of the study was to detect the pathogen, namely Fusarium fujikuroi, with more accuracy for two rice cultivars. The proposed method uses less time and increases grain yield. Wheat crops were also examined under the same automated detector. Other researchers (Pantazi et al., 2017b) proposed a tool that is capable of detecting and discriminating between healthy *Silybum marianum* plants and those that are infected by smut fungus Microbotyum silybum. Another study (Pantazi et al., 2017) presented a system that detects nitrogen-stressed and healthy winter canopies and yellow rust-infected based on a hierarchical self-organizing classifier and hyperspectral reflectance image data. The useful usages of fertilizers and fungicides as per the plant's requirement was the main objective achieved in the study.

4.3   Weed recognition

It is also one of the first problems in agriculture. The detection and discrimination of weeds are quite difficult from the crops. ML algorithms can be a useful tool that can be integrated with sensors for more accurate detection and discrimination, which can minimize the need for herbicides. One study (Pantazi et al., 2016) proposed a methodology strategy and developed a model for crop and weed species recognition. The proposed model is based on ML and hyperspectral imaging. The main objective of the study is to detect and discriminate various types of maize (*Zea mays*) as crop plant and Tarraxacum officinale, *Sinapis arvensis*, *Ranunculus repens*, *Medicago lupulina*, and Urtica dioicaas, a weed species. Based on counter propagation (CP)-ANN, one study (Pantazi et al., 2017a) proposed a method with the support of multispectral images captured by unmanned aircraft systems that can identify *Silybum marianum*. This weed causes significant losses to the crop yield, and it is quite difficult to isolate it.

4.4   Crop quality

The identification of features connected with crop quality is important to increase product price and reduce waste. Researchers (Maione et al., 2016) suggested a method based on ML techniques used in the chemical composition of samples for predicting and classifying the geographical origin of rice samples. The study's result showed that Rb, K, Cd, and Mg are the most relevant chemical components for the classification of the samples. One study (Zhang et al., 2017) proposed a methodology strategy and developed a model that detects and classifies botanical and nonbotanical foreign matter embedded inside the cotton lint during harvesting. The main objective of the study was to improve the quality by minimizing fiber damages. Another study (Hu et al., 2017) considered the ML method supported with hyperspectral reflectance imaging to identify and differentiate Korla fragrant pear into deciduous-calyx or persistent-calyx categories.

4.5   Species recognition

Researchers (Jha et al., 2019) proposed methodology on agricultural automation practices like IoT, wireless communication, ML, AI, and DL. Automation is the key to gain productivity and strengthen soil fertility. The proposed system is for leaf and flower identification and plant watering.

4.6 Soil management

ML is used in predicting and identifying agricultural soil properties like soil conditions, temperature, soil drying, and moisture content available in the soil. Researchers (Coopersmith et al., 2014) proposed a method for the evaluation of soil drying through the support of evapotranspiration and prediction data from Urbana, Illinois, in the United States, which helps in agricultural planning. The main motive of the proposed method was the provision of remote farm management decisions. One study (Morellos et al., 2016) proposed a methodology strategy and developed a model that predicts soil conditions. In the study, the author adopted a visible-near-infrared (Vis-NIR) spectrophotometer to collect soil spectra from 140 unprocessed and wet samples of the top layer of Luvisol soil types. The samples were collected from an arable field in Premslin, Germany, in August 2013. One study (Nahvi et al., 2016) presented a model based on a self-adaptive evolutionary extreme learning machine (SAE-ELM) with the support of weather data. In the study, estimation of daily soil temperature took place at six different depths, that is, 5, 10, 20, 30, 50, and 100 cm, in two different climate condition regions of Iran: Bandar Abbas and Kerman. A different study (Johann et al., 2016) proposed a novel method to estimate soil moisture primarily based on the ANN model with the support of a dataset from force sensors on a no-till chisel opener.

Table 2 shows the most popular methods and models based on ML in smart agriculture.

5 Role of deep learning in agriculture

DL is a promising technology for the agricultural sector. DL is a subset of ML where ANNs, algorithms inspired by the human brain, learn from large amounts of data (Lecun et al., 2015; Schmidhuber, 2014). DL can be used for crop management, prediction, and more. DL technology in modern farming with evolved algorithms is efficient and effective in the agroindustry. DL in data analysis helps farmers analyze crops to get the desired output. DL, with its selflearning capability, is capable of using IoT for the advancement of water and soil management to empower yield production healthily. In regards to adverse effects of climate change and various environmental and economic factors affecting crops, DL helps farmers tackle these problems by species breeding to get specific genes for plants to adapt to climatic changes and become disease resistant. DL technology is a game changer in modern agriculture that can help sustain the agriculture sector. Algorithms makes crop prediction and crop management models much more precise and effective. The following subsection describes and analyzes the different specific application of DL in agriculture.

5.1 Leaf disease detection

For detecting cucumber leaf diseases, especially zucchini yellow mosaic virus and melon yellow spot virus, researchers (Kawasaki et al., 2015) proposed a

TABLE 2 Summary of role of machine learning in agriculture.

Application goals and scenarios	Author and year	Method adopted	Results obtained	Advantages and disadvantages
Identifies the immature green citrus	Sengupta and Suk (2013)	An early yield mapping system	Acceptable accuracy	Also helps growers/farmers in optimizing their grove in terms of profits and increased yields
Reduce human resources labor requirements	Amatya et al. (2015)	Machine vision system	Effective and supportive	Help farmers in reducing human resources
To detect tomatoes	Senthilnath et al. (2015)	User-defined framework based on EM and remote sensors	Gain more satisfactory results	Cost-effective and can also apply to other vegetables
Estimates the grassland's biomass	Ali et al. (2016)	User-defined model based on ANNs and multitemporal remote sensing data	Acceptable accuracy	This approach helps save the environment and reduce cost
For wheat yield predictions	Pantazi et al. (2016)	A technique based on satellite imagery	Prediction is more accurate	Enhances the existing system performances
For agriculture yield predictions	Kung et al. (2016)	The user-defined method based on ENN	Acceptable accuracy	The study supports farmers in maintaining the market supply, demand, and crop quality
To classifies the coffee fruits.	Ramos et al. (2017)	Nondestructive method	High classification accuracy	Helps coffee growers in optimizing economic benefits

Continued

TABLE 2 Summary of role of machine learning in agriculture—cont'd

Application goals and scenarios	Author and year	Method adopted	Results obtained	Advantages and disadvantages
For the rice development stage prediction	Ying-xue et al. (2017)	A model based on SVM and essential geographical data	Prediction is more accurate	Enhances farming performances
Crop yield prediction and nitrogen status estimation	Chlingaryan et al. (2018)	Hybrid system-combining ML with other technology	Cost-effective and compressive solutions for farming	Provides cost-effective and compressive solutions for better crop and environmental state estimation
To take soil parameters and predict crop yield	Murugesan et al. (2019)	UGV	Better accuracy in crop prediction	Ability to work in a variety of crops and environments
For detection of yellow rust-infected or healthy wheat	Moshou et al. (2004)	ANN model and spectral reflectance features	Better results obtained	This approach can also be implemented in other crops.
To discriminate between healthy and infected winter wheat canopies	Moshou et al. (2013)	LS-SVM classifier along with multisensory optical fusion	High classification accuracy rate.	Cost-effective
For detecting and screening of Bakanae disease in rice seedling	Chung et al. (2016)	A user-defined method based on ML	Detected pathogen namely Fusarium fujikuroi with more accuracy for two rice cultivars	The proposed method uses less time and increases grain yield

Detecting and discriminating the healthy *Silybum marianum* plants	Pantazi et al. (2017b)	User-defined tool based on ML	High accuracy obtained	Greater efficiency
To detect nitrogen-stressed and healthy winter canopies and yellow rust-infected	Pantazi et al. (2017)	Hierarchical selforganizing classifier and hyperspectral reflectance image data.	Gain more satisfactory results	Also provides useful usages of fertilizers and fungicides as per the plant's requirement
To detect and discriminates various types of maize	Pantazi et al. (2016)	User-defined model based on ML and hyperspectral imaging	High accuracy obtained	Cost-effective
To identify Silybum marianum	Pantazi et al. (2017a)	The method based on CP-ANN	Effective and supportive	Helps identify and isolate Silybum marianum, which causes major loss to crop yield
For predicting and classifying the geographical origin of rice samples	Maione et al. (2016)	User-defined based on ML techniques	The result showed that Rb, K, Cd, and Mg are the most relevant chemical component for the classification of the samples.	Higher prediction rate
To improve the quality by minimizing fiber damages	Zhang et al. (2017)	User-defined model	The effect is ideal.	Cost-effective
For identifying and differentiating Korla fragrant	Hu et al. (2017)	The method based on ML and hyperspectral reflectance imaging	Gain more satisfactory results	Higher classification rates

Continued

TABLE 2 Summary of role of machine learning in agriculture—cont'd

Application goals and scenarios	Author and year	Method adopted	Results obtained	Advantages and disadvantages
Agricultural automation	Jha et al. (2019)	IoT, wireless communication, ML, AI, and DL	Gain productivity and strengthen soil fertility	Botanical farm for flower and leaf identification and watering using IoT
For the evaluation of soil drying	Coopersmith et al. (2014)	User-defined method support with evapotranspiration and prediction data from Urbana, IL, USA	Improve smart farming	Greater efficiency
For predicting soil conditions	Morellos et al. (2016)	User-defined model based on ML supported with adopted Vis-NIR spectrophotometer	Acceptable and effective results	Improve smart farming
For estimation of daily soil temperature taken at six different depths	Nahvi et al. (2016)	SAE-ELM with the support of weather data	Supportive and effective results obtained	Greater efficiency
To estimate soil moisture	Johann et al. (2016)	ANN model	Highly accurate compared to existing techniques	Improve the agriculture environment

methodology strategy and developed a convolutional neural network-based (CNN-based) system. The proposed method utilizes square crop and square deformation strategies as a preprocessing step with the overall accuracy of 94.90%. Another study (Sladojevic et al., 2016) proposed a DL model that uses CaffeNet for leaf disease detection. The proposed method is created with the database containing 4483 images that include 13 various types of healthy leaves and plant diseases. The proposed method has an accuracy of 96.30% (classification accuracy), which is better than the SVM. Researchers (Chen et al., 2020) planned to acquaint a framework on deep convolutional neural network (DCNN) for plant leaf disease identification and data used by a pretrained model for doing specific tasks. The proper approach presents a substantial performance improvement concerning other state-of-the-art methods. This would be extremely beneficial in preventing massive crop damage and increasing production. The average accuracy of the proposed approach reaches 92.00% for the class prediction of rice plant images. Experimental results demonstrate the validity of the proposed approach, and it is accomplished efficiently for plant disease detection.

5.2   Plant disease detection

One study (Mohanty et al., 2016) presented a framework based on CaffeNet and supported by AlexNet and GoogleNet. The authors' proposed model identified 26 diseases and 14 crop species using the PlantVillage public data set of 54,306 images of diseased and healthy plant leaves. The 0.9935 F1 score indicates the precision of the proposed method. Another study (Lu et al., 2017) considered DL and developed a model that identifies paddy crop disease. The developed CNN model is an upgraded version of AlexNet CNN architecture and LeNet-5. The trained CNN model has an average recognition precision of 95.48% for 10 paddy crop diseases. To prevent overfitting and to enhance the capability of the proposed model, stochastic pooling is preferred. One study (Amara et al., 2017) classified banana leaf diseases using the support of a DL model that uses LeNet and achieved the precision of 96% and an F1 score of 0.968. The image dataset comprises of 3700 images of banana disease acquired from PlantVillage. Another study (Lu et al., 2017) proposed a framework based on supervised DL that diagnoses the wheat diseases. The proposed framework considered 50,000 images of the wheat crop, including infected leaves and healthy leaves. In the proposed framework, four different CNN models performed recognition of seven wheat disease classes. The maximum average recognition accuracy of 97.95% was achieved with the support of the VGG16 model, which has fully connected layers. In a different study, researchers (Brahimi et al., 2017) classified nine tomato diseases based on CNN models, especially GoogleNet and AlexNet, with the support of the visualization method to visualize and detect symptoms. The dataset used for the study comprises of 14,828 images. The study's result showed that the CNN model is a better choice compared to the SVM and random forest (RF). For the identification of plant disease, researchers (Ferentinos, 2018) proposed five different deep CNN models that include Google Net, AlexNetOWTBn, AlexNet, Overfeat, and VGG. The proposed framework considered 87,848 individual leaf images from 58 different classes of plant disease combinations of 25 different plant species. The highest classification accuracy achieved using the VGG-CNN model was 99.53%. Based on DL, researchers (Jiang et al., 2019) developed an INAR-SSD model to detect five apple leaf diseases. The dataset consisted of 26,377 images. The INAR-SSD performance was about 78.80% mAP along with a detection speed of 23.13 FPS.

5.3   Land cover classification

One study (Chen et al., 2014) developed a framework based on a hybrid of PCA, autoencoder, and logistic regression that is capable of producing the precision result of 98.00%, which is 1% more precise than RBF-SVM. In the study, the authors identified 13 different land cover classes at the Kennedy Space Center (KSC) and nine different classes in Pavia. The database used in the framework was collected from the KSC, Florida, USA, and an urban site in the city of Pavia, Italy. Another study (Luus et al., 2015) developed a framework based on Theano. The proposed framework supports land cover classification with an average accuracy of 93.48% (classification accuracy). Land owned by the University of California, Merced, was used as a dataset in the study in which the authors identified 21 land-use classes that contain a variety of spatial patterns. Other researchers (Lu et al., 2017) proposed a methodology strategy based on deep CNN that is used to extract information about cultivated land with the help of a dataset comprised of images from UAVs at the Sichuan province, China, Guanghan country, Pengzhow country.

5.4   Crop type classification

One study (Kussul et al., 2017) proposed a methodology to classify crops like wheat, soybean, maize, sugar beet, and sunflower. The study uses a database comprised of 19 multitemporal scenes collected by Landsat-8 and Sentinel-1A RS satellites from a test site in Ukraine. The overall classification accuracy of the proposed method is 94.60%, which is better than the RF (i.e., 88%) and multilayer perception (MLP) (i.e. 92.7%). Another study (Ghosal et al., 2018) considered a deep machine vision-based methodology that identifies, classifies, and measures plant stresses, including abiotic and biotic, using a database comprised of 25,000 images of healthy and stressed leaflets in the fields. Deep CNN model accomplishes the classification accuracy of 94.13%.

5.5   Plant recognition

A study (Reyes et al., 2015) proposed a model based on CaffeNet and supported by AlexNet. The dataset is comprised of 91,759 images distributed in 13,887 plant observations collected by LifeCLEF in 2015. In the study, the authors recognize seven different views of various plant: branch, entire plant, flower, stem, fruit, and scans. The overall LifeCLEF metric is about 48.60%, which is worse than the local descriptors in representing images and KNN. Another study (Lee et al., 2015) developed a model based on CaffeNet and supported by AlexNet with a maximum classification accuracy of 99.60%, which is better than SVM (95.1%) and ANN (58%). In the study, the authors recognize 44 different plant species using the Malaya Kew Leaf dataset that is comprised of 44 classes collected at the Royal Botanic Garden, Kew England. Another group of researchers (Grinblat et al., 2016) presented a framework based on Pylearn2 that supported the identification of plants from vein patterns of white, soya, and red beans and has a classification accuracy of 96.90%. The dataset was comprised of 866 leaf images provided by INTA Argentina, that is, 172 white bean, 272 red bean, and 422 soybean leaves. Another study (Anami et al., 2020) introduced a technique based on DCNN with VGG-16 CNN model for the identification of crops using field images. The proposed framework was for automatic recognition and classification of biotic and abiotic paddy crop stress using field images. The trained models achieved an average accuracy of 92.89%. The generality of the proposed approach can make it applicable to a wide range of field crops, such as wheat, maize, barley, soybean, and more.

5.6   Segmentation of root and soil

One study (Douarre et al., 2016) proposed a methodology strategy based on CNN with SVM supported by MatConvNet for identification of roots from soils with a quality measurement of 0.23 (simulation) and 0.57 (real roots). The soil images used in the study were generated from X-ray tomography.

5.7   Crop yield estimation

Researchers (Kuwata & Shibasaki, 2015) presented a work based on CaffeNet to estimate maize yield with a root mean square error of 6.298, which is better than support vector regression (8.204). The dataset is downloaded from the climate research unit, and moderate resolution imaging spectroradiometer-enhanced vegetation index comprised data of maize yield from 2001 to 2010. Another study (Kamilaris & Prenafeta-Boldú, 2018) defined work on a CNN and presented the advantage and disadvantages of the CNN. This approach is for the implementation of the CNN in a sugarcane plantation in Costa Rica, and future potential of DL is also discussed in the other areas.

5.8   Fruit counting

At present, DL-based approaches are dominating the field of image segmentation and object detection (Badrinarayanan et al., 2017). The overwhelming success of these techniques is often attributed to the huge amount of training data from which the networks learn features that ideally generalize across environments. Previously, fruit counting is dominated by circular Hough transformation (CHT) (Pedersen & Kjeldgaard, 2007). CHT requires extensive parameter tuning and fails to handle occlusions. These issues led to the development of more sophisticated methods for fruit counting. One study (Chen et al., 2017) suggested a data-driven approach for counting oranges and apples based on DL. First, they introduced a labeling platform to label the fruits on input images. Then, with the use of a blob detector neural network, the candidate region was extracted. Again, another neural is utilized for counting the number of fruits within the image. Finally, regression analysis is applied between algorithmic count and manual count to evaluate the performance. This method is used for oranges and apples with the intersection of union (IoU) 0.813 and 0.838, respectively. Another study (Häni et al., 2018) addressed the problem of accurately counting fruits directly from images. They presented a solution that uses AlexNet CNN, which modified and fine-tuned their training data. The methodology achieved accuracy in the range of 80% to 94%. The detection and counting of fruits got more attention after the development of faster R-CNN. In another study, researchers (Hashim et al., 2018) demonstrated a quick, simple, and reliable method of nondestructive identification of the impact of cold storage on mango. The proposed method may be used to effectively distinguish separate fruits after low temperature preservation.

5.9 Obstacle detection

One study (Steen et al., 2016) considered a framework on CaffeNet based on AlexNet in the area of obstacle detection with a high classification accuracy of 99.9% in row crops and 90.8% in grass mowing. The study is about identifying ISO barrel-shaped obstacles in row crops and grass mowing using a total of 437 images as a dataset for the framework. Another study (Christiansen et al., 2016) suggested a model based on AlexNet and VGG supported by CaffeNet, which has 0.72 F1 score to detect obstacles.

5.10 Identification of weeds

In one study, researchers (Xinshao & Cheng, 2016) developed a model based on PCANet and LMC classifiers that classify 91 weed seed types with an average classification accuracy of 90.96%, which is better than the other features extraction techniques. The dataset used in the framework contains 3980 images, including 91 different types of weed seed. A different study (Dyrmann et al., 2016) proposed Theano-based Lasagne library for Python supported by variation in VGG16 to classify weed from crop species with 85.20% classification accuracy using the dataset of 10,413 images collected from BBCH 12–16, including 22 weed and crops species at early growth stages. Another study

(Sørensen et al., 2017) proposed a method based on DenseNet to identify thistle in winter wheat with a classification accuracy of 97.00%. Based on CNN supported with crop lines algorithm, researchers (Bah et al., 2018) presented work for identification of weeds in bean, beet, and spinach fields. The dataset comprises of vegetable images captured by drone at about 20 m. In the study, the best accuracy was obtained in the beet field. Finally, one study (Yu et al., 2019) proposed a model based on DCNN with the support of GoogleNet, VGGNet, and DetectNet for weed detection in turfgrass using images captured using digital cameras. The study's result showed that DCNN is most suitable for weed detection.

5.11   Prediction of soil moisture

To predict soil moisture content over an irrigated cornfield, researchers (Song et al., 2016) developed deep belief network-based macroscopic cellular automata (DBN-MCA) with root mean square error of 6.77. The soil data was collected from an irrigated cornfield (an area of 22 km^2) in the Zhangye oasis in northwest China.

5.12   Cattle race classification

A study (Santoni et al., 2015) suggested a model based on gray level cooccurrence matrix CNN (GLCM–CNN) supported by DL MATLAB Toolbox for cattle race classification with an average classification accuracy of 93.76%.

Table 3 shows the most popular methods and models based on DL in smart agriculture.

6   Role of IoT in agriculture

To connect objects with a network for information exchange and communication, IoT technology is used. IoT is capable of making billions of interconnected devices that are also termed smart objects. These smart objects are proficient at collecting environmental information and communicating with other systems through the internet (Meiklejohn et al., 2013). IoT-based applications enable devices to monitor and control in different domains, including processes, home appliances, health monitoring applications, smart homes, smart cities, smart agriculture, and more (Chang & Lin, 2018). IoT applications have unique importance throughout the lifespan of the agriculture sector, such as cultivate yields, irrigation, harvesting, postharvesting, crop storage, processing, transportation, and sales. For agriculture applications, there are a variety of specialized sensors available, for instance, soil moisture sensor, humidity, leaf moisture, solar emissions, infrared radiations, rain predictor, and more. In the scenario of IoT, sensors can be installed in different fields like greenhouses, seed storages, cold storages, agriculture machinery, transportation system, and livestock;

TABLE 3 Summary of role of deep leaning in agriculture.

Application goals and scenarios	Author and year	Method adopted	Results obtained	Advantages and disadvantages
For detecting cucumber leaf diseases	Kawasaki et al. (2015)	A CNN-based system	Overall accuracy of 94.90%	Help farmers increase productivity
For leaf disease detection	Sladojevic et al. (2016)	DL model with the support of CaffeNet	Classification accuracy of 96.30%	The proposed model is better than the SVM
Plant leaf disease identification	Chen et al. (2020)	DCNN	High accuracy about 92.00%	Great efficiency
To identify 26 diseases and 14 crop species	Mohanty et al. (2016)	CaffeNet, AlexNet, and GoogleNet	0.9935 as F1 score	Cost-effective
To identify paddy crop diseases	Lu et al. (2017)	Trained CNN model.	Average recognition precision of 95.48%	The developed CNN model is an upgraded version of AlexNet CNN architecture and LeNet-5
For classification of banana diseases	Amara et al. (2017)	DL model with the support of LeNet	Classification accuracy of 96.00% and 0.968 as F1 score	Better performance among existing models
For recognition of seven wheat disease classes	Lu et al. (2017)	VGG16 model	The maximum average recognition accuracy of 97.95%	Enhances farming performances
To classify 9 tomato diseases	Brahimi et al. (2017)	CNN model, GoogleNet, and AlexNet	Higher accuracy	CNN model is a better choice compared to the SVM and RF
For the identification of plant disease	Ferentinos (2018)	GoogleNet, AlexNetOWTBn, AlexNet, Overfeat, and VGG	VGG-CNN model achieved the highest classification accuracy of 99.53%	Enhances farming performances

Objective	Reference	Method	Result	Remarks
To detect five apple leaf diseases	Jiang et al. (2019)	INAR-SSD model	78.80% mAP and detection speed of 23.13 FPS	The system can be improved more
To identify 13 different land cover classes at KSC and 9 different classes in Pavia	Chen et al. (2014)	Framework based on hybrid of PCA, autoencoder, and logistic regression	98.00% classification accuracy	This framework was 1% more precise than RBF-SVM
For land cover classification	Luus et al. (2015)	User-defined model based on Theano	The average accuracy of 93.48%	Capable of identifying 21 land-use classes that contain a variety of spatial patterns
To extract information about cultivated land	Lu et al. (2017)	Deep CNN	Satisfactory results	Better performance
To classify crops like wheat, soybean, maize, sugar beet, and sunflower	Kussul et al. (2017)	A user-defined model with the support of by Landsat-8 and Sentinel-1A RS satellites	Classification accuracy of 94.60%	Better than RF and MLP
To identify, classify, and measure plant stresses	Ghosal et al. (2018)	Deep machine vision-based system	Classification accuracy of 94.13%	Great efficiency
To recognize seven different views of various plant: branch, entire plant, flower, stem, fruit, and scans	Reyes et al. (2015)	A model based on CaffeNet supported by AlexNet	Average accuracy	The overall LifeCLEF metric is about 48.60%, which is worse than the local descriptors in representing images and KNN
To recognize 44 different plant species using the Malaya Kew Leaf dataset	Lee et al. (2015)	A model based on CaffeNet supported by AlexNet	Maximum classification accuracy of 99.60%	The proposed method was better than SVM (95.1%) and ANN (58%)

Continued

TABLE 3 Summary of role of deep leaning in agriculture—cont'd

Application goals and scenarios	Author and year	Method adopted	Results obtained	Advantages and disadvantages
For identification of plants from vein patterns of white, soya and red beans	Grinblat et al. (2016)	A framework based on Pylearn2	Classification accuracy of 96.90%	Better performance
The identification of crops using field images	Anami et al. (2020)	DCNN Framework with VGG-16 CNN model	The trained models achieve an average accuracy of 92.89%	Applicable to a wide range of field crops
For identification of roots from soils	Douarre et al. (2016)	CNN with SVM supported by MatConvNet	Quality measure of 0.23 (simulation) and 0.57 (real roots)	Great efficiency
To estimate maize yield	Kuwata and Shibasaki (2015)	User-defined model based on CaffeNet.	Root mean square error of 6.298	Better than SVR
Sugarcane plantation in costa rice	Kamilaris and Prenafeta-Boldú (2018)	CNN	Better results obtained	This approach can also be implemented in other areas
For counting of oranges and apples	Chen et al. (2017)	A data-driven approach based on DL	This method is applied for oranges and apples with the IoU 0.813 and 0.838, respectively	Applicable to a wide range of field crops

Application	Reference	Method	Result	Remarks
For accurately counting fruits directly from images	Häni et al. (2018)	AlexNet CNN	The accuracy in the range of 80% to 94%	Faster R-CNN is better than the proposed method
In the area of obstacle detection	Steen et al. (2016)	CaffeNet based on AlexNet	High classification accuracy of 99.9% in row crops and 90.8% in grass mowing	Great efficiency
To detect obstacles	Christiansen et al. (2016)	AlexNet and VGG supported by CaffeNet	0.72 F1 score	Better performances
To classify 91 weed seed types	Xinshao and Cheng (2016)	PCANet and LMC classifiers	Average classification accuracy of 90.96%	Better than the other feature extraction techniques
To classify weed form crop species	Dyrmann et al. (2016)	Theano-based Lasagne library for Python supported by variation in VGG16	85.20% as classification accuracy	Enhances farming performances
To identify thistle in winter wheat	Sørensen et al. (2017)	DenseNet	Classification accuracy of 97.00%	Great performances
For identification of weeds in bean, beet, and spinach fields	Bah et al. (2018)	CNN supported with crop lines algorithm	Best accuracy was obtained in the beet field	Can improve more
For weed detection in turf grass using the images	Yu et al. (2019)	DCNN with support of GoogleNet, VGGNet, and DetectNet	Better performances	DCNN is most suitable for weed detection
To predict soil moisture content over an irrigated cornfield	Song et al. (2016)	DBN-MCA	Root mean square error of 6.77	Can improve more
For cattle race classification	Santoni et al. (2015)	GLCM–CNN supported by DL MATLAB Toolbox	Average classification accuracy of 93.76%	Better performances

and their data can be stored in the cloud for monitoring and control (Sawa, 2019). Researchers (Farooq et al., 2020) conducted a survey of IoT technology and its application in the agricultural domain. Using supervised learning, the authors presented the main issue and challenges in the field of agriculture. The framework and contextualization of a range of solutions in agriculture were also discussed. The following subsection described the progress of IoT in smart farming.

6.1   Climate condition monitoring

In one study (Brandt et al., 2017), the Food and Agriculture Organization of the United Nations introduced an approach related to the weather/climate, namely climate-smart agriculture, which identifies the climate conditions and helps in improving the agriculture system to a great extent. IoT had been deployed with the support of WSN to monitor weather conditions by using sensors and devices (Martín et al., 2017).

6.2   Crop yield

One study (Ayaz et al., 2019) was intended to apply wireless sensor and IoT in the agriculture domain. The development of the ventilate, wireless sensor, VAVS, cloud computer, and a new method for improving the crop yield and handling were also discussed. The IoT-based sensors and communication is mandatory in agriculture to maximize crop production.

6.3   Soil patter

To monitor soil moisture content, humidity and moisture sensors were deployed in one study (De Morais et al., 2019). The soil monitoring test is one of the most delicate tests that increases crop productivity and also suggests the best suitable fertilization technique. However, IoT technology supports identification of contaminated soil, which protects the field from crop loss and over fertilization.

6.4   Pest and crop disease monitoring

A study (Zang & Wang, 2014) proposed a system for monitoring wheat diseases, pests, and weeds based IoT technology with the support of ZigBee network. The dataset was collected by IoT. The proposed system is easy to operate, and users can even monitor using a PC or hand-held terminal. One of the major issues is crop raiding, which is generally due to contraction of the cultivated field into the different wildlife haunts. A different study (Giordano et al., 2018) had developed a methodology based on IoT application with the support of low-power devices and an open-source system for crop protection from both weather conditions and wild animal attacks. Another study (Awan et al., 2019) considered blockchain technology for the development of smart farming. A smart farming model is developed to uplift the traditional agriculture using blockchain technology and IoT. The proposed technique can be used to reduce food waste and the cause of foodborne diseases.

6.5   Irrigation monitoring system

With the installation of various sensing devices, irrigation monitoring systems aid farmers by reducing monthly bills for irrigation and limited water resources (Keswani et al., 2018). A more generalized, advanced system was proposed by researchers (Hellin et al., 2014) that uses cellular technology for controlling the process of irrigation. In the proposed method, sensor data can be transferred to the system database using mobile technology. One study (Mohanraj et al., 2016) suggested a framework consisting of KM-knowledge base and monitoring modules for field monitoring and automation using IoT in agriculture domain. A knowledge data flow model was constructed connecting scattered sources to the crop structures, and a comparison between the development system and the existing system was presented. The system overcomes the limitations of traditional agricultural procedures by utilizing water resources efficiently and also reducing labor cost. For monitoring water quality, researchers in one study (Ikhwan & Thamrin, 2017) proposed a model based on IoT using sensor nodes for empowering the wireless communication to measure physical and chemical constraints of water, such as temperature, pH, oxygen, and conductivity. For supervision of the collected database about water management system on the internet, cloud computing services were utilized. The proposed system also controls the water consumption in the field. Another study (Nawandar & Satpute, 2019) designed and developed a low-cost irrigation system based on an IoT with the support of HTTP and MQTT protocols. The proposed system's results promises to be beneficial with its intelligence, portability, and low cost.

6.6   Optimum time for plant and harvesting

A study (Kamilaris et al., 2016) proposed an IoT-based framework applying real-time collection processing and analysis of data. This will provide real-time provisions or smart solutions and decision support by experts to researchers and farmers. Also, this smart farming framework increases productivity and protects the environment by using fewer resources like water, fertilizer, and so on.

6.7   Tracking and tracing

One study (Satyanarayana, 2013) developed a model that monitors soil condition with the support of the ZigBee network along with other devices, such as GPRS, CMS, and GPS. However, the proposed technique is expensive but highly utilized in the field of agriculture because of its accurate location monitoring and tracking property. Another study (Farooq et al., 2019) proposed a framework on technologies involving IoT in the agriculture domain. The author also presented a discussion on network technologies involving network architecture and layers and the connection of IoT-based agriculture system to relevant technologies.

6.8 Farm management system

A farm management system is a crucial element for processing, planning, and decision-making in smart farming (Gardasˇevic et al., 2017). One study (Elijah et al., 2018) considered the integration of IoT with data analytics for enabling smart agriculture. The author classified all the advantages and challenges in the implementation of IoT in the agricultural sector. The main aim is to draw attention to research in the development of LPWA communications. Also, as the cost of IoT devices, data storage, processing, and transfer reduces with time, small- and medium-scale farmers will be able to deploy the IoT systems.

6.9 Agricultural drone

Agricultural drones, that is, UAVs, are used to improve different practices and process of smart farming. Agricultural processes include screening, scouting reports, crop health assessment, nitrogen measurement, spraying, and monitoring soil conditions. One study (Bodake et al., 2018) proposed a methodology based on the integration of IoT and GIS to map and capture the image of crop health with the support of drones. The proposed method is specially deployed for monitoring bacteria and fungus on the farm.

Table 4 shows the most popular methods and models based on IoT in smart agriculture.

7 Role of wireless sensor networks in agriculture

For sensing and analyzing the various parameters that are required in the agriculture domain, WSN technologies are available. To utilize sensors in agriculture, many applications have been developed. Sensor networks are the best options to make a strong bond between cyberspace and the real world. By design, sensors are appropriate for connecting agriculture to the IoT. WSN are cheap devices capable of working in specific environments for an extended period without battery replacement (Louis & Dunston, 2018). The concept of precision farming is made clear, and the study of vital elements of precision and smart farming is done. The concept of GIS, a distinct information system, is discussed in one study (Yanxia et al., 2007) in detail. The system utilizes GIS techniques, agro-techniques, scientific research results, expert experience, and computer technique in creating a comprehensive precision farming expert

TABLE 4 Summary of role of internet of things in agriculture.

Application goals and scenarios	Author and year	Method adopted	Results obtained	Advantages and disadvantages
To identify climate conditions	Brandt et al. (2017)	User-defined, model based on IoT and WSN	Satisfactory results obtained	Can improve more
For improving the crop yield and handling	Ayaz et al. (2019)	Ventilate, wireless sensor, VAVS, and cloud computing	Better performance	IoT-based methods are essential to maximizing crop production
To monitor soil moisture	De Morais et al. (2019)	Humidity and moisture sensors and IoT technology	Higher efficiency	Most excellent test that increase crop productivity
For monitoring wheat diseases, pests, and weeds	Zang and Wang (2014)	Monitoring system based on IoT technology and ZigBee network	Acceptable accuracy	Easy to operate; users could monitor using PC
For crop protection from weather conditions and wild animal attacks	Giordano et al. (2018)	IoT application with the support of low-power devices and an open-source system	Great efficiency	Also solves the issue of crop raiding
Uplift the traditional agriculture	Awan et al. (2019)	Smart farming model	Improve smart farming	Reduce food waste and the cause of foodborne diseases
For controlling the process of irrigation	Hellin et al. (2014)	Cellular technology	Better results obtained	Performance of the existing system increases

Continued

TABLE 4 Summary of role of internet of things in agriculture—cont'd

Application goals and scenarios	Author and year	Method adopted	Results obtained	Advantages and disadvantages
Field monitoring and automation	Mohanraj et al. (2016)	KM-knowledge base monitoring module	The trained models achieve high accuracy and utilizing water resource efficiently	Requires less labor cost
For empowering irrigation monitoring system	Ikhwan and Thamrin (2017)	The user-defined system based on IoT	The effect is ideal	The proposed system also controls water consumption in the field.
For monitoring water quality	Nawandar and Satpute (2019)	Low-cost irrigation system based on IoT with the support of HTTP and MQTT protocols	System's results promises to be beneficial with its intelligence	Portability and low cost
Increases the productivity	Kamilaris et al. (2016)	Real-time data collection and analysis	DL is better than exact AI technologies	High accuracy, reliability and robustness
To monitor and soil condition	Satyanarayana (2013)	ZigBee network, along with other devices such as GPRS, CMS, GPS	The results showed exact location monitoring and property tracking	The proposed technique is expensive.
Agricultural challenges and security requirements	Farooq et al. (2019)	IoT-based network architecture	Improve smart farming security	Cost-effective
To draw attention to research in the development of LPWA Communications	Elijah et al. (2018)	Integration of IoT with data analytics	Satisfactory results	Helps in enabling smart agriculture
For monitoring bacteria and fungus on the farm	Bodake et al. (2018)	IoT, GIS, and drones	Better performances	Helps in enabling smart agriculture

system that is of great intelligence. This section reviews the progress of image processing in the agricultural and food processing.

7.1   Irrigation management

A study (Rawidean et al., 2014) proposed a framework on WSNs for resource optimization and monitoring in agriculture. The proposed approach is for gathering real-time information about crops. The implementation of WSNs will optimize the uses of water and fertilizer and maximize the yield of crops. Another study (Ojha et al., 2015) reviewed the WSN application, issues, and challenges in the implementation of WSN. The authors presented various case studies proposed in the literature to discuss WSN deployment for farming applications. The current use of WSN in irrigation, crop management, and more as well as an approach for further implementation of WSNs in agriculture were the main points in the presented article.

7.2   Soil moisture prediction

The open-source feature of Tiny OS is discussed by (Jao et al., 2013) in detail. The detailed design and implementation of WSNs, both hardware and software, was presented. An experiment was conducted to validate the performance of MDA300CA driver. A single node experiment and a multiple node experiment were shown, and the readings were analyzed. The readings helped in knowing the soil type, that is, whether it was dry, moist, or water-saturated soil. (Joshi et al., 2017) had defined work on soil monitoring systems. The proposed WSN system is for controlling parameters of soil, and this system is embedded on a web server uses Raspberry Pi and IoT for monitoring and controlling soil parameters.

7.3   Precision farming

One study (Bencini et al., 2012) came up with the design, optimization, and development of a practical solution for application to the agro-food chain monitoring and control. The main features of VineSense were described. Moreover, some critical agronomic results achieved by the use of VineSense in different scenarios were sketched out, thus emphasizing the positive effects of the WSN technology in the agricultural environment. Another study (Piyare & Lee, 2013) proposed an extensible and flexible architecture for integrity WSN with cloud computing for data collection and sharing using REST-based web services. The evaluation illustrates that the data can be accessed by users anywhere and on any mobile device with internet access. This proposed methodology is an energy-efficient approach to increase the lifetime of senses nodes. A different study (Bhanu et al., 2014) designed and developed an agricultural monitoring system to reduce manual work. This system measures the parameters and provides the information to farmers. Detects even minor changes in parameters.

The WNS system architecture and data architecture were discussed with the continuous monitoring of many environmental parameters; the grower can analyze the optimal environmental conditions to achieve maximum crop productiveness and to achieve remarkable energy savings. In one study, researchers (Gangurde & Bhende, 2015) defined the WSN as a game changer in precision agriculture. The proposed WSN system can be used to control agricultural parameters and enhance growth. One study (Jawad et al., 2017) presented a comparison among different wireless technologies or protocols and proposed a system that uses ZigBee and Lora wireless protocols, which are convenient because of low-power consumption and high communication range. Also introduced a classification of energy-efficient techniques algorithm and energy harvesting and techniques. Another study (Siva Rama Krishnan & Arun Kumar, 2019) suggested a strategy for the practical implementation of smart farming using routing recommended in the WSN. The data is taken and sent through the RF transmitter and received by a single server that processes the data, and further details are generated. The authors define the approach to control some parameters for the effective utilization of available resources.

7.4 Climate condition monitoring

WSNs trace down climate conditions to automate and analyze the corresponding parameters. Web and smartphone applications show real-time parameters, like temperature, humidity, and CO_2, and give access for farmers to remotely open their greenhouse (Roham et al., 2015). Researchers (Rodríguez et al., 2017) proposed a methodology and developed a system for the monitoring and predicting of data in precision agriculture in a rose greenhouse based on WSNs. The roses in a greenhouse were taken for this case study. The proposed design of WSNs can measure parameters like temperature, humidity, and light. Integrated with API for monitoring and predicting.

Table 5 shows the most popular methods and models based on IoT in smart agriculture.

8 Role of data mining in agriculture

"Big data" refers to a huge quantity of data gathered from the different channels for extended periods. Data collected from sensors, social networking, and business data is called big data. The big data have many challenges, like capturing, storage, investigation, and research. To cut production costs, big data is useful in the agriculture domain for maintaining supply chain management of agricultural products (Chen et al., 2019). DM and data analysis are key to increasing production at a low rate and getting maximum yield with maximum profit. DM uses existing technologies to bring a revolutionary change in the field of

TABLE 5 Summary of role of wireless sensor networks in agriculture.

Application goals and scenarios	Author and year	Method adopted	Results obtained	Advantages and disadvantages
Precision and smart farming	Yanxia et al. (2007)	GIS technique	The trained models help in precision farming	Sustainable farming
Resource optimization and monitoring in agriculture	Rawidean et al. (2014)	WSN-based techniques	Optimization increased to a great extent	Also maintains the moisture level and healthiness of plants
Comparison among different wireless technologies or protocols	Ojha et al. (2015)	WSN, ZigBee, LoRa, and IoT	Low-power consumption and high communication range	Energy-efficient
Study of soil state or soil type	Jao et al. (2013)	Tiny OS along with WSN	An experiment was conducted to validate the performance of MDA300CA driver	Also able to define whether soil is dry, moist, or water-saturated
Controlling of soil parameters	Joshi et al. (2017)	Soil monitoring with WSN systems	Better results obtained	Cost-effective
Food chain monitoring and control	Bencini et al. (2012)	VineSense	More accurate than existing techniques	Improves the agriculture environment
For precision farming	Piyare and Lee (2013)	WSN, cloud computing, and REST-based web services	The trained models helps in precision farming	The proposed methodology is energy-efficient approach to increase the lifetime of senses nodes

Continued

TABLE 5 Summary of role of wireless sensor networks in agriculture—cont'd

Application goals and scenarios	Author and year	Method adopted	Results obtained	Advantages and disadvantages
To reduce manual work in farming	Bhanu et al. (2014)	Agricultural monitoring system based on WSN	Improve smart farming	Reliable, cost-effective, and maximum crop productiveness
For control of agricultural parameters and to enhance growth	Gangurde and Bhende (2015)	User-defined module based on WSN	Great efficiency	Performance of the existing system increases
Cloud computing with WSN	Jawad et al. (2017)	Integrated WSN, cloud REST-based web services	The effect is ideal	Easily access from anywhere
Optimization of crop supervision	Siva Rama Krishnan and Arun Kumar (2019)	Recommendation routing in WSN	Better results obtained	Effective utilization of available resources
To trace down climate conditions	Roham et al. (2015)	Web and smartphone application based on WSN	This method show low cost and high portability	Easily controllable for farmer
Support and management tools for the agricultural sector	Rodríguez et al. (2017)	WSN technology integrated with API	The results show that SVMs seem to provide the best prediction model	Enhances greenhouse environmental conditions forecasting

agriculture (MiloviC & Radojevic, 2011). One study (Vanitha et al., 2019) intended to highlight some of the common DM techniques and presented their application in the field of agriculture. The further use of DM to predict crop yield in agriculture sector were discussed. The following subsection addresses the progress of DM in the smart farming and agricultural industry.

8.1 Irrigation management

To manage the irrigation system called FITRA, researchers (Kokkonis et al., 2017) presented a fuzzy neural network algorithm. This algorithm uses sensor information. Many soil moisture sensors were being used to limit utilization and increment production. The framework naturally embraces the changing ecological conditions. Another study (Padalalu et al., 2017) proposed an automated irrigation system so that proper supervision and management of water required in the field is filled. To monitor the field, different sensors were installed in the field so that different parameters, such as soil temperature, humidity, and soil type (pH) can be monitored. Naïve Bayes algorithm was adopted for a specific amount of water according to the crop needs. By adopting this proposed method, proper water management can be achieved. In a different study, researchers (Xie et al., 2017) suggested a framework to support irrigation systems. The framework includes irrigation demand estimation, solar energy prediction based on SVR technique, and scheduling optimization.

The framework utilizes hourly numerical weather prediction (NWP) and the time of use (ToU) model. The study's results are quite promising, as 7.97% of water resources and energy can be saved and even amortized cost reduced by 25.34% as compared to the method based on soil moisture. One study (Goldstein et al., 2018) proposed a methodology that predicts irrigation by applying DM methods. In the study, various models were adopted and applied using classification and regression algorithms. For better performance, gradient boosted regression trees (GBRTs) and boosted trees classifiers (BTCs) were used instead of a linear regression model. The main advantage of this model is that its irrigation action helps keep the soil moisture within the suitable limits and helps the system in saving water. One group of researchers (González Perea et al., 2019) proposed a model that predicts occurrences in the irrigation process. The proposed model is based on a decision tree that is combined with an NSGA II. This is also used to optimize the different parameters of the decision tree. Various datasets are being used like crop type data, climatic data, phonological plant, and so forth. Results of this model are quite promising.

8.2 Prediction and detection of plant diseases

One study (Padol & Yadav, 2016) suggested that the discovery of a few plant illnesses could be possible using a blend of DM strategies and picture handling to beat the absence of human perception and even to diminish costs. Based on the manipulator, researchers (Schor et al., 2016) developed a robotic disease detection system with the features of different detection poses. The main objective of the work was to develop a method that can overcome the drawback of PCA-based and coefficient variation-based (CV-based) models, which were generally used in the detection of tomato spotted wilt virus (TSWV) and powdery mildew (PM) that threaten greenhouse bell peppers. Based on the hidden Markov model (HMM), researchers (Patil & Thorat, 2016) suggested a framework for early disease detection in grapes. The proposed model analyzes the input data, like leaf moisture, temperature, and relative humidity, which enable the model to classify grape diseases such as bacterial leaf cancer, rust, anthracnose, downy mildew, and PM. The proposed method was better than the statistical method as per the results of the study. To deduce the probability of Cd stress in rice, one study (Liu et al., 2019) considered a Bayesian method based on temporal characteristics and satellite data and to verify the Cd stress probability soil Cd concentration was used. The overall accuracy of the proposed method was 81.57%.

8.3 Pest monitoring

For mapping pests and disease risks, one study (Marques da Silva et al., 2015) suggested an algorithm that can be used for calculating "accumulated degree-days" with the support of land surface data collected by meteorological satellite. In the study, linear regression was also adopted to deal with the missing data and logistic regression that was used to analyzes the results of land surface temperature in monthly degree-days data. Another study (Boniecki et al., 2015) suggested a neural classifier based on MLP neural network topology that can identify likely parasites in apple orchards, such as apple moth, apple aphid, apple blossom weevil, apple clearwing, and apple leaf sucker. The proposed classifier includes 16 color characteristics, 7 form factors, and a total of 23 parameters.

8.4 Optimum management of inputs (fertilizer and pesticides)

One study (Lottes et al., 2016) presented a system for detection of sugar beet plants based on RF classification and a Markov random field (MRF). The study was carried out on three different sugar beet fields. By implementing the method, the robot was able to perform necessary spraying and remove weeds. Another study (Viani et al., 2016) proposed a novel fuzzy logic to predict the dose of the pesticides to be applied. The fuzzy logic was also used for the management of pests, weeds, and diseases by studying various data like weather data, risk of infection, and stage of the development of the plant. Finally, a study (Chlingaryan et al., 2018) surveyed research literature about the accurate prediction of crop yield and the estimation of nitrogen status in the field of precision agriculture using DM.

8.5   Crop yield prediction

One study (Ruß, 2009) showed how data collection, from precise geo-tagging to climate study, will help a lot to farmers. It is an excellent way to use data in the prediction of yield. The author talks about techniques like vector regression, which is immensely helpful in predicting the yield. And likewise, many other methods can be implemented as the author says, which indeed brings a revolutionary change in the agricultural field. Another study (Kaur et al., 2014) proposed a system based on finding a suitable data model that helps in achieving high accuracy and price prediction. Genetic, algorithm-based neural networks can be constructed for price prediction. The Coimbatore market was selected for the price of a tomato as an example and simulated the results using MATLAB. One researcher (Geetha, 2015) defined work on DM from the perspective of the agricultural field. The author also discussed different DM techniques for solving different agrarian problems. The author, in his work, integrates the work of various authors so that it is useful for researchers to get information on the current scenario of DM techniques and their applications in the context of agriculture. The author also presented a subarray to provide a survey of various data money techniques used in agriculture. Other researchers (Kung et al., 2016) suggested the use of cloud computing and IoT, which encompassed with big data and robots can genuinely encourage farm work and increase production with reduced labor or workforce. The use of cloud computing and big data are the keys in the coming future to enhance the agricultural field and increase production.

One study (Gandhi & Armstrong, 2016) presented work on DM for decision-making in agriculture. The various DM techniques, like AI, neural network, and Bayesian networks, improve existing agriculture systems. The authors also propose an approach to use complex agriculture data sets for crop yield prediction with an integration of both seasonal and special using GIS technology. Another study (Bhagawati et al., 2016) proposed a strategy for making agriculture sustainable and resilient and finding a wide application of DM in agriculture. The proposed system depends on translation and a multidisciplinary approach. The suggested approach illustrates how precision agriculture can increase production and productivity. In another study, researchers (Patel & Kathirya, 2017) focused on yield prediction of crops and proposed methodology while considering the uses DM in agriculture. DM in agriculture is a rising research field in crop yield analysis. The IT sector, like DM techniques, play a crucial role in smart farming in agriculture domain. Another set of researchers (Majumdar et al., 2017) proposed a methodology for analyzing agriculture data and finding optimal parameters to maximize the crop production using DM techniques like PAM CLARA. The proposed system is capable of analyzing soil and other factors for increasing crop production under different climatic conditions. There are various DM techniques, such as k-means, KNN, ANNs, and SVMs, being used for very recent applications of DM techniques in the domain of agriculture for prize prediction of the crop. Other researchers (Cai et al., 2019) presented various ML methods (such as RF, SVM and NN) and regression methods, like least absolute shrinkage and selection operator (LASSO). Before using ML methods, exploratory data analysis was carried out with the satellite and climate data, which enrich the performance of the proposed framework. Finally, one study (Tian et al., 2019) proposed a method to identify the corn cultivated area, especially in Hebei Province based on cloud computing technology with the support of high-resolution images (about 10 m). Input for RF classifier, metric composite for sentinel 1 and sentinel 2 images were calculated. An overall accuracy of 89.89% was obtained.

8.6 Climate condition monitoring

For the analysis of various environmental parameters such as Food Price Index, area under cultivation, and annual precipitation (AP), researchers (Sellam & Poovammal, 2016) proposed a method and analysis that establishes the relationship between them. The study was carried out in rice cultivation in India. One study (Balakrishnan & Muthukumarasamy, 2016) developed a forecast model based on time series analysis with the support of AdaSVM and AdaNAIVE, which were far better than the SYM and Naïve Bayes models in terms of accuracy and classification error. For smart farming and performing intelligent irrigation, it can be possible to predict soil temperature, air temperature, and humidity, and one study (Varman et al., 2017) suggested different sensors likely temperature and humidity sensors, including with invariant data. Another study (Rajeswari et al., 2018) proposed a model that helps the farmer by providing the analysis for the best crop sequence; it also suggests the next crop that will grow for better production and the total production in an area of interest. C5.0 classification algorithm and association rule DM method were adopted to collect some valuable information from the input data. The proposed model also monitors real-time soil samples.

Table 6 shows the most popular methods and models based on DM in smart agriculture.

9 Conclusion

Farming will become more essential than ever in the coming decades. Smart agriculture and precision farming are beginning, but they may be the precursors for much greater usage of technology in the farming environment. Smart farming is supposed to close the divide between farmers in both emerging and industrialized countries. Technological progress, development in IoT, and mobile implementation have significantly led to the acceptance of technology in agriculture. It is no wonder that most historically practiced agricultural operations have modified dramatically. Smart farming methods and methodologies such as the usage of computers, software, sensors, and information technologies can be

TABLE 6 Summary of role of data mining in agriculture.

Application goals and scenarios	Author and year	Method adopted	Results obtained	Advantages and disadvantages
To manage irrigation system called FITRA	Kokkonis et al. (2017)	Fuzzy neural network algorithm	Highly efficient	The framework naturally embraces changing ecological conditions
For proper supervision and management of water	Padalalu et al. (2017)	An automated irrigation system based on Naïve Bayes algorithm	Proper water management achieved	Improve the existing system
To support irrigation system	Xie et al. (2017)	SVR, NWP, and ToU	The results are quite promising as 7.97% of water resources and energy can be saved	Also, cost is reduced by 25.34% as compared to other methods based on soil moisture
Predict irrigation	Goldstein et al. (2018)	DM techniques, GBRT, BTC, and regression algorithm	Average prediction rate	The result showed better performances in saving water
To predict the occurrences irrigation process	González Perea et al. (2019)	User-defined model based on decision tree combined with a NSGA II	Maximum prediction accuracy	Also used to optimize the different parameters of decision tree
For discovery of a few plant illnesses.	Padol and Yadav (2016)	User-defined system based on DM technique	Results showed handling to beat the absence of human perception and even to diminish costs	Better performances
For different detection pose	Schor et al. (2016)	Robotic disease detection system	Better results obtained	Improve PCA, CV, and PM used for TSEVdetection

Continued

TABLE 6 Summary of role of data mining in agriculture—cont'd

Application goals and scenarios	Author and year	Method adopted	Results obtained	Advantages and disadvantages
For early disease detection in grapes	Patil and Thorat (2016)	User-defined model based on HMM	Highly efficient	The proposed method was better than the statistical method
To deduce the probability of Cd stress in rice	Liu et al. (2019)	Bayesian method based on temporal characteristics and satellite data	81.57% was the overall accuracy	Can be improved
For mapping pests and disease risks	Marques da Silva et al. (2015)	User-defined model based on land surface data and logistic regression	Better mapping	Better performance
To identify parasites in apple orchards	Boniecki et al. (2015)	Neural classifier based on MLP	Results are promising and cost-effective	Performance of the existing system increases
For detection of sugar beet plants	Lottes et al. (2016)	User-defined model based on RF classification and MRF	Better performance	Also able to perform necessary spraying and remove weeds
For the management of pests, weeds, and diseases	Viani et al. (2016)	Fuzzy logic	Highly efficient	Improve the existing system
The prediction of yield	Ruß (2009)	Vector regression	Immensely helpful in predicting the yield	Precision farming is possible
Prediction of crop	Kaur et al. (2014)	K-Means, KNN, ANN, SVM	High accuracy and, generally, for price prediction	Effective utilization of available resources and cost-effective

Application	Reference	Method	Result	Outcome
For price prediction of tomato	Geetha (2015)	Genetic, algorithm-based neural networks and MATLAB	High accuracy	Better performances
DM for decision-making in agriculture	Gandhi and Armstrong (2016)	AI, neural network, Bayesian networks, and GIS technology	Better results obtained	Improve the agriculture environment
For increasing production and productivity	Bhagawati et al. (2016)	Translation and multidisciplinary approach	Results are promising and cost-effective	Sustainable and resilient
Crop yield analysis	Patel and Kathirya (2017)	Big data and DM	High accuracy on yield prediction of a crop	Cost-effective
Optimal parameters to maximize the crop production	Majumdar et al. (2017)	PAM CLARA	More accurate than existing techniques	Increasing crop production under different climatic conditions
For crop yield prediction	Cai et al. (2019)	RF, SVM, NN, and LASSO	Uses satellite and climate data, which enrich the performance of the proposed framework	Better performance
To identify the corn cultivated area especially in Hebei Province	Tian et al. (2019)	Cloud computing technology and RF classifier	89.89% was obtained as overall accuracy	Can be improved
For the analysis of various environmental parameters	Sellam and Poovammal (2016)	User-defined method based on DM techniques	Satisfactory results obtained	The study was carried out in rice cultivation in India

Continued

TABLE 6 Summary of role of data mining in agriculture—cont'd

Application goals and scenarios	Author and year	Method adopted	Results obtained	Advantages and disadvantages
For climate condition monitoring	Balakrishnan and Muthukumarasamy (2016)	Forecast model based on time series analysis with the support of AdaSVM and AdaNAIVE	High accuracy and low classification error	Better than the SYM and Naïve Bayes model
For prediction of soil temperature, air temperature, and humidity	Varman et al. (2017)	Different sensor with invariant DM techniques	Results are promising and cost-effective	Precision farming is possible
For the best crop sequence and suggestion about next crop to be grow	Rajeswari et al. (2018)	C5.0 classification algorithm and association rule DM method	Better production and the total production in an area of interest	The proposed model also monitors real-time soil samples

linked to technical development. Evidently, smart farming is a brilliant farming idea that can help farmers reap several benefits, including increased production, enhanced quality, and decreased costs if properly applied. Such creativity needs resources, expertise, and technical skills. You need more than just farming passion; you need the right technology and expertise to analyze your farm's data, account and track developments, and predict demand and price changes. This chapter aims to provide a brief summary to researchers working in field of agriculture and smart farming. Almost all the peer-reviewed quality articles of the past 5 years were reviewed. Because each article reviewed involves different datasets, metrics, preprocessing method, models, and parameters, it is difficult to generalize and perform comparison between the papers. The bottom line is that while smart farming is relevant in agriculture and promises improved yields, research on best practices that match with your farming goals and needs is advisable.

References

Abate, G. T., Bernard, T., de Brauw, A., & Minot, N. (2018). The impact of the use of new technologies on farmers' wheat yield in Ethiopia: Evidence from a randomized control trial. *Agricultural Economics (United Kingdom)*, *49*, 409–421.

Ali, I., Cawkwell, F., Dwyer, E., & Green, S. (2016). *Modeling managed grassland biomass estimation by using multitemporal remote sensing data—A machine learning approach* (pp. 1–16).

Amara, J., Bouaziz, B., Algergawy, A., 2017. A deep learning-based approach for Banana leaf diseases classification. B. Mitschang et al. (Hrsg.): BTW 2017—Workshopband, lecture notes in informatics (LNI), Gesellschaft für Informatik, Bonn 79–88.

Amatya, S., Karkee, M., Gongal, A., & Zhang, Q. (2015). ScienceDirect detection of cherry tree branches with full foliage in planar architecture for automated sweet-cherry harvesting. *Biosystems Engineering*, 1–13.

Anami, B. S., Malvade, N. N., & Palaiah, S. (2020). Deep learning approach for recognition and classification of yield affecting paddy crop stresses using field images. *Artificial Intelligence in Agriculture*, *4*, 12–20.

Aravind, K. R., Raja, P., & Pérez-ruiz, M. (2017). Task-based agricultural mobile robots in arable farming : A review. *Spanish Journal of Agricultural Research*, *15*, 1–16.

Awan, S. H., Ahmed, S., Safwan, N., Najam, Z., Hashim, M. Z., & Safdar, T. (2019). Role of internet of things (IoT) with Blockchain Technology for the Development of Smart Farming. *Journal of Mechanics of Continua and Mathematical Sciences*, *14*, 170–188.

Ayaz, M., Member, S., & Member, M. A. S. (2019). *Internet-of-things (IoT) based smart agriculture : towards making the fields talk.* (IEEE Access XX).

Badrinarayanan, V., Kendall, A., & Cipolla, R. (2017). SegNet: A deep convolutional encoder-decoder architecture for image segmentation. *IEEE Transactions on Pattern Analysis and Machine Intelligence*, *39*, 2481–2495.

Bah, M. D., Dericquebourg, E., Hafiane, A., & Canals, R. (2018). Deep learning based classification system for identifying weeds using high-resolution UAV imagery. In *In science and information conference* (pp. 176–187). Springer, Cham: Springer International Publishing.

Balakrishnan, N., & Muthukumarasamy, G. (2016). Crop production—ensemble machine learning model for prediction. *International Journal of Computer Science and Software Engineering*, *5*, 148–153.

Bencini, L., Maddio, S., Collodi, G., Di Palma, D., Manes, G., & Manes, A. (2012). *Development of wireless sensor networks for agricultural monitoring*. (Lecture Notes in Electrical Engineering).

Bhagawati, K., Sen, A., Shukla, K. K., & Bhagawat, R. (2016). Application of data Mining in Agriculture Sector. *International Journal of Computer Science Trends and Technology (IJCST)*, *3*, 66–69.

Bhanu, B. B., Rao, K. R., Ramesh, J. V. N., & Hussain, M. A. (2014). Agriculture field monitoring and analysis using wireless sensor networks for improving crop production. In *IFIP international conference on wireless and optical communications networks, WOCN*.

Bodake, K., Ghate, R., Doshi, H., Jadhav, P., & Tarle, B. (2018). Soil based fertilizer recommendation system using internet of things. *MVP Journal of Engineering Sciences*, *1*.

Bogue, R. (2016). Robots poised to revolutionise agriculture. *Industrial Robot: An International Journal Iss An International Journal*, *32*, 468–471.

Boniecki, P., Koszela, K., Piekarska-Boniecka, H., Weres, J., Zaborowicz, M., Kujawa, S., ... Raba, B. (2015). Neural identification of selected apple pests. *Computers and Electronics in Agriculture*, *110*, 9–16.

Bosilj, P., Duckett, T., & Cielniak, G. (2018). Connected attribute morphology for unified vegetation segmentation and classification in precision agriculture. *Computers in Industry*, *98*, 226–240.

Brahimi, M., Boukhalfa, K., Moussaoui, A., & Brahimi, M. (2017). Deep learning for tomato diseases : Classification and symptoms visualization deep learning for tomato diseases : Classification and symptoms visualization. *Applied Artificial Intelligence*, *31*, 299–315.

Brandt, P., Kvaki, M., Butterbach-bahl, K., & Ru, M. C. (2017). How to target climate-smart agriculture ? Concept and application of the consensus-driven decision support framework " targetCSA". *Agricultural Systems journal*, *151*, 234–245.

Butz, P., Hofmann, C., & Tauscher, B. (2006). Recent developments in noninvasive techniques for fresh fruit and vegetable internal quality analysis. *Journal of Food Science*, *70*, R131–R141.

Cai, Y., Guan, K., Lobell, D., Potgieter, A. B., Wang, S., Peng, J., ... Peng, B. (2019). Integrating satellite and climate data to predict wheat yield in Australia using machine learning approaches. *Agricultural and Forest Meteorology*, *274*, 144–159.

Chahal, N., & Anuradha. (2015). A study on agricultural image processing along with classification model. In *2015. Souvenir of the 2015 IEEE international advance computing conference, IACC* (pp. 942–947).

Chang, H., & Lin, T. (2018). Real-time structural health monitoring system using internet of things and cloud computing. In *Eleventh U.S. national conference on earthquake engineering*.

Chen, J., Chen, J., Zhang, D., Sun, Y., & Nanehkaran, Y. A. (2020). Using deep transfer learning for image-based plant disease identi fi cation. *Computers and Electronics in Agriculture*, *173*, 105393.

Chen, W., Feng, G., Zhang, C., Liu, P., Ren, W., Cao, N., & Ding, J. (2019). Development and application of big data platform for garlic industry chain. *Computers, Materials and Continua*, *58*, 229–248.

Chen, Y., Lin, Z., & Zhao, X. (2014). Deep learning-based classification of hyperspectral data. *IEEE Journal of Selected Topics in Applied Earth Observations and Remote Sensing*, *7*, 2094–2107.

Chen, S. W., Shivakumar, S. S., Dcunha, S., Das, J., Okon, E., Qu, C., ... Kumar, V. (2017). Counting apples and oranges with deep learning: A data-driven approach. *IEEE Robotics and Automation Letters*, *2*, 781–788.

Chlingaryan, A., Sukkarieh, S., & Whelan, B. (2018). Machine learning approaches for crop yield prediction and nitrogen status estimation in precision agriculture : A review. *Computers and Electronics in Agriculture*, *151*, 61–69.

Christiansen, P., Nielsen, L. N., Steen, K. A., Jørgensen, R. N., & Karstoft, H. (2016). DeepAnomaly: Combining background subtraction and deep learning for detecting obstacles and anomalies in an agricultural field. *Sensors (Switzerland), 16*.

Chung, C., Huang, K., Chen, S., Lai, M., Chen, Y., & Kuo, Y. (2016). Detecting Bakanae disease in rice seedlings by machine vision. *Computers and Electronics in Agriculture, 121*, 404–411.

Coopersmith, E. J., Minsker, B. S., Wenzel, C. E., & Gilmore, B. J. (2014). Machine learning assessments of soil drying for agricultural planning. *Computers and Electronics in Agriculture, 104*, 93–104.

Costa, C., Antonucci, F., Pallottino, F., Aguzzi, J., Sun, D. W., & Menesatti, P. (2011). Shape analysis of agricultural products: A review of recent research advances and potential application to computer vision. *Food and Bioprocess Technology, 4*, 673–692.

De Morais, C. M., Sadok, D., & Kelner, J. (2019). An IoT sensor and scenario survey for data researchers. *Journal of the Brazilian Computer Society Research, 25*.

DePalma, K., Smith, B., & McDonald, A. G. (2019). Effect of processing conditions, biochemical properties, and microstructure on tofu production from yellow field peas (*Pisum sativum*). *Journal of Food Science, 84*, 3463–3472.

Douarre, C., Schielein, R., Frindel, C., & Gerth, S. (2016). Deep learning based root-soil segmentation from X-ray tomography images. *bioRxiv*, 1–22.

Dyrmann, M., Karstoft, H., & Midtiby, H. S. (2016). Plant species classification using deep convolutional neural network. *Biosystems Engineering, 151*, 72–80.

Eitzinger, A., Cock, J., Atzmanstorfer, K., Binder, C. R., Läderach, P., Bonilla-Findji, O., … Jarvis, A. (2019). GeoFarmer: A monitoring and feedback system for agricultural development projects. *Computers and Electronics in Agriculture, 158*, 109–121.

Elijah, O., Member, S., & Rahman, T. A. (2018). An overview of internet of things (IoT) and data analytics in agriculture : Benefits and challenges. *IEEE Internet of Things Journal, 5*, 3758–3773.

Farmer, M. E., & Jain, A. K. (2005). A wrapper-based approach to image segmentation and classification. *IEEE Transactions on Image Processing, 14*, 2060–2072.

Farooq, M. S., Riaz, S., Abid, A., Abid, K., & Naeem, M. A. (2019). A survey on the role of IoT in agriculture for the implementation of smart farming. *IEEE Access PP, 1*.

Farooq, M. S., Riaz, S., Abid, A., Umer, T., & Zikria, Y. B. (2020). Role of IoT Technology in Agriculture : A systematic literature review. *Electronics, 9*.

Femat-Diaz, A., Vargas-Vazquez, D., Huerta-Manzanilla, E., Rico-Garcia, E., & Herrera-Ruiz, G. (2011). Scanner image methodology (SIM) to measure dimensions of leaves for agronomical applications. *African Journal of Biotechnology, 10*, 1840–1847.

Feng, C.-H., Makino, Y., Yoshimura, M., Thuyet, D. Q., & García-Martín, J. F. (2018). Hyperspectral imaging in tandem with R statistics and image processing for detection and visualization of pH in Japanese big sausages under different storage conditions. *Journal of Food Science, 83*, 358–366.

Ferentinos, K. P. (2018). Deep learning models for plant disease detection and diagnosis. *Computers and Electronics in Agriculture, 145*, 311–318.

Freixenet, J., Muñoz, X., Raba, D., Martí, J., & Cufí, X. (2002). Yet another survey on image segmentation: Region and boundary information integration. *Lecture Notes in Computer Science (including subseries Lecture Notes in Artificial Intelligence and Lecture Notes in Bioinformatics), 2352*, 408–422.

Gandhi, N., & Armstrong, L. J. (2016). A review of the application of data mining techniques for decision making in agriculture. In *2nd International conference on contemporary computing and informatics, IC3I 2016* (pp. 1–6).

Gangurde, P., & Bhende, M. (2015). A novel approach for precision agriculture using wireless sensor network. *International Journal of Computer Science and Mobile Computing, 46*, 1158–1165.

Gao, H., Zhu, F., & Cai, J. (2010). A review of non-destructive detection for fruit quality. *IFIP Advances in Information and Communication Technology, 317*, 133–140.

Gardasˇevic, G., Veletic, M., Maletic, N., Vasiljevic, D., Radusinovic, I., & Tomovic, S. (2017). The IoT architectural framework, design issues and application domains. *Wireless Personal Communications, 92*(1), 127–148.

Geetha, M. C. S. (2015). A survey on data mining techniques in agriculture. *International Journal of Innovative Research in Computer and Communication Engineering, An 3*, 887–892.

Ghosal, S., Blystone, D., Singh, A. K., Ganapathysubramanian, B., Singh, A., & Sarkar, S. (2018). An explainable deep machine vision framework for plant stress phenotyping. *Proceedings of the National Academy of Sciences of the United States of America, 115*, 4613–4618.

Giordano, S., Seitanidis, I., Ojo, M., Adami, D., & Vignoli, F. (2018). IoT solutions for crop protection against wild animal attacks. In *IEEE international conference on environmental Engineering (EE). IEEE* (pp. 1–5).

Goldstein, A., Fink, L., Meitin, A., Bohadana, S., Lutenberg, O., & Ravid, G. (2018). Applying machine learning on sensor data for irrigation recommendations: Revealing the agronomist's tacit knowledge. *Precision Agriculture, 19*, 421–444.

González Perea, R., Camacho Poyato, E., Montesinos, P., & Rodríguez Díaz, J. A. (2019). Prediction of irrigation event occurrence at farm level using optimal decision trees. *Computers and Electronics in Agriculture, 157*, 173–180.

Gonzalez Viejo, C., Fuentes, S., Torrico, D. D., Howell, K., & Dunshea, F. R. (2018). Assessment of beer quality based on a robotic pourer, computer vision, and machine learning algorithms using commercial beers. *Journal of Food Science, 83*, 1381–1388.

Grinblat, G. L., Uzal, L. C., Larese, M. G., & Granitto, P. M. (2016). Deep learning for plant identification using vein morphological patterns. *Computers and Electronics in Agriculture, 127*, 418–424.

Häni, N., Roy, P., & Isler, V. (2018). Apple counting using convolutional neural networks. In *IEEE international conference on intelligent robots and systems* (pp. 2559–2565).

Hashim, N., Onwude, D. I., & Osman, M. S. (2018). Evaluation of chilling injury in mangoes using multispectral imaging. *Journal of Food Science, 83*, 1271–1279.

Hellin, H. N., Torres-Sánchezb, R., Soto-Vallesc, F., Albaladejo-Péreza, C., López-Riquelmec, J. A., & Domingo-Miguel, R. (2014). A wireless sensors architecture for efficient irrigation water management. *Agricultural Water Management*.

Hu, H., Pan, L., Sun, K., Tu, S., Sun, Y., Wei, Y., & Tu, K. (2017). Differentiation of deciduous-calyx and persistent-calyx pears using hyperspectral reflectance imaging and multivariate analysis. *Computers and Electronics in Agriculture, 137*, 150–156.

Ikhwan, M., & Thamrin, N. M. (2017). IoT implementation for indoor vertical farming watering system. In *International conference on electrical, electronics and system engineering (ICEESE), Kanazawa* (pp. 89–94).

Jao, J., Sun, B., & Wu, K. (2013). *A prototype wireless sensor network for precision agriculture* [IEEE 33rd international conference on distributed computing systems workshops] (pp. 280–285).

Jawad, H. M., Nordin, R., Gharghan, S. K., Jawad, A. M., & Ismail, M. (2017). Energy-efficient wireless sensor networks for precision agriculture: A review. *Sensors (Switzerland), 17*.

Jha, K., Doshi, A., Patel, P., & Shah, M. (2019). Arti fi cial intelligence in agriculture a comprehensive review on automation in agriculture using artificial intelligence. *Artificial Intelligence in Agriculture, 2*, 1–12.

Jhuria, M., Kumar, A., & Borse, R. (2013). Image processing for smart farming: Detection of disease and fruit grading. In *2013 IEEE 2nd international conference on image information processing* (pp. 521–526). IEEE ICIIP.

Jiang, P., Chen, Y., & Liu, B. I. N. (2019). Real-time detection of apple leaf diseases using deep learning approach based on improved convolutional neural networks. *IEEE Access*, *7*, 59069–59080.

Johann, A. L., De Araújo, A. G., Delalibera, H. C., & Hirakawa, A. R. (2016). Soil moisture modeling based on stochastic behavior of forces on a no-till chisel opener. *Computers and Electronics in Agriculture*, *121*, 420–428.

Joshi, P., Kanade, S., & Joshi, S. P. (2017). Wireless sensors application for controlling of crop field parameters. *International Education and Research Journal*, *3*, 98–101.

Kamilaris, A., Gao, F., Boldu, P., Francesc, X., & Intizar Ali, M. (2016). Agri-IoT : A semantic framework for internet of things-enabled smart farming applications. In *IEEE 3rd world forum on internet of things (WF-IoT)*.

Kamilaris, A., & Prenafeta-Boldú, F. X. (2018). A review of the use of convolutional neural networks in agriculture. *Journal of Agricultural Science*, *156*, 312–322.

Kapur, R. (2018). Usage of technology in the agricultural sector. *Acta Scientific Agriculture*, *2*, 78–84.

Kaur, M., Gulati, H., & Kundra, H. (2014). Data Mining in Agriculture on crop Price prediction: Techniques and applications. *International Journal of Computer Applications*, *99*, 1–3.

Kawasaki, Y., Uga, H., Kagiwada, S., & Iyatomi, H. (2015). Basic study of automated diagnosis of viral plant diseases using convolutional neural networks Yusuke. In G. Bebis, et al. (Eds.), *Advances in visual computing. ISVC 2015. Lecture notes in computer science* (pp. 842–850).

Keller, M., Rosenberg, M., Brettel, M., & Friederichsen, N. (2014). How virtualization, Decentrazliation and network building change the manufacturing landscape: An industry 4.0 perspective. *International Journal of Mechanical, Aerospace, Industrial Mechatronic and Manufacturing Engineering*, *8*, 37–44.

Keswani, B., Mohapatra, A. G., Mohanty, A., Khanna, A., Rodrigues, J. J. P. C., Gupta, D., & Hugo, V. (2018). Adapting weather conditions based IoT enabled smart irrigation technique in precision agriculture mechanisms. *Neural Computing and Applications*, *1*.

Kokkonis, G., Kontogiannis, S., & Tomtsis, D. (2017). FITRA—A neuro-fuzzy computational algorithm approach based on an embedded water planting system. In *ACM international conference proceeding series* (pp. 0–7).

Kumar, S. A., & Ilango, P. (2018). The impact of wireless sensor network in the field of precision agriculture: A review. *Wireless Personal Communications*, *98*, 685–698.

Kung, H., Kuo, T., Chen, C., & Tsai, P. (2016). Accuracy analysis mechanism for agriculture data using the ensemble neural network method. In *Sustainability* (pp. 1–11). MDPI.

Kussul, N., Lavreniuk, M., Skakun, S., & Shelestov, A. (2017). Deep learning classification of land cover and. *IEEE Geoscience and Remote Sensing Letters*, *14*, 778–782.

Kuwata, K., & Shibasaki, R. (2015). Estimating crop yields with deep learning and remotely sensed data. In *IEEE international geoscience and remote sensing symposium (IGARSS)* (pp. 858–861).

Lamb, D. W., & Brown, R. B. (2001). Remote-sensing and mapping of weeds in crops. *Journal of Agricultural and Engineering Research*, *78*, 117–125.

Lasi, H., Fettke, P., Kemper, H. G., Feld, T., & Hoffmann, M. (2014). Industry 4.0. *Business and Information Systems Engineering*, *6*, 239–242.

Lecun, Y., Bengio, Y., & Hinton, G. (2015). Deep learning. *Nature*, *521*, 436–444.

Lee, S. H., Chan, C. S., Wilkin, P., & Remagnino, P. (2015). Deep-plant: Plant identification with convolutional neural networks. In *Proceedings—International conference on image processing, ICIP. IEEE* (pp. 452–456).

Liakos, K. G., Busato, P., Moshou, D., & Pearson, S. (2018). Machine learning in agriculture : A review. *Sensors*, 1–29.

Liao, Y., Deschamps, F., Loures, E.d. F. R., & Ramos, L. F. P. (2017). Past, present and future of industry 4.0—A systematic literature review and research agenda proposal. *International Journal of Production Research*, *55*, 3609–3629.

Liu, M., Wang, T., Skidmore, A. K., Liu, X., & Li, M. (2019). Identifying rice stress on a regional scale from multi-temporal satellite images using a Bayesian method. *Environmental Pollution*, *247*, 488–498.

Lottes, P., Hoeferlin, M., Sander, S., Muter, M., Schulze, P., & Stachniss, L. C. (2016). An effective classification system for separating sugar beets and weeds for precision farming applications. In *Proceedings—IEEE international conference on robotics and automation* (pp. 5157–5163).

Louis, J., & Dunston, P. S. (2018). Automation in construction integrating IoT into operational work fl ows for real-time and automated decision-making in repetitive construction operations. *Automation in Construction*, *94*, 317–327.

Lu, H., Fu, X., Liu, C., Li, L. G., He, Y. X., & Li, N. W. (2017). Cultivated land information extraction in UAV imagery based on deep convolutional neural network and transfer learning. *Journal of Mountain Science*, *14*, 731–741.

Lu, J., Hu, J., Zhao, G., Mei, F., & Zhang, C. (2017). An in-field automatic wheat disease diagnosis system. *Computers and Electronics in Agriculture*, *142*, 369–379.

Lu, Y., Yi, S., Zeng, N., Liu, Y., & Zhang, Y. (2017). Identification of rice diseases using deep convolutional neural networks. *Neurocomputing*, *267*, 378–384.

Luus, F. P. S., Salmon, B. P., Van Den Bergh, F., & Maharaj, B. T. J. (2015). Multiview deep learning for land-use classification. *IEEE Geoscience and Remote Sensing Letters*, *12*, 2448–2452.

Lytos, A., Lagkas, T., Sarigiannidis, P., Zervakis, M., & Livanos, G. (2020). Towards smart farming: Systems, frameworks and exploitation of multiple sources. *Computer Networks*, *172*, 107147.

Maione, C., Lemos, B., Dobal, A., Barbosa, F., & Melgaço, R. (2016). Classification of geographic origin of rice by data mining and inductively coupled plasma mass spectrometry. *Computers and Electronics in Agriculture*, *121*, 101–107.

Majumdar, J., Naraseeyappa, S., & Ankalaki, S. (2017). Analysis of agriculture data using data mining techniques: Application of big data. *Journal of Big Data*, *4*.

Mans, M. S., Fardad, H., Enteshari, R., & Mansouri, Y. S. (2010). Isolating healthy bananas from unhealthy ones based on feature extraction and clustering method using neural network. *Modern Applied Science*, *4*, 51–60.

Marques da Silva, J. R., Damásio, C. V., Sousa, A. M. O., Bugalho, L., Pessanha, L., & Quaresma, P. (2015). Agriculture pest and disease risk maps considering MSG satellite data and land surface temperature. *International Journal of Applied Earth Observation and Geoinformation*, *38*, 40–50.

Martín, J., Eduardo, L., Alejandro, J., Alejandra, M., Manuel, J., Teresa, D., … Ernesto, L. (2017). Review of IoT applications in agro-industrial and environmental fields. *Computers and Electronics in Agriculture*, *142*, 283–297.

Maynard, A. D. (2015). Navigating the fourth industrial revolution. *Nature Nanotechnology*, *10*, 1005–1006.

Meiklejohn, S., Pomarole, M., Jordan, G., Levchenko, K., Mccoy, D., Voelker, G. M., & Savage, S. (2013). A fistful of bitcoins : Characterizing payments among men with no names. In *2013 Conference on internet measurement conference* (pp. 127–140). ACM.

Mendoza, F., & Aguilera, J. M. (2004). Application of image analysis for classification of ripening bananas. *Journal of Food Science*, *69*, 471–477.

MiloviC, B., & Radojevic. (2011). Application of data mining in telecommunications companies. In *Proceedings of the 11th international symposium on operational research in Slovenia, SOR 2011* (pp. 87–92).

Mohanraj, I., Ashokumar, K., & Naren, J. (2016). Field monitoring and automation using IOT in agriculture domain. *Procedia—Procedia Computer Science, 93*, 931–939.

Mohanty, S. P., Hughes, D. P., & Salathé, M. (2016). Using deep learning for image-based plant disease detection. *Frontiers in Plant Science, 7*, 1–10.

Moreda, G. P., Muñoz, M. A., Ruiz-Altisent, M., & Perdigones, A. (2012). Shape determination of horticultural produce using two-dimensional computer vision - a review. *Journal of Food Engineering, 108*, 245–261.

Morellos, A., Pantazi, X., Moshou, D., Alexandridis, T., Whetton, R., Tziotzios, G., … Mouazen, A. M. (2016). ScienceDirect special issue : Proximal soil sensing machine learning based prediction of soil total nitrogen, organic carbon and moisture content by using VIS-NIR spectroscopy. *Biosystems Engineering*, 1–13.

Moshou, D., Bravo, C., Oberti, R., West, J., Bodria, L., Mccartney, A., & Ramon, H. (2005). Plant disease detection based on data fusion of hyper-spectral and multi-spectral fluorescence imaging using Kohonen maps. *Real-Time Imaging, 11*, 75–83.

Moshou, D., Bravo, C., West, J., Wahlen, S., Mccartney, A., & Ramon, H. (2004). Automatic detection of ' yellow rust ' in wheat using reflectance measurements and neural networks. *Computers and Electronics in Agriculture, 44*, 173–188.

Moshou, D., Pantazi, X., & Kateris, D. (2013). Water stress detection based on optical multisensor fusion with a least squares support vector machine classifier 5. *Biosystems Engineering, 117*, 15–22.

Murugesan, R., Sudarsanam, S. K., Malathi, G., Vijayakumar, V., Neelanarayanan, V., Venugopal, R., … Malolan, V. (2019). Artificial intelligence and agriculture 5. 0. *International Journal of Recent Technology and Engineering (IJRTE) ISSN:2277-3878, 8*, 1870–1877.

Nahvi, B., Habibi, J., Mohammadi, K., & Shamshirband, S. (2016). Using self-adaptive evolutionary algorithm to improve the performance of an extreme learning machine estimating soil temperature. *Computers and Electronics in Agriculture, 124*, 150–160.

Nawandar, N. K., & Satpute, V. R. (2019). IoT based low cost and intelligent module for smart irrigation system. *Computers and Electronics in Agriculture, 162*, 979–990.

Ojha, T., Misra, S., & Singh, N. (2015). Wireless sensor networks for agriculture : The state-of-the-art in practice and future challenges. *Computers and Electronics in Agriculture, 118*, 66–84.

Padalalu, P., Mahajan, S., Dabir, K., Mitkar, S., & Javale, D. (2017). Smart water dripping system for agriculture/farming. In *2017 2nd international conference for convergence in technology, I2CT 2017* (pp. 659–662).

Padol, P. B., & Yadav, A. A. (2016). SVM classifier based grape leaf disease detection. *Conference on Advances in Signal Processing, CASP, 2016*, 175–179.

Pandurng, J. A. (2015). Image processing applications in agriculture : A survey. *International Journal of Advanced Research in Computer Science and Software Engineering Digital, 5*, 622–624.

Pantazi, X. E., Moshou, D., Alexandridis, T., Whetton, R. L., & Mouazen, A. M. (2016). Wheat yield prediction using machine learning and advanced sensing techniques. *Computers and Electronics in Agriculture, 121*, 57–65.

Pantazi, X. E., Moshou, D., & Bochtis, D. (2017). Detection of biotic and abiotic stresses in crops by using hierarchical self organizing classifiers. *Precision Agriculture.*

Pantazi, X., Moshou, D., & Bravo, C. (2016). ScienceDirect special issue : Robotic agriculture active learning system for weed species recognition based on hyperspectral sensing. *Biosystems Engineering*, 1–10.

Pantazi, X. E., Tamouridou, A. A., Alexandridis, T. K., Lagopodi, A. L., Kashefi, J., & Moshou, D. (2017a). Evaluation of hierarchical self-organising maps for weed mapping using UAS multispectral imagery. *Computers and Electronics in Agriculture*, *139*, 224–230.

Pantazi, X. E., Tamouridou, A. A., Alexandridis, T. K., Lagopodi, A. L., Kontouris, G., & Moshou, D. (2017b). Detection of Silybum marianum infection with Microbotryum silybum using VNIR field spectroscopy. *Computers and Electronics in Agriculture*, *137*, 130–137.

Patel, A. A., & Kathirya, D. R. (2017). Data Mining in Agriculture: A review. *AGRES—An International e. Journal*, *6*, 637–645.

Patil, S. S., & Thorat, S. A. (2016). Early yield prediction using image analysis of apple fruit and tree canopy features with neural networks. In *2nd International conference on cognitive computing and information processing, CCIP 2016*.

Pedersen, & Kjeldgaard, S. J. (2007). Circular Hough transform. *Aalborg University, Vision, Graphics, and Interactive Systems*, *123*(6), 181.

Pivoto, D., Waquil, P. D., Talamini, E., Finocchio, C. P. S., Dalla Corte, V. F., & de Vargas Mores, G. (2018). Scientific development of smart farming technologies and their application in Brazil. *Information Processing in Agriculture*, *5*, 21–32.

Piyare, R., & Lee, S. R. (2013). Towards internet of things (IOTS): Integration of wireless sensor network to cloud services for data collection and sharing. *International Journal of Computer Networks & Communications*, *5*, 59–72.

Poojith, A., Reddy, B. V. A., & Kumar, G. V. (2014). Image processing in agriculture. *International Journal of Innovative Research in Electrical, Electronics, Instrumentation and Control Engineering*, *2*, 207–230.

Prabha, D. S., & Kumar, J. S. (2013). Three dimensional object detection and classification methods: A study. *International Journal of Engineering Research and Science & Technology*, *2*, 33–42.

Prakash, K., Saravanamoorthi, P., Sathishkumar, R., & Parimala, M. (2017). A study of image processing in agriculture. Int. J. *Advanced Networking and Applications*, *22*, 3311–3315.

Rajeswari, S., Suthendran, K., & Rajakumar, K. (2018). A smart agricultural model by integrating IoT, mobile and cloud-based big data analytics. In *International conference on intelligent computing and control, I2C2 2017* (pp. 1–5).

Ramos, P. J., Prieto, F. A., Montoya, E. C., & Oliveros, C. E. (2017). Automatic fruit count on coffee branches using computer vision. *Computers and Electronics in Agriculture*, *137*, 9–22.

Rawidean, M., Kassim, M., Mat, I., & Harun, A. N. (2014). Wireless sensor network in precision agriculture application. In *International conference on computer, information and telecommunication systems (CITS)*.

Rehman, A., & Hussain, I. (2016). Modern agricultural technology adoption its importance, role and usage for the improvement of agriculture. *American-Eurasian Journal of Agricultural & Environmental Sciences*.

Reyes, A. K., Caicedo, J. C., & Camargo, J. E. (2015). *Fine-tuning deep convolutional networks for plant recognition*. CLEF (working notes) (p. 1391).

Ribeiro, P. G. A. (2016). Fleets of robots for environmentally-safe pest control in agriculture. *Precision Agriculture*, *18*, 574–614.

Rodríguez, S., Gualotuña, T., & Grilo, C. (2017). A system for the monitoring and predicting of data in precision agriculture in a rose greenhouse based on wireless sensor networks. *Procedia Computer Science*, *121*, 306–313.

Roham, V. S., Pawar, G. A., Patil, A. S., & Rupnar, P. R. (2015). Smart farm using wireless sensor network. *International Journal of Computer Applications*, 8–11.

Roldán, J. J., Cerro, J., De, J., Ramos, D. G., Aunon, G., Garzón, M., & De León, J. (2017). *Robots in agriculture : State of art and practical experiences.*

Ruß, G. (2009). *Data mining of agricultural yield data: A comparison of regression models, lecture notes in computer science (including subseries lecture notes in artificial intelligence and lecture notes in bioinformatics).*

Saiz-Rubio, V., & Rovira-Más, F. (2020). From smart farming towards agriculture 5.0: A review on crop data management. *Agronomy, 10.*

Santoni, M. M., Sensuse, D. I., Arymurthy, A. M., & Fanany, M. I. (2015). Cattle race classification using gray level co-occurrence matrix convolutional neural networks. *Procedia Computer Science, 59,* 493–502.

Satyanarayana, G. V. (2013). Wireless sensor based remote monitoring system for agriculture using ZigBee and GPS. In *Advances in communication and control systems 2013 (CAC2S 2013) wireless* (pp. 110–114).

Sawa, T. (2019). Blockchain technology outline and its application to field of power and energy system. *Electrical Engineering in Japan, 206,* 1–5.

Schmidhuber, J. (2014). *Deep learning in neural networks : An overview* (pp. 1–88).

Schor, N., Bechar, A., Ignat, T., Dombrovsky, A., Elad, Y., & Berman, S. (2016). Robotic disease detection in greenhouses: Combined detection of powdery mildew and tomato spotted wilt virus. *IEEE Robotics and Automation Letters, 1,* 354–360.

Sellam, V., & Poovammal, E. (2016). Prediction of crop yield using regression analysis. *Indian Journal of Science and Technology, 9.*

Sengupta, S., & Suk, W. (2013). Special issue : Image analysis in agriculture identification and determination of the number of immature green citrus fruit in a canopy under different ambient light conditions 5. *Biosystems Engineering, 117,* 51–61.

Senthilnath, J., Dokania, A., & Kandukuri, M. (2015). ScienceDirect special issue : Robotic agriculture detection of tomatoes using spectral-spatial methods in remotely sensed RGB images captured by UAV. *Biosystems Engineering,* 1–17.

Siva Rama Krishnan, S., & Arun Kumar, T. (2019). A practical implementation smart farming using recommendation routing in WSN. *International Journal of Recent Technology and Engineering, 7,* 335–345.

Sladojevic, S., Arsenovic, M., Anderla, A., Culibrk, D., & Stefanovic, D. (2016). Deep neural networks based recognition of plant diseases by leaf image classification. *Computational Intelligence and Neuroscience Volume, 2016,* 11.

Song, X., Zhang, G., Liu, F., Li, D., Zhao, Y., & Yang, J. (2016). Modeling spatio-temporal distribution of soil moisture by deep learning-based cellular automata model. *Journal of Arid Land, 8,* 734–748.

Sørensen, R. A., Rasmussen, J., Nielsen, J., & Jørgensen, R. N. (2017). Thistle detection using convolutional neural networks: EFITA 2017 presentation. In *EFITA WCCA congress. 2–6. June 2017.*

Steen, K. A., Christiansen, P., Karstoft, H., & Jørgensen, R. N. (2016). Using deep learning to challenge safety standard for highly autonomous machines in agriculture. *Journal of Imaging, 2,* 2–9.

Surya, P., & Satheesh, K. (2014). Image processing methods and its role in agricultural sector—A study. *International Journal of Business Intelligents, 03,* 366–373.

Tewari, V. K., Pareek, C. M., Lal, G., Dhruw, L. K., & Singh, N. (2020). *Image processing based real-time variable rate chemical spraying system for disease control in paddy crop.* (Artificial Intelligence in Agriculture).

Tian, F., Wu, B., Zeng, H., Zhang, X., & Xu, J. (2019). Efficient identification of corn cultivation area with multitemporal synthetic aperture radar and optical images in the Google earth engine cloud platform. *Remote Sensing, 11,* 629.

Timalsina, T. R. (2019). Agricultural transformation around Koshi Hill region: A rural development perspective. *NUTA Journal, 6,* 95–101.

Vanitha, C., Archana, N., & Sowmiya, R. (2019). Agriculture analysis using data mining and machine learning techniques. In *2019 5th international conference on advanced computing and communication systems, ICACCS 2019. IEEE* (pp. 984–990).

Varman, S. A. M., Baskaran, A. R., Aravindh, S., & Prabhu, E. (2017). Deep learning and IoT for smart agriculture using WSN. In *IEEE international conference on computational intelligence and computing research, ICCIC 2017. IEEE* (pp. 1–6).

Viani, F., Robol, F., Bertolli, M., Polo, A., Massa, A., Ahmadi, H., & Boualleague, R. (2016). *A wireless monitoring system for phytosanitary treatment in smart farming applications* [2016 IEEE antennas and propagation society international symposium, APSURSI 2016—Proceedings] (pp. 2001–2002).

Vibhute, A., & Bodhe, K. S. (2012). Applications of image processing in agriculture: A survey. *International Journal of Computer Applications, 52,* 34–39.

Xie, T., Huang, Z., Chi, Z., & Zhu, T. (2017). Minimizing amortized cost of the on-demand irrigation system in smart farms. In *Proceedings - 2017 3rd international workshop on cyber-physical systems for smart water networks, CySWATER 2017* (pp. 43–46).

Xinshao, W., & Cheng, C. (2016). Weed seeds classification based on PCANet deep learning baseline. In *2015 Asia-Pacific signal and information processing association annual summit and conference, APSIPA ASC, 2015* (pp. 408–415).

Yanxia, G., Baozhong, W., & Zhenhui, R. (2007). Research of precision farming expert system based on GIS. In *The eighth international conference on electronic measurement and instruments ICEMI* (pp. 858–861).

Ying-xue, S., Huan, X., & Li-jiao, Y. (2017). Support vector machine-based open crop model (SBOCM): Case of rice production in China. *Saudi Journal of Biological Sciences, 24,* 537–547.

Yu, J., Sharpe, S. M., Schumann, A. W., & Boyd, N. S. (2019). Deep learning for image-based weed detection in turfgrass. *European Journal of Agronomy, 104,* 78–84.

Zang, S., Chen, X., Wang, S., 2014. Research on the monitoring system of wheat diseases, pests and weeds based on IOT. In: The 9th international conference on computer science & education (ICCSE 2014) August 22–24, 2014 Vancouver, Canada. SaP10.5. 981–985.

Zhang, M., Li, C., & Yang, F. (2017). Classification of foreign matter embedded inside cotton lint using short wave infrared (SWIR) hyperspectral transmittance imaging. *Computers and Electronics in Agriculture, 139,* 75–90.

Chapter 2

A systematic review of artificial intelligence in agriculture

Parvinder Singh and Amandeep Kaur

Department of Computer Science and Technology, Central University of Punjab, Bathinda, Punjab, India

1 Precision farming

1.1 Introduction

The Food and Agriculture Organization of the United Nations (FAO), a specialized agency steering an international endeavor to defeat hunger worldwide, claims global population will reach peak height with 9.2 billion by the year 2050 (Amin, 2017; Rose et al., 2016).

According to different agencies and experts, grain consumption will increase worldwide exponentially in the coming years, which will cause an explosion of the food crisis. This global crisis will not be solved only by planting more crops or breeding more cattle. Further, this problem becomes more serious due to the splitting of agriculture land in small pieces and highly inconsistent availability of natural resources, such as water, organic fertilizers, and more, across the world. Therefore, the exigent growth of agriculture products is also necessary, and making use of new techniques and methods is essential for efficient and sustainable agricultural methods to balance the supply chain, according to the consumer demand.

Precision agriculture (PA) is a collection of new technologies and different strategies, management tools, and practices that provide new, smarter methods to curb the global food crisis by increasing crop growth, effectively managing natural resources, and regulating the use of agricultural land. PA can also be defined as "doing the right thing, at the right time, in the right place, in the right way" (Karydas & Silleos, 2000; Srinivasan, 2006). For this, PA uses different technologies and information management tools to control the spatial and temporal mutability in order to reduce the environmental degradation and increase the effective use of natural resources with highly productivities of agricultural products (Dimitriadis & Goumopoulos, 2008). PA includes plant monitoring, driverless tractors, automated irrigation systems, automatic spraying of

Deep Learning for Sustainable Agriculture. https://doi.org/10.1016/B978-0-323-85214-2.00011-2

pesticides using drones, and more. In other words, it is an intelligent decision support system that makes the decision by analyzing the data that is collected by effectively monitoring crops and their environment throughout the year.

PA increases the production capacity and minimizes the overall cost using different AI-based applications. Over the last few years, traditional agriculture methods have been affecting the environment badly, while the profit margin is continuously decreasing. Because of this, farmers are committing suicide in developing countries, hence, for forthwith benefit to the farmer, it is requisite to develop new and smarter methods for efficient agriculture. PA provides management tools for smart irrigation, exact use of pesticides, fertilizers, herbicides, insecticides, seeds, and more, which this also endows autonomous and robotic labor. Furthermore, PA helps in steadily increasing profits, reducing the waste of natural resources, and improving the quality of the climate (Lee & Ehsani, 2015). Fig. 1 pictorially represents some smart tools, such as soil analysis drones, farming robots, and hyperspectral imaging systems for PA.

PA has emerged as an interdisciplinary research area at the interface of diverse technological disciplines, mobile computing, the Internet of Things (IoT), wireless sensor networks, robotics, artificial intelligence (AI), deep learning, and many more, and it is a major cause of the exponential growth in the field of PA.

(A)　　　　　　　　　　　(B)

(C)　　　　　　　　　　　(D)

FIG. 1　PA technologies. (A) Soil analysis drone (Talaviya et al., 2020). (B) Strawberry harvesting robot (Pathan et al., 2020). (C) Autonomous agriculture robot (Pathan et al., 2020). (D) Hyperspectral imaging: from the lab to the field robot (Pathan et al., 2020).

According to Cox (2002), PA includes techniques that extend our ability to control operations automatically and that are useful for information gathering, processing, and decision-making to improve agricultural production. Furthermore, Cox (2002) states that the general heading of PA includes applications of livestock production and spatially variable field operations that are possible via satellite global positioning system (GPS).

1.2   Related work using AI

Considering the importance of PA, a lot of theoretical and experimental progress has been made in last three decades toward the development of this area. Image processing has become a major technique since the 1990s for monitoring the growth of plants and crops (Takakura, 1991). AI and machine learning have also played a major role in order to develop control systems in PA. As an example, a smart system for irrigation scheduling for greenhouse environments using neural networks was developed in the 1990s (Ehret et al., 2001). Neural networks have also been used to monitor the water status by identifying a nonlinear relation with textural features of pictorial information generated from the plant canopy (Murase et al., 1994).

The foundation of PA is based on different innovative system approaches, such as geographic information systems (GIS), GPS, multispectral and hyperspectral, ground-based computer vision and modeling, remote sensing, and more (Gibbons, 2000; Waheed et al., 2006). According to Gibbons (2000) an advanced information technology (IT) infrastructure provides a systematic approach for timely management of plants and crops. Using the actuator and sensors, a proactive computing model was presented in one study (Goumopoulos et al., 2007) as the deployment of an intelligent system for the application of PA. Therefore, PA integrates different technologies, collect multifarious data, and increases the production while minimizing the cost through effective analysis of this data (Amin, 2017).

PA is analogous of smart farming (SF) and is inclusive of electronics and communication technology into mechanical machinery appliances (Pivoto et al., 2018). One can also view SF as the use of sensors and actuators in agriculture production systems (Ahmed et al., 2016; Pedersen et al., 2008). Considering the major challenges of agricultural productions, such as plants sensitivity for climate changes, weather restrictions, environmental impact, productivity, and food sustainability (Dimitriadis & Goumopoulos, 2008; Gebbers & Adamchuk, 2010), an intelligent, flexible, and fast-responding system is essential. SF is an important system that can address these challenges. It can better understand the multivariate, unpredictable, and complicated agricultural ecosystems by continuously monitoring and analyzing various physical measures and phenomena (Kamilaris & Prenafeta-Boldú, 2018; Tyagi, 2016). Further, Narvaez et al. (2017) presented precision horticulture to redress the different difficulties encountered by agribusiness due to atmosphere changes, accessibility of agricultural land, lack of man power, and land debasement. In recent years, computer vision and image processing have speedy growth in agriculture because of high power computation, low-cost equipment, and introduction of nondestructive food assessment methods (Patrício & Rieder, 2018).

Artificial neural networks (ANNs) and fuzzy logic are useful in classification and can predict and forecast different requirements, like water required for a particular crop (Jha et al., 2019). Classification is a vital process in PA to classify the crops into different classes for crop mapping. In one study (Noguchi et al., 1998), generic -optimized (GA-optimized) fuzzy logic was used to classify crops. ANNs were been used to differentiate weeds from the crops in one study (Gliever & Slaughter, 2001) and also used to estimate the height and width of the soybean crops based on weed segmentation in another study (Heckmann et al., 2017). Maier and Dandy applied neural networks for predicting water resource variables (Maier & Dandy, 2000). Fuzzy logic is applied for grading the crops and plants of cauliflower, apples, mangoes, and even tomatoes (Pathan et al., 2020). Fuzzy logic and ANNs extract features such as size, shape, color, aroma, plant canopy, and more from the input data or from captured images of plants to perform the grading or classification (Mustafa et al., 2009).

An autonomous robot is a programmable machine that can automatically perform the complex series of actions. Autonomous robots have competence with a dynamic process of adopting and learning (Hagras et al., 2002). Robots use different sensors for inputting information and processing information using a control unit. The control unit of a robot is designed using fuzzy logic (Hagras et al., 2000). Autonomous robots can be used in industrial production and service application to assist humans in their tasks (Ben-Ari & Mondada, 2018). Autonomous robots are very useful machinery for PA to perform different tasks, such as seeding and planting, weed removing, drone spraying, harvesting, and so on (Pathan et al., 2020; Slaughter et al., 2008). Some robots models are shown in Fig. 2.

Lee et al. (1999) designed robotics for weed control, which was based on the exactitude of a chemical application system and a vision machine system. Autonomous robots consist of eye-hand systems and gripper systems for automatic inspection and treatment of diseases of plants (Acaccia et al., 2003). Robots use different navigation systems, but most of robots of PA use human-operated mobiles/laptops and GPS to move among the rows of plants (Pathan et al., 2020).

Agriculture plays a major role in the gross domestic product of any developing country; therefore, to increase the economic returns with shortened energy input and environmental impact on farming, Hakkim et al. (2016) defined PA futures with different technologies, such as soil management, crop management, rate controllers, stick irrigation, and variable-rate fertilizer (VRT) for cereals, vegetables, and fruits. Furthermore, Pire et al. described different factors of new technologies behind the success of PA. (Ullah et al., 2017) reviewed different tools and technologies based on AI and machine learning

FIG. 2 Different types of autonomous robots used in PA. (A) The agricultural robot sprayer (Adamides et al., 2014). (B) The agricultural drone sprayer (Talaviya et al., 2020). (C) The agricultural robot platform (Ball et al., 2016). (D) Strawberry harvesting robot (Xiong et al., 2020).

to overcome major challenges and issues in agriculture. In this digital era, PA has four major steps: (1) data collection; (2) data analysis; (3) decisions management; and (4) farming. These steps are implemented using different tools and technologies based on ANNs and fuzzy logic. IoT is also a fast-growing, interdisciplinary technology and a foundation of PA (Khanna & Kaur, 2019). IoT is the network of physical objects that contains embedded technology to communicate and sense or interact with their internal states or the external environment.

1.3 Objective and design consideration

Until the last two decades, primarily three major levels of technology were used in agriculture: hand-tool technology, animal-drawn technology, and mechanical-power technology (Tekin & Sindir, 2002). Voss (1974) described four different stages of agriculture mechanization process, stated as:

(1) Hand tools are cheap and easily available.
(2) Animal power is used in the place of human labor.
(3) Mechanical power is also used in some operations of agriculture, but not in all.

(4) Mechanization of agricultural processes are based on power equipment and have not included electronics components.

Although these technologies and the levels of mechanization of farming improve the productivity, they could not handle the in-field variability of soil conditions, environment, and crops. Also, the previously mentioned technologies could not help in continuous monitoring of crop life cycle. The present era of digitalization has given birth to the concept of PA; hence, the following two new stages are introduced in the agriculture mechanization process (Tekin & Sindir, 2002).

(5) In this stage, agriculture production makes use of IT and an intermediate level of information systems. Agribusiness use computers and software for keeping stock information, keeping the historical records, and analyzing the what-if models. An agriculture vehicle like a tractor could have an automatic lift controller, power brakes, power steering, and inherent monitoring systems to display fuel consumption, work rate, forward and backward speed, and distance traveled. Other agricultural tools like seeder and fertilizer machines and harvesters, and sprayers have computerized control systems and data-logging facilities.

(6) At this level, agriculture is known as precision farming, also called SF. It uses different advanced technologies such as AI, machine learning, fuzzy logic, robotics, and IoT in farming. Precision farming can be efficient in managing the in-field variability of soil conditions, environmental conditions, and crops. PA includes continuous monitoring of plants, driverless tractors, automated irrigation systems, and automatic spraying of pesticides using drones.

Fundamental objectives of PA are as follows:

- Reduce the application cost of chemical, pesticides, and fertilizers.
- Make and use less chemicals, pesticides, and fertilizers.
- Make the best decisions by measuring the performance of several seed types, soils, chemicals, and fertilizers
- Maximize profit, field performance, agricultural produce, and productivity with little investment.
- Minimize environmental and soil pollution with the proper use of chemicals.
- Analyze data collected from the continuous monitoring for better decision-making in farm management.
- Improve bumper yield, disease detection, and treatment in plants, and analyze crop phenotyping to produce hybrid seeds.
- Improve the management of farm records, which are essential in crop sale, land sale, and successions.
- Analyze the performance and productivity of each field area by tracking and mapping the performance of the field in square meters.

A lot of progress has been made in the last decade in IT infrastructure and its components, like hardware networking and software. Significant development and price drop of electronics components is a major factor for the exponential growth in SF. Major technologies that are desired within PA and have made significant impression are as follows (Balafoutis et al., 2017):

- GIS are required for decision support systems in PA.
- Remote sensing and satellite technology are used to get information regarding crop environment characteristics and crop life cycle.
- Soil health management tools are required for soil sampling and analysis, collecting the information on soil characteristics, finding requirement of fertilizers and chemicals for fertile land, and for growing and developing crops.
- Smart positioning systems, such GPS, are required to apply practices of PA that seek location information.
- Wireless sensor networks are required for continual monitoring of crops, and monitors, such as yield monitor, are required to measure the effect of SF.
- Mapping systems are required for analyzing, displaying, and decision-making based on data collected through different sensors.
- GA, ANNs, fuzzy logic, robotics, IoT, and deep learnings are used in disease detection and treatment in plants and to analyze crop phenotyping to produce hybrid seeds.

1.4 Challenges and future scope

In developing countries, productivity level is significantly less in comparison to per capita of investment; hence, the performance level of production is not significant. This is due to small and scattered agricultural land, poverty and illiteracy among farmers, variability of soil conditions, environmental conditions, and crops.

PA systems depend on the vivid capabilities of AI, machine learning, and IoT to improve the growth of farming productions and deliver new monitoring competencies. In SF, sensors are placed within the ground to measure different physical inputs, such as soil moisture, temperature, and pH levels. Environmental sensors measure the amount of sun exposure, rain fall, wind speed, air temperature, and humidity. Aerial drones are useful to observe crops and the effects of pesticides and chemicals on the plant life cycle. Further, AI and machine learning tools are used to process the data collected from different sensors for the decision-making.

Despite the advantages, the smart agriculture system faces several challenges (Fakhruddin, 2017). The major issues and challenges toward the success of PA are detailed in the following list:

(1) Unstable climate. An unstable climate is a great challenge for PA. In rainy or stormy seasons, devices like sensors may be damaged. In winter, field

equipment might not communicate with control devices due to fog. Therefore, hardware components of SF should be reliable and flexible.

(2) Portability of different standards. SF includes different tools and technologies based on different technological standards. But for complete success of PA, data should be uniform in nature. Hence, interoperability has become a great concern, and PA is still fragmented.

(3) Lack of technical education. In precision farming implementation of necessary IoT architecture, sensor network and machine learning is essential. A little error in technical use can be disastrous. Farmers and agriculture tool manufacturers are not completely aware of the latest technologies. So, it is essential for our society to be acquainted with new tools and technologies.

(4) Network connectivity. Strong, reliable internet connectivity is essential for PA, which is a big problem in remote locations, farmlands, and hilly terrains. Unless the network performance, bandwidth, speed, and reception of GPS signals are improved, precision farming will not succeed.

(5) Big data analysis. PA is speedily becoming a source of big data. Technical agriculture is helpful only when farmer can make sense of available data. Large multicrop lands generate petabit data and millions of data points. It is difficult to monitor every data point, so big data is also another challenge in PA. Therefore, AI tools should find out data points for monitoring for best knowledge discovery.

(6) Lack of configuration and scalability. As we know, farms vary in size, geography, and climate conditions. Hence, scalability is a big challenge in PA. So, our technology must be highly scalable and configurative according to requirements and situations.

(7) Nonawareness of different varying agricultural functions. The agriculture production function for all the crops is not the same. It differs according to geographic conditions and crop growth cycles. If our AI tools do not carry these varying functions, there may be malfunctions in the overall system. For example, spraying too much pesticides results in crop damage. So, in agriculture automation, varying functions is an immense issue.

(8) The effective management of SF requires division of land into different zones according to the characteristics of soils. Therefore, the individual zones have their own fertilizer, chemical, pesticide, and seed requirements. This management is another big deal.

(9) Efficient energy management. In PA, the need for powerful data centers, gateways, and hubs leads to heavy energy consumption. Another important component is a sensor. Sensors are deployed in remote areas of the fields. Sensors lose their battery power after a period and stop working. Hence, energy depletion is another big challenge.

(10) Mostly, PA machinery and methods are designed only for traditional outdoor farming. Hence, optimal use of the environmental factors, such as

light, temperature, and water availability for indoor farming, requires more attentions.

(11) Technical failures. PA depends upon correct functioning of hardware and software. Hardware failure or sensor malfunction can be dangerous for crops. For example, any deficiency in a smart irrigation system might result in plants being underwatered or overwatered.

(12) E-wastes. In digital farming, different tools and devices are implemented. But by the time, they malfunction, they are outdated. Therefore, they are dumped, which causes a new risk of e-waste in PA.

(13) Human unemployment Agriculture is a main source for living most of the people in our society. Due to SF, there will be an explosion of unemployed labor in upcoming years, and it will become a global problem.

(14) Cyber security. PA mostly uses electronics equipment. There is always a risk of malware, data theft, and software viruses and bugs, so tighter security is the need for complete implementation of SF.

(15) Expensive instruments. Tools and technologies used in SF are very expensive, and long-term benefits are unpredictable. Expense is another major issue, and a lot of research is required to reduce the cost of components used in PA.

2   Plant disease detection

2.1   Introduction

Food security is the main challenge in underdeveloped and developing countries like India. Crop disease is the major cause of loss both in terms of quality and quantity in agriculture produce. The symptoms of crop disease effecting the different parts of a plant are detected manually by farmers. Later, farmers share the symptoms with agriculture experts, usually by visiting the nearest office or placing a phone call. This kind of assessment requires experts to do the tests, is subjective in nature and prone to human error, and requires more human effort and time. To reduce the effort and time required, especially in large fields, researchers have proposed automated computerized methods for crop disease detection using image processing and classification techniques (Cristin et al., 2020).

Most common plant diseases are fungal in nature. Other diseases are caused by viral and bacterial organisms. The diseases could be noninfectious or contagious. Careful checking of visual appearance of a plant can give a good indication regarding the type of pathogen and disease category. Visual indicators are changes in the color or shape of a plant. The symptoms are leaf wilting, lesions, and leaf spots (Jim, 2012).

The development of automated computer-based systems for plant disease detection holds great significance. Especially when the system is integrated with drones or remote sensing to scan large farms areas at any time. Such automatic modules help in fast disease detection that are more accurate than manual methods of plant disease detection. Timely disease detection helps control diseases better with less use of pesticides and other sprays, leading to cost savings for farmers.

Initial work in this area was done using image-processing techniques that come under the purview of computer and machine vision. For a detailed review of image processing techniques in plant disease detection, readers may refer to Sharif et al. (2018). A brief description of image-processing steps for crop disease detection and classification follows.

Step 1: Image acquisition
Hyperspectral remote sensing images help in rapid detection of disease in plants but are expensive to capture and process. Thus, most techniques in the literature use images acquired using visible light cameras; such cameras are even available on a mobile phone today.

Step 2: Image preprocessing and conversion to appropriate color models
Most of the collected images of different parts of the plant, like leaves, fruit, and stems, suffer from low contrast, noise, shadows, and nonuniform illumination due to uncontrolled conditions during image capture. This leads to the requirement of image preprocessing to make the image more suitable for further processing, like segmentation and feature extraction. The generally used technique for contrast improvement is histogram equalization. This technique is fully automatic and easy to implement, but it may lead to over enhancement and add image distortions. Many advance techniques for contrast enhancement are proposed in literature (Weizheng et al., 2008) and may be explored for improved results. For noise removal, a commonly used technique that gives good results is median filtering. The issue of shadow and nonuniform illumination is handled by different researchers with the help of color model conversion (Narvekar et al., 2014). Some researchers have worked in RGB color space; others have done conversion to XYZ, HSI, or CMYK color models before further processing of images.

Step 3: Image segmentation
After the image is preprocessed, it is segmented to select the region of interest (ROI). Segmentation is twofold. Segmentation is first done to isolate the leaf, fruit, or flower from the background. A second segmentation is then done to isolate healthy tissue from diseased tissue. That is the diseased part of the leaf, fruit, or some other part, and it suppresses the background (Barbedo, 2019). Many of the existing papers use threshold, edge, or clustering techniques for segmentation. The threshold-based techniques can be used when there is only one type of foreground in the image, but they are not suitable for complex images (Iqbal et al., 2018). Otsu method, which is a global technique, is commonly used. For improved results, local techniques, like Sauvola thresholding, which tend to give better results in images with

nonuniform illumination, may be explored. Canny edge detection is used in some papers for segmentation. Edge-based techniques are suitable when the images have good contrast and low noise. Many papers use k-means clustering for segmenting the diseased part, as it is simple to implement and an image can be divided into a number of clusters. The method could be slow to segment.

Step 4: Feature extraction

In most of the proposed work for automatic disease detection in plants, handcrafted features extraction is used from the ROI. This helps to collect unique information from the image to represent the disease symptoms. It is desirable for features to have good discrimination power, not be very sensitive for distortions in the images, and easy to compute, and require less space and invariant to transformations like rotation, scale, and translation. The calculated features are used to train the classifiers to differentiate between healthy and diseased plants. There are various types of features that are broadly classified into shape, color, and texture. The researchers generally use a combination of these features to improve the recognition accuracy. The detailed description of shape-based features is given in Yang et al. (2008). In plant disease. Shape-based features like region area, Fourier descriptor, and wavelets are used. The color and texture features are more commonly used features in this research area. One of the most straightforward visual features of an image is the color because the human eye is sensitive to colors. Color features are the basic characteristic of the content of images. Using color features, humans can recognize most images and objects included in the image. Images can be represented by color histograms that show the proportion of pixels of each color within the image (Afifi & Ashour, 2012). The texture features provide us with information regarding the placement of various intensities or colors in the image. These features can be used for image analysis, classification, and segmentation. Humeau-Heurtier (2019) provides a comprehensive survey of the texture feature extraction methods.

Step 5: Training

Machine learning algorithms are supplied with feature vectors and trained to categorize features associated with each disease to be recognized. The trained algorithm can then be used to recognize features from new images captured from the field. Classification deals with matching a given input feature vector with one of the distinct classes learned during training. The designer may use more than one learning algorithm for training and classification.

2.2 Deep learning in image processing

Computer vision is currently used in a number of applications from video games to selfdriving cars. Image classification is a specific part of computer vision that has many diverse real-world applications. However, it also has been traditionally very difficult to pull off successfully due to the enormous amount of different factors (camera angles, lighting, color balance, resolution, etc.) that go into creating an image. Today, deep neural networks are a portion of the most established machine learning algorithms that give good classification results from character recognition and remote sensing applications to medical images.

In machine learning there are various classifiers that are supervised, semi-supervised, or unsupervised. Deep learning is a subfield of machine learning, which uses a set of algorithms that attempts to model high-level abstractions present in data by using a deep architecture possessing multiple processing layers, having linear and nonlinear transformation functions. Deep learning is based on ANNs, which attempts to mimic the way the human brain works. The feed forward neural networks, comprising of many hidden layers, are good examples of models with deep architecture. The standard back propagation algorithm popularized in 1980 is still an effective way of training the neural networks.

In their review of image segmentation techniques, Pal & Pal (1993) predicted that due to the noise robust and parallel architecture of the neural networks, they would become widely applied in image processing, particularly in real-time applications. Their prediction turned out to be true today with AI everywhere around us, especially the deep neural networks.

Deep learning algorithms, specifically convolutional neural networks (CNNs), have become a widely used methodology in various images processing, segmentation, pattern recognition, and classification techniques (Dhingra et al., 2018). It is emerging as a promising technique even in PA and other related applications in this area. CNN is particularly useful in image processing, as it is an end-to-end learning machine and overcomes the shortcomings of techniques based on handcrafted feature extraction. CNN is called an end-to-end learning machine, as in this deep neural network, there is no need for feature extraction to train the model but a raw image may be given directly to the CNN to obtain the target output. If the training data is large and unbiased, the CNN-based techniques for classification give much better results than the state-of-the-art feature extraction-based classification techniques (Aloysius & Geetha, 2017).

CNNs were developed by LeCun et al. (1990) and later improved on by LeCun et al. (1998). It was specifically designed to classify handwritten digits and was successful in recognizing visual patterns directly from the input image without any preprocessing. But, due to lack of sufficient training data and computing power, this architecture failed to perform well in complex problems. Researchers (Krizhevsky et al., 2017) came up with a CNN model that succeeded in bringing down the error rate on ILSVRC competition (Berg et al., 2010). Over the years, their work has become one of the most influential in the field of computer vision and is used by many for trying out variations in CNN architecture. AlexNet was able to achieve remarkable results compared to the previous model of learning and without any unsupervised pretraining to keep the net simple. The architecture can be considered a major variant of LeNet having five convolutional layers followed by three fully connected layers. There have been variations of AlexNet since its huge success in ILSVRC-2012 competitions. This chapter will serve as a guide for beginners in the area. Many frameworks are available for deep learning, of which Google's TensorFlow is the latest and fastest growing.

2.3 Review of plant disease detection using image processing and deep learning

Oide et al. (1995) were one of the first researchers to use CNN neural networks for plant images. As the CNN networks were evolving, some of the major issues were hardware limitations and a need for better learning methods for large-scale deep neural networks. Most of these problems are solved today with powerful hardware available at nominal prices, cloud-based solutions, and a number of good training algorithms (Sladojevic et al., 2016). AlexNet, a type of CNN proposed by Krizhevsky et al. (2012), competed in the ImageNet Large Scale Visual Recognition Challenge in 2012 and outperformed most of the existing machine learning algorithms. The main difference between previous image classification techniques and CNN is that most of the traditional methods first extract the image feature and then use these hand-crafted features for image classification. There are various challenges in selecting suitable feature extraction techniques. The computationally simple features are generally not rotation, scale, and translation invariant. Image quality, like low contrast, nonuniform illumination, and noise, effect the accuracy of features. In CNN we have to only train the weights and select filter parameters in the hidden layers to generate image features. For training the weights and parameters, the backpropagation training algorithm is in use in CNN (Toda & Okura, 2019). With time, deeper CNN architectures were proposed with an increased number of layers. In VGG-19 (Lu et al., 2017) there are 19 layers, GoogleNet (Oide et al., 1995) has 22 layers, and ResNet (Srivastava et al., 2014) has 152 layers. Recent generations of CNN have led to significant improvement in problems like image recognition, classification, and analysis.

Plant disease detection is a challenging problem, as there are subtle changes in the leaves and other parts of the plants that are difficult to classify (Jadhav et al., 2020). Some researchers are focusing on layer-to-layer visualization of features to find the optimal number of feature for better classification of diseases in plants and reduction in number of parameters (Jadhav et al., 2020; Toda & Okura, 2019). For understanding and comparing various visualization techniques, the reader may refer to Brahimi et al. (2017) and Bharali et al. (2019).

2.4 Performance analysis of some state-of-art techniques

The plant disease detection through the images is a challenging research area. The changes in the disease part of the plant are very subtle; there are intra-disease variations and inter-disease similarities. Due to this, many researchers are developing models to classify either a single disease or multiple diseases in the same category of plants. There is very limited work in the development of a generalized model that can recognize different types of diseases in various types of plants. Some researchers use CNN with transfer learning (use of deep neural networks trained for other tasks having large dataset and further using the pre-trained networks for other classification problems). Techniques like CNN require large datasets that are limited for plant diseases. There is one public dataset (PlantVillage) that is widely used by researchers in this area. It has 38 plant disease categories with more than 50 000 standardized images of around 14 types of plants. Achieving a higher accuracy with real-time plant image datasets captured with natural background, nonuniform illumination, different weather conditions, and so on pose greater challenges. We are comparing some promising recent techniques using CNN in Table 1 with different frameworks, with and without transfer learning, either public or selfgenerated dataset. The results are compared in terms of accuracy.

2.5 Research gaps and future scope

With the recent advances in CNN and its frameworks, classification results in various computer vision applications have significantly improved in terms of accuracy. There are many challenges in general and specific to plant disease detection that need to be overcome. Some of the major challenges are described in the following list:

(1) The accuracy on natural field images is significantly low compared to results on curated images as in the PlantVillage dataset (Picon et al., 2019). The difference in result is due to image acquisition under diverse conditions. Images have different backgrounds from field to field.

(2) There is a need to develop large scale datasets of healthy and diseased plant parts to better train the deep neural network model. The larger dataset increases variability, which helps extract better features leading to improved learning.

(3) A deep learning architecture with a large number of layers improves results. But due to the complexity of the network, it is difficult to interpret how the results are obtained. Some researchers are working on feature visualization techniques to see the feature extracted by various hidden layers and features leading to better classification.

(4) Some researchers are focusing only on classifying a single disease or multiple diseases in the same plant. Others are focusing to generalize the model to detect any disease in any plant. Each technique has its merits and

TABLE 1 Recent CNN techniques for plant disease classification.

S. No	Study	Framework	With or without transfer learning	Data set	Dataset size	Accuracy
1.	Brahimi et al. (2018, 2017)	AlexNet GoogleNet	With transfer learning	Public data set (Plant Village)	14 828	98.66% with pretraining 97.35% without pretraining
2.	Sladojevic et al. (2016)	Caffe	Without transfer learning	Developed dataset from internet with 15 classes and 13 diseases	3000 original images extended to 30 000 by transformations	96.3%
3.	Jadhav et al. (2020)	AlexNet GoogleNet	With transfer learning	Dataset created from soya been fields for four diseases	With 649 training data images for AlexNet and 550 for GoogleNet	98.75% (AlexNet) 96.25% (GoogleNet)
4.	Lu et al. (2017)	Modified CNN inspired by AlexNet	Without transfer learning	Dataset generated from experiments in 1 rice field and 10 diseases	500 images	95%
5.	Chen et al. (2020)	MobileNet-V2 extended with classification activation map	With transfer learning	Public data set (PlantVillage) and selfgenerated dataset	All 38 classes in PlantVillage dataset with 50 000+ images; 200 images in created dataset	99.85% on public data set with 31.4%

Continued

TABLE 1 Recent CNN techniques for plant disease classification—cont'd

S. No	Study	Framework	With or without transfer learning	Data set	Dataset size	Accuracy
6.	Picon et al. (2019)	Modified CNN with complementary plant information with plant images	Without transfer learning	Self-created dataset of 17 diseases and five plants	100 000 images captured through mobile phone	98%
7.	Ferentinos (2018)	Modified AlexNet and VGG		Open dataset 87 848 images, with 25 different plants and 58 diseases		99.5%

limitations. More effort is required to decide which model is better for future developments.

(5) Different diseases with similar initial symptoms may lead to misclassification.

3 Soil health monitoring using AI

3.1 Introduction

The agriculture output depends on the health of the soil. Soil needs to be prepared to have the right quantity of nutrients through proper use of fertilizers. The fertilizers used must be as per the soil health and the kind of crop grown. For good growth of plants, proper nutrients are needed, including: soil organic matter, magnesium, potassium, pH, and correct water quantity. The main soil parameters for high crop yield are soil PH and moisture content. Administering the correct dose of fertilizers helps reduce soil pollution and cost. This will also aid in water conservation.

The soil texture is another parameter that is important to select the type of crop that can be grown in a given soil. The soil texture is detected using surface images through image analysis by using features like color histograms of the images. The movement of nutrients and water in the soil depends on the soil texture.

3.2 Brief history

Traditional approaches for soil properties mostly work by taking soil samples from the fields and testing the soil in labs by using costly equipment. This approach is tedious and time-consuming, as multiple samples are collected from fields to evaluate soil health. The time complexity and expense is especially high for mapping at regional, national, and international levels. In the manual process, as the data are spatially coarse and in-field variability in soil health is difficult to capture, the results are subjective. The soil health can be monitored using IoT systems or mobile applications or with remote sensing. These techniques have the potential to overcome the limitations of the traditional approaches.

The paper by Chung et al. (2010) gives a soil texture classification algorithm using RGB channel information. The paper by Bhatnagar & Chandra (2020) proposes a IoT-based image processing system to monitor soil health. The method explores the use of remote sensing and machine learning to predict soil properties like magnesium (mg), potassium (k), and PH for corn yield. The paper analyzes various machine learning classification algorithms for soil health and concludes that neural network classification gives the highest accuracy. The paper presents a technique using image processing and neural networks to give soil PH and six different nutrient levels. A larger data set is needed for better results.

Multispectral reflectance-based methods are promising but are computationally intensive and complex, but deep learning has led to many advances in this area. The researchers are working to create regional, national, and international soil maps. Padarian et al. (2019) state that diffuse reflectance infrared spectroscopy allows rapid acquisition of soil properties in the fields.

Soil properties are primarily derived from three sources. Experienced soil experts, existing soil maps, and soil samples collected from fields. Local soil survey is done by expert experience. As different experts have different experiences, this method does not reflect the continuous spatial distribution of soil characteristics, hence, limiting its use.

3.3 Opportunity of AI in soil health monitoring

The paper presents a CNN model trained on spectral soil data to predict six soil properties. CNN does not need preprocessing or handcrafted features of the soil images. One study (Puno et al., 2017) investigates the use of image processing and ANN for soil health.

Wu et al. (2019) use geo spatial data for soil mapping, the data is extracted from high-resolution remote sensing images using a CNN-based learning algorithm. In this work, the relationship between soil properties and environmental variables is derived using tree-based ML algorithm regression with random forest and XGBoost (Wu et al., 2019).

3.4 Current status

Digital soil mapping is an important area of soil research. Digital mapping of soil will help farmers use fertilizers and water as needed. This will be cost-saving for farmers and conserve water. Very limited work is done in soil health monitoring in most of the countries of the world. High-precision quantitative soil property mapping is urgently needed in the field of PA. The emergence of deep learning techniques in AI and better hardware at cheaper cost holds promise to use high-definition remote sensing images for digital mapping of soil.

4 Scope and challenges of AI in agriculture

AI plays an important role in PA. PA generates big data from various sensors. AI techniques help make sense of available data. The knowledge extracted from big data helps in better farming decision like best time to sow a crop, precise fertilizer and water requirement, type of crop suitable as per the soil quality, optimized harvesting, and many more. Thus, AI-based precision farming leads to better quality and yield of crop at lower cost. Intelligent machines are used for many repetitive tasks without any human intervention. The smart irrigation systems help conserve water.

AI helps reduce the excess use of pesticides and thus saves our food and environment from adverse effects. This is a disruptive technology that will result in major changes in how farming is done using less space with more yield and limiting or omitting agrochemical use. With a wide potential of its use in agriculture, we need to overcome certain challenges, some of them are listed in the next section.

Developed countries are widely using precision farming, but in developing countries farming is still done using traditional methods. For these countries to develop intelligent farming, systems there is a strong requirement of experts in AI, data analytics, and machine learning. Large scale datasets need to be developed. Further, many machine learning prototype models are developed for agriculture applications, but these models sometimes fail in real environments due to various uncontrolled parameters like weather and soil conditions (Wu et al., 2019).

5 Conclusions

Looking after the crops manually is very labor intensive with high losses. Precision farming will help manage each plant as per its requirement. The AI-based agriculture helps reduce the manpower required to handle different farming processes leading to an increase in farmer profit and high-quality yield with little or no traces of pesticides in the produce. AI-based irrigation systems help conserve the water. AI techniques are growing in the agriculture sector at a fast pace in problems like plant and soil health for better utilization of fertilizers and water. Timely disease detection in plants is needed to take corrective measures and reduce the use of pesticides and other harmful chemicals.

With many benefits of using the AI in agriculture, there are some challenges, like improving and creating better datasets and developing AI-based algorithms that work in natural environments and are computationally efficient.

References

Acaccia, G. M., Michelini, R. C., Molfino, R. M., & Razzoli, R. P. (2003, March). Mobile robots in greenhouse cultivation: Inspection and treatment of plants. In *Memories. Paper presented in 1st International Workshop on Advances in Services Robotics. Bardolino, Italia.*

Adamides, G., Katsanos, C., Christou, G., Xenos, M., Papadavid, G., & Hadzilacos, T. (2014, August). User interface considerations for telerobotics: The case of an agricultural robot sprayer. In *Second international conference on remote sensing and geoinformation of the environment (RSCy2014): Vol. 9229* (p. 92291W). International Society for Optics and Photonics.

Afifi, A. J., & Ashour, W. M. (2012). Image retrieval based on content using color feature. *ISRN computer graphics: Vol. 2012.* Hindawi: International Scholarly Research Notices.

Ahmed, H., Juraimi, A. S., & Hamdani, S. M. (2016). Introduction to robotics agriculture in pest control: A review. *Pertanika Journal of Scholarly Research Reviews, 2*(2).

Aloysius, N., & Geetha, M. (2017, April). A review on deep convolutional neural networks. In *2017 International conference on communication and signal processing (ICCSP)* (pp. 0588–0592). IEEE.

Amin, U. (2017, December). A survey on precision agriculture: Technologies and challenges. In *The 3rd international conference on next generation computing (ICNGC2017b)*.

Balafoutis, A. T., Beck, B., Fountas, S., Tsiropoulos, Z., Vangeyte, J., van der Wal, T., ... Pedersen, S.M. (2017). Smart farming technologies—Description, taxonomy and economic impact. In *Precision agriculture: Technology and economic perspectives* (pp. 21–77). Cham: Springer.

Ball, D., Upcroft, B., Wyeth, G., Corke, P., English, A., Ross, P., ... Bate, A. (2016). Vision-based obstacle detection and navigation for an agricultural robot. *Journal of Field Robotics, 33*(8), 1107–1130.

Barbedo, J. G. A. (2019). Plant disease identification from individual lesions and spots using deep learning. *Biosystems Engineering, 180*, 96–107.

Ben-Ari, M., & Mondada, F. (2018). Robots and their applications. In *Elements of robotics* (pp. 1–20). Cham: Springer.

Berg, A., Deng, J., & Fei-Fei, L. (2010). *Large scale visual recognition challenge* (p. 2010). www.image-net.org/challenges.

Bharali, P., Bhuyan, C., & Boruah, A. (2019, May). Plant disease detection by leaf image classification using convolutional neural network. In *International conference on information, communication and computing technology* (pp. 194–205). Singapore: Springer.

Bhatnagar, V., & Chandra, R. (2020). IoT-based soil health monitoring and recommendation system. In *Internet of things and analytics for agriculture: Vol. 2* (pp. 1–21). Singapore: Springer.

Brahimi, M., Arsenovic, M., Laraba, S., Sladojevic, S., Boukhalfa, K., & Moussaoui, A. (2018). Deep learning for plant diseases: Detection and saliency map visualisation. In *Human and machine learning* (pp. 93–117). Cham: Springer.

Brahimi, M., Boukhalfa, K., & Moussaoui, A. (2017). Deep learning for tomato diseases: Classification and symptoms visualization. *Applied Artificial Intelligence, 31*(4), 299–315.

Chen, J., Zhang, D., & Nanehkaran, Y. A. (2020). Identifying plant diseases using deep transfer learning and enhanced lightweight network. In *Multimedia tools and applications* (pp. 1–19). Springer.

Chung, S. O., Cho, K. H., Kong, J. W., Sudduth, K. A., & Jung, K. Y. (2010). Soil texture classification algorithm using RGB characteristics of soil images. *IFAC Proceedings Volumes, 43* (26), 34–38.

Cox, S. (2002). Information technology: The global key to precision agriculture and sustainability. *Computers and Electronics in Agriculture, 36*(2–3), 93–111.

Cristin, R., Kumar, B. S., Priya, C., & Karthick, K. (2020). Deep neural network based rider-cuckoo search algorithm for plant disease detection. *Artificial Intelligence Review*, 1–26.

Dhingra, G., Kumar, V., & Joshi, H. D. (2018). Study of digital image processing techniques for leaf disease detection and classification. *Multimedia Tools and Applications, 77*(15), 19951–20000.

Dimitriadis, S., & Goumopoulos, C. (2008, August). Applying machine learning to extract new knowledge in precision agriculture applications. In *2008 panhellenic conference on informatics* (pp. 100–104). IEEE.

Ehret, D., Lau, A., Bittman, S., Lin, W., & Shelford, T. (2001). *Automated monitoring of greenhouse crops*. EDP Sciences.

Fakhruddin, H. (2017). *Precision agriculture: Top 15 challenges and issues.* https://teks.co.in/site/blog/precision-agriculture-top-15-challenges-and-issues/. Accessed-03/10/2020.

Ferentinos, K. P. (2018). Deep learning models for plant disease detection and diagnosis. *Computers and Electronics in Agriculture, 145*, 311–318.

Gebbers, R., & Adamchuk, V. I. (2010). Precision agriculture and food security. *Science*, *327*(5967), 828–831.

Gibbons, G. (2000). *Turning a farm art into science—An overview of precision farming*. http://www.precisionfarming.com.

Gliever, C., & Slaughter, D. C. (2001, July). Crop versus weed recognition with artificial neural networks. In *ASAE meeting paper*. No. 01-3104.

Goumopoulos, C., Kameas, A., & O'Flynn, B. (2007, July). Proactive agriculture: An integrated framework for developing distributed hybrid systems. In *International conference on ubiquitous intelligence and computing* (pp. 214–224). Berlin, Heidelberg: Springer.

Hagras, H., Callaghan, V., & Colley, M. (2000, April). Online learning of the sensors fuzzy membership functions in autonomous mobile robots. In *Proceedings 2000 ICRA. Millennium conference. IEEE international conference on robotics and automation. Symposia proceedings (Cat. No. 00CH37065): Vol. 4* (pp. 3233–3238). IEEE.

Hagras, H., Colley, M., Callaghan, V., & Carr-West, M. (2002). Online learning and adaptation of autonomous mobile robots for sustainable agriculture. *Autonomous Robots*, *13* (1), 37–52.

Hakkim, V. A., Joseph, E. A., Gokul, A. A., & Mufeedha, K. (2016). Precision farming: The future of Indian agriculture. *Journal of Applied Biology and Biotechnology*, 068–072. [Online] (November).

Heckmann, D., Schlüter, U., & Weber, A. P. (2017). Machine learning techniques for predicting crop photosynthetic capacity from leaf reflectance spectra. *Molecular Plant*, *10*(6), 878–890.

Humeau-Heurtier, A. (2019). Texture feature extraction methods: A survey. *IEEE Access*, *7*, 8975–9000.

Iqbal, Z., Khan, M. A., Sharif, M., Shah, J. H., ur Rehman, M. H., & Javed, K. (2018). An automated detection and classification of citrus plant diseases using image processing techniques: A review. *Computers and Electronics in Agriculture*, *153*, 12–32.

Jadhav, S. B., Udupi, V. R., & Patil, S. B. (2020). Identification of plant diseases using convolutional neural networks. *International Journal of Information Technology*, 1–10.

Jha, K., Doshi, A., Patel, P., & Shah, M. (2019). A comprehensive review on automation in agriculture using artificial intelligence. *Artificial Intelligence in Agriculture*, *2*, 1–12.

Jim, I. (2012). *Signs and symptoms of plant disease: Is it fungal, viral or bacterial?*. https://www.canr.msu.edu/news/signs_and_symptoms_of_plant_disease_is_it_fungal_viral_or_bacterial. Accessed-12/10/2020.

Kamilaris, A., & Prenafeta-Boldú, F. X. (2018). Deep learning in agriculture: A survey. *Computers and Electronics in Agriculture*, *147*, 70–90.

Karydas, C., & Silleos, N. (2000, October). Precision agriculture: Current state and prospects in Greece. In *Proceedings of the 2nd special conference of applications of informatics to the agricultural sector*. Hellenic Operational Research Association: Chania, Greece.

Khanna, A., & Kaur, S. (2019). Evolution of internet of things (IoT) and its significant impact in the field of precision agriculture. *Computers and Electronics in Agriculture*, *157*, 218–231.

Krizhevsky, A., Sutskever, I., & Hinton, G. (2012). ImageNet classification with deep convolutional neural networks. In *Proc. advances in neural information processing system*. Morgan Kaufmann Publishers, Inc.

Krizhevsky, A., Sutskever, I., & Hinton, G. E. (2017). Imagenet classification with deep convolutional neural networks. *Communications of the ACM*, *60*(6), 84–90.

LeCun, Y., Boser, B. E., Denker, J. S., Henderson, D., Howard, R. E., Hubbard, W. E., & Jackel, L. D. (1990). Handwritten digit recognition with a back-propagation network. In *Advances in neural information processing systems* (pp. 396–404).

LeCun, Y., Bottou, L., Bengio, Y., & Haffner, P. (1998). Gradient-based learning applied to document recognition. *Proceedings of the IEEE, 86*(11), 2278–2324.

Lee, W. S., & Ehsani, R. (2015). Sensing systems for precision agriculture in Florida. *Computers and Electronics in Agriculture, 112*, 2–9.

Lee, W. S., Slaughter, D. C., & Giles, D. K. (1999). Robotic weed control system for tomatoes. *Precision Agriculture, 1*(1), 95–113.

Lu, Y., Yi, S., Zeng, N., Liu, Y., & Zhang, Y. (2017). Identification of rice diseases using deep convolutional neural networks. *Neurocomputing, 267*, 378–384.

Maier, H. R., & Dandy, G. C. (2000). Neural networks for the prediction and forecasting of water resources variables: A review of modelling issues and applications. *Environmental Modelling & Software, 15*(1), 101–124.

Murase, H., Honami, N., & Nishiura, Y. (1994). A neural network estimation technique for plant water status using the textural features of pictorial data of plant canopy. *Greenhouse Environment Control and Automation, 399*, 255–262.

Mustafa, N. B. A., Ahmed, S. K., Ali, Z., Yit, W. B., Abidin, A. A. Z., & Sharrif, Z. A. M. (2009, November). Agricultural produce sorting and grading using support vector machines and fuzzy logic. In *2009 IEEE international conference on signal and image processing applications* (pp. 391–396). IEEE.

Narvaez, F. Y., Reina, G., Torres-Torriti, M., Kantor, G., & Cheein, F. A. (2017). A survey of ranging and imaging techniques for precision agriculture phenotyping. *IEEE/ASME Transactions on Mechatronics, 22*(6), 2428–2439.

Narvekar, P. R., Kumbhar, M. M., & Patil, S. N. (2014). Grape leaf diseases detection & analysis using SGDM matrix method. *International Journal of Innovative Research in Computer and Communication Engineering, 2*(3), 3365–3372.

Noguchi, N., Reid, J. F., Zhang, Q., & Tian, L. F. (1998). *Vision intelligence for precision farming using fuzzy logic optimized genetic algorithm and artificial neural network*. American Society of Agricultural Engineers, St. Joseph, MI, ASAE paper (p. 983034).

Oide, M., Ninomiya, S., & Takahashi, N. (1995). Perceptron neural network to evaluate soybean plant shape. In *Proceedings of ICNN'95—International conference on neural networks: Vol. 1* (pp. 560–563). IEEE.

Padarian, J., Minasny, B., & McBratney, A. B. (2019). Using deep learning to predict soil properties from regional spectral data. *Geoderma Regional, 16*, e00198.

Pal, N. R., & Pal, S. K. (1993). A review on image segmentation techniques. *Pattern Recognition, 26* (9), 1277–1294.

Pathan, M., Patel, N., Yagnik, H., & Shah, M. (2020). Artificial cognition for applications in smart agriculture: A comprehensive review. In *Artificial intelligence in agriculture*. Elsevier.

Patrício, D. I., & Rieder, R. (2018). Computer vision and artificial intelligence in precision agriculture for grain crops: A systematic review. *Computers and Electronics in Agriculture, 153*, 69–81.

Pedersen, S. M., Fountas, S., & Blackmore, S. (2008). Agricultural robots—Applications and economic perspectives. In *Service robot applications*.

Picon, A., Seitz, M., Alvarez-Gila, A., Mohnke, P., Ortiz-Barredo, A., & Echazarra, J. (2019). Crop conditional convolutional neural networks for massive multi-crop plant disease classification over cell phone acquired images taken on real field conditions. *Computers and Electronics in Agriculture, 167*, 105093.

Pivoto, D., Waquil, P. D., Talamini, E., Finocchio, C. P. S., Dalla Corte, V. F., & de Vargas Mores, G. (2018). Scientific development of smart farming technologies and their application in Brazil. *Information Processing in Agriculture, 5*(1), 21–32.

Puno, J. C., Sybingco, E., Dadios, E., Valenzuela, I., & Cuello, J. (2017, December). Determination of soil nutrients and pH level using image processing and artificial neural network. In *2017 IEEE 9th international conference on humanoid, nanotechnology, information technology, communication and control, environment and management (HNICEM)* (pp. 1–6). IEEE.

Rose, D. C., Sutherland, W. J., Parker, C., Lobley, M., Winter, M., Morris, C., … Dicks, L.V. (2016). Decision support tools for agriculture: Towards effective design and delivery. *Agricultural Systems, 149*, 165–174.

Sharif, M., Khan, M. A., Iqbal, Z., Azam, M. F., Lali, M. I. U., & Javed, M. Y. (2018). Detection and classification of citrus diseases in agriculture based on optimized weighted segmentation and feature selection. *Computers and Electronics in Agriculture, 150*, 220–234.

Sladojevic, S., Arsenovic, M., Anderla, A., Culibrk, D., & Stefanovic, D. (2016). Deep neural networks based recognition of plant diseases by leaf image classification. *Computational Intelligence and Neuroscience, 2016*.

Slaughter, D. C., Giles, D. K., & Downey, D. (2008). Autonomous robotic weed control systems: A review. *Computers and Electronics in Agriculture, 61*(1), 63–78.

Srinivasan, A. (Ed.). (2006). *Handbook of precision agriculture: Principles and applications* CRC press.

Srivastava, N., Hinton, G., Krizhevsky, A., Sutskever, I., & Salakhutdinov, R. (2014). Dropout: A simple way to prevent neural networks from overfitting. *The Journal of Machine Learning Research, 15*(1), 1929–1958.

Takakura, T. (1991, January). Sensors in controlled environment agriculture (CEA): Measuring growth and development. In *International workshop on sensors in horticulture 304* (pp. 99–102).

Talaviya, T., Shah, D., Patel, N., Yagnik, H., & Shah, M. (2020). Implementation of artificial intelligence in agriculture for optimisation of irrigation and application of pesticides and herbicides. In *Artificial intelligence in agriculture*. Elsevier.

Tekin, A. B., & Sindir, K. O. (2002). Prospects and challenges for precision farming in Turkey. In *Proceedings of the union of scientist rousse, energy and efficiency and agricultural engineering (EE & AE 2002)* (pp. 4–6).

Toda, Y., & Okura, F. (2019). How convolutional neural networks diagnose plant disease. *Plant Phenomics, 2019*, 9237136.

Tyagi, A. C. (2016). Towards a second green revolution. *Irrigation and Drainage, 4*(65), 388–389.

Ullah, A., Ahmad, J., Muhammad, K., & Lee, M. Y. (2017). A survey on precision agriculture: technologies and challenges. In *The 3rd international conference on next generation computing (ICNGC 2017)* (pp. 1–3).

Voss, C. (1974). Different forms and levels of farm mechanization and their effect on production and employment. In *Agricultural Services Div. Expert panel on the effects of farm mechanization on production and employment*. Rome (Italy): FAO. Rome (Italy) 4 Feb 1975.

Waheed, T., Bonnell, R. B., Prasher, S. O., & Paulet, E. (2006). Measuring performance in precision agriculture: CART—A decision tree approach. *Agricultural Water Management, 84*(1–2), 173–185.

Weizheng, S., Yachun, W., Zhanliang, C., & Hongda, W. (2008, December). Grading method of leaf spot disease based on image processing. In *2008 international conference on computer science and software engineering: Vol. 6* (pp. 491–494). IEEE.

Wu, T., Luo, J., Dong, W., Sun, Y., Xia, L., & Zhang, X. (2019). Geo-object-based soil organic matter mapping using machine learning algorithms with multi-source geo-spatial data. *IEEE Journal of Selected Topics in Applied Earth Observations and Remote Sensing, 12*(4), 1091–1106.

Xiong, Y., Ge, Y., Grimstad, L., & From, P. J. (2020). An autonomous strawberry-harvesting robot: Design, development, integration, and field evaluation. *Journal of Field Robotics, 37*(2), 202–224.

Yang, M., Kpalma, K., & Ronsin, J. (2008). A survey of shape feature extraction techniques. *Pattern Recognition*, 43–90.

Chapter 3

Introduction to deep learning in precision agriculture: Farm image feature detection using unmanned aerial vehicles through classification and optimization process of machine learning with convolution neural network

Halimatu Sadiyah Abdullahi[a] and Ray E. Sheriff[b]
[a]Faculty of Engineering & Informatics, University of Bradford, Bradford, United Kingdom, [b]School of Engineering, University of Bolton, Bolton, United Kingdom

1 Introduction

Food is a necessity to human life and requires its continuous supply and production to cater to the needs of the increasing population through sustainable agriculture. To achieve the required rate of food production to meet up with the rising population (Rozin et al., 1999) expected to increase from seven to nine billion in 2050 (Benton, 2014; EC, 2014), the application of the emerging technologies in the agricultural sector is employed to maximize production across vegetation. Technology can aid/improve agriculture in several ways (FAO, 2009) from preplanning to postharvest by the use of computer vision technology (Gomes & Leta, 2012) and through image processing to determine the soil nutrient composition and to regulate the right amount, time, and place of application of farm input resources, such as fertilizers, herbicides, water, weed detection, early detection of pest and diseases (Deavis et al., 2009; Tilman et al., 2002), and more. Also, environmental factors like the weather, groundwater reserves, and the health of the soil largely affect agricultural

Deep Learning for Sustainable Agriculture. https://doi.org/10.1016/B978-0-323-85214-2.00013-6
81

production, causing changes in yield on the plantation in different areas of the same farm field (Mohanty, 2010). Precision agriculture (PA) aims to minimize this variability by combining remote sensing technology with artificial intelligence (AI) (Cox, 2002). PA is the technology that improves farming techniques by preparing the land before planting, ensuring equally fertile vegetation across the plantation, and monitoring the plantations during in-season growth. PA involves remote sensing, the use of geographical information system (GIS), global positioning system (GPS), and data analysis (Godfray et al., 2010; Gomes & Leta, 2012). This technology enables the collection of field data in a nondestructive way and makes the data available for analysis and implementation on the field (McBratney et al., 2005). PA is made necessary due to the spatial and temporal variability of the field revealing information as patterns and spatial relationships. The phases of remote sensing involve the energy interaction with the atmosphere and interaction with the target, then the interaction of the energy with the selected sensor (camera), data transmission and processing, image analysis, and then the application of results to the required treatment areas (Bongiovanni & Lowenberg-Deboer, 2004; Khorram et al., 2012). Simple applications on the farm involve determining the location of sampling sites, plotting maps for use in the field, examining the distribution of soil types in relation to yields and productivity. Some other applications utilize the advantage of the analytical capabilities of GIS and remote sending software for the vegetation classification to predict crop yield, environmental impacts, modeling of the surface water drainage forms, tracking animal movement patterns, and other varieties of applications (McLoud, 2007). For the image acquisition process, satellites, mobile phones, and unmanned aerial vehicles (UAVs) are being used. A wide variety of imagery is available from satellites using both active and passive sensors, both of which operate from the microwave to the ultraviolet regions of the electromagnetic wave spectrum (Mulla, 2013). All of these vary in their spatial, spectral, radiometric, and temporal resolution, playing an important role by identifying which applications the sensors are best suited for (Hayhurst et al., 2016; Wright et al., 2004). With the satellites, the images obtained are preprocessed, matched together, and can provide information about crop identification, crop area determination, and crop condition. The challenge of this method of data acquisition is the associated cost of obtaining the data. The images are obtained only during visit cycles, limiting its availability on-demand for real-time applications and its poor resolution considering its long distance from the ground (Hayhurst et al., 2016). The use of a mobile phone has the ability to produce excellent images but is limited in its ability to cover the entire field within a specific period set out, limited in taking aerial images, and limited in its ability to control the movement disturbances and illumination when taking images (Espinoza & Ross, 2013; Hayhurst et al., 2016; Zurich et al., 2009). The process of taking images has recently advanced from the use of expensive resources (aircraft, satellites) and periodic availability to

UAVs at more affordable costs and in real-time or near real-time (Costa et al., 2012; McBride & Daberkow, 2003). To obtain images with the required resolution in near real-time, the use of UAVs was proposed and considered as the best and most efficient means of data collection on the field (Alsalam et al., 2017). The use of UAVs in agriculture is fast becoming widespread, with the implementation of aerospace engineering, and sensor technology is reducing in cost. UAVs employ cameras to collect images and sensors to compile a set of data to help with monitoring and decision making on the farm (Barnard, 2007; Radoglou-Grammatikis et al., 2020). Analyzing images of the plantation gives information that impacts management decisions on the farm for immediate treatment from preplanting to postharvest stages. The information obtained is derived from the plant's image shape, height, texture, color, and growth rate to develop a pattern to model farmland (Lottes et al., 2017). UAVs gather information at very high resolutions, which allow the differences in plantations to be easily noticed in centimeters, as seen with the naked eye (Martinelli et al., 2015). They also provide immediate visual information about large areas of crops, which help farmers with fast decision making. With the need to optimize production on a farm land, the problems of image analysis for making on-time informed decisions on a farm has become very apparent. Previously, remote sensing through PA was achieved in two basic steps: feature extraction and classification.

The challenges in automatic plant image recognition are dependent on the ideal and best capture conditions to work suitably. For example, the presence of complex backgrounds that are not easily separated from the region of interest of the plant images, ill-defined boundaries for symptoms, and certain plant diseases being similar result in a range of characteristics that may be present simultaneously. Hence, the need to employ complex image processing to overcome some of these challenges (Arnal Barbedo, 2013; Eastman, 2001).

This research approaches the challenges of data analysis in real-time and managing large databases by building upon existing methods, developing a new algorithm, using a recent image processing technique, and proposing improvements with deep learning (DL) techniques (Fuentes et al., 2017). The new method, which is currently gaining recognition, is the DL (Lecun et al., 2015) technique. DL is a kind of machine learning computational field like the artificial neural network (ANN). It is about "deeper" neural networks that provide a hierarchical illustration of the data through several convolution operations, thus allowing larger learning capabilities and higher performance and precision (Sladojevic et al., 2016). DL is used here to extract and classify features of plant images to determine its health condition for developing a treatment plan to make quick farm management decisions with the aim of optimizing yield on the plantation.

In summary, work done in this chapter begins by evaluating new methods of obtaining data in nondestructive ways with the use of UAVs to analyses the images using convolution neural networks (CNNs).

2 Deep learning overview

There have been major improvements in the state-of-the-art techniques for performing image analysis outside the agro-vision literature within the last five years, especially with computers today being able to classify images automatically and dsescribe the various elements from an image in English. This is done through DL technology that learns the patterns naturally occurring in the images with the development of parallel computing using graphics processing units (GPUs) (Wolfert et al., 2017; Zhang et al., 2019). In DL, a CNN, also known as ConvNets, is a class of the deep neural networks most commonly applied to analyzing visual imagery. It accommodates a great number of model input parameters, all showing potential in capturing the large variability in data obtained (Alex et al., 2012). In machine learning, CNN constitutes a class of deep, feed-forward ANN that has been applied effectively to computer vision applications (Schmidhuber, 2015).

CNN has been in practice since the early 1990s with changes in the year 2010 to achieve excellent results, but more presently, CNNs are achieving very high performances on very challenging tasks. This is due to their ability to learn a great number of parameters with a large number of well-labeled data (Chen et al., 2014). CNN learns complex problems quite fast because of weight sharing and more complex models used, which permits massive parallelization (Pan & Yang, 2010). CNNs can increase their possibility of correct classifications, given that there are sufficiently large data sets (for example, up to thousands of measurements, depending on the complexity of the problem being studied) available for describing the task. They consist of various convolutional, pooling, and/or fully connected (FC) layers (Canziani et al., 2016). The convolutional layers are the feature extractors from the input images whose dimensionality is considerably reduced by the pooling layers, while the FC layers act as the classifiers. Typically, at the last layer, the FC layers exploit the high-level features studied in order to classify the input images into the predefined classes (Schmidhuber, 2015).

ImageNet is considered one of the major databases of labeled images used in training the CNN using GPU-accelerated DL frameworks, such as the Caffe2, Microsoft Cognitive Toolkit, MXNet, PaddlePaddle, Pytorch, TensorFlow, Chainer, and inference optimizers such as TensorRT (Opala, 2018). The basic structure of the CNN is shown in Fig. 1.

The CNN layers comprise 13 layers of the filters. The model consists of convolution layers, pooling layers, linearization, and FC layers (Schmidhuber, 2015). The convolutional layer is the essential building block unit of CNN, and it consists of several basic building blocks. The layers implement basic functionalities like normalization, convolution, pooling and FC layers. The layers' parameters comprise a set of learnable filters, which possess a small receptive field that convolves with the input to generate an output feature map (Zhang et al., 2019).

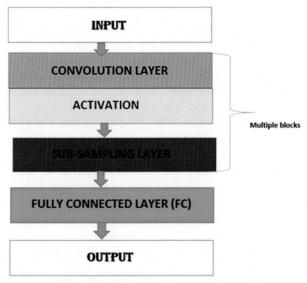

FIG. 1   Basic structure of a typical CNN block.

The convolutional layer is the first layer that extracts features from an input image. Convolution conserves the connection between pixels by learning features from the images using small squares of the input data. It is a mathematical operation that takes two inputs like the image matrix and a filter. Regardless of the convolution output, the input normalization is not usually necessary; it is applied after rectified linear unit (ReLU) nonlinearity and the first and second convolutional layer as it reduces top-1 (percentage of the time the classifier did not output the correct class of the highest score) and top-5 (percentage of time the classifier did not include the correct class among its top 5 guesses) error rates. CNN in neurons within a hidden layer is segmented into "feature maps," and the neurons within a feature map share the same weight and bias and search for the same feature (Razavian et al., 2014; Yamashita et al., 2018). The neurons are unique, as they are connected to other neurons in the lower layers. For the first hidden layer, the neurons within a given feature map are connected to different regions of the input image. Then the hidden layer is segmented into feature maps again where each neuron of the feature map looks for an identical feature at other positions of the input image. Fundamentally, the feature map is the result of applying convolution across a given image. This convolution layer extracts features by computing a dot multiplication between the weights of the neurons and a small region of the input volume, often termed kernels. These neurons are arranged as stacks of two-dimensional filters that cover the depth of the input volume, thus resulting in a three-dimensional structure. During a forward pass, each kernel is convolved across the width and height of the input volume to produce a two-dimensional feature map.

There are different architectures of CNNs developed each year that all compete to classify images correctly, detect objects, perform image segmentation, and execute other advanced tasks. The most commonly used CNN architectures (Khan et al., 2019) are discussed in this section. The evolution and emergence of the different architectures from the ILSVRC is shown in Fig. 2.

It all began with LeNet in 1998 and ultimately, after almost 15 years, led to the groundbreaking models winning the ImageNet Large Scale Visual Recognition Challenge, which includes AlexNet in 2012, GoogleNet in 2014, and ResNet in 2015, and an ensemble of previous models in 2016 (Alom et al., 2018).

The residual network (ResNet) is reported to be one of the most revolutionary works in the computer vision/DL community in the last couple of years. ResNet allows the possibility to train up to thousands of layers and still achieve very good performances. By taking advantage of ResNet's powerful representational ability, the performance of many computer vision applications for feature identification has been boosted (He et al., 2016). ResNet-50 was used in this experiment, which is a 50-layer deep CNN with residual blocks that can be termed a shortcut of connections between its layers. The residual connections aid in combating the challenge of vanishing gradients with the case of networks with a larger number of layers. This helps in better training the network and increasing the accuracy (Khan et al., 2019).

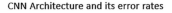

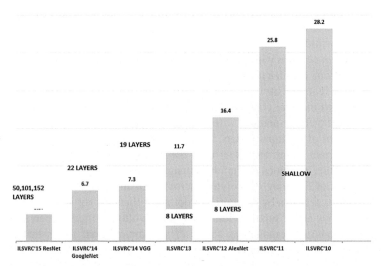

FIG. 2   Development of the CNN architectures.

3 CNN training

In CNN, a network can be trained from scratch with a large dataset, by fine-tuning an existing model, or by making use of "off-the-shelf CNN features." Fine-tuning involves transferring weights of the first n layers learned from a previously based network to the new network. The dataset obtained for the new network is now trained to perform specific tasks (Liu et al., 2015). Through transfer learning, CNNs can efficiently learn generic image features, and the features can be used with simple classifiers to solve most computer vision challenges. The process involves taking off the last layer of the trained CNN model and using the activations of the last connected layer as features. Through research it has been shown that this approach can be used for a dataset with a small number of images and generalizes well (Razavian et al., 2014). Thus, this approach was used in the dataset analysis of this research with the dataset formed.

Generally, during training, CNN learns by tuning the parameters of the network in a way where the input space is properly mapped to the output space. CNNs have a fixed number of weights governed by the choice of filter size and the number of filters, which are independent on the number of input size. The weights are updated through backpropagation, which is an algorithm used for training supervised learning of ANNs using the gradient descent, where the gradient of the error function given with respect to the neural networks' weights are calculated (Ferentinos, 2018; Sladojevic et al., 2016).

3.1 CNN in agricultural applications

In standard agricultural applications, DL methods have recently been used in a number of analyses, such as to obtain plant statistics, to distinguish value crops and weeds types in the fields, in classification problems for high-resolution remote sensing images, and more.

Deep CNN was applied for classifying different crop types to estimate distinct biomass quantities (Mortensen et al., 2016). The technique involved using red, green, and blue (RGB) images of field plots captured at a height of about 3 m above the soil level, which achieved an overall accuracy of 80% with the evaluation of a per-pixel basis.

A visual system was prosed and developed (Chen et al., 2017) to obtain a robust count of fruits in the field subject to the dramatic lighting changes and with heavy obstructions from neighboring vegetation. The research combined the use of CNN for blob region application and a counting algorithm based on another CNN to estimate the fruit count in each region. Their method generalized across both data sets and was able to perform well even on the highly occluded fruits that were challenging for human labelers to interpret.

CNN was used with adaptive boosting (Bhatt et al., 2019) to detect plant diseases in ensembles and obtained an accuracy of over 88% when compared to other methods using CNN only, then, a perception system developed on a fusion of RGB imagery and near infrared imagery (NIR) for both crop and weed classification employing a pixel-wise to acquire predictions for detecting features in the vegetation (Potena et al., 2017). An accuracy of approximately 97% on performance was achieved for the vegetation detection, which is directly comparable to a threshold-based approach based on the normalized difference vegetation index (NDVI), and a 98% for the crop and weed classification if the visual appearance stayed unchanged between the training and testing cycles.

Apart from the previously mentioned applications, one commonly researched area of focus in the agricultural sector is the accurate classification of plant diseases to determine the most suitable treatment plan on the farm. The focus on plant diseases all comes down to the fact that it is one of the major threats to global food security, estimated to contribute to about 10%–16% of the losses in the worldwide harvest of crops. This is estimated to amount to losses of up to US$220 billion going forward (Noiret, 2016; Strange & Scott, 2005).

The misuse and often equal distribution of the use of chemicals, such as bactericides, fungicides, and so on, to control plant diseases has been causing adverse side effects in the agro-ecosystem. Therefore, there is a tremendous need to develop an effective early disease detection technique to control plant diseases for food security and sustainability of the agro-ecosystem.

Recently, researchers (Bhatt et al., 2019) used CNN with adaptive boosting to extract plant diseases in ensembles and obtained an accuracy of over 88% when compared to other methods of using CNN alone. Several other researchers (Altieri & Nicholls, 2003; van der Zanden, 2008) have mentioned other factors affecting crop yield besides plant diseases. The occurrence of weeds on farmland, thereby competing for nutrients from the plants, water-stressed plants, and malnourished plants were also found to be major factors affecting plant growth and causing harvest losses. This can occur at any stage of the plant's development. The most important nutrient of any plant life is nitrogen and then potassium and phosphorous. Ensuring that plants acquire their required nutrient in the right amount at the right time will increase production further and cut down a lot of the harvest losses incurred on the farmland.

The novelty explored in this chapter is the development of an automatic detection system to identify plant health status with consideration of other factors and plant diseases during image capture for optimization of farm products with PA and CNN.

4 Methodology

4.1 Data collection and processing

This section describes the formation of a comprehensive dataset. The data is used to develop a model for the accurate classification results of the plant features. A UAV was used to collect the data for this analysis. The UAV used

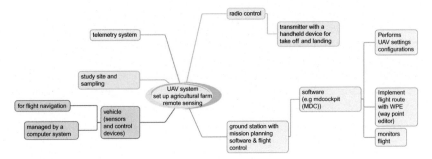

FIG. 3 UAV preparation steps for image capture.

was contracted from a private owner in the northern part of Nigeria, with its specification listed in the following section, and it was operated by staff to collect the images.

Product specification

Payload: RGB Gimbal with IR pointer.
Range: 10 km.
Endurance: 60–90 min.
SPEED: 32–81 km/h.
Operating altitude: 100–500 ft. (30–152 m).
Wingspan: 4.5 ft. (1.4 m).
Length: 0.9 m.
Weight: 1.9 kg.
GCS: Dell laptop, Intel Core i7.
Launch and recovery method: Hand launches, Deep stall landing.
Farm location: Nigeria/maize plantation.
UAV name: DJI Phantom 3 Professional.

The UAV was equipped with the new generation hyperspectral sensors with programmed tasks matched by programming pack available on the DJI Phantom 3 professional drone. The ethics and regulations of flying the UAV were strictly adhered to by following the authorized flight path plans. The process of preparing the drone for image capture is explained in Fig. 3.

The system set up to take the images is made up of five major steps involving the telemetry system, radio control connection, the ground station set up for controlling and transmitting the images, sensors on board, and the process of studying the site for uploading the map for the relevant flight path.

4.2 UAV specification

The DJI PHANTOM captured aerial images on a sunny afternoon on July 12, 2016, with an annual average temperature of 26.5°C and precipitation of 1217 mm. The flight height was a maximum of 10 km above the plantation, which was also varied according to the height of the plantation covering an area of 8000 m^2. Most of the images taken were sharp, while some had a degree of blurriness to them resulting from motion of the platform created by wind, yet, they were all usable in the analysis. Some of the raw images taken are represented in Fig. 4 before they were cropped and resized to be used for the analysis as shown in Fig. 5. The images consist of the up-close images of the plantation taken from all angles and from the top and sides for a complete view of the plantation.

4.3 Image processing and labeling

4.3.1 Image processing

The images collected were appropriately and properly labeled for accurate classification results from training to evaluation stages. They were labeled with the help of the expert farmers who are professionals at spotting the different plant health conditions toward a better agricultural development. This process is crucial, as any potential mislabeling could produce false results during training and eventually testing (Sladojevic et al., 2016). To increase consistency and performance of the model, the images were resized to 224 × 224 pixels (with fastai library, which automatically converts fixed-size models to dynamically sized models) (Sladojevic et al., 2016) written in a custom script (keras) (Chollet, 2015) designed to output the specified input requirements based on the chosen CNN architecture.

A sample dataset of 4000 maize leaves were selected carefully from the overall images and labeled into four distinct groups: (1) diseases, which contained three different classes; the healthy class; discolored plants; and water-stressed plants. The justification for selecting this sample size is due to the closely related classes of images being distinguished and also based on the ImageNet output, where samples have been trained in the order of 1000 data examples per class (considering there were four classes of data). This is also in the interest of confirming the accuracy of the classes in the dataset to reliably develop the model. A sample of the division of the four categories is shown in Table 1 as they were randomly selected. This database creation is the first of its kind with multiple features.

Appropriate format, labels, and sample size are central to the effective implementation of machine learning approaches, including CNN models.

The data was initially split into 60% for training and 40% for testing/validation. For the 60/40 division, the neural network trains 60% of the data, and it is then artificially increased; specifically, image augmentation was applied. This ensures sufficient variance. Hence, data augmentation is employed online and in a randomized manner.

FIG. 4 Aerial images of the plantation.

FIG. 5 Aerial images of the maize farm.

TABLE 1 Distribution of plant leaves images.

Description	Quantity
Healthy leaves	1600
Diseased leaves	800
Water-stressed leaves	900
Discolored leaves	700

4.3.2 Data augmentation strategy

In order to efficiently train a deep neural network, millions of images are usually required. Data augmentation has been used to increase the amount of training images and reduce class imbalance (Shorten & Khoshgoftaar, 2019). For this reason, the images were specifically augmented by resizing the images randomly, cropping, taking its aspect ratio, rotating 90, 180, and 270 degrees, flipping (mirroring each of the rotated images) the images, centering the crop (cutting the center of the image by the same size), and using pixel normalization to increase the dataset and avoid overfitting during the training process. Table 2 shows the results of the augmentation and summarizes the data augmentation protocol used in this analysis performed one after the other, and Fig. 6 shows an example of the augmented images using the flipping and rotating method.

Therefore, the images were resized to 224 × 224 RGB in a script written in Python and were stored as JPEG format. Images were augmented thus, creating a total of 600,0000 train and test images. Data augmentation increased the size of the database, helping reduce the risk of model overfitting during the training process (Takahashi et al., 2019). This is because complex, deep neural networks learn millions of parameters, and mathematically, it has been proven that the data samples need to be at least equal or more than the learned parameters (Takahashi et al., 2019).

4.3.3 Software and hardware configuration

The DL framework used in these experiments is known as Facebook's PyTorch ('PyTorch', 2020), a machine learning library with both a C language back end and a Python front end. The Facebook PyTorch framework was chosen because it is open-source and available freely for use, and it works based on dynamic graph model. Therefore, the model can be manipulated at runtime during the computation.

The hardware used to run all of the experiments is the Google Colab (Bonner, 2019), a cloud-based research tool that provides free access to state-of-the-art Python machine libraries.

TABLE 2 Data augmentation protocol.

Description	Range	Enumeration
Random resize-crop	Input image cropped and resized randomly between 0.7 and 1.0 of the original size (5 random values).	2400 training samples × 5 Subtotal 12,000
Random aspect ratio	Images are resized randomly with different aspect ratio ranging from 0.7 to 1.35 the original size (5 random values).	12,000 samples × 5 Subtotal 60,000
Random rotation	Random rotation between −16 to 16 degrees (5 random rotations).	60,000 samples × 4 Subtotal 240,000
Horizontal Flip	Images are randomly flipped with default probability of 0.5.	2400,00 × 5/4 Subtotal 300, 000
Center crop	Images are randomly cropped to a size of 224 × 224 around the center.	300, 000 × 2 Subtotal 600, 000
Pixel normalization	Images are normalized from 0 to 255-pixel values to a range of 0–1.	Data size does not change.
Zscore normalization	All images are zscore normalized by subtracting the mean pixel and dividing by standard deviation	Data size does not change.

The hardware specification is:

- GPU: Tesla K80 GPU
- CPU: Intel(R) Xeon(R) CPU @ 2.30 GHz
- RAM: ~12 GB
- HD: 311 GB

An epoch is set when an entire dataset is passed forward and backward through the neural network once. The batch size is the total number of training samples present in a single batch/set of iteration. The entire dataset cannot be passed into the neural network at once, so the dataset is divided into a number of batches or parts. Iterations is the number of batches required to complete one epoch. Dropout is a regularization technique used in dropping out hidden input layers of the neural network randomly to prevent overfitting. Weight decay is also a regularization technique applied during training; after each update, the weights are multiplied by a factor slightly less than 1 to prevent the weights from growing too large. This can be seen as gradient descent on a quadratic regularization term (Khan et al., 2018).

FIG. 6 Examples of the augmented images (flipping and rotation).

TABLE 3 Parameter selection for training.

Parameter	Value
Epoch	100
Batch size	32
Dropout layer	0.3
Learning rate	0.1–10
Weight decay	0.001

In the experiment, the first step taken was to download a pretrained residual neural network (ResNet-50) that was trained on the huge ImageNet dataset with the parameter selection in Table 3. The process of fine-tuning is repeatedly changed to alter the pretrained parameters of the CNN hidden layers of the final layers and its hyperparameters. The best suited model for plant feature detection was achieved through this process and finalized for predictions.

The results were achieved from the pretrained ResNet-50 model by freezing all of the weights of the CNN layers with the last layer removed and four new layers added, which is retrained as shown in Fig. 7. The layers are the FC layer, a ReLU, a dropout layer and the classification softmax layers. This approach aids in achieving excellent results and can be used on a relatively small size of dataset. It also trains faster as compared to training from scratch. ResNet-50 selected is specifically a 50-layered residual neural network that has been proven to minimize complexity and inference time during training (Alom et al., 2019).

The customization layer is organized by adding a linear FC layer with 512 nodes, which are later fed into a ReLU activation layer. The dropout layer of 0.3 is chosen as a threshold that is added to regularize and, as a result, ensure generalization. Later, a final linear node is added to classify the outputs.

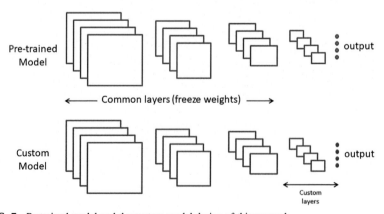

FIG. 7 Pretrained model and the custom model design of this research.

To perform the classification, the last linear layer that has two nodes for the multiclass experiment containing four nodes are used (three diseases and a healthy class). Specifically, the logarithmic softmax function as defined in Eqs. (1) and (2) was used to compute the loss. The optimization algorithm used in the analysis throughout is the efficient Adam optimization algorithm (Kingma & Ba, 2015).

$$\pi_\theta(s, a) = softmax = \frac{e^\phi(s, a)T^\theta}{\sum_{k=-1}^{N} e^\phi(s, a_k)^{T\theta}} \tag{1}$$

$$\log(\pi_\theta(s, a)) = \log\left(e^\phi(s, a)^{T\theta}\right) - \log\left(\sum_{N=1}^{k} e^{\phi(s, a_k)^{T\theta}}\right) \tag{2}$$

where θ is the optimal parameters, T is the time step, $\phi(s, a)$ is a vector, and $\pi(s, a)$ denotes the probability of taking action a in state s.

5   Experiment and results

5.1   Binary classification

The first step of this research was to use machine learning to automatically identify the images of health and unhealthy maize leaves. Here, the three categories of unhealthy images are collapsed into a single class, then the data is split into a 60:40 ratio for training and validation.

Fig. 8 shows a snippet (in Python) of a customized layer that is added to the frozen ResNet-50 layer. Then the deep neural network is trained through 100 iterations (epochs).

```
# Change the final layer of ResNet50 Model for Transfer Learning
fc_inputs = resnet50.fc.in_features

#add the custom layers
resnet50.fc = nn.Sequential(
    nn.Linear(fc...inputs, 512),
    nn.ReLU(),
    nn.Dropout(0.3),
    nn.Linear(512, 2), #2 is the output to classify health or un healthy
    nn.LogSoftmax(dim=1) # For using logarithmic softmax
)
```

FIG. 8   Snippet of the customized layer in Python.

```
        Validation : Loss : 0.0019, Accuracy: 100.0000%, Time: 11.0696s
Epoch: 94/100
Epoch : 093, Training: Loss: 0.0160, Accuracy: 99.4025%,
        Validation : Loss : 0.0000, Accuracy: 100.0000%, Time: 11.0127s
Epoch: 95/100
Epoch : 094, Training: Loss: 0.0061, Accuracy: 99.7760%,
        Validation : Loss : 0.0002, Accuracy: 100.0000%, Time: 11.0048s
Epoch: 96/100
Epoch : 095, Training: Loss: 0.0078, Accuracy: 99.7760%,
        Validation : Loss : 0.0001, Accuracy: 100.0000%, Time: 11.0041s
Epoch: 97/100
Epoch : 096, Training: Loss: 0.0131, Accuracy: 99.4772%,
        Validation : Loss : 0.0000, Accuracy:  99.4500%, Time: 10.9933s
Epoch: 98/100
Epoch : 097, Training: Loss: 0.0553, Accuracy: 98.0583%,
        Validation : Loss : 0.0026, Accuracy:  99.5000%, Time: 10.9702s
Epoch: 99/100
Epoch : 098, Training: Loss: 0.0151, Accuracy: 99.3279%,
        Validation : Loss : 0.0001, Accuracy: 100.0000%, Time: 11.0130s
Epoch: 100/100
Epoch : 099, Training: Loss: 0.0068, Accuracy: 99.7013%,
        Validation : Loss : 0.0000, Accuracy: 100.0000%, Time: 11.2428s
```

FIG. 9   Training summary.

During the forward pass, input images are passed through the model to obtain an output. The loss function is then used to compare the network's prediction to the ground truth classes. The error is then computed and propagated backward in order to adjust the weights of the neural network for better prediction. This is repeated through all the epochs (iterations). A screenshot of the training process is shown in Fig. 9.

Fig. 10 shows how the losses vary for each of the training and validation divisions. It is obvious from the graph, which can also be spotted easily, that both losses settle (reduce) a lot quicker; this is evidence that the deep neural network is learning fast on the new set of images. It is also an advantage associated with fine-tuning. With the set of results being generated, further training was not required through thousands of iterations, rather just 50–100 iterations,

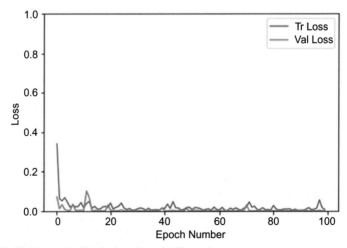

FIG. 10   Training and validation loss through 100 epochs.

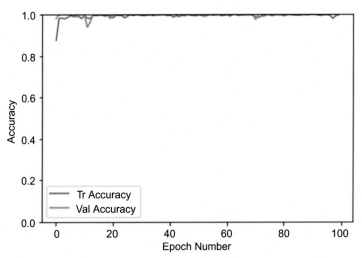

FIG. 11 Training and validation accuracy.

that produced an extremely good validation result of 100% on the unseen data. The results are displayed in the graph on Figs. 10 and 11. Precisely, a 100% validation accuracy was observed before reaching an epoch of a hundred (100). However, training continued as it was noticed that only small improvements occurred on the training loss until the 100th epoch was reached and training accuracy had peaked.

As shown in Fig. 11, a 100% accuracy was achieved in unseen data even before epoch 100; however, training was continued until the training accuracy reached its peak. The initial experiment, which is a binary classification via fine-tuned ResNet-50 neural network, achieved a perfect result of 100% accuracy on unseen data. This is a promising result, which demonstrates the power of a carefully chosen, tuned, and trained neural network. This is also evidence that careful data collection and manual labeling by professionals aid machine learning and automation. In summary, this answers the first question of this research. It can be concluded that, yes, machine learning can be used to identify healthy and unhealthy maize leaves. Despite this convincing result, there is still one big challenge, which is whether machine learning can be used to do fine-grained classification of subclasses that fall under the big umbrella known as "unhealthy leaves." Since lack of nutrients, water shortage, and/or diseases all cause the leaves to appear as unhealthy, there is a need to investigate if the same model, which achieved 100% accuracy, will be able to subclassify the data.

5.2 Multiclass classification

The experiment here consists of the training of an efficient yet light neural network to identify a multiclass fine-grained classification using a deep neural network. The classes identified from the plants were diseased, discolored, and water-stressed plant from the class of the unhealthy leaves dataset obtained from the binary classification. A key feature of PA is an accurate classification of multiple plant conditions using a set of plantation images. The methods described in the previous section were incapable of performing multifeature automatic and real-time detection of multiple plant conditions. To date, no research has yet been carried out to develop an end-to-end model for the overall plant diagnosis system. Previous studies have focused on the detection of a single disease at any given time, making it difficult to implement comprehensive real-time PA systems.

The network framework utilized a pretrained CNN classification model to extract feature maps from the input images and compute the centers of feature maps as stored patterns to infer the test image class before classifying the images.

Fig. 12 is a snippet (in Python) of a customized layer that is added to the frozen ResNet-50 layer. Then the deep neural network is trained through 250 iterations (epochs).

During the forward pass, input images are passed through the model to obtain one of four outputs. The loss function is then used to compare the network's prediction to the ground truth classes. Similar to the procedure in binary classification, error is then computed and propagated backward in order to adjust the weights of the neural network for better prediction. This is repeated through all the epochs (iterations). A screenshot of the training process is shown in Fig. 13.

```python
# Change the final layer of ResNet50 Model for Transfer Learning

fc_inputs = resnet50.fc.in_features


#add the custom layers

resnet50.fc = nn.Sequential(

    nn.Linear(fc...inputs, 512),

    nn.ReLU(),

    nn.Dropout(0.3),

    nn.Linear(512, 4), #4 is the output to classify health , diseased, water-

stressed and discoloured

    nn.LogSoftmax(dim=1) # For using logarithmic softmax

)
```

FIG. 12 Snippet of the customized layer in Python (multiclass classification).

```
Epoch : 237, Training: Loss: 0.0944, Accuracy: 96.7857%,
        Validation : Loss : 0.0785, Accuracy: 96.6146%, Time: 25.6612s
Epoch: 239/250
Epoch : 238, Training: Loss: 0.1027, Accuracy: 95.9091%,
        Validation : Loss : 0.0801, Accuracy: 96.6146%, Time: 25.5823s
Epoch: 240/250
Epoch : 239, Training: Loss: 0.0788, Accuracy: 97.0455%,
        Validation : Loss : 0.0902, Accuracy: 95.8333%, Time: 25.7606s
Epoch: 241/250
Epoch : 240, Training: Loss: 0.0856, Accuracy: 96.8182%,
        Validation : Loss : 0.0816, Accuracy: 95.8333%, Time: 25.5425s
Epoch: 242/250
Epoch : 241, Training: Loss: 0.0835, Accuracy: 96.7532%,
        Validation : Loss : 0.1018, Accuracy: 95.5729%, Time: 25.7868s
Epoch: 243/250
Epoch : 242, Training: Loss: 0.0939, Accuracy: 96.6234%,
        Validation : Loss : 0.0701, Accuracy: 96.8750%, Time: 25.7381s
Epoch: 244/250
Epoch : 243, Training: Loss: 0.0773, Accuracy: 97.0455%,
        Validation : Loss : 0.0876, Accuracy: 95.5729%, Time: 25.7195s
Epoch: 245/250
Epoch : 244, Training: Loss: 0.0916, Accuracy: 96.7857%,
        Validation : Loss : 0.0919, Accuracy: 95.5729%, Time: 25.6769s
Epoch: 246/250
Epoch : 245, Training: Loss: 0.0949, Accuracy: 96.2662%,
        Validation : Loss : 0.0753, Accuracy: 96.6146%, Time: 25.6700s
Epoch: 247/250
Epoch : 246, Training: Loss: 0.0855, Accuracy: 96.9805%,
        Validation : Loss : 0.0627, Accuracy: 97.6562%, Time: 25.6654s
Epoch: 248/250
Epoch : 247, Training: Loss: 0.0852, Accuracy: 96.5260%,
        Validation : Loss : 0.0877, Accuracy: 97.3958%, Time: 26.0482s
Epoch: 249/250
Epoch : 248, Training: Loss: 0.0835, Accuracy: 96.7532%,
        Validation : Loss : 0.0656, Accuracy: 96.3542%, Time: 25.8720s
Epoch: 250/250
Epoch : 249, Training: Loss: 0.0976, Accuracy: 96.7857%,
        Validation : Loss : 0.0841, Accuracy: 96.8750%, Time: 25.6811s
```

FIG. 13   Results from 250 epochs show identification accuracy of 96.87% on unseen data.

Also, Fig. 14 shows how the losses vary for training and validation. It can be seen that both losses settle very quickly; this is evidence that the neural network is learning fast on the dataset, and it is also an obvious advantage of fine-tuning. Thousands of iterations were not required; rather, just 250 iterations produced good validation accuracy of 96.87% on unseen data. Fig. 15 shows consistent performance gain right from epoch 1.

6   Discussion

The model deals with problems of working with noisy and low-resolution images. The model can accurately perform automatic image processing with the evaluation performed using the rigorous technique. The analysis has clearly shown that DL of CNN explored in the experiments offers superior performance compared to work from other authors and also other traditional approaches of machine learning techniques. From the data obtained, it is apparent that not only

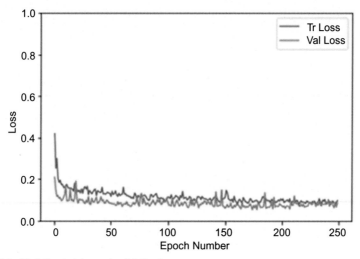

FIG. 14   Variation training and validation loss.

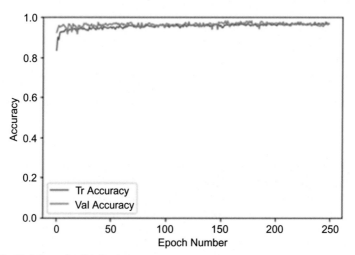

FIG. 15   Training and validation accuracy.

are plant features affected by diseases but also there are a number of other factors to be considered for yield optimization. This is where PA plays a key role by identifying these other conditions and factoring them into the decision-making process of implementing treatment solutions. The study used pretrained CNN models to obtain the best performance in the detection of multiple plant features before they are classified using the fine-tuning based on transfer learning and the different architecture of CNN. It is also seen that the resolution of the data

and accompanying distinct features determine the ability of the DL architecture to detect the features accurately. Bad images yield bad results, and indistinct features can develop inaccurate and distorted results.
The contributions of this chapter include:

- the development of an efficient neural network training strategy; and
- the classification of other plant defects, such as water stress, discoloration due to lack of nutrients rather than parasitic attack, and weeds.

6.1 Advantages of the developed model

- The model used images from plants taken in-field, thus avoiding the traditional process of collecting samples and analyzing them in the laboratory.
- The model also considered the possibility that a plant can be simultaneously affected by more than one condition, including diseases, nutrient deficiency, water deficiency, and discoloration in the same sample.
- The approach employed used colored input images captured under different conditions with various resolutions and different sensors.
- The model can competently deal with different illumination conditions, the size of objects, and background variations in the surrounding area of the plant images, thereby eliminating the preprocessing step.
- This approach also practicalizes a near real-time application that is usable in the field with a reduction in the cost of obtaining the images.
- The model identifies the most suitable deep-learning architecture for the task outlined by considering three main families of detectors of the DL architecture.

7 Conclusion

In this research, the recurrent problems associated with increasing food production were explained and solutions were experimented from field data collected using CNN.

This chapter focuses on effectively and efficiently extracting features and classifying them for making fast and accurate management decisions on the farm for an early intervention process to optimize yield. This eventually leads to more sustainable farming toward smarter and more secure food production. Remarkable progress has been made in image recognition owing to the availability of large-scale datasets and the recent revitalization of the DL network of CNN. This process is a data-driven learning process used with well-labeled datasets and decides, to a great extent, the performance of the model. ImageNet offers a very comprehensive database of more than 1.2 million natural images categorized into 1000 plus classes (Alex et al., 2012). Although no large-scale annotated agricultural image dataset compares to ImageNet, data acquisition and annotation for each category, plant type, condition, and stage of a plantation's development is difficult.

It is desired for each of the classes of the features to be accurately classified and distinguished. Information gathered from experts revealed that the key problems in plant stages development are not only diseases but also factors like nutrient deficiency, irrigation problems, and weeds. These factors are well covered in literature, but no focus has been put into solving the problems that appear in plant images after collection.

The models built on the new and improved database improved feature detection and segmentation problems in the plant image dataset. Also, the model has demonstrated that a robust deep learning-based multiclass detection for the overall real-time plant health detection and recognition using DL is possible.

The model can at this time effectively perform pest identification, minimize or control herbicide use, control the application of plant nutrients, identify weeds across the plantation, and identify the irrigation needs of the farm.

References

Alex, K., Sutskever, I., & Hinton, G. E. (2012). Imagenet classification with deep convolutional neural networks. In *Neural Information Processing Systems (NIPS)* (pp. 1097–1105). Available at: https://blog.acolyer.org/2016/04/20/imagenet-classification-with-deep-convolutional-neural-networks/. (Accessed 18 March 2017).

Alom, Z., Taha, T. M., Yakopcic, C., Westberg, S., Nasrin, M. S., & Asari, V. K. (2018). *The History Began from AlexNet: A Comprehensive Survey on Deep Learning Approaches.* Available at: https://arxiv.org/ftp/arxiv/papers/1803/1803.01164.pdf. (Accessed 22 July 2019).

Alom, M. Z., Taha, T. M., Yakopcic, C., Westberg, S., Sidike, P., Nasrin, M. S., … Asari, V.K. (2019). A state-of-the-art survey on deep learning theory and architectures. *Electronics, 8* (3), 292. https://doi.org/10.3390/electronics8030292.

Alsalam, B. H. Y., Morton, K., Campbell, D., & Gonzalez, F. (2017). Autonomous UAV with vision based on-board decision making for remote sensing and precision agriculture. In *IEEE Aerospace Conference Proceedings* (pp. 1–12). IEEE. https://doi.org/10.1109/AERO.2017.7943593.

Altieri, M. A., & Nicholls, C. I. (2003). Soil fertility management and insect pests: Harmonizing soil and plant health in agroecosystems. *Soil and Tillage Research, 72*(2), 203–211. https://doi.org/10.1016/S0167-1987(03)00089-8. Elsevier.

Arnal Barbedo, J. G. (2013). Digital image processing techniques for detecting, quantifying and classifying plant diseases. *SpringerPlus, 2*(1), 1–12. https://doi.org/10.1186/2193-1801-2-660. Springer.

Barnard, J. (2007). *'Small UAV command, control and communication issues', with UAVs with UAVs* (pp. 75–85).

Benton, T. (2014). Food futures. *Food Science & Technology, 28*(2), 20–22.

Bhatt, P., Sarangi, S., Shivhare, A., Singh, D., & Papppula, S. (2019). *Identification of diseases in corn leaves using convolutional neural networks and boosting* (pp. 894–899). https://doi.org/10.5220/0007687608940899.

Bongiovanni, R., & Lowenberg-Deboer, J. (2004). Precision agriculture and sustainability. *Precision Agriculture, 5*(4), 359–387. https://doi.org/10.1023/B:PRAG.0000040806.39604.aa.

Bonner, A. (2019). *Getting started with OpenAI Gym – Towards Data Science*. Available at: https://towardsdatascience.com/getting-started-with-google-colab-f2fff97f594c. (Accessed 1 August 2019).

Canziani, A., Paszke, A., & Culurciello, E. (2016). *An analysis of deep neural network models for practical applications* (pp. 1–7). Available at: http://arxiv.org/abs/1605.07678.

Chen, Z., Lam, O., Jacobson, A., & Milford, M. (2014). Convolutional neural network-based place recognition. In *Australasian Conference on Robotics and Automation, ACRA*. Available at: https://arxiv.org/ftp/arxiv/papers/1411/1411.1509.pdf. (Accessed 7 January 2018).

Chen, S. W., Shivakumar, S. S., Dcunha, S., Das, I., Okon, E., Qu, C., ... Kumar, V. (2017). Counting apples and oranges with deep learning: A data-driven approach. *IEEE Robotics and Automation Letters, 2*(2), 781–788. https://doi.org/10.1109/LRA.2017.2651944.

Chollet, F. (2015). *GitHub—keras-team/keras: Deep Learning for humans*. Available at: https://github.com/keras-team/keras. (Accessed 1 July 2020).

Costa, F. G., Ueyama, J., Braun, T., Pessin, G., Osorio, F. S., & Vargas, P. A. (2012). The use of unmanned aerial vehicles and wireless sensor network in agricultural applications. In *2012 IEEE International Geoscience and Remote Sensing Symposium* (pp. 5045–5048). https://doi.org/10.1109/IGARSS.2012.6352477.

Cox, S. (2002). Information technology: The global key to precision agriculture and sustainability. In *Computers and electronics in agriculture* (pp. 93–111). https://doi.org/10.1016/S0168-1699(02)00095-9.

Deavis, R. J., Baillie, C. P., & Schmidt, E. J. (2009). Precision agriculture technologies— relevance and application to sugarcane production. *Area, 2*(1), 103–116.

Eastman, J. (2001) 'Guide to GIS and image processing', in Clark University, *USA* pp. 17–34.

EC. (2014). *Research and innovation for sustainable agriculture and food and nutrition security*. Brussels, Belgium: European Commission.

Espinoza, L., & Ross, J. (Eds.). (2013). *Maize (corn) | diseases and pests, description*. Propagation: Uses. Available at: https://plantvillage.psu.edu/topics/corn-maize/infos. (Accessed 17 January 2020).

FAO. (2009). 'FAO's Director-general on how to feed the world in 2050. *Population and Development Review*, 837–839. https://doi.org/10.1111/j.1728-4457.2009.00312.x.

Ferentinos, K. P. (2018). Deep learning models for plant disease detection and diagnosis. *Computers and Electronics in Agriculture, 145*, 311–318. https://doi.org/10.1016/j.compag.2018.01.009.

Fuentes, A., Yoon, S., Kim, S. C., & Park, D. S. (2017). A robust deep-learning-based detector for real-time tomato plant diseases and pests recognition. *Sensors (Switzerland), 17*(9), 2022. https://doi.org/10.3390/s17092022. Multidisciplinary Digital Publishing Institute.

Godfray, H. C. J., Crute, I. R., Haddad, L., Muir, J. F., Nisbett, N., Lawrence, D., ... Whiteley, R. (2010). The future of the global food system. *Philosophical Transactions of the Royal Society B: Biological Sciences, 365*(1554), 2769–2777. https://doi.org/10.1098/rstb.2010.0180.

Gomes, J. F. S., & Leta, F. R. (2012). Applications of computer vision techniques in the agriculture and food industry: A review. *European Food Research and Technology, 235*(6), 989–1000. https://doi.org/10.1007/s00217-012-1844-2. Springer-Verlag.

Hayhurst, K. J., Maddalon, J. M., Neogi, N. A., & Verstynen, H. A. (2016). Safety and certification considerations for expanding the use of UAS in Precision Agriculture. In *International Society of Precision Agriculture, 13th Annual Conference* (pp. 1–15). Available at: https://ntrs.nasa.gov/archive/nasa/casi.ntrs.nasa.gov/20160010343.pdf.

He, K., Zhang, X., Ren, S., & Sun, J. (2016). Deep residual learning for image recognition. In *Proceedings of the IEEE Computer Society Conference on Computer Vision and Pattern Recognition* (pp. 770–778). https://doi.org/10.1109/CVPR.2016.90.

Khan, S., Rahmani, H., & Syed Afaq Ali Shah, M. B. (2018). *A guide to convolutional neural networks for computer vision*. Morgan & Claypool Publishers. Available at: https://www.waterstones.com/book/a-guide-to-convolutional-neural-networks-for-computer-vision/salman-khan/hossein-rahmani/9781681732787. (Accessed 28 September 2020).

Khan, A., Sohail, A., Zahoora, U., & Qureshi, A. S. (2019). *A survey of the recent architectures of deep convolutional neural networks* (pp. 1–62). Available at: http://arxiv.org/abs/1901.06032.

Khorram, S., Koch, F. H., Van der Wiele, C. F., & Nelson, S. A. C. (2012). Future trends in remote sensing. In *Principles of applied remote sensing* (pp. 125–129). Cham: Springer International Publishing. https://doi.org/10.1007/978-1-4614-3103-9_8.

Kingma, D. P., & Ba, J. L. (2015). Adam: A method for stochastic optimization. In *3rd International Conference on Learning Representations, ICLR 2015 - Conference Track Proceedings* (pp. 1–15).

Lecun, Y., Bengio, Y., & Hinton, G. (2015). Deep learning. *Nature, 521*(7553), 436–444. https://doi.org/10.1038/nature14539.

Liu, T., Fang, S., Zhao, Y., Wang, P., & Zhang, J. (2015). *Implementation of training convolutional neural networks*. Available at: http://arxiv.org/abs/1506.01195.

Lottes, P., Khanna, R., Pfeifer, J., Siegwart, R., & Stachniss, C. (2017). UAV-based crop and weed classification for smart farming. In *Proceedings—IEEE International Conference on Robotics and Automation* (pp. 3024–3031). IEEE. https://doi.org/10.1109/ICRA.2017.7989347.

Martinelli, F., Scalenghe, R., Davino, S., Panno, S., Scuderi, G., Ruisi, P., … Dandekar, A.M. (2015). Advanced methods of plant disease detection. A review. *Agronomy for Sustainable Development, 35*(1), 1–25. https://doi.org/10.1007/s13593-014-0246-1. Springer Paris.

McBratney, A., Whelan, B., Ancev, T., & Bouma, J. (2005). Future directions of precision agriculture. *Precision Agriculture, 6*(1), 7–23. https://doi.org/10.1007/s11119-005-0681-8.

McBride, W. D., & Daberkow, S. G. (2003). Information and the adoption of precision farming technologies. *Journal of Agribusiness, 21*.

McLoud, P. G. R. (2007). *Precision agriculture: NRCS Support for Emerging Technologies*. Available at: http://www.nrcs.usda.gov/Internet/FSE_DOCUMENTS/stelprdb1043474.pdf.

Mohanty, B. (2010). *Financing agriculture—Emerging scenario, state of india's livelihoods report 2010. India.* Available at: http://www.accessdev.org/downloads/soil_report_2010.pdf#page=86.

Mortensen, A. K., Dyrmann, M., Karstoft, H., Nyholm Jørgensen, R., & Gislum, R. (2016). Semantic segmentation of mixed crops using deep convolutional neural network. In *CIGR-AgEng Conference* (pp. 1–6). Available at: www.elementar.de.

Mulla, D. J. (2013). Twenty five years of remote sensing in precision agriculture: Key advances and remaining knowledge gaps. *Biosystems Engineering, 114*(4), 358–371. https://doi.org/10.1016/j.biosystemseng.2012.08.009.

Noiret, B. (2016). Food security in a changing climate: A plea for ambitious action and inclusive development. *Development (Basingstoke), 59*(3–4), 237–242. https://doi.org/10.1057/s41301-017-0092-y. Palgrave Macmillan UK.

Opala, M. (2018). *Deep Learning Frameworks Comparison – Tensorflow, PyTorch, Keras, MXNet, The Microsoft Cognitive Toolkit, Caffe, Deeplearning4j, Chainer, Netguru Blog on Machine Learning.* Available at: https://www.netguru.com/blog/deep-learning-frameworks-comparison. (Accessed 15 July 2019).

Pan, S. J., & Yang, Q. (2010). A survey on transfer learning. *IEEE Transactions on Knowledge and Data Engineering, 22*(10), 1345–1359. https://doi.org/10.1109/TKDE.2009.191. IEEE.

Potena, C., Nardi, D., & Pretto, A. (2017). Fast and accurate crop and weed identification with summarized train sets for precision agriculture. In *Advances in intelligent systems and computing* (pp. 105–121). Cham: Springer. https://doi.org/10.1007/978-3-319-48036-7_9.

'PyTorch'. (2020). Available at: https://ai.facebook.com/tools/pytorch/. (Accessed 1 July 2020).

Radoglou-Grammatikis, P., Sarigiannidis, P., Lagkas, T., & Moscholios, I. (2020). A compilation of UAV applications for precision agriculture. *Computer Networks*, *172*(February), 107148. https://doi.org/10.1016/j.comnet.2020.107148. Elsevier B.V.

Razavian, A. S., Azizpour, H., Sullivan, J., & Carlsson, S. (2014). CNN features off-the-shelf: An astounding baseline for recognition. In *IEEE Computer Society Conference on Computer Vision and Pattern Recognition Workshops* (pp. 512–519). https://doi.org/10.1109/CVPRW.2014.131.

Rozin, P., Fischler, C., Imada, S., Sarubin, A., & Wrzesniewski, A. (1999). Attitudes to food and the role of food in life in the U.S.a., Japan, Flemish Belgium and France: Possible implications for the diet-health debate. *Appetite*, *33*(2), 163–180. https://doi.org/10.1006/appe.1999.0244.

Schmidhuber, J. (2015). Deep Learning in neural networks: An overview. *Neural Networks*, *61*, 85–117. https://doi.org/10.1016/j.neunet.2014.09.003.

Shorten, C., & Khoshgoftaar, T. M. (2019). A survey on image data augmentation for deep learning. *Journal of Big Data*, *6*(1). https://doi.org/10.1186/s40537-019-0197-0. Springer International Publishing.

Sladojevic, S., Arsenovic, M., & Andras Anderla, D. S. (2016). Deep neural networks based recognition of plant diseases by leaf image classification. *Computational Intelligence and Neuroscience*, *2016*. Available at: http://dxdoi.org/10.1155/2016/3289801.

Strange, R. N., & Scott, P. R. (2005). Plant disease: A threat to global food security. *Annual Review of Phytopathology*, *43*(1), 83–116. https://doi.org/10.1146/annurev.phyto.43.113004.133839.

Takahashi, R., Matsubara, T., & Uehara, K. (2019). Data augmentation using random image cropping and patching for deep CNNs. *IEEE Transactions on Circuits and Systems for Video Technology*, *14*(8), 1. https://doi.org/10.1109/tcsvt.2019.2935128.

Tilman, D., Cassman, K. G., Matson, P. A., Naylor, R., & Polasky, S. (2002). Agricultural sustainability and intensive production practices. *Nature*, *418*(6898), 671–677. https://doi.org/10.1038/nature01014.

Van der Zanden, A. M. (2008). Environmental factors affecting plant growth | OSU extension service. In *OSU extension service*. Available at: https://extension.oregonstate.edu/gardening/techniques/environmental-factors-affecting-plant-growth. (Accessed 12 October 2020).

Wolfert, S., Ge, L., Verdouw, C., & Bogaardt, M. J. (2017). Big data in smart farming – A review. *Agricultural Systems*, *153*, 69–80. https://doi.org/10.1016/j.agsy.2017.01.023. Elsevier.

Wright, D., Rasmussen, V., Ramsey, R., Baker, D., & Ellsworth, J. (2004). Canopy reflectance estimation of wheat nitrogen content for grain protein management. *GIScience & Remote Sensing*, *41*(4), 287–300. https://doi.org/10.2747/1548-1603.41.4.287.

Yamashita, R., Nishio, M., Do, R. K. G., & Togashi, K. (2018). Convolutional neural networks: An overview and application in radiology. *Insights into Imaging*, *9*(4), 611–629. https://doi.org/10.1007/s13244-018-0639-9. Insights into Imaging.

Zhang, Q., Zhang, M., Chen, T., Sun, Z., Ma, Y., & Yu, B. (2019). Recent advances in convolutional neural network acceleration. *Neurocomputing*, *323*, 37–51. https://doi.org/10.1016/j.neucom.2018.09.038.

Zurich, E. T. H., Eisenbeiß, H., & Zürich, E. T. H. (2009). *UAV photogrammetry*. University of Technology Dresden. Available at: http://www.igp-data.ethz.ch/berichte/Blaue_Berichte_PDF/105.pdf. (Accessed 29 March 2015).

Chapter 4

Design and implementation of a crop recommendation system using nature-inspired intelligence for Rajasthan, India

Lavika Goel[a], Akshina Jindal[b], and Shray Mathur[b]
[a]*Department of Computer Science and Engineering, Malaviya National Institute of Technology (MNIT), Jaipur, Rajasthan, India,* [b]*Department of Computer Science and Information Systems, Birla Institute of Technology and Science, Pilani, Rajasthan, India*

1 Introduction

For farmers and farm managers, selecting the type of crop to be grown in a particular field with the purpose of gaining the maximum yield is a difficult task since many factors have to be considered simultaneously. In fact, instead of considering all the factors simultaneously for selection of crop, farmers only account for a few due to lack of awareness and nonavailability of an expert. An elucidation to this predicament is an expert system that takes into account all the existing information to select the most favored crop for a particular location. The traditional approach to crop selection involved the use of a manually designed knowledge base and a rule-based system. These were designed by taking the help of field experts. The value of field parameters used to be manually gathered using questionnaires and surveys or with the help of previous datasets, in the process of selecting a crop for a particular location. This process, however, does not take into account the constant change in the environment. Moreover, conducting field surveys frequently is also a major challenge. The proposed approach aims to develop a computationally intelligent expert system by incorporating remote sensing for crop selection in India.

The computational intelligence techniques are chosen because there is no defined formula to find the ideal solution to a problem this complex. But we are capable of finding the most significant factors and training a computational intelligence to find patterns that give us good results. Existing rule-based systems are not enough because they cannot learn from past experiences. Unlike a

Deep Learning for Sustainable Agriculture. https://doi.org/10.1016/B978-0-323-85214-2.00005-7
109

human expert, who knows when to "break the rules," an expert system cannot automatically modify its knowledge base, adjust existing rules, or add new ones. The knowledge engineer is still responsible for revising and maintaining the system. Therefore, evolutionary computing techniques can lead to more effective solutions and to complicated and intractable pattern recognition and learning problems. These techniques use methods that are close to a human way of reasoning and, hence, will provide the best decision in the form of crop selection. The focus would be to automatize the crop selection process by developing a web-enabled application that can be used by farmers to select a crop that is most suitable in terms of yield for a particular location. The input required from the farmer would be only the location and the processing of the input location's images, and thereafter, crop recommendations would be handled by the proposed system. The farmers would be able to receive the recommendation once they entered the input location and postprocessing by the proposed system. Hence, the use of the developed expert system can overcome a farmer's difficulty in crop selection. It will facilitate the farmers to make better crop planning decisions that will result in optimum utilization of their land, capital, and other resources, as previously mentioned.

2 Literature survey

Crop selection has been a challenging problem since the dawn of agriculture, and people have tried a lot of different approaches to tackle this problem. The most common approach used was the rule-based approach. People tried to build expert systems that would recommend crops. Crudely, it means, for example, a rule like this: if soil can retain a lot of water and rainfall is high, then rice should be grown. But later on, people tried to incorporate machine learning instead of rule-based expert systems.

For predicting crop yield, multilayered perceptron (Cai & Wang, 2006) and back propagation (Rumelhart et al., 1986) is used. Artificial neural networks are used for the same purpose but only for wheat (Ma & Simon, 2017). There is a lot of work on the problem of crop selection and crop sequencing in particular. Classification tools for selection purpose and heuristics are used for crop sequencing (Donagemma et al., 2016; Kumar et al., 2015). But the major limitation of this study is that it does not incorporate many important factors. Only a limited number of factors were taken into consideration. In states like Rajasthan where water is scarce, such approaches will not work that well. First, we need to consider more factors, and second, these approaches are not fully automated. We are trying to create a fully automated system. One more reason that puts this project apart from other approaches is that we are using nature-inspired algorithms for optimization.

Biogeography-based optimization (Mohamed et al., 2019) and plate tectonics-based optimization (Goel et al., 2012) algorithms are the two mainly used algorithms. We propose our own hybrid biogeography-based optimization–plate tectonics-based optimization) (BBO-PBO) algorithm for better results. In the results section, we showcase a preliminary hybrid algorithm that gives good results and suggestions for improving on a simple BBO or PBO. Adam optimization algorithm (Kingma & Ba, 2014) is also a valuable approach, and we are planning to test and compare it with the remaining algorithms.

3 Proposed methodology

This sections deals with the protocol followed from data preprocessing to prediction of crop type. Each layer in the system architecture is described in this section.

3.1 Preprocessing layer

Data has been preprocessed to be fed into the classifier. The images in the Geo-TIFF format had to be converted to matrices to perform relevant feature extraction (Li & Schreiber, 2006). Two major steps in preprocessing were data download and image tiling.

3.1.1 Download and tiling

We used a Rajasthan area crop yield statement from 2016 to find the top six crops grown in varied regions in this state. Depending upon the crop yields, we selected one or two districts where each of these crops were majorly grown. The six crops selected were maize, wheat, mustard, bajra, barley, and soybean. For area selection, it was ensured that there was no overlapping such that one area corresponds to only one crop. For each selected district, corresponding Landsat images were downloaded for the year 2016 and according to the sowing seasons of each particular crop (Fig. 1).

The original Geo-TIFF images were of 7731 × 7871 pixels. These images were tiled into smaller images of size 1200 × 1200 to give more datapoints and also allow for more robust feature extraction.

3.2 Feature extraction

Crop-based features necessary for crop growth were extracted either from the satellite images or from knowledge-based sources.

3.2.1 Image-based features

Soil texture plays a key role in determining the type of crop that can be grown on a given piece of land. Therefore, we look to extract sand and clay content values of fields from satellite images based on reflectance values.

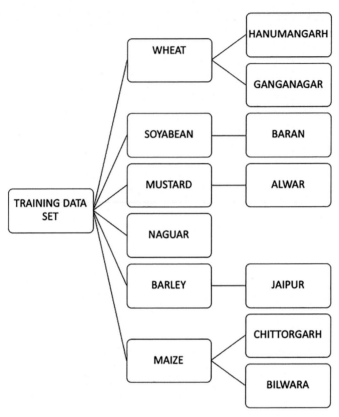

FIG. 1   Dataset layout.

3.2.1.1   Sand and clay content

Soil quality plays a significant role in determining the nature of plant ecosystems and the capacity of the earth to sustain life, particularly human life. The study of soils, including their physical and chemical properties, is essential for agricultural management. Soil quality must be maintained to ensure sustainable production of food and conservation of natural resources. In this context, soil mapping is important to provide spatial information, which can be performed using remote sensing techniques.

Soil type is defined by the contents of sand, silt, and clay in the soil. The texture of soil is considered a crucial property for a variety of soil functions and properties. A few indispensable soil properties in terms of soil classification would be soil structure, water retention capacity, aeration, organic matter content, susceptibility to erosion, cation exchange capacity, and these are all influenced by the soil type. In addition, it has been shown in the study carried out by

Chakraborty and Mistri (2015) that soil texture is one of the most important factors in selection and growth of agricultural crops.

The models used to extract the soil type are based on particle size fractions of sand and clay. Silt has been observed to have a low correlation with the Landsat 8 bands and has therefore not been used for prediction. It has been observed that clay has the most negative correlation with the bands of Landsat 8, especially in the near infrared (band 5) and shortwave infrared 2 (band 7). Sand, on the other hand, while has been observed to have a low correlation with band 1, has a greater positive value for all the other bands. The estimated correlation between clay and sand with the Landsat 8 bands has been displayed in Eqs. (1) and (2). The soil texture has been estimated by using the models developed in one study (Yao et al., 1999). Though these models were developed in Brazil, they were developed with the aim of being applicable to other regions; therefore, we have extrapolated these models to the districts of Rajasthan as well. These models have been developed by employing multiple linear regression models and have shown the $R2$ values to be 0.64 for clay and 0.63 for sand.

$$CLAY_{content} = 281 - 13*B_7 + 9.4B_3 + 1.1*B_5 \qquad (1)$$

$$SAND_{content} = 585.5 + 29.5*B_7 - 12.8*B_5 - 5.3*B_3 \qquad (2)$$

Here, B_x are the reflectance values for band number x.

3.2.2 Knowledge-based features

The amount of rainfall that falls on a piece of land and the temperature of the location have a crucial effect on the type of crop grown; therefore, these are the meteorological features that we have decided to include in our study.

3.3 Optimization layer

There are a variety of optimization algorithms in the field of machine learning. Gradient descent, genetic algorithms (GAs), and particle swarm optimization (PSO) are some examples of it. Derivative-based optimization algorithms have some drawbacks, such as failing to give results when the function is not smooth (differentiable) and the possibility that the algorithm will be stuck at local minima. On the other hand, evolutionary algorithms guarantee global minimum (or maximum as required). We mainly exploit two algorithms, namely, BBO (Goel et al., 2012) and PBO. We also consider hybrid BBO-PBO models and their hybrids with Adam optimization algorithm. Adam optimizer has been selected as a result of the comparative analysis between the performance of standard optimizers like root mean square propagation (RMSprop), stochastic gradient descent (SGD), and so on. It should be noted that these algorithms do not bother with the cost to reach the solution but only concerned with achieving the final optimal solution. Once the weights for all the crops are derived using the optimization technique, they can be used to predict which crop must be grown on the given location. For this purpose we have used the softmax function, which gives us a probability distribution of the suitability of different crops for the given location that can then be used to predict the most appropriate crop for the area under study.

3.3.1 Plate tectonics optimization

PBO is another machine learning technique that is derived from nature. This algorithm is inspired by the theory of plate tectonics, which says that Earth's outer shell is divided into several plates that glide over the mantle, the rocky inner layer above the core. The plates act like a hard and rigid shell compared to the Earth's mantle. This algorithm is modeled on the basis of the movement of the plates of the Earth. There are two underlying concepts that form the basis of plate tectonics theory: the first is the dynamics of the movements of the Earth's plates, and the second is crust formation. Temperatures at different point of a plate are considered as different candidate solutions. These temperatures are characteristic of the solution and are proportional to the plate mobility index (PMI). The PMI of a solution is analogous to the habitat suitability index (HSI) in BBO. The value of PMI is completed for each solution. Like BBO, PBO is also an iterative algorithm. Within each iteration, the value of PMI for each solution is calculated. Initially, the number decision variables used to calculate the PMI are limited. With each iteration, the number of decision variables are increased according to a threshold value. Each decision variable is assigned a weight. After each iteration, the weights are normalized. This step helps in incorporating dynamic data into the algorithm. PBO due to its very nature is computationally faster than BBO. Dynamic incorporation of new conditions is another very useful advantage of PBO. It allows PBO to reach faster convergence and additional refinement of solution. To summarize, PBO, due to its strengths, outperforms other evolutionary algorithms like BBO in a specific set of problems:

1. Optimization environment is dynamic while in other evolutionary algorithms, like BBO, PSO, and GA, it is static.
2. By changing decision variables and their weights, PBO generates new solutions, while in BBO we perform a probabilistic adaptation of an old solution by migration.
3. In BBO our solutions change directly via migration, but in PBO they do not change directly. They are changed via change in associated weights.
4. Iterative improvement in PBO as we go on incorporate lower prioritized variables with normalized weights iteratively, but in BBO we use migration to change existing solutions, and to retain the best solution, we perform elitism.
5. Computational effort for PBO is much lower, as the problem of creating an infeasible solution is absent here, while in the case of BBO, higher computational effort is required due to a waiting period from feasibility check.

Pseudo code for PBO model
1. Form an initial set of candidate solutions.
2. Calculate the PMI for each solution.
3. Reduce the tolerance value in order to incorporate lower prioritized decision variables and, hence, formulate the new set of decision variables C_j^α. $\alpha = \alpha - T$ is the iterative refinement in the tolerance value.
4. Alter the weights corresponding to the new set of decision variables by replacing $W_{C_j^\alpha}$ by $WC_j^\alpha \Big/ \sum_{j=1}^{p} WC_j^\alpha$ for each C_j^α such that $\sum_{j=1}^{p} W_{C_j^\alpha} = 1$ and the next iterations performed with these weights.
5. Return to the second step until the PMI reaches 0 at which point the corresponding solution is the best fit solution.

3.3.2 BBO

BBO is a nature-inspired optimization algorithm. This algorithm is derived from mathematical models for biogeography (Goel et al., 2012). Biogeography is the study of the distribution of species and ecosystems in geographic space and through geological time. It describes migration of species from one island to another. These islands are modeled as habitats. Each habitat has a set of suitability index variables (SIVs). The suitability of a particular habitat is dependent on these set of variables. Geographical areas that are well-suited as residences for biological species are said to have a high HSI. The HSI of a habitat is modeled using the SIVs. Habitats with a high HSI tend to have a large number of species, while those with a low HSI have a small number of species. Species from a habitat with high HSI tend to migrate to a habitat of lower HSI. The probability of a species of a low HSI habitat to migrate is much less. The emigration and immigration from a habitat are governed by the immigration rate (λ) and emigration rate (μ). Here the immigration and emigration of species is analogous to the sharing of SIVs between different habitats. Finally, a good solution is one with the highest value of the HSI. In BBO, initially, the parameters and habitats of the model are initialized. The choice of the SIVs and the formulation of the HSI is problem dependent.

Pseudo code for BBO Optimization algorithm
    Initialize a population of N candidate solutions $\{x_k\}$
    While not (terminal criterion)
    For each x_k, set the emigration probability $\mu_k \propto$ *fitness of* x_k, with $\mu_k \in [0,1]$
      For each x_k, set immigration probability $\lambda_k = 1 - \mu_k$
      $\{z_k\} \leftarrow \{x_k\}$
      For each individual $z_k(k = 1, 2, ..., N)$

For each independent variable index $s \in [1, n]$
   Use λ_k to probabilistically decide whether to immigrate to z_k
   If immigrating then
      Use $\{\mu_k\}$ to probabilistically select the emigrating individual x_j
      $z_k(s) \leftarrow x_j(s)$
   End if
   Next independent variable index: $s \leftarrow s + 1$
   Probabilistically mutate z_k
  Next individual: $k \leftarrow k + 1$
 $\{x_k\} \leftarrow \{z_k\}$
Next generation

The whole optimization process is iterative. At each iteration there are two major steps: migration and mutation.

Migration: After the initialization of the habitats, their HSIs are computed. On the basis of the computed HSIs, we decide the λ and μ for each habitat. Then we select a habitat based on its immigration rate λ. Then for each remaining habitat, we probabilistically decide whether an SIV is to be migrated from that habitat or not on the basis of its μ. If this habitat is selected, we randomly choose an SIV from the habitat to be mutated and replace it with the corresponding SIV of the selected habitat.

Mutation: During mutation, we probabilistically select whether a habitat is to be mutated or not. This is done on the basis λ and μ. Then we select a suitable SIV from the given habitat and replace it with a randomly generated SIV. This gives the habitats with a low HSI a chance to improve and hence is beneficial for our final decision.

Pseudo code for Adam optimization algorithm
1. Initialize α as step size, $\beta 1$ and $\beta 2$ are exponential decay rates for moment estimates.
2. Initialize m_o—first moment vector as zero: second moment vector as zero and t: time step as zero.
3. While θ_t not converged do
  3.1. $t \leftarrow t + 1$
  3.2. $g_t = \nabla_\theta(f_t(\theta_t))$
  3.3. $m_t = \beta_1 * m_{t-1} + (1 - \beta_1) * g_t$
  3.4. $v_t = \beta_2 * v_{t-1} + (1 - \beta_2) * g_t^2$
  3.5. $\hat{m}_t = {}^{m_t}/_{1 - \beta_1^t}$
  3.6. $\hat{v}_t = {}^{v_t}/_{1 - \beta_2^t}$
  3.7. $\theta_t = \theta_{t-1} - \alpha * \left(\frac{\hat{m}_t}{\sqrt{\hat{v}_t}} \right) + \in$
 endwhile
return θ_t

3.3.3 Adaptive moment estimation optimization

This optimization algorithm can be used instead of the classical SGD procedure to update network weights iterative based in the training data. Adam was presented by Diederik Kingma from OpenAI (Li & Schreiber, 2006) and Jimmy Ba (Noble & Daniel, 1987) from the University of Toronto in their 2015 ICLR paper (poster) titled "Adam: A Method for Stochastic Optimization." Adam is derived from the term "adaptive moment estimation." This algorithm became famous due to its very straightforward implementation and its efficiency. The key idea of Adam optimization algorithms is "the method computes individual adaptive learning rates for different parameters from estimates of first and second moments of the gradients," unlike SGD where we maintain a single learning rate (termed alpha) for all weight updates, and the learning rate does not change during training. Adam configuration parameters are:

1. α: Learning rate/step size
2. β_1: The exponential decay rate (first moment estimates)
3. β_2: The exponential decay rate (second moment estimates)
4. ε: very small number to prevent any division by zero

Generally, we keep $\alpha = 0.001$, $\beta_1 = 0.9$, $\beta_2 = 0.999$, and $\varepsilon = 10^{-8}$.

Adam optimization algorithm is famous for achieving good results in lesser time, making it more efficient than preexisting gradient-based algorithms (Yao et al., 1999). For the SGD algorithm, we keep the same learning rate (alpha) throughout the training process. For all weight, updating alpha is the same (Kingma & Ba, 2014). But what happens if we keep different learning rates for different weight updating, and as the learning process continues, we keep on adapting our learning rate?

Variations of a normal gradient descent algorithm follow:

1. *Adaptive Gradient Algorithm (AdaGrad)*: This algorithm keeps different learning rates for different parameters, and for computation of those learning rates, it takes help from the first and second moments of its gradients. In problems where we have gradients that are sparse in nature, this modification has proven to be highly successful.
2. *RMSprop*: In this algorithm, we keep different learning rates for different parameters, but the computation process is different. We calculate gradients of weights first and then consider the average of recent magnitudes of them. From this, we calculate a learning rate for that parameter. In short, we observe how weights are getting updated for a particular parameter, and based on that, we assign a learning rate for that parameter. The RMSprop technique looks at the average first moment and then makes decisions regarding tuning of learning rate for a parameter, but in the case of Adam, it looks at both first and second moments of gradients and then makes a decision regarding tuning of

1	Adam	SGD	Adagrad	Adamax	Nadam
2	1.99637292	2.1047115	1.6912759	1.84997	1.958618
3	0.09293283	1.1857154	0.4458449	0.245305	0.136641
4	0.04704489	0.8355882	0.1530682	0.07858	0.009975
5	0.00137877	0.5639499	0.0356014	0.005652	0.001047
6	0.00071436	0.4268754	0.0186273	0.003475	0.000448
7	0.0005338	0.3221564	0.006062	0.001578	0.000171
8	0.00013005	0.239053	0.0033669	0.001033	9.76E-05
9	9.4324E-05	0.1803214	0.0023479	0.000819	7.16E-05
10	7.0198E-05	0.1415419	0.0017978	0.000684	5.45E-05
11	5.4261E-05	0.1144432	0.0014519	0.00058	4.26E-05
12	0.00016955	0.0897802	0.0002922	0.000276	8.33E-06
13	5.92E-06	0.0724069	0.0001788	0.00012	5.32E-06
14	3.6788E-06	0.0609374	0.0001291	0.000105	3.82E-06
15	2.6667E-06	0.0526006	0.0001007	9.54E-05	2.85E-06
16	2.0468E-06	0.0456042	8.181E-05	8.65E-05	2.17E-06
17	1.6487E-06	0.0401632	6.874E-05	7.88E-05	1.72E-06
18	1.3745E-06	0.0359203	5.941E-05	7.22E-05	1.43E-06
19	1.1694E-06	0.032427	5.226E-05	6.62E-05	1.2E-06
20	8.9169E-07	0.0270461	4.197E-05	5.6E-05	9.05E-07
21	8.2255E-07	0.0255729	3.932E-05	5.29E-05	8.29E-07

FIG. 2 Comparison of Adam to other optimize.

learning rate for a parameter. This modification makes Adam algorithm much more robust and efficient. Fig. 2 depicts how Adam loss is much less than other optimizers like SGD, AdaGrad, AdaMax, and Nadam.

3.3.4 PBO-BBO hybrid

A hybrid version that we proposed used different batches to initialize weights with factors that are most significant initialized at the beginning.

Pseudo code for PBO/BBO hybrid
    Read input with f factors.
    Generate n candidate solutions (also called the population size).
    Set algorithm parameter α as the number of batches.
    Lower and Upper bounds of weights as *lb and ub*.
    Set x as the number of iterations for BBO.
    Create α uniform intervals that lie between *lb and ub*.
    For i in range (α):
- Generate random weights from i^{th} interval of size for only f/α factors.
- Run BBO to optimize these weights for x iterations.
- $x = x * 2$

Final run gives the best solution. The flowchart in Fig. 3 explains the workflow of the hybrid algorithm.

To tackle our problem, we propose a new hybrid PBO/BBO algorithm. We used PBO for then initialization stage and then ran BBO on it. A detailed explanation with pseudo code is given in later sections. Suppose that there are 10 factors we are considering for crop selection, and we know that not all of them are equally important. So, we can make use of PBO, which allows us to dynamically keep on changing our search space. Hence, we will first incorporate highly important factors, as they are the major decision variables, and then we keep on adding less important factors. In each incorporation we keep on increasing the size of the search space, which leads to a better solution and faster convergence. This algorithm is still in very preliminary stages, so further testing is required.

3.3.5   PBO-Adam hybrid

The algorithm borrows quite a few concepts from plate tectonics and mathematically formulates it to optimize arbitrary f-dimensional functions when it is solved. The basic idea is that, due to f factors, our solution space is an f-dimensional curve navigated by our algorithm for the minimum error. By breaking the factors in different pieces, we reduce the computational work and allow the algorithm to divide the space and quickly navigate to the optimum solution. Factors that are most prominent for our classifier are fed first. Interactions all multiplied after each batch processing because we want the initial optimizations to be very rough. As we add more factors, more iterations allow us to fine-tune the answer for lower error. This algorithm is illustrated in Fig. 4.

Weight updating is done with the help of Adam optimization algorithm.

Pseudo code for PBO/Adam hybrid
1. Read input with f factors.
2. Generate n candidate solutions (also called the population size). Set algorithm parameter α as the number of batches.

3. Generate weights using Glorot uniform method.
4. Initialize the learning rate (*lr*) and prod as the factor by which *x* increases. Set *x* as the number of iterations that Adam runs for.
5. For *i* in range (*α*):
   - Generate random weights and append to existing weights.
   - Run Adam to optimize these weights for *x* iterations.
6. $x = x * prod$
7. $lr = \frac{lr}{2}$

Final run gives the best solution.

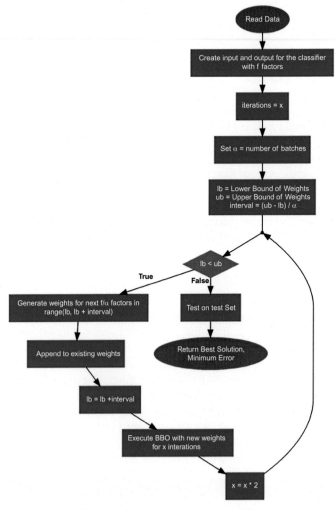

FIG. 3 Flowchart for PBO/BBO hybrid.

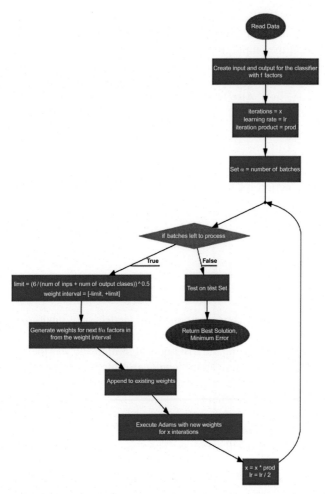

FIG. 4 Flowchart for PBO/ADAMS hybrid.

Here in this hybrid algorithm, we propose to remove BBO from the previous hybrid algorithm and place the Adam optimization algorithm instead. Adam optimization is a gradient-based technique, unlike BBO, which is a nature-inspired algorithm. PBO is used for the initialization phase where factors are distributed in batches of size alpha, and we keep on adding less significant factors in later stages and make algorithms run for a larger number of iteration so that our algorithm will finally end up at global minimum.

3.4 Softmax classification layer

The output from the previous layers is used as the input to the softmax layer. This layer outputs a probability score stating the expectance of a data sample to belong to a particular crop type. It is a $n*1$ matrix where n is the number of crops. The softmax function is used to model multiclass classification problems where we want the output to be a probability distribution of the different possible classes (Noble & Daniel, 1987). Let us assume that the factors affecting the decision are defined by the vector X and the weight for class k are defined by $W^k = [w_1^k w_2^k w_3^k ... w_n^k]$. Also let the total number of classes be K. Then the probability of a class k to be the correct class given a set of parameters X is:

$$p(k|X) = \frac{e^{w^k * X^T}}{\sum e^{w^j * X^T}}$$

The loss function for the softmax classifier is the cross entropy loss. The cross entropy loss H can be given as:

$$H = -1 * \sum p(x) * \log q(x)$$

4 Results

We first tested all the hybrid and nonhybrid models on a randomly generated dataset to get an overall view of the performance of the models. The random dataset was first tested using the BBO-only algorithm and was then tested using the hybrid PBO-BBO optimization technique. Table 1 shows the absolute errors for 20 iterations and has been used to compare the performance of the optimization techniques on the dataset.

At the 15th iteration, the error reported by the hybrid version suddenly jumps. This is when the next batch is initialized. Four successive batches run BBO for 15, 30, 60, and 120 iterations. The absolute error for different iterations is also shown in Fig. 5.

Absolute value had to be taken because of the lower initial value of error in the hybrid algorithm due to the inclusion of only two factors. The jumps in error we see are when a new range of factors is incorporated in the algorithm. Although it did give satisfactory results at the end, it took significantly longer to achieve them. Fig. 5 shows a slower convergence in the hybrid algorithm; however, the algorithm did eventually manage to reach a point where its error was almost as low as the BBO-only version, and it predicted crops with about 99% accuracy.

Now, we will see how our newly proposed PBO/Adam hybrid algorithm works in comparison with a plain BBO algorithm. Note that we are taking BBO algorithm as comparator because it is a standard and widely used nature-inspired algorithm. We will run the PBO/Adam hybrid algorithm on the same dataset so that we can compare the results easily. For the purposes of this run, after every iteration, we have doubled the iterations for each subsequent batch and halved the learning rate, which was initially 0.03. Table 2 shows error along with iteration number for both PBO/Adam and BBO.

TABLE 1 Comparison of errors of the BBO-only and PBO-BBO hybrid optimization techniques.

Iterations	Error(BBO Only)	Error(PBO-BBO)
0	2.146008416	0.802646767
1	2.142993286	0.76215821
2	1.45340939	0.632267627
3	1.45340939	0.597098821
4	1.25228848	0.597098821
5	1.25228848	0.536057676
6	1.060338592	0.524341231
7	0.760345537	0.519293139
8	0.760345537	0.514983106
9	0.760345537	0.508374307
10	0.542329629	0.508374307
11	0.542329629	0.508374307
12	0.542329629	0.508296347
13	0.372784539	0.507195293
14	0.334679196	0.507195293
15	0.183846899	0.691771368
16	0.183846762	0.614999058
17	0.183846762	0.574390274
18	0.183846762	0.546063602
19	0.175459535	0.546063602
20	0.163967176	0.480497508

We can see that the PBO/Adam hybrid outperforms the BBO. Starting from epoch 1, its error is always less than that of the BBO's error. After 300 iterations, error generated by the BBO is almost 0.0003 while the hybrid algorithm gives 0.000005, which is significantly lower than that of the BBO's error. Graphical representation will help readers to understand difference between the two algorithms. Fig. 6 shows the graph of errors generated by both algorithms.

Finally, the BBO-only and PBO/Adam were trained and tested on the newly generated dataset using feature extraction. The evaluation metric used was the

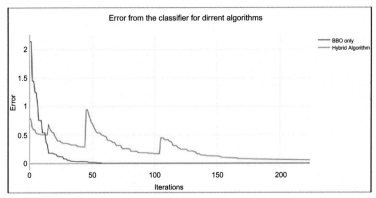

FIG. 5   Error comparison for BBO and PBO/BBO.

TABLE 2 Comparison of errors of the BBO-only and PBO-Adam hybrid optimization techniques.

Epoch	BBO	PBO-Adam hybrid
0	3.27919242	1.73305398
1	3.27919242	1.47481345
2	2.88759214	1.35510473
4	2.57641396	1.25034575
6	1.92629025	1.20219536
8	1.68864249	1.15109242
10	0.71467005	1.23334128
12	0.53558253	0.68422502
15	0.35855317	0.29156289
20	0.19051317	0.13241501
30	0.0560806	0.13555464
40	0.04131696	0.01337125
50	0.03694463	0.00318711
100	0.01389424	0.00023549
150	0.00436062	0.038605389
200	0.00104588	1.7208E-05
250	0.00042188	8.1817E-06
300	0.000289475	5.00455E-06

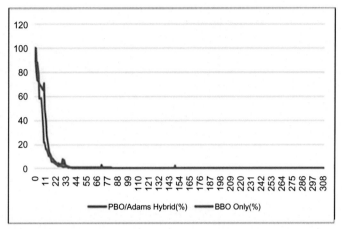

FIG. 6   Error comparison for BBO and PBO/Adam.

area under the receiver operating characteristic (ROC) curve. For BBO, 150 iterations and a population size of 30 were chosen, while for PBO/Adam, 10 iterations were chosen and iter_product is 2. The results are tabulated in Figs. 7 and 8 and Table 3.

As expected, the PBO-Adam hybrid performs much better than the PBO-only optimizer. The area under the ROC curve (AUC) obtained for PBO/Adam is 0.95, which clearly states that the model is able to learn the dataset variations well on the real data set and the randomly generated datasets.

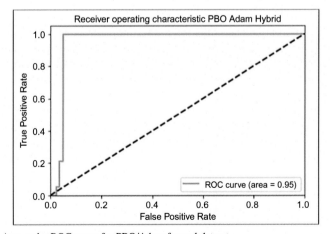

FIG. 7   Area under ROC curve for PBO/Adam for real dataset.

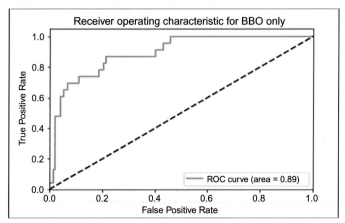

FIG. 8 Area under ROC curve for BBO only for real dataset.

TABLE 3 Results for PBO, BBO, and PBO/Adam real dataset.

Optimizer	AUC-ROC
BBO only	0.89
PBO/Adam	0.95

5   Conclusion and future work

While BBO has been successful in reducing the error to a great degree with the new dataset, the previous results show that the PBO/Adam hybrid outperforms the classic BBO optimizer models. Also, such classifiers work well with satellite-based crop data sets, as can be inferred from the real data set results. Henceforth, the use such a crop recommendation system, which incorporates either nonhybrid or hybrid nature-inspired algorithms, can help the farmers make better decision about the type of crop to be grown at a particular location. In the future, the proposed models can be improved using several neural net layers and changing different hyperparameters. Other than the model, higher resolution satellite images can be used to get more robust crop-based features. Certain other factors responsible for crop growth, like soil moisture, soil pH, soil salinity, soil depth, groundwater level, land elevation, and so on, can be extracted and can be helpful in predicting the correct crop for a particular region. Since soil feature extraction based on the reflectance values using remote sensing technology, for Rajasthan, it is important to corroborate these values with actual ground truth values from a large number of field-specific sample points. These ground truth values can be used to fine-tune the current models that have been used for feature extraction. This will not only help in getting more precise and accurate feature values but will also help increase the accuracy of crop prediction for a given piece of land.

References

Cai, Z., & Wang, Y. (2006). A multiobjective optimization-based evolutionary algorithm for constrained optimization. *IEEE Transactions on Evolutionary Computation: A Publication of the IEEE Neural Networks Council, 10*(6), 658–675.

Chakraborty, K., & Mistri, B. (2015). Importance of soil texture in sustenance of agriculture: A study in Burdwan-I CD Block, Burdwan, West Bengal. *Eastern Geographer, 21*, 475–482.

Donagemma, G. K., et al. (2016). Characterization, agricultural potential, and perspectives for the management of light soils in Brazil. *Pesquisa Agropecuaria Brasileira, 51*(9), 1003–1020.

Goel, L., Gupta, D., & Panchal, V. K. (2012). Biogeography and plate tectonics based optimization for water body extraction in satellite images. In *Advances in intelligent and soft computing* (pp. 1–13). Springer India: New Delhi.

Kingma, D. P., & Ba, J. (2014). Adam: A method for stochastic optimization. *arXiv. [cs.LG]*. Available at: http://arxiv.org/abs/1412.6980.

Kumar, R., et al. (2015). Crop Selection Method to maximize crop yield rate using machine learning technique. In *2015 International conference on smart technologies and management for computing, communication, controls, energy and materials (ICSTM)*IEEE.

Li, C.-K., & Schreiber, S. J. (2006). On dispersal and population growth for multistate matrix models. *Linear Algebra and its Applications, 418*(2–3), 900–912.

Ma, H., & Simon, D. (2017). *Evolutionary computation with biogeography-based optimization* (1st ed.). London, England: ISTE Ltd and John Wiley & Sons.

Mohamed, E. S., et al. (2019). Mapping soil moisture and their correlation with crop pattern using remotely sensed data in arid region. *Egyptian Journal of Remote Sensing and Space Sciences*. https://doi.org/10.1016/j.ejrs.2019.04.003.

Noble, B., & Daniel, J. W. (1987). *Applied linear algebra* (3rd ed.). Upper Saddle River, NJ: Pearson.

Rumelhart, D. E., Hinton, G. E., & Williams, R. J. (1986). Learning representations by backpropagating errors. *Nature, 323*(6088), 533–536.

Yao, X., Liu, Y., & Lin, G. (1999). Evolutionary programming made faster. *IEEE Transactions on Evolutionary Computation : A Publication of the IEEE Neural Networks Council, 3*(2), 82–102.

Further reading

Caswell, H. (1989). *Matrix population models: Construction, analysis and interpretation*. Sunderland, MA: Sinauer Associates.

Gallo, B., et al. (2018). Multi-temporal satellite images on topsoil attribute quantification and the relationship with soil classes and geology. *Remote Sensing, 10*(10), 1571.

Gustafson, S., & Burke, E. K. (2006). The Speciating Island model: An alternative parallel evolutionary algorithm. *Journal of Parallel and Distributed Computing, 66*(8), 1025–1036.

Ho, Y. C., & Pepyne, D. L. (2002). Simple explanation of the no-free-lunch theorem and its implications. *Journal of Optimization Theory and Applications, 115*(3), 549–570.

Kolesnikova, A., Song, C.-H., & Lee, W. D. (2009). Applying UChooBoost algorithm in precision agriculture. In *Proceedings of the international conference on advances in computing, communication and control—ICAC3 '09*. New York, NY, USA: ACM Press.

Krishna Kumar, K., et al. (2004). Climate impacts on Indian agriculture. *International Journal of Climatology: A Journal of the Royal Meteorological Society, 24*(11), 1375–1393.

Okparanma, R. N., & Mouazen, A. M. (2013). Determination of total petroleum hydrocarbon (TPH) and polycyclic aromatic hydrocarbon (PAH) in soils: A review of spectroscopic and nonspectroscopic techniques. *Applied Spectroscopy Reviews, 48*(6), 458–486.

Stroud, P. D. (2001). Kalman-extended genetic algorithm for search in nonstationary environments with noisy fitness evaluations. *IEEE Transactions on Evolutionary Computation : A Publication of the IEEE Neural Networks Council, 5*(1), 66–77.

Sujjaviriyasup, T., & Pitiruek, K. (2013). Agricultural product forecasting using machine learning approach. *International Journal of Mathematical Analysis, 7*, 1869–1875.

Younis, S. M. Z., & Iqbal, J. (2015). Estimation of soil moisture using multispectral and FTIR techniques. *Egyptian Journal of Remote Sensing and Space Sciences, 18*(2), 151–161.

Zhu, Y., Yang, Z., & Song, J. (2006). A genetic algorithm with age and sexual features. In *Lecture Notes in Computer Science* (pp. 634–640). Berlin, Heidelberg: Springer Berlin Heidelberg.

Chapter 5

Artificial intelligent-based water and soil management

Ahmed Elbeltagi[a], Nand Lal Kushwaha[b], Ankur Srivastava[c], and Amira Talaat Zoof[d]

[a]Agricultural Engineering Department, Faculty of Agriculture, Mansoura University, Mansoura, Egypt, [b]Division of Agricultural Engineering, ICAR-Indian Agricultural Research Institute, New Delhi, India, [c]School of Engineering, The University of Newcastle, Callaghan, NSW, Australia, [d]Civil Engineering Department, Faculty of Engineering, Mansoura University, Mansoura, Egypt

1 Introduction

Agriculture is the bedrock of sustainability of the global economy. Pressure on the farming systems will increase with the continuing expansion of the human population. Agricultural technology and precision farming, new scientific fields that have developed and are now also known as digital agriculture, use data-intensive approaches to improve agricultural productivity while minimizing its environmental effects (Liakos et al., 2018). A number of different sensors provide the data produced in modern agricultural operations, enabling a better understanding of the operating environment (the interaction between crop, soil, and weather conditions) and the process itself (data from machinery), contributing to more precise and make a rapid decision. The vision for artificial intelligence-driven (AI-driven) machines started with developments in information technology in the 20th century, after the arrival of computers (Adamala & Srivastava, 2018; Dharmaraj & Vijayanand, 2018; Srivastava et al., 2017, 2018).

AI algorithms are depicted by the beginning function, which uses interconnected information processing units to convert the input into output by detecting relationships and patterns in data. Artificial neural networks (ANNs) are considered the best procedures for extracting information from imprecise and nonlinear data (Adisa et al., 2019; Elbeltagi et al., 2020a, 2020b, 2020d; Srivastava et al., 2020a, 2020b), as shown in Fig. 1.

The fundamental advantage of this form of network is that no arithmetical model is needed, as ANNs are trained from examples and recognize patterns in a series of independent and dependent data without any previous hypothesis about

Deep Learning for Sustainable Agriculture. https://doi.org/10.1016/B978-0-323-85214-2.00008-2

129

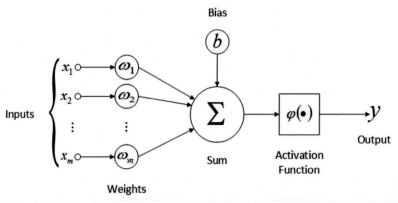

FIG. 1   Architecture of artificial neural network (Elbeltagi et al., 2020d).

their natural distribution and interrelations (Moghaddam et al., 2010). The limitations are not applicable to ANNs of the conventional approaches by obtaining the required information using the recorded data. Instead of the engineering equation, using an ANN requires sufficient input variables and output (Akcayol & Cinar, 2005). It is a better alternative to the normal empirical model based on linear regression and polynomial regression (Kose, 2008). We have divided the chapter into two major parts: first for the applications of AI in water management, and second for soil management. Then we presented in the conclusion the major points with the recommendations.

2   Applications of artificial intelligence in water management

2.1   Evapotranspiration estimation

Evapotranspiration (ET_o) represents a basic role in environmental, hydrological, and agricultural practices and plays a key role in managing and designing irrigation systems under fully irrigated and rain-fed farming (Djaman et al., 2015; Elbeltagi et al., 2020e; Kumari & Srivastava, 2020; Liu et al., 2019; Paul et al., 2018; Srivastava et al., 2018, 2020a). It can be measured directly or estimated by calculating reference ET_o. There have been a number of equations used to estimate ET_o. However, the FAO-56 Penman–Monteith (FAO-56 PM) method (Allen et al., 1998) has been confirmed to be superior in comparison with other techniques that are often used as the reference equation (Elbeltagi et al., 2020a; Huang et al., 2020; Malamos et al., 2015; Srivastava et al., 2017, 2020b; Yang et al., 2019). AI methods have been widely applied for estimation reference ET_o at several regions, for example, Motamedi et al. (2015) implemented soft computing approaches: support vector machine-firefly approach (SVM-FFA), genetic programming (GP), ANN, and SVM–wavelet. Their results stated that SVM–wavelet gave high satisfactory findings for ET_o prediction, while the developed SVM–wavelet and SVM-FFA models produced higher determination coefficients in comparison with ANN and GP computational methods. Petković et al. (2020) applied neuro-fuzzy logic based on weather conditions and the global findings indicated that global radiation has the strongest influence on the ET_o. A combination of average temperature and global radiation is the optimal combination for the ET_o estimation. Zhu et al. (2020) used the particle swarm optimization (PSO) algorithm and an unique hybrid PSO-ELM (extreme learning system) mode for estimating daily ET_o. The findings indicated that machine learning (ML) models generated more accurate ET_o estimates, compared with the empirical models with the same inputs. The hybrid PSO-ELM model exhibited higher performance and accuracy than the other algorithms for daily ET_o estimation as indicated by the statistical results. Shan et al. (2020) estimated the daily ET_o by applying the multivariate adaptive regression splines (MARS) model and illustrated that the MARS model surpassed back propagation neural network (BPNN) and empirical models at different growing stages, suggesting that the best MARS accurately modeled ET_o and climate factors and crop growth indicators. Furthermore, Yu et al. (2020) explored the uncertainty of AI by applying the ANN, SVR, and ELM models to model everyday reference ET_o. The outcomes revealed that, because of the comparable simulation ability and lower uncertainty, both the SVR and ELM models are highly recommended for ET_o estimation. Elbeltagi et al. (2020b) used deep learning to model long-term crop ET_o dynamics and found that the research outputs show that the determination coefficients between real vs expected monthly ET_c varied from 0.95 to 0.97 for calibration and from 0.94 to 0.95 for the validation period for the study locations, and the established models provided satisfactory results for water managers to conserve water and achieve farm water sustainability. A multilayer feed-forward network with one or two hidden neuron layers and an approach of sigmoid transfer feature and training algorithm for Bayesian regularization or Levenberg–Marquardt are used by Abrishami et al. (2019).

The results demonstrated the sufficient capacity and reasonable precision of ANNs to estimate daily ET_o. The ANN and mathematical methods of Hargreaves (H), Priestley-Taylor (PT), Makkink (M), and mass transfer were implemented by Antonopoulos & Antonopoulos (2017) to estimate the ET_o with everyday meteorological data. The 4-6-1 ANN layouts that were chosen have 4, 6, and 1 as neurons in the input, hidden, and output layers that correspond to ET_o, using a function of sigmoid transfer. In addition, the outputs of PT and M methods were correlated with outputs of Penman–Monteith (PM) method, following the method of H, which overestimates higher ET_o values. Moreover, Elbeltagi et al. (2020c) predicted the monthly crop coefficients (k_c) of maize, which considers a significant factor for calculation ET_o based on ANN models and declared that the accuracy of the best ANN model and correlation coefficients for prediction k_c were closed to 1. Thus, the developed model was proven to generate a high performance for the simulation process and recommend predicting the accurate value of k_c with limited climatic factors (Srivastava et al., 2017).

2.2 Crop water content prediction

Monitoring of the status of plant and crop heterogeneity are common physiological parameters limiting photosynthesis efficiency, and productivity of biomass in plants is needed at the farm level for irrigation scheduling, management, and planning (Maza et al., 2020; Srivastava et al., 2020b). A few literature reviews have applied and implemented AI methods for estimating crop water content, for example, Zakaluk & Ranjan (2006) applied ANNs for modeling leaf water potential (LWP) using RGB digital images. Also, The partial least squares (PLS), least squares SVM regression (LSSVR), and radial basis function (RBF) neural network for determining leaf water content (LWC) were introduced by Jin et al. (2017). Their findings showed that visible and near-infrared (VIS/NIR) spectroscopy combined with RBF-LSSVR or RBF-neutral network (RBF-NN) is a beneficial, nondestructive instrument for determining LWC.

Moreover, the water status of a vine was predicted using an ANN system and it was reported that the determination coefficient obtained between ANN outputs and measurements of ground-truth ranged from 0.56 to 0.87, including bands 550, 570, 670, 700, and 800 nm. Furthermore, Chen et al. (2012) used ANN methods and back propagation to assess the quality of peach tree leaf water and to conduct quantitative analyses between spectral indices. The research findings exhibit a linear relationship between the LWC of peach tree and reflectance spectral index.

2.3 Water footprint modeling

An indicator that relates production to the total consumption of water resources is the water footprint (WF), which was proposed by Hoekstra et al. (2011). Green and blue WFs represent rainfall (R) and agricultural water use, respectively. In general, the WF makes it possible to determine the basic and secondary consumption of freshwater resources required for the production of a given product (Elbeltagi et al., 2020a, 2020c; Hoekstra, 2008; Paul et al., 2018). A few methods have been applied for estimating the colors of WF, such as Elbeltagi et al. (2020a), who predicted the green and blue WF (WF_g and WF_b, respectively) of maize crop by using ANN technology (Table 1). The outcomes of ANN models stated that the deviation percentages between the observed vs simulated WFs varied from -2.6% to 6.63% for the blue WFs and from -2.4% to 3.16% for the green WFs.

2.4 Groundwater simulation

Assessment of the quality and quantity of surface and subsurface water is important in hydro-environmental management to sustain the natural systems and a safe, livable environment on and under the earth's surface. Dogan

TABLE 1 Comparison between the predicted and actual blue and green WFs for the two locations.

Location	Year	Actual WF$_b$ m^3/ton	Predicted WF$_b$ m^3/ton	Difference (predicted-actual)	Deviation
Blue WF					
Ad Daqahliyah	2013	780.60	798.69	18.09	0.0230
	2014	860.28	837.18	−23.1	−0.0260
	2015	864.75	864.06	−0.69	−0.0008
	2016	861.75	860.94	−0.825	−0.0009
Al Gharbiyah	2013	1026.63	1025.88	−0.75	−0.0007
	2014	1017.25	1014.70	−2.55	−0.0025
	2015	1077.09	1063.68	−13.41	−0.0124
	2016	1042.76	1046.66	3.89	0.0037
Green WF					
Ad Daqahliyah	2013	2.498	2.515	0.0164	0.0066
	2014	6.030	6.030	−0.0001	0.0000
	2015	43.910	43.910	0.0000	0.0000
	2016	1.753	1.742	−0.0107	−0.0061
Al Gharbiyah	2013	0.901	0.929	0.0285	0.0316
	2014	2.588	2.589	0.0008	0.0003
	2015	27.572	27.572	0.0000	0.0000
	2016	1.161	1.138	−0.0237	−0.0204

Elbeltagi et al. (2020c), studied the impact of climate changes on the WF colors of wheat and maize production using deep neural networks (DNN). Their results highly recommend the optimal use of the eastern delta to save blue water by 16.58% and 40.25% of total requirements for wheat-maize in contrast to others. Li et al. (2020) used path analysis of the WF, and the findings gained exhibited that the WFs were close to 190.74 G m^3 per year, including 55.41%, 22.65%, and 21.94% for the green, blue, and gray water, respectively.

et al. (2008) developed ANN for predicting the groundwater levels (GWLs) and stated that the monthly data series was equipped with all models, and their performance was compared. Results of predicting GWLs indicated that ANN performed better outcomes than multiple-linear regression and multiple-nonlinear regression (MNLR). Mohammadi et al. (2015) compared the ANN outputs with the observed outputs with different combinations of testing and validation dataset by means of the model evaluation parameters and revealed that the ANN tool can be executed for the GWL prediction. In addition, Djurovic et al. (2015) used two soft computing techniques—an adaptive neuro-fuzzy inference method (ANFIS) and an ANN—and proposed that both of these techniques are useful tools for the simulation of hydrological processes in agriculture. A number of common data-driven models, including ANNs, SVMs, and the M5 Model Tree, were evaluated and compared by Huang & Tian (2015). The findings show that the methodologies will simplify and strengthen the GWL forecast procedure. A low mean squared error value of 0.0014 and a high coefficient of 0.99 resulted when considering the validity of the ANN model. This implies that ANN can be used with relatively good precision to predict GWL in a complex basement terrain. Kombo et al. (2020) used a hybrid k-nearest neighbor-random forest to predict differences in GWLs of an aquifer, and the model generated satisfactory results. The occurrence of the ensemble model and the emotional ANN, the generalized neural regression network, and the conventional feed-forward neural network (FFNN) were investigated by Roshni et al. (2020). The study concluded that the EANN-GA model yields significantly better extreme event predictions and could therefore be a promising method for developing alarm systems for real-world water problems.

2.5 Pan evaporation estimation

Accurate simulation of pan evaporation (E_p) is important for monitoring and managing water resources, planning and scheduling of irrigation practices, irrigation needs, reservoir evaporation estimation, water budget of lakes, water allocation, and hydrologic modeling studies, especially in arid and semiarid regions (Rezaie-Balf et al., 2019). Several studies have been conducted for estimating E_p based on AI methods. For example, Seifi & Soroush (2020) applied novel hybrid meta-heuristic ANN-based methods in different climates, including genetic algorithm (GA), grey wolf optimization, and whale optimization algorithm, and found high E_p predictions using these models with limited climatic data. In addition, Rahimikhoob (2009) calculated daily E_p using ANN and found that both empirical and ANN techniques were similar to the observed values, but better estimates were provided by the ANN method than by the calibrated Hargreaves method. Moreover, chi-squared automatic interaction detector, neural networks, classification, and regression tree were used by Kisi et al. (2016), who revealed that an ANN model performed slightly better than the other models in both applications. Furthermore, functional link ANN (FLANN) was applied by Majhi and Naidu (2020), who reported that, in comparison to multilayer ANNs (MLANN), the proposed FLANN models have an improved estimate of E_p. Heuristic methods—the multilayer perceptrons neural network (MLPNN), coactive neuro-fuzzy inference system (CANFIS), radial basis neural network (RBNN), selforganizing map neural network (SOMNN), and climate models—were applied to predict E_p by Malik et al. (2017), and the results showed that CANFIS models with six input variables performed better than other models in estimating monthly E_p.

Also, the capabilities of ANN, least squares, fuzzy logic, adaptive neuro-fuzzy inference system (ANFIS), and LS-SVR techniques were analyzed to enhance E_p accuracy and it was found that the approaches to fuzzy logic and LS-SVR can be used effectively from the available climate data to model the everyday evaporation process. Besides, Tabari et al. (2010) used ANN and MNLR methods and indicated that ANN method estimates the best variables of daily E_P compared to MNLR models. More to this point, Alsumaiei (2020) applied ANN in hyper-arid climates and stated that air temperature (AT) and wind velocity were defined as the optimal meteorological variables that most affected the performance of ANN.

3 Applications of artificial intelligence in soil management

The major focus for soil management in agriculture for enhancing crop productivity is on the maintenance and improvement of dynamic soil parameters (Suchithra & Pai, 2020). ANNs are more suitable than mathematical approaches for solving complex problems in agricultural systems. Without specific physical consideration, ANN has the ability to identify and learn the underlying relations between input and output (Fig. 2). The construction of its massively equivalent distribution and the capacity to learn and then generalize the problem are the advantages of using ANN. In soil management field, ANNs have been implemented to plan irrigation strategies and to estimate the wetting portion for hidden soil layers using drip irrigation. Due to oversimplification and the illiteracy of dynamic nonlinear interactions, the use of statistical methods in soil management estimation has been limited. The use of nonlinear approaches such as ANN is another approach to working with dynamic systems. In the description and forecast, ANN was used effectively. The theoretical advantages of this

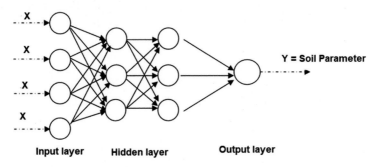

FIG. 2 Multilayer perceptron neural network developed for the estimation of soil parameter.

approach include greater credibility of prediction, cost-effective estimation, and the resolution of complex nonlinearity and uncertainty problems (Ayoubi et al., 2011).

3.1 Soil water content determination

Arif et al. (2013) has developed an ANN model with minimal meteorological data to predict soil moisture in paddy fields. ANN model dynamics was to measure soil moisture with reference inputs, ET_o, and R. Initially, ET_o was estimated using the maximum, average, and minimum values and approximate AT, like the model inputs. The models were carried out between the two under varying environmental cultivation conditions of paddy. The model testing process was implemented in the first period, using the observation data, while validating the procedure was performed on the basis of actual data in the second period. Dynamic measured soil moisture of the ANN model with R^2 values for preparation and validation of 0.80 and 0.73, processes, meanwhile, showed that close linear correlations of soil moisture levels between observed and expected values were recorded. The ANN model, therefore, measures soil moisture accurately with a minimal meteorological dataset.

3.2 Soil temperature monitoring

It has been shown that forecasting weather parameters such as soil temperature (ST), AT, wind speed, humidity (RH), and R is useful for purposes in agriculture. It has also been found that certain temperature parameters are extremely linked to solar radiation of these conditions. ST is one of the most critical variables influencing agriculture production. It is, however, very expensive to achieve precise ST readings. Therefore, it is important to build predictive models to forecast ST without using historical data on ST. It is a daunting mission.

ST and other agro-climatic variables involved may have complex interrelationships. Such problems can be efficiently solved using ANNs. ANN have been found to provide better solutions than traditional statistical methods when applied to poorly defined and poorly understood complex systems. Various ANN models such as, RBNNs and FFNNs have been employed to model various meteorological variables (Napagoda & Tilakaratne, 2012).

ST considers climate factor, which defines the soil's levels of physical, chemical, and biological reactions. In space and time, however, calculated values are very sparse and often not available for a given position. For estimating STs at different depths, ranged from 5 to 100 cm, used ANNs and CANFIS with few input variables (mean AT). The meteorological data collection over 14 years obtained for Gorgan in northern Iran and Zabol in southeastern Iran were used. Model performances proved that both ANNs and CANFIS models performed better in Zabol. The accuracy of the models gradually decreased from the surface down to the different soil depths and indicated the capabilities of the ANNs in estimation of STs in the two regions.

3.3 Soil fertilizer estimation

Precision fertilization represents an important component of precision agriculture technology; the basic concept is to use GPS to segment the field into grids, then check for soil nutrients and measure the required fertilizer input by using the fertilization model and fertilize based on a variable rate applicator. Practical experience shows that precise fertilization can minimize the use of fertilizers, improve crop production, balance nutrients in the soil, and minimize emissions in the atmosphere.

A novel neural network ensemble approach has been suggested to measure the fertilization rate more accurately (Yu et al., 2020), in which the k-means clustering method is used to choose optimal networks individually and a Lagrange multiplier is used to integrate these chosen networks. A fertilization model is built on the basis of the previously mentioned ANN ensemble system. The rates of soil nutrients and fertilization are taken as ANN inputs, and the production is taken as the output. This model transforms assessing fertilization rate to overcome programming problems, which can be applied to measure the overall yield and maximum benefit fertilization rate and to predict the yield. Additionally, on fertilizer impact results, this fertilization model has been checked. The findings suggest that using the neural network ensemble, the value prediction is more reliable than that obtained for individual neural networks.

3.4 Soil mapping

High-resolution soil land maps are considered to be the most important variables for supporting the decision in forestry, agriculture, environmental protection, and flood control. Soil properties are commonly derived mostly from field surveys. Land soil surveys are normally time-consuming and costly, with deployment limitations over a wide region. As such, for research purposes, high-resolution soil land maps are only available for specific areas and are not commonly acquired. ANN models have been presented in the chapter to generate high-resolution soil property maps. It was found that ANNs can be used with fair precision and low cost to forecast texture, drainage classes, and organic material of soil across landscapes (Zhao et al., 2017).

Advanced computer-based methods that are being used for digital soil mapping (DSM) are ANN. These methods allow soil classes to be mapped using surrogate landscape data in a cheaper, more consistent, and scalable way. This work contrasts the performance of two MLPs, selforganizing map (SOM), and ANN methods for DSM. Tests have been performed by researchers (Behrens et al., 2005) at Rhineland-Palatinate, covering 600 km^2, using the feed-forward ANN with back propagation, the best network topology was estimated at one layer and cells ranged from 15 to 30 based on the unit of soil. A total of 69, 53, and 3 different terrain attributes, geologic-petro graphic units, and forms of land use were obtained from accessible maps and databases to identify soil accuracy and to train the ANN. Of the expected soil units ($n = 33$), 80% had ANN training errors below 0.1. For the trained network outputs, validation returned a mean precision of over 92%. Altogether, the methodology presented, based on ANN and an expanded approach to digital terrain analysis, is time-saving and cost-effective and provides remarkable results.

4 Conclusion and recommendations for water-soil management

In the agriculture field, AI technology has been applied as an approach in different farming techniques for prediction, planning, management, and scheduling. The idea of cognitive computing is one that, as a computer model, imitates the process of human thinking. The findings of AI-powered agriculture as turbulent technology render its service to improve efficiency in the interpretation, acquisition, and response to different conditions.

This chapter assesses the value of AI methods in agriculture water management, such as ET_o estimation, crop water content prediction, WF modeling, groundwater simulation, and E_p estimation. The chapter also evaluates the performance of different AI methods for soil management, such as soil water content determination, ST monitoring, soil fertilizer estimation, and soil mapping. The results obtained from the previous researches revealed that the accuracy and performance of the developed ANN models were highly acceptable and can help promote the decision-making process for water managers, water users, and development planners to improve water-use efficiency and monitor the soil status. We recommend extending use of AI in all agricultural application for creating new agricultural system based on databases and rapid decisions for sustainable agro system development.

References

Abrishami, N., Sepaskhah, A. R., & Shahrokhnia, M. H. (2019). Estimating wheat and maize daily evapotranspiration using artificial neural network. *Theoretical and Applied Climatology, 135* (3–4), 945–958.

Adamala, S., & Srivastava, A. (2018). Comparative evaluation of daily evapotranspiration using artificial neural network and variable infiltration capacity models. *Agricultural Engineering International: CIGR Journal, 20*(1).

Adisa, O. M., Botai, J. O., Adeola, A. M., Hassen, A., Botai, C. M., Darkey, D., & Tesfamariam, E. (2019). Application of artificial neural network for predicting maize production in South Africa. *Sustainability, 11*(4), 1145.

Akcayol, M. A., & Cinar, C. (2005). Artificial neural network based modeling of heated catalytic converter performance. *Applied Thermal Engineering, 25*(14–15), 2341–2350.

Allen, R. G., Pereira, L. S., Raes, D., Smith, M., & Ab, W. (1998). *Allen_FAO1998* (pp. 1–15). Rome, Italy: Food and Agriculture Organization.

Alsumaiei, A. A. (2020). Utility of artificial neural networks in modeling pan evaporation in hyperarid climates. *Water, 12*(5), 1508.

Antonopoulos, V. Z., & Antonopoulos, A. V. (2017). Daily reference evapotranspiration estimates by artificial neural networks technique and empirical equations using limited input climate variables. *Computers and Electronics in Agriculture, 132*, 86–96.

Arif, C., Mizoguchi, M., & Setiawan, B. I. (2013). Estimation of soil moisture in paddy field using artificial neural networks. *arXiv.* preprint arXiv:1303.1868.

Ayoubi, S., Shahri, A. P., Karchegani, P. M., & Sahrawat, K. L. (2011). Application of artificial neural network (ANN) to predict soil organic matter using remote sensing data in two ecosystems. *Biomass and Remote Sensing of Biomass*, 181–196.

Behrens, T., Förster, H., Scholten, T., Steinrücken, U., Spies, E. D., & Goldschmitt, M. (2005). Digital soil mapping using artificial neural networks. *Journal of Plant Nutrition and Soil Science, 168*(1), 21–33.

Chen, X., Han, W., & Li, M. (2012). Spectroscopic determination of leaf water content using linear regression and an artificial neural network. *African Journal of Biotechnology, 11*(10), 2518–2527.

Dharmaraj, V., & Vijayanand, C. (2018). Artificial intelligence (AI) in agriculture. *International Journal of Current Microbiology and Applied Sciences, 7*(12), 2122–2128.

Djaman, K., Balde, A. B., Sow, A., Muller, B., Irmak, S., N'Diaye, M. K., ... Saito, K. (2015). Evaluation of sixteen reference evapotranspiration methods under sahelian conditions in the Senegal River valley. *Journal of Hydrology: Regional Studies, 3*, 139–159.

Djurovic, N., Domazet, M., Stricevic, R., Pocuca, V., Spalevic, V., Pivic, R., ... Domazet, U. (2015). Comparison of groundwater level models based on artificial neural networks and ANFIS. *The Scientific World Journal, 2015*, 13. https://doi.org/10.1155/2015/742138. 742138.

Dogan, A., Demirpence, H., & Cobaner, M. (2008). Prediction of groundwater levels from lake levels and climate data using ANN approach. *Water SA, 34*(2), 199–208.

Elbeltagi, A., Aslam, M. R., Malik, A., Mehdinejadiani, B., Srivastava, A., Bhatia, A. S., & Deng, J. (2020). The impact of climate changes on the water footprint of wheat and maize production in the Nile Delta, Egypt. *Science of the Total Environment, 743*, 140770.

Elbeltagi, A., Aslam, M. R., Mokhtar, A., Deb, P., Abubakar, G. A., Kushwaha, N. L., ... Deng, J. (2020). Spatial and temporal variability analysis of green and blue evapotranspiration of wheat in the Egyptian Nile Delta from 1997 to 2017. *Journal of Hydrology*, 125662.

Elbeltagi, A., Deng, J., Wang, K., & Hong, Y. (2020). Crop water footprint estimation and modeling using an artificial neural network approach in the Nile Delta, Egypt. *Agricultural Water Management, 235*, 106080.

Elbeltagi, A., Deng, J., Wang, K., Malik, A., & Maroufpoor, S. (2020). Modeling long-term dynamics of crop evapotranspiration using deep learning in a semi-arid environment. *Agricultural Water Management, 241*, 106334.

Elbeltagi, A., Zhang, L., Deng, J., Juma, A., & Wang, K. (2020). Modeling monthly crop coefficients of maize based on limited meteorological data: A case study in Nile Delta, Egypt. *Computers and Electronics in Agriculture, 173*, 105368.

Hoekstra, A. Y. (2008). Water neutral: Reducing and offsetting the impacts of water footprints, value of water research report series no. 28, UNESCO-IHE, Delft, the Netherlands. www.waterfootprint. org 34/Business water footprint accounting Hoekstra. *Value of Water Research Report Series.*

Hoekstra, A. Y., Chapagain, A. K., Aldaya, M. M., & Mekonnen, M. M. (2011). *The water footprint assessment manual: Setting the global standard.* London: Earthscan.

Huang, Q. A., Tang, C. Y., Chen, Z. S., Li, S. F., & Li, J. H. (2020). Numberical simulation of evapotranspiration with limited data in the Pearl River Basin. In *Materials science forum: Vol. 980* (pp. 512–524). Trans Tech Publications Ltd.

Huang, M., & Tian, Y. (2015, October). Prediction of groundwater level for sustainable water management in an arid basin using data-driven models. In *2015 International conference on sustainable energy and environmental engineering*Atlantis Press.

Jin, X., Shi, C., Yu, C. Y., Yamada, T., & Sacks, E. J. (2017). Determination of leaf water content by visible and near-infrared spectrometry and multivariate calibration in Miscanthus. *Frontiers in Plant Science, 8*, 721.

Kisi, O., Genc, O., Dinc, S., & Zounemat-Kermani, M. (2016). Daily pan evaporation modeling using chi-squared automatic interaction detector, neural networks, classification and regression tree. *Computers and Electronics in Agriculture, 122*, 112–117.

Kombo, O. H., Kumaran, S., Sheikh, Y. H., Bovim, A., & Jayavel, K. (2020). Long-term groundwater level prediction model based on hybrid KNN-RF technique. *Hydrology, 7*(3), 59.

Kose, E. (2008). Modelling of colour perception of different age groups using artificial neural networks. *Expert Systems with Applications, 34*(3), 2129–2139.

Kumari, N., & Srivastava, A. (2020). An approach for estimation of evapotranspiration by standardizing parsimonious method. *Agricultural Research, 9*(3), 301–309.

Li, X., Chen, D., Cao, X., Luo, Z., & Webber, M. (2020). Assessing the components of, and factors influencing, paddy rice water footprint in China. *Agricultural Water Management, 229*, 105939.

Liakos, K. G., Busato, P., Moshou, D., Pearson, S., & Bochtis, D. (2018). Machine learning in agriculture: A review. *Sensors, 18*(8), 2674.

Liu, X., Xu, J., Yang, S., & Lv, Y. (2019). Surface energy partitioning and evaporative fraction in a water-saving irrigated rice field. *Atmosphere, 10*(2), 51.

Majhi, B., & Naidu, D. (2020). Pan evaporation modeling in different agroclimatic zones using functional link artificial neural network. In *Information processing in agriculture* (pp. 134–147). KeAi Chinese Roots Global Impact.

Malamos, N., Barouchas, P. E., Tsirogiannis, I. L., Liopa-Tsakalidi, A., & Koromilas, T. (2015). Estimation of monthly FAO penman-monteith evapotranspiration in GIS environment, through a geometry independent algorithm. *Agriculture and Agricultural Science Procedia, 4*, 290–299.

Malik, A., Kumar, A., & Kisi, O. (2017). Monthly pan-evaporation estimation in Indian Central Himalayas using different heuristic approaches and climate based models. *Computers and Electronics in Agriculture, 143*, 302–313.

Maza, M., Srivastava, A., Bisht, D. S., Raghuwanshi, N. S., Bandyopadhyay, A., Chatterjee, C., & Bhadra, A. (2020). Simulating hydrological response of a monsoon dominated reservoir catchment and command with heterogeneous cropping pattern using VIC model. *Journal of Earth System Science, 129*(1), 1–16.

Moghaddam, M. G., Ahmad, F. B. H., Basri, M., & Rahman, M. B. A. (2010). Artificial neural network modeling studies to predict the yield of enzymatic synthesis of betulinic acid ester. *Electronic Journal of Biotechnology, 13*(3), 3–4.

Mohammadi, A., Costelloe, J. F., & Ryu, D. (2015). Prediction of groundwater levels using artificial neural network: a case study of Gandhinagar and Kalol Taluka. In *21St Int. Congr. Model. Simul* (pp. 2346–2352).

Motamedi, S., Shamshirband, S., Petkovic, D., Ch, S., Hashim, R., & Arif, M. (2015). Soft computing approaches for forecasting reference evapotranspiration. *Computers and Electronics in Agriculture, 113*, 164–173.

Napagoda, N. A., & Tilakaratne, C. D. (2012). Artificial neural network approach for modeling of soil temperature: A case study for Bathalagoda area. *Sri Lankan Journal of Applied Statistics, 13*, 39–59.

Paul, P. K., Kumari, N., Panigrahi, N., Mishra, A., & Singh, R. (2018). Implementation of cell-to-cell routing scheme in a large scale conceptual hydrological model. *Environmental Modelling & Software, 101*, 23–33.

Petković, B., Petković, D., Kuzman, B., Milovančević, M., Wakil, K., Ho, L. S., & Jermsittiparsert, K. (2020). Neuro-fuzzy estimation of reference crop evapotranspiration by neuro fuzzy logic based on weather conditions. *Computers and Electronics in Agriculture, 173*, 105358.

Rahimikhoob, A. (2009). Estimating daily pan evaporation using artificial neural network in a semi-arid environment. *Theoretical and Applied Climatology, 98*(1–2), 101–105.

Rezaie-Balf, M., Kisi, O., & Chua, L. H. (2019). Application of ensemble empirical mode decomposition based on machine learning methodologies in forecasting monthly pan evaporation. *Hydrology Research, 50*(2), 498–516.

Roshni, T., Jha, M. K., & Drisya, J. (2020). Neural network modeling for groundwater-level forecasting in coastal aquifers. *Neural Computing and Applications*, 1–18.

Seifi, A., & Soroush, F. (2020). Pan evaporation estimation and derivation of explicit optimized equations by novel hybrid meta-heuristic ANN based methods in different climates of Iran. *Computers and Electronics in Agriculture, 173*, 105418.

Shan, X., Cui, N., Cai, H., Hu, X., & Zhao, L. (2020). Estimation of summer maize evapotranspiration using MARS model in the semi-arid region of Northwest China. *Computers and Electronics in Agriculture, 174*, 105495.

Srivastava, A., Deb, P., & Kumari, N. (2020). Multi-model approach to assess the dynamics of hydrologic components in a tropical ecosystem. *Water Resources Management, 34*(1), 327–341.

Srivastava, A., Kumari, N., & Maza, M. (2020). Hydrological response to agricultural land use heterogeneity using variable infiltration capacity model. *Water Resources Management, 34*(12), 3779–3794.

Srivastava, A., Sahoo, B., Raghuwanshi, N. S., & Chatterjee, C. (2018). Modelling the dynamics of evapotranspiration using variable infiltration capacity model and regionally calibrated Hargreaves approach. *Irrigation Science, 36*(4–5), 289–300.

Srivastava, A., Sahoo, B., Raghuwanshi, N. S., & Singh, R. (2017). Evaluation of variable-infiltration capacity model and MODIS-terra satellite-derived grid-scale evapotranspiration estimates in a River Basin with tropical monsoon-type climatology. *Journal of Irrigation and Drainage Engineering, 143*(8), 04017028.

Suchithra, M. S., & Pai, M. L. (2020). Improving the prediction accuracy of soil nutrient classification by optimizing extreme learning machine parameters. *Information Processing in Agriculture, 7*(1), 72–82.

Tabari, H., Marofi, S., & Sabziparvar, A. A. (2010). Estimation of daily pan evaporation using artificial neural network and multivariate non-linear regression. *Irrigation Science, 28*(5), 399–406.

Yang, Y., Cui, Y., Bai, K., Luo, T., Dai, J., Wang, W., & Luo, Y. (2019). Short-term forecasting of daily reference evapotranspiration using the reduced-set penman-Monteith model and public weather forecasts. *Agricultural Water Management, 211*, 70–80.

Yu, H., Wen, X., Li, B., Yang, Z., Wu, M., & Ma, Y. (2020). Uncertainty analysis of artificial intelligence modeling daily reference evapotranspiration in the northwest end of China. *Computers and Electronics in Agriculture, 176*, 105653.

Zakaluk, R., & Ranjan, R. S. (2006). Artificial neural network modelling of leaf water potential for potatoes using RGB digital images: A greenhouse study. *Potato Research*, *49*(4), 255–272.

Zhao, Z., Meng, F. R., Yang, Q., & Zhu, H. (2017). Using artificial neural networks to produce high-resolution soil property maps. In *Advanced applications for artificial neural networks* IntechOpen.

Zhu, B., Feng, Y., Gong, D., Jiang, S., Zhao, L., & Cui, N. (2020). Hybrid particle swarm optimization with extreme learning machine for daily reference evapotranspiration prediction from limited climatic data. *Computers and Electronics in Agriculture*, *173*, 105430.

Chapter 6

Machine learning for soil moisture assessment

Alka Rani[a], Nirmal Kumar[b], Jitendra Kumar[c], Jitendra Kumar[a], and Nishant K. Sinha[a]

[a]ICAR-Indian Institute of Soil Science, Nabibagh, Bhopal, Madhya Pradesh, India, [b]ICAR-National Bureau of Soil Survey and Land Use Planning, Nagpur, Maharashtra, India, [c]ICAR-Vivekananda Parvatiya Krishi Anusandhan Sansthan, Almora, Uttarakhand, India

1 Introduction

Soil moisture is a vital component in regulating water and energy circulation between land and atmosphere (Willmott et al., 1985). It also influences chemical and biological processes in the soil (Moyano et al., 2013; Orchard & Cook, 1983; Weitz et al., 2001). Soil moisture impacts and is influenced by meteorological or climatic parameters like precipitation, temperature, and evapotranspiration, thereby playing a significant role in weather and climate change studies (Berg et al., 2014; Koster et al., 2004; Seneviratne et al., 2010). The soil moisture information is crucial for precipitation estimates, weather forecasting (Capecchi & Brocca, 2014; Drusch et al., 2009; Wanders et al., 2015), and monitoring and forecasting natural disasters like droughts (Bolten et al., 2009; Rahmani et al., 2016), floods (Alvarez-Garreton et al., 2015; Massari et al., 2014), and landslides (Bittelli et al., 2012; Brocca et al., 2012). Soil moisture determines the water availability to the crops; thus, its data is vital for irrigation management in agriculture (Rodríguez-Iturbe & Porporato, 2007) and crop yield prediction (Dai et al., 2011; Ines et al., 2013). Soil moisture content determines the partitioning of rainfall into soil moisture storage and runoff (Koren et al., 2000); therefore, it is required for estimation or modeling of runoff and soil erosion (Lørup & Styczen, 1990; Raclot & Albergel, 2006; Zhang et al., 2011).

The soil moisture is heterogeneous with space and time. So, the regular measurement of soil moisture is required for its applications. The conventional approaches for measuring soil moisture include gravimetric method, neutron scattering, gamma-ray attenuation, electromagnetic sensors like Time-domain reflectometer, Frequency-domain reflectometer, and electrical resistance

Deep Learning for Sustainable Agriculture. https://doi.org/10.1016/B978-0-323-85214-2.00001-X

143

blocks, tensiometer, fiber optic sensors, and more. These techniques only provide point measurements (Topp, 2003). However, soil moisture at spatial and temporal level is required for regional planning. It is challenging to apply conventional and in-situ measurement methods over a large area, as it will be very laborious and time-consuming. The establishment of a dense network of soil moisture measuring sensors is very expensive. Remote sensing techniques can be used for regular monitoring of soil moisture status at spatial and temporal scales (Ahmed et al., 2011). The remote sensing approach utilizes electromagnetic radiations in optical, infrared, and mainly microwave wavelengths for estimating soil moisture content using various empirical and mechanistic models. Several methods are being used for estimating soil moisture through satellite remote sensing. The optical remote sensing explores the linear relationship between land surface reflectance and soil moisture content either directly or through the development of empirical spectral indices (Jackson et al., 1976; Kogan, 1995; Liu et al., 2003). Thermal remote sensing estimates soil moisture through thermal inertia and temperature index (Maltese et al., 2013; Minacapilli et al., 2009; Verhoef, 2004). Microwave remote sensing provides surface soil moisture estimates under all weather conditions with reasonable accuracy by using direct relation between soil dielectric constant and water content (Ahmed et al., 2011; Baghdadi et al., 2004). Out of all these bands, the microwave band is most suitable for estimating soil moisture as it can penetrate through the atmosphere and vegetation to detect soil moisture in the surface layer (Ahmed et al., 2011). The radiometer, scatterometer, and Synthetic Aperture Radar (SAR), on-board air-borne or space-borne platforms, operating in microwave waveband, are being widely used to retrieve soil moisture content.

Over the last decade, the application of machine learning (ML) algorithms like linear regression, artificial neural networks (ANNs), deep learning, support vector machines (SVMs), classification and regression tree (CART), random forest (RF), and so on, have increased significantly in the arena of soil moisture research due to their non-parametric nature and ability to capture complex and non-linear relationships (Padarian et al., 2020). ML approaches could be used to develop pedotransfer functions (PTFs) for the estimation of soil hydraulic properties and prediction models for forecasting soil moisture (Kalkhajeh et al., 2012; Amanabadi et al., 2019; Pekel, 2020). In data-driven precision irrigation or the Internet of Things-based (IoT-based) smart irrigation, the use of ML algorithms is inevitable for real-time soil moisture monitoring and need-based, site-specific irrigation to the plants (Shekhar et al., 2017). The satellite-derived remotely sensed soil moisture products, like Soil Moisture Active Passive (SMAP), Soil Moisture and Ocean Salinity (SMOS), European Space Agency Climate Change Initiative (ESA CCI), Advanced Scatterometer (ASCAT), and so on, are of coarser spatial resolution (> 9 km), which limit their applicability at the watershed or regional scale as soil moisture is highly variable with space and time (Cui et al., 2018). Therefore, there is a need to downscale these soil moisture products at a finer spatial resolution, which can also be done by developing models using ML with several covariates like vegetation, slope, soil texture, etc. (Peng et al., 2017). The ML approaches have opened up new opportunities in soil moisture assessment. In this chapter, we present an overview of the applicability of ML algorithms for soil moisture estimation in various domains.

2 Overview of machine learning

ML is a type of Artificial Intelligence (AI) that enables the machines or systems to learn from their data or experience rather than through predefined equations or rule-based programming. According to Mitchell (1997), "Machine learning is the study of computer algorithms that allow computer programs to automatically improve through experience." So, in ML, the system learns from experience just like human beings. ML is done through a variety of algorithms. These algorithms try to solve real-world problems in a heuristic manner. First of all, the data is collected by the user, and its quality is checked and improved for applying any ML algorithm. Based on the desired objective, an appropriate ML algorithm is selected. The algorithm is applied to the training data, which builds a model to represent the data. The performance or accuracy of the model is evaluated on testing data. If the model performance is not good, it can be improved by selecting different algorithms, adding more data, or improving the data quality. When the model performs satisfactorily, then it is deployed for performing the desired task. There are broadly three types of algorithms in ML—supervised learning, unsupervised learning, and reinforcement learning—which are discussed below briefly:

Supervised learning: In supervised learning, the labeled training dataset is provided in which output is already known. The model is trained to predict the desired output by applying the algorithm to the input dataset. The model is trained until it attains the required accuracy on the training dataset. Supervised learning is mainly used for classification and regression. Examples of supervised ML algorithms are SVMs, linear regression, logistic regression, Naïve Bayes, neural networks, RF, and so forth. These algorithms are mostly used for soil moisture assessment in various domains of soil moisture research.

Unsupervised learning: In unsupervised learning, unlabeled data is provided so that the algorithms learn and infer from the data without external supervision. Unsupervised ML is used for finding the hidden patterns, grouping similar kinds of data, exploratory data analysis, and dimensionality reduction. Thus, it mainly deals with clustering and association. The typical examples of unsupervised ML algorithms are k-means, hierarchical clustering, apriori algorithm, expectation-maximization algorithm, principal component analysis, and so on.

Reinforcement learning: In reinforcement learning, the algorithm navigates through an uncertain environment by taking actions. The feedback of actions in the form of reward or penalty further guides the algorithm to maximize its performance. In it, predefined data is not provided as the interaction of the algorithm with the environment creates data. In reinforcement learning, decisions are taken sequentially. The most commonly used algorithms under reinforcement learning are the Q-learning algorithm, State–action–reward–state–action algorithm (SARSA), Deep Deterministic Policy Gradient (DDPG) Algorithm, and more. It is also combined with deep learning in some applications.

3 Machine learning algorithms applied in soil moisture research

In soil moisture research, mainly supervised ML algorithms are applied. Out of all the supervised ML algorithms, the most commonly used algorithms in soil moisture assessment having ample available literature are briefly discussed in this chapter.

3.1 Linear regression

Linear regression is the simplest and most commonly used method for prediction. It predicts by considering the linear relationship between the dependent variable and independent variables. If there is only one independent variable, then it is called a simple linear regression. If there is more than one independent variables, then it is referred to as multiple linear regression (MLR). The simple linear equation can be denoted by the following equation:

$$y = \alpha + \beta x.$$

where, y: Dependent or response variable
  α: Intercept
  β: Slope
  x: Independent or predictor variable
MLR can be represented in the form of the following equation:

$$y = \beta_0 + \beta_1 x_1 + \beta_2 x_2 + \cdots + \beta_i x_i + \epsilon$$

where, y: Dependent or response variable
  x_i: Independent or predictor variables
  β_0 : y-intercept
  β_i: slope coefficients for each independent variable
  ϵ: error term or residuals
  Linear regression performs well when data is linearly separable and predictor variables are independent of each other. It should not be applied if less data is available, as it is prone to noise and overfitting. Linear regression is also sensitive to outliers. The multicollinearity among the variables should be removed before applying it. The usage of MLR is generally referred to as a traditional approach in soil moisture research.

3.2 Artificial neural network/deep neural network

ANNs, developed by McCulloch & Pitts (1943), are greatly inspired by the functioning of the human brain having interconnected neurons for processing the data. An ANN also has interconnected nodes similar to neurons that communicate messages to each other. A simple ANN is depicted in Fig. 1. An ANN has an input layer (*x* variable), one or more hidden layers, and an output layer (*y* variable). The signals are passed according to an activation function (*f*) and weighted (*w* values) corresponding to their importance. For "*n*" number of input nodes, the ANN can be represented by the following equation:

$$y(x) = f\left(\sum_{i=1}^{n} w_i x_i\right)$$

An ANN is characterized by the activation function, interconnection pattern between the different layers of neurons, which is known as network architecture, and training or learning algorithm for determining the adaptive weights on the connections. There are several choices for activation function like threshold or unit step, Gaussian, sigmoid, hyperbolic tangential, rectified linear unit, and so forth. The network architecture depends upon the number of layers, the number of nodes in each layer, and the nature of the flow of information in the network, which can be both forward and backward. The commonly used learning algorithms are radial basis function, feed-forward propagation, backpropagation, and perceptron algorithms. The overall goal of learning or training is to adjust weights or biases such that the cost function is minimum. A type of ANN with a multilayer feed-forward network, and fuzzy reasoning to signalize an input space to an output space is known as adaptive neuro-fuzzy inference system (ANFIS). ANN can be used for classification and regression problems.

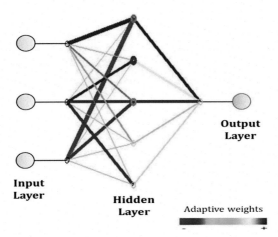

FIG. 1 A simple ANN with one hidden layer.

It can capture non-linear and complex relationships. However, it is prone to underfit or overfit the training data. The deep neural network (DNN) is ANN with multiple hidden layers and increased number of neurons per hidden layer for solving complex problems. DNN is more accurate than ANN but requires more time and computational power.

3.3   Support vector machine

SVM is a supervised ML algorithm for both classification and regression. It is derived from statistical learning theory by Boser et al. (1992). The process of finding out the correct hyperplane for classification with the help of support vectors, that is, the points of each class present at the margin is the basic principle of SVMs. Fig. 2 depicts all components of SVM. When SVM is used for regression, then it is generally referred to as support vector regression (SVR).

SVM can be linear or non-linear. Linear SVM can be further categorized into hard margin and soft margin. In hard margin SVM, the data is completely linearly separable by a hyperplane, but not in soft margin SVM. In soft margin SVM, positive slack variables ξ are introduced that represent penalty to the data points on the incorrect side of the margin boundary. The value of the slack variable increases with the increase in its distance from the margin. When the data is non-linear, then non-linear SVM is used in which the original input space is mapped to higher-dimensional feature space by the use of kernel functions on training sets. The most commonly used kernels are the radial basis, polynomial, and sigmoidal. SVM is more robust to outliers and noise. It provides several choices for the model parameters and kernels, which need to be tested for

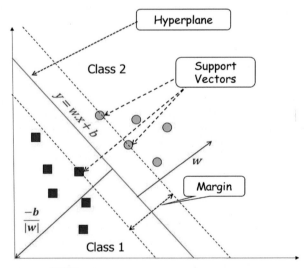

FIG. 2   Components of SVM.

selecting the best SVM. It performs well under high-dimensional spaces. As it is a black box algorithm, so, it is difficult to understand and interpret the final SVM model, variable weights, and individual impact.

3.4 Classification and regression tree

CART is a decision tree algorithm that was first introduced by Breiman et al. (1984). This algorithm constructs an inverted tree-like graphical structure from the data comprising of a series of logical decisions at their root node, branches, and leaf nodes for classification or regression as depicted in Fig. 3. The input and output data can be both categorical and continuous for classification and regression. Each node in CART represents a decision rule that splits the data into two or more homogeneous sets. The topmost node of the tree is known as the root node, which gives rise to internal nodes. The internal nodes have both parent and child nodes containing decision rules. The branches represent the outcome of the respective test or decision rule. The leaf node or terminal node does not have any children, and they represent the final output. The variable is selected at each split based on its contribution in minimizing the cost metric. The cost metrics are Gini impurity, misclassification error, or entropy for classification, and mean squared error for regression. Initially, the preliminary criteria for construction, division, and stopping of a tree are given. When the fully grown CART model is constructed, then the pruning is done to remove branches that do not significantly reduce the cost metric. This further simplifies the CART model. CART is sometimes referred to as Cubist while used for regression, as it yields a rule-based model having several rules with their specific conditions.

CART is simple, non-linear, and non-parametric. CART model is easy to understand and interpret due to its white box nature. It can be implemented with little data preparation as the normalization or scaling of input data is not

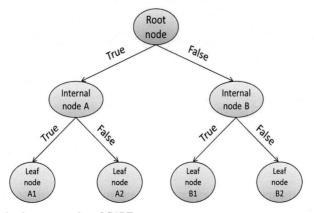

FIG. 3 A simple representation of CART.

required. It is prone to overfitting if data has more noise. It can produce results with high variance when the data having small variation is provided. It has a low bias that makes it difficult to incorporate any new data. The small change in data results in large changes in the CART model structure. The model becomes complex when the data size is very large, which can lead to overfitting.

3.5 Random forest

RF is an ensemble ML technique that was developed by Breiman (2001). In this technique, a "forest" of multiple random uncorrelated decision trees are constructed from the subsets of the training dataset, and their outputs are ensembled to give the final output. The final output is computed by taking the mode of the classes predicted by the individual decision tree in the case of classification, whereas the mean prediction of individual trees is taken in regression. The schematic diagram of the RF is depicted in Fig. 4. RF algorithm has higher accuracy, is compatible with a large dataset, eliminates the need for pruning decision trees, and prevents the problem of overfitting, which makes it better than CART. The relative importance of each variable in prediction can also be measured. However, while doing regression, it should be noted that this algorithm predicts within the range of training data and cannot predict extreme values accurately.

3.6 Extremely randomized trees

This algorithm is similar to RF except the multiple trees are constructed without bootstrapping (sampling without replacement), and splits in nodes are made randomly instead of best splits. It was introduced by Geurts et al. (2006). This

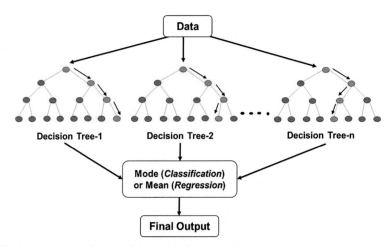

FIG. 4 A schematic diagram of the random forest algorithm.

algorithm constructs trees from the whole training dataset. This algorithm is faster computationally than the RF model because it does not have to calculate the best split.

4 Applications of machine learning for soil moisture assessment

ML algorithms are being used for soil moisture assessment in various domains of soil moisture research. The research studies highlighting the application of different ML algorithms with their respective accuracy in soil moisture assessment are briefly discussed in this chapter.

4.1 Pedotransfer functions

ML algorithms are used for the development of PTFs, which can be used for the prediction of soil properties. PTFs are the equations or algorithms that express the relationship between different soil properties. PTFs predict the soil properties that are unavailable or difficult to measure through the use of easily available or measurable soil properties (Pachepsky & Van Genuchten, 2011). Therefore, they serve as an alternative to the expensive field and laboratory methods. Several PTFs are being developed by researchers for the prediction of soil hydraulic properties using ML algorithms. Kalkhajeh et al. (2012) developed PTFs for predicting soil saturated hydraulic conductivity (Ks) in southwest Iran through MLR, ANFIS, and ANN with multilayer perceptron (MLP) and radial basis function (RBF) models using available soil data. They reported that the coefficient of determination (R^2) between measured and predicted Ks from PTFs developed using MLR, ANFIS, MLP, and RBF were 0.53, 0.71, 0.81, and 0.82, respectively. The PTFs developed from ANN with MLP and RBF had higher accuracy in comparison to other algorithms, which can be used for predicting Ks. However, for prediction of infiltration rate and deep percolation using soil parameters such as clay, silt, bulk density, water saturation percentage, and organic carbon, the PTFs based on ANFIS had higher accuracy than ANN followed by MLR (Sarmadian & Mehrjardi, 2010). Kaingo et al. (2018) developed PTF for predicting soil moisture-holding capacity from the sand, clay, bulk density, and organic carbon using SVR with the linear kernel, which was found to perform marginally better than MLR.

ML techniques can be used for the modeling and prediction of the soil water retention curve (SWRC), which depicts the non-linear relationship between soil matric potential and volumetric soil water content. Amanabadi et al. (2019) developed PTFs based on MLR, scaled numerical models, ANN, and ANFIS, which predict SWRC using basic soil properties like sand, silt, clay, saturated water content, matric potential, bulk density, particle density, and porosity. They reported that ANN (RMSE = 0.029) predicted SWRC better than ANFIS (RMSE = 0.035), scaled model (RMSE = 0.060), and MLR (RMSE = 0.071), regardless of the soil texture. Achieng (2019) compared several ML algorithms for modeling SWRC and found that RBF-based SVR outperformed SVR with linear and polynomial kernels, single layer ANN, and DNN in loamy sand soil.

There is always a problem of selecting optimal parameters in the SVM and ANN so that the final model provides accurate results. Therefore, for optimization of parameters, many new algorithms like genetic algorithms or firefly algorithms can be used. Azadmard et al. (2020) used a genetic algorithm with ANN for the prediction of near-saturated soil hydraulic properties such as unsaturated hydraulic conductivity, saturated hydraulic conductivity, macroscopic capillary length, and van Genucthen scaling and shape parameters in Moghan plain, northwestern Iran, which performed much better than MLR approach. Ghorbani et al. (2017) used a firefly algorithm for the optimization of parameters of SVR for prediction of field capacity and permanent wilting point using sand, silt, clay, bulk density, and organic matter content as inputs that outperformed SVR and ANN models in terms of accuracy. Thus, the usage of genetic or firefly algorithms significantly improved the performance of SVM and ANN models by selecting optimal parameters based on data. Overall, we may conclude that MLR is the least accurate method for PTF development, whereas ANN and SVR were found to be the most accurate and preferred methods.

4.2 Prediction models for soil moisture estimation/forecasting

The estimation and forecasting of soil moisture are crucial for meteorological studies, estimation of runoff and soil erosion, drought and flood forecasting, and judicious use and management of water resources. There are two ways for predicting soil moisture. The first way is to use an empirical approach to establish the relationship between soil moisture content with meteorological, hydrological, and soil parameters. The second way is the use of a physical or simulation model having some theoretical basis like soil water balance, thermal or dielectric properties of soil water, and so forth. ML algorithms have proved their wide applicability in the development of prediction models based on empirical approach for estimation or forecasting of soil moisture. Gorthi & Dou (2011) used precipitation, air, and soil temperature, and Soil Adjusted Vegetation Index computed from the reflectance data in visible and NIR region as inputs in the ANN model to provide soil moisture content in the 6 cm soil depth as output. Pekel (2020) applied decision tree regression or CART to estimate soil moisture by taking air temperature, time, relative humidity, and soil temperature as input variables. Deep learning regression network (DLRN) with big data fitting capability was proposed by Cai et al. (2019) for constructing soil moisture prediction models with initial soil moisture, daily precipitation, land temperature, average wind speed, relative humidity, average temperature, and pressure as inputs. The DLRN model predicted soil moisture with high accuracy ($R^2 = 0.98$), as it has excellent generalization capability and scalability. As numerical models like HYDRUS-2D require a large amount of input data for simulating the time-series of soil moisture, it can be done efficiently by ML algorithms like SVM and ANFIS if limited input data is available (Karandish & Šimůnek, 2016). Although the accuracy of ML algorithms is comparatively lower than numerical models, they can serve as a better alternative under limited and missing data conditions.

The soil moisture content can be predicted at deeper depth from the surface data. Zaman & McKee (2014) predicted the soil moisture content 4 days ahead at 1 and 2 m depths from the current soil moisture collected from 5, 10, 30, and 50 cm depths by applying a multivariate relevance vector machine (MVRVM) model. The MVRVM model is based on a sparse Bayesian learning approach in which the machine learns the input and output pattern with higher accuracy. Soil moisture forecasting using past soil moisture data and SVM was successfully done by Wu et al. (2007). The soil moisture and meteorological data of the current and previous day were taken to forecast the soil moisture content after four and seven days by using SVM and ANN in which the former performed better (Gill et al., 2006). A similar approach was used by Khalil et al. (2005) to forecast soil moisture content 5 days ahead using SVM and sparse Bayesian learning-based relevance vector machine (RVM) algorithm having comparable accuracy. An ensemble approach based on ANN was developed by Prasad et al. (2018) for fore-casting monthly upper and lower layer soil moisture. They used climate indices, atmospheric, and hydro-meteorological parameters as inputs in the second-order Volterra, M5 model tree (decision tree), RF, and an extreme learning machine (single layer feed-forward neural network) models for prediction of soil moisture contents. The outputs of individual models were channeled as input in the feed-forward ANN known as ANN multimodel ensemble committee of models (ANN-CoM) for providing a monthly forecast of soil moisture. This ANN-CoM model performed better than individual models. Therefore, it is evi-dent that ML algorithms are playing a major role in developing prediction models for soil moisture estimation and forecasting.

4.3   Soil moisture retrieval through remote sensing

In remote sensing, the electromagnetic radiations in optical, infrared, and mainly microwave wavelength are used for estimating soil moisture content without coming in physical contact with the soil. Generally, the radiometer, scatterometer, and SAR, on-board air-borne or space-borne platforms, operat-ing in microwave waveband, are used to retrieve soil moisture content. How-ever, optical and infrared bands are also used in some conditions or as complementary to the microwave data. Apart from satellite remote sensing, unmanned aerial vehicles (UAVs) and ground-based sensors are also used to retrieve soil moisture. Through remote sensing, the soil moisture content at the regional level can be estimated, and their spatio-temporal variation pattern can be studied. The soil moisture status retrieved from the satellite data can be used for planning at the regional level, whereas the data from UAVs and ground-based sensors can be used at the field scale. ML algorithms are considerably used for estimation of soil moisture from the remote sensing data because of their ability to integrate data with unknown probability density functions (Ali et al., 2015). However, a large amount of training data is required for applying ML algorithms to produce accurate results. The general methodology followed for estimating the soil moisture from remote sensing datasets by using ML algorithms is depicted in Fig. 5. The remote sensing images and ancillary data, like land use, soil properties, and so on, are used as the explanatory or independent variables, and soil moisture is taken as a response or dependent variable. After preprocessing, the data is split into a training and testing set. About 70%–80% of data is used for training, and the remaining 20%–30% is used for testing. The ML algorithm is applied to the training dataset with soil moisture as the output variable. The ML model is trained by optimizing its parameter such that it yields good accuracy on training and testing data. This trained and validated ML model is then used for the estimation of soil moisture by using the independent variables as inputs to give soil moisture as output.

Several studies have been reported by researchers indicating the wide usage of ML algorithms in estimating soil moisture from remote sensing data. Lakhankar et al. (2009) reported that ANN performed better than MLR for retrieving soil moisture data from the C-band backscatter data of RADARSAT-1 satellite besides with Normalized Difference Vegetation Index (NDVI) and soil texture data. Ahmad et al. (2010) used backscatter and incidence angle data from Tropical Rainfall Measuring Mission (TRMM), and NDVI data from Advanced Very High Resolution Radiometer (AVHRR) for estimating soil moisture content and reported that SVM outperformed feedforward backpropagation ANN and MLR. Torres-Rua et al. (2016) successfully estimated surface soil moisture from satellite images and energy balance products by employing relevance vector regression (RVR), which is the Bayesian treatment of SVR. Han et al. (2018) applied the CART algorithm for estimating soil moisture at 1 km spatial resolution in China using precipitation, temperature, and soil properties as explanatory variables. Hajdu et al. (2018) also used Sentinel-1 data with vegetation and topographic parameters to estimate soil moisture in the hilly area of New Zealand through the RF model ($R^2 = 0.86$). Chatterjee et al. (2020) retrieved surface soil moisture using Sentinel-1 backscatter data along with ancillary data, including digital elevation model (DEM), soil property, and land cover maps by applying Cubist, RF, and MLR algorithms. He found that Cubist algorithm ($R^2 = 0.68$ and RMSE $= 0.06 \text{ m}^3 \text{ m}^{-3}$) performed better than RF and MLR. Eroglu et al. (2019) used ANN to retrieve soil moisture from NASA's Cyclone Global Navigation Satellite System reflectometry signals and surface roughness, NDVI, terrain parameters, and vegetation water content as ancillary parameters. Subsequently, Senyurek et al. (2020) evaluated the performance of ANN, RF, and SVM on the same data to estimate soil moisture for the contiguous United States and reported that the RF model (RMSE $= 0.052 \text{ cm}^3/\text{cm}^3$) outperformed ANN (RMSE $= 0.061 \text{ cm}^3/\text{cm}^3$) and SVM (RMSE $= 0.065 \text{ cm}^3/\text{cm}^3$).

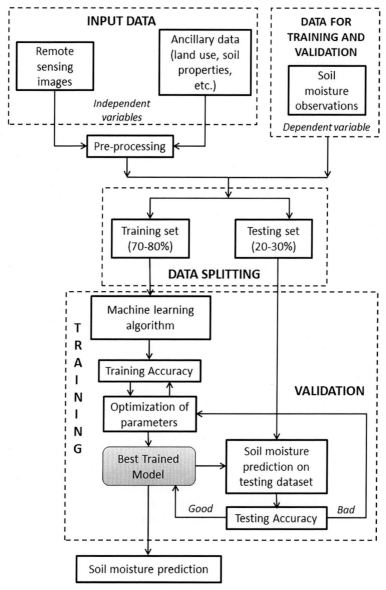

FIG. 5 A general methodology for soil moisture estimation through remote sensing using ML algorithm.

The ML algorithms can also be used for the derivation of site-specific calibration functions of SAR data to relate spectral measurements to gridded topographic features to estimate near-surface soil moisture patterns (Nasta et al., 2019). ML algorithms are also reported to retrieve soil moisture from ground-based radar data. Gupta et al. (2017) applied an ANN algorithm on

X-band data of ground-based scatterometer to retrieve soil moisture from bare soil at VV polarization. Similarly, Baghdadi et al. (2012) used C-band polarimetric SAR data to estimate soil moisture using the MLP-ANN technique with RMSE $= 0.098$ cm^3/cm^3 without a-priori information on soil parameters and RMSE $= 0.065$ cm^3/cm^3 with the application of a-priori information.

Apart from microwave data, visible and infrared data are also reported to estimate soil moisture. Hajjar et al. (2020) used the RGB pixel values of digital images to estimate moisture content in vineyard soils through ANN with MLP and SVR. The SVR model outperformed MLP when evaluated with thermo-gravimetric soil moisture content. Using visible and near-infrared (VNIR) hyper-spectral data along with long wave infrared (LWIR) data, Keller et al. (2018) estimated soil moisture status at a grassland site by applying various regression models and concluded that the extremely randomized trees model performed best. Araya et al. (2020) collected reflectance data through UAVs with multispectral sensors and used it along with precipitation, potential evapotranspiration, and topographic data to estimate soil moisture in the field using several ML algorithms such as ANN, SVR, RVR, RF, and boosted regression trees. He reported that boosted regression trees performed best with a mean absolute error of 3.8% volumetric soil moisture content. The boosted regression trees algorithm is a decision tree ensemble model in which the ensemble is enhanced by the gradient boosting approach. Therefore, it is clear that ML algorithms, mostly ANN, SVM, and RF, are proving their wide applicability and acceptability in soil moisture retrieval through ground-based, UAV, and satellite remote sensing.

4.4   Irrigation scheduling

Irrigation scheduling is making a decision about when and how much water should be applied through irrigation to replenish the crop water demand. Optimum irrigation scheduling is crucial for saving water and energy. In this regard, the data on soil moisture is necessary for making an appropriate decision. This soil moisture data can be either collected through soil moisture sensors installed in the field or estimated through remote sensing or data on other factors. ML algorithms are used for predicting soil moisture from various available datasets, which can further assist in irrigation scheduling. Hassan-Esfahani et al. (2015) used ANN on Landsat images and point-based soil moisture observations to predict spatial root zone soil moisture and provided it as a component in the soil water balance equation along with other components, that is, actual evapotranspiration and precipitation. The change in soil moisture content computed from the soil water balance equation and water requirement of oats and alfalfa crops were considered to compute the optimal irrigation water allocation through a central pivot irrigation system. Hedley et al. (2013) reported that the RF model predicted soil moisture and water table depth better than MLR to quantify soil variability concerning soil water storage in an irrigated maize field, which could be used for precision irrigation.

Due to recent advances in the IoT and wireless sensor network technologies, efforts are being made to develop smart and automated irrigation systems that can schedule irrigation in crops without human intervention. Several researchers have tried to develop such automated irrigation systems by collecting data from various sensors installed in the field in near real-time. These systems generally employ ML algorithms to predict soil moisture in the upcoming days so that decisions about irrigation scheduling can be made through a decision support system. The water pump for irrigating crops automatically switch on or off for the required duration as directed by the decision support system. Shekhar et al. (2017) developed an intelligent IoT-based automated irrigation system in which soil moisture and temperature data were collected from the wireless sensor network installed in the field, and the k-nearest neighbor (KNN) ML algorithm was deployed for making predictions about irrigation requirements. Based on the irrigation requirement, this system was able to irrigate the field automatically with the required amount of water without human intervention. Goap et al. (2018) also designed an IoT-based smart irrigation management system in which weather forecast data and sensor data on soil moisture, soil and air temperature, ultraviolet radiation, and relative humidity of crop field were collected. SVM and k-means algorithms were applied to these collected datasets to predict the soil moisture in the upcoming first, second, and third days. This soil moisture prediction in conjunction with weather forecast data was used to automatically schedule irrigation in the crop field. Adeyemi et al. (2018) utilized feed-forward ANN to predict volumetric soil moisture content 1 day ahead based on past soil moisture, precipitation, and climatic measurements. These soil moisture predictions were then combined with the AQUACROP model to decide on irrigation scheduling in potato crops. This technique resulted in the saving of water by 20%–46%. This technology is still in the infancy stage, and research advancements are going on so that this IoT-based smart irrigation system may become successful in farmers' fields.

4.5 Downscaling of satellite-derived soil moisture products

Satellite remote sensing is an effective tool for regular monitoring of spatial and temporal variability in soil moisture. However, most of the available satellite-derived soil moisture products like SMAP, SMOS, and ESA CCI-SM are of coarse spatial resolution, which limits their applicability at the regional or watershed level. These freely available and common satellite-derived soil moisture products with their respective spatial resolution are depicted in Table 1. The coarser resolution of these soil moisture products emphasizes the need for their downscaling at a finer spatial resolution. ML algorithms are used for downscaling these soil moisture products by developing their relationship with dynamic and static ancillary variables having finer spatial resolution, like vegetation indices, topographic indices, soil texture, land use, and so on. The downscaled soil moisture products are further validated with in situ soil moisture

TABLE 1 Satellite-derived soil moisture products with their respective spatial resolution.

Satellite	Soil moisture product name	Source	Spatial resolution	Temporal availability
Soil Moisture Active Passive (SMAP)	L3_SSM	NASA	36 km × 36 km	Daily
	L3_SSM_E		9 km × 9 km	Daily
	SMAP L4		9 km × 9 km	3 h
Soil Moisture and Ocean Salinity (SMOS)	SMOS Level 3 CATDS	ESA	25 km × 25 km	Daily, 3 days, 10 days, monthly
MetOp Advanced Scatterometer (ASCAT)	H101, H16	EUMETSAT	12.5 km × 12.5 km	Daily, weekly, monthly
	H102, H103		25 km × 25 km	
European Space Agency Climate Change Initiative (ESA CCI)	CCI_SM	ESA	25 km × 25 km	Daily
Advanced Microwave Scanning Radiometer 2 (AMSR 2)	AMSR2/ GCOM-W1 (LPRM)	NASA	10 km × 10 km	Daily

observations. The general methodology followed for downscaling of satellite-derived soil moisture products using ML algorithms is depicted in Fig. 6. The downscaled soil moisture product can be used for irrigation scheduling, drought and flood monitoring and forecasting, crop yield forecasting, estimation of run-off and soil erosion, weather and climate change studies, and more by serving as an input in empirical or mechanistic models. Several researchers have used ML algorithms for downscaling soil moisture products by developing their relation with different types of covariate or ancillary data. In this regard, the studies reported by various researchers with their respective accuracy are mentioned in Table 2. From the literature survey, we may conclude that ML algorithms are contributing significantly to downscaling soil moisture products.

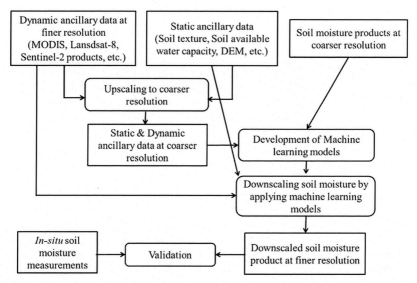

FIG. 6 A general methodology for downscaling satellite-derived soil moisture products using ML algorithms.

5 Conclusions

The ML algorithms have immense applications for soil moisture assessment in various domains of soil moisture research, which include the development of PTFs for predicting soil hydraulic properties, formulation of soil moisture prediction models from the data collected through ground-based sensors or remote sensing, soil moisture forecasting to assist in site-specific and automatic irrigation scheduling in IoT-based smart irrigation systems, and for downscaling satellite-derived soil moisture products at a finer spatial resolution. The applicability of ML algorithms has increased with the advancement in computing technology. These algorithms can model nonlinear and complex relationships without assuming any probability distribution for the input data. The elimination of the scaling and normalization of input data has also increased their relevance. These algorithms can be applied without describing any physical or mechanistic relationship among different variables in the data. The performance of an ML algorithm-based model greatly relies on the quality of data and choice of optimal parameters. The parameters of an ML model can be optimized either by following a heuristic approach or by using advanced algorithms like genetic or firefly. The black box ML algorithms like ANN and SVM create difficulty in understanding the relation of target variables with input variables and interpreting the model structure. However, white box algorithms like CART and RF are very easy to understand and interpret. Each ML algorithm has its respective benefits and limitations. Therefore, the selection of an

TABLE 2 ML algorithms applied for downscaling soil moisture products by various researchers.

Reference	Soil moisture data	Covariate data	Downscaled resolution	ML algorithm	Performance
Calla et al. (2013)	SMOS	Land surface temperature (LST) and NDVI from MODIS	1 km	MLR	Difference is <4.12% for 60% and ~11% for 90% of total datasets
Srivastava et al. (2013)	SMOS	LST from MODIS	5 km	MLR	$R^2 = 0.698$, RMSE = 0.013
				SVM	$R^2 = 0.698$, RMSE = 0.013
				RVM	$R^2 = 0.691$, RMSE = 0.013
				ANN	$R^2 = 0.751$, RMSE = 0.011
Sánchez-Ruiz et al. (2014)	SMOS	NDVI and Normalized Difference Water Index from MODIS	500 m	MLR	Correlation coefficient (r) = 0.61–0.72, cRMSD = 0.04 m^3/m^3
Im et al. (2016)	AMSR-E	LST, NDVI, Enhanced Vegetation Index, Leaf Area Index, albedo and evapotranspiration from MODIS	1 km	RF	$r = 0.71$–0.84, RMSE = 0.049–0.057
				Boosted regression trees	$r = 0.75$–0.77, RMSE = 0.052–0.078
				Cubist	$r = 0.61$–0.70, RMSE = 0.051–0.063
Liu et al. (2018)	ESA CCI	LST, NDVI, DEM, reflectance in red, blue, NIR, and MIR band	1 km	CART	RMSE = 0.076
				KNN	RMSE = 0.074
				Bayesian	RMSE = 0.075
				RF	RMSE = 0.073

Bai et al. (2019)	SMAP	SAR data from Sentinel-1, vegetation indices, and LST from MODIS	1 km and 3 km	RF	$r = 0.55-0.86$, RMSE = $0.013-0.025$
Guevara & Vargas (2019)	ESA CCI	Primary and secondary terrain parameters from DEM	1 km	KNN	RMSE = $0.057 \ m^3/m^3$
Long et al. (2019)	ESA CCI	NDVI, albedo, LST, soil texture, and precipitation	1 km	RF	$r = 0.72$, RMSE = 0.041
Zappa et al. (2019)	ASCAT, SMAP	Soil texture, topography, and fraction of absorbed green radiation	30 m	RF	$r = 0.68-0.76$, cRMSD = $0.054-0.061 \ m^3/m^3$

appropriate algorithm is necessary depending upon the purpose. Several researchers have reported that advanced ML algorithms, like SVM, ANN, RF, and so forth, provide accurate results as compared to traditional MLR algorithms in soil moisture research. Therefore, the utility of these advanced ML algorithms is increasing in this data-driven technological era for soil moisture assessment.

Abbreviations

AI	Artificial Intelligence
AMSR	Advanced Microwave Scanning Radiometer
ANFIS	adaptive neuro-fuzzy inference system
ANN	artificial neural network
ASCAT	Advanced Scatterometer
AVHRR	Advanced Very High Resolution Radiometer
CART	classification and regression tree
cRMSD	centered Root Mean Square Difference
DDPG	deep deterministic policy gradient
DEM	digital elevation model
DLRN	deep learning regression network
DNN	deep neural network
ESA CCI	European Space Agency Climate Change Initiative
IoT	Internet of Things
Ks	soil saturated hydraulic conductivity
KNN	k-nearest neighbors
LST	land surface temperature
LWIR	long wave infrared
ML	machine learning
MLP	multilayer perceptron
MLR	multiple linear regression
MODIS	Moderate Resolution Imaging Spectroradiometer
MVRVM	multivariate relevance vector machine
NDVI	Normalized Difference Vegetation Index
PTF	pedotransfer function
r	correlation coefficient
R^2	coefficient of determination
RBF	radial basis function
RF	random forest
RMSE	Root Mean Square Error
RVR	relevance vector regression
SARSA	state–action–reward–state–action algorithm
SMAP	Soil Moisture Active Passive
SMOS	Soil Moisture and Ocean Salinity
SVM	support vector machine

SVR	support vector regression
SWRC	soil water retention curve
TRMM	Tropical Rainfall Measuring Mission
UAV	unmanned aerial vehicle
VNIR	visible and near-infrared

References

Achieng, K. O. (2019). Modelling of soil moisture retention curve using machine learning techniques: Artificial and deep neural networks vs support vector regression models. *Computers & Geosciences, 133*, 104320.

Adeyemi, O., Grove, I., Peets, S., Domun, Y., & Norton, T. (2018). Dynamic neural network modelling of soil moisture content for predictive irrigation scheduling. *Sensors, 18*(10), 3408.

Ahmad, S., Kalra, A., & Stephen, H. (2010). Estimating soil moisture using remote sensing data: A machine learning approach. *Advances in Water Resources, 33*(1), 69–80.

Ahmed, A., Zhang, Y., & Nichols, S. (2011). Review and evaluation of remote sensing methods for soil-moisture estimation. *SPIE Reviews, 2*(1), 028001.

Ali, I., Greifeneder, F., Stamenkovic, J., Neumann, M., & Notarnicola, C. (2015). Review of machine learning approaches for biomass and soil moisture retrievals from remote sensing data. *Remote Sensing, 7*(12), 16398–16421.

Alvarez-Garreton, C., Ryu, D., Western, A. W., Su, C. H., Crow, W. T., Robertson, D. E., & Leahy, C. (2015). Improving operational flood ensemble prediction by the assimilation of satellite soil moisture: Comparison between lumped and semi-distributed schemes. *Hydrology and Earth System Sciences, 19*(4), 1659–1676.

Amanabadi, S., Vazirinia, M., Vereecken, H., Vakilian, K. A., & Mohammadi, M. H. (2019). Comparative study of statistical, numerical and machine learning-based pedotransfer functions of water retention curve with particle size distribution data. *Eurasian Soil Science, 52*(12), 1555–1571.

Araya, S. N., Fryjoff-Hung, A., Anderson, A., Viers, J. H., & Ghezzehei, T. A. (2020). Advances in soil moisture retrieval from multispectral remote sensing using unmanned aircraft systems and machine learning techniques. *Hydrology and Earth System Sciences Discussions*, 1–33.

Azadmard, B., Mosaddeghi, M. R., Ayoubi, S., Chavoshi, E., & Raoof, M. (2020). Estimation of near-saturated soil hydraulic properties using hybrid genetic algorithm-artificial neural network. *Ecohydrology & Hydrobiology, 20*(3), 437–449. https://doi.org/10.1016/j.ecohyd.2019.09.001.

Baghdadi, N., Cresson, R., El Hajj, M., Ludwig, R., & La Jeunesse, I. (2012). Estimation of soil parameters over bare agriculture areas from C-band polarimetric SAR data using neural networks. *Hydrology and Earth System Sciences, 16*(6), 1607–1621.

Baghdadi, N., Gherboudj, I., Zribi, M., Sahebi, M., King, C., & Bonn, F. (2004). Semi-empirical calibration of the IEM backscattering model using radar images and moisture and roughness field measurements. *International Journal of Remote Sensing, 25*(18), 3593–3623.

Bai, J., Cui, Q., Zhang, W., & Meng, L. (2019). An approach for downscaling SMAP soil moisture by combining sentinel-1 SAR and MODIS data. *Remote Sensing, 11*(23), 2736.

Berg, A., Lintner, B. R., Findell, K. L., Malyshev, S., Loikith, P. C., & Gentine, P. (2014). Impact of soil moisture–atmosphere interactions on surface temperature distribution. *Journal of Climate, 27*(21), 7976–7993.

Bittelli, M., Valentino, R., Salvatorelli, F., & Pisa, P. R. (2012). Monitoring soil-water and displacement conditions leading to landslide occurrence in partially saturated clays. *Geomorphology, 173*, 161–173.

Bolten, J. D., Crow, W. T., Zhan, X., Jackson, T. J., & Reynolds, C. A. (2009). Evaluating the utility of remotely sensed soil moisture retrievals for operational agricultural drought monitoring. *IEEE Journal of Selected Topics in Applied Earth Observations and Remote Sensing, 3*(1), 57–66.

Boser, B. E., Guyon, I. M., & Vapnik, V. N. (1992, July). A training algorithm for optimal margin classifiers. In *Proceedings of the fifth annual workshop on computational learning theory* (pp. 144–152).

Breiman, L. (2001). Random forests. *Machine Learning, 45*(1), 5–32.

Breiman, L., Friedman, J. H., Olshen, R. A., & Stone, C. J. (1984). *Classification and regression trees. 432* (pp. 151–166). Belmont, CA: Wadsworth: International Group.

Brocca, L., Ponziani, F., Melone, F., Moramarco, T., Berni, N., & Wagner, W. (2012). *Improving landslide movement forecasting using ASCAT-derived soil moisture data* (p. 2307). EGUGA.

Cai, Y., Zheng, W., Zhang, X., Zhangzhong, L., & Xue, X. (2019). Research on soil moisture prediction model based on deep learning. *PLoS One, 14*(4), e0214508.

Calla, O. P. N., Kalla, A., Rathore, G., Gadri, K. L., Sharma, R., & Agrahari, S. K. (2013, July). Downscaling of SMOS derived soil moisture and validation with ground truth data. In *2013 IEEE international geoscience and remote sensing symposium-IGARSS* (pp. 735–738). IEEE.

Capecchi, V., & Brocca, L. (2014). A simple assimilation method to ingest satellite soil moisture into a limited-area NWP model. *Meteorologische Zeitschrift, 23*, 105–121.

Chatterjee, S., Huang, J., & Hartemink, A. E. (2020). Establishing an empirical model for surface soil moisture retrieval at the US climate reference network using sentinel-1 backscatter and ancillary data. *Remote Sensing, 12*(8), 1242.

Cui, C., Xu, J., Zeng, J., Chen, K. S., Bai, X., Lu, H., … Zhao, T. (2018). Soil moisture mapping from satellites: An intercomparison of SMAP, SMOS, FY3B, AMSR2, and ESA CCI over two dense network regions at different spatial scales. *Remote Sensing, 10*(1), 33.

Dai, X., Huo, Z., & Wang, H. (2011). Simulation for response of crop yield to soil moisture and salinity with artificial neural network. *Field Crops Research, 121*(3), 441–449.

Drusch, M., Scipal, K., De Rosnay, P., Balsamo, G., Andersson, E., Bougeault, P., & Viterbo, P. (2009). Towards a Kalman filter based soil moisture analysis system for the operational ECMWF integrated forecast system. *Geophysical Research Letters, 36*(10).

Eroglu, O., Kurum, M., Boyd, D., & Gurbuz, A. C. (2019). High spatio-temporal resolution CYGNSS soil moisture estimates using artificial neural networks. *Remote Sensing, 11*(19), 2272.

Geurts, P., Ernst, D., & Wehenkel, L. (2006). Extremely randomized trees. *Machine Learning, 63* (1), 3–42.

Ghorbani, M. A., Shamshirband, S., Haghi, D. Z., Azani, A., Bonakdari, H., & Ebtehaj, I. (2017). Application of firefly algorithm-based support vector machines for prediction of field capacity and permanent wilting point. *Soil and Tillage Research, 172*, 32–38.

Gill, M. K., Asefa, T., Kemblowski, M. W., & McKee, M. (2006). Soil moisture prediction using support vector machines 1. *JAWRA Journal of the American Water Resources Association, 42* (4), 1033–1046.

Goap, A., Sharma, D., Shukla, A. K., & Krishna, C. R. (2018). An IoT based smart irrigation management system using machine learning and open source technologies. *Computers and Electronics in Agriculture, 155*, 41–49.

Gorthi, S., & Dou, H. (2011, January). Prediction models for the estimation of soil moisture content. In *International design engineering technical conferences and computers and information in engineering conference: Vol. 54808* (pp. 945–953).

Guevara, M., & Vargas, R. (2019). Downscaling satellite soil moisture using geomorphometry and machine learning. *PLoS One, 14*(9), e0219639.

Gupta, D. K., Prasad, R., Kumar, P., & Vishwakarma, A. K. (2017). Soil moisture retrieval using ground based bistatic scatterometer data at X-band. *Advances in Space Research, 59*(4), 996–1007.

Hajdu, I., Yule, I., & Dehghan-Shear, M. H. (2018, July). Modelling of near-surface soil moisture using machine learning and multi-temporal sentinel 1 images in New Zealand. In *IGARSS 2018-2018 IEEE international geoscience and remote sensing symposium* (pp. 1422–1425). IEEE.

Hajjar, C. S., Hajjar, C., Esta, M., & Chamoun, Y. G. (2020). Machine learning methods for soil moisture prediction in vineyards using digital images. In *Vol. 167. E3S web of conferences* (p. 02004). EDP Sciences.

Han, J., Mao, K., Xu, T., Guo, J., Zuo, Z., & Gao, C. (2018). A soil moisture estimation framework based on the CART algorithm and its application in China. *Journal of Hydrology, 563*, 65–75.

Hassan-Esfahani, L., Torres-Rua, A., & McKee, M. (2015). Assessment of optimal irrigation water allocation for pressurized irrigation system using water balance approach, learning machines, and remotely sensed data. *Agricultural Water Management, 153*, 42–50.

Hedley, C. B., Roudier, P., Yule, I. J., Ekanayake, J., & Bradbury, S. (2013). Soil water status and water table depth modelling using electromagnetic surveys for precision irrigation scheduling. *Geoderma, 199*, 22–29.

Im, J., Park, S., Rhee, J., Baik, J., & Choi, M. (2016). Downscaling of AMSR-E soil moisture with MODIS products using machine learning approaches. *Environmental Earth Sciences, 75*(15), 1120.

Ines, A. V., Das, N. N., Hansen, J. W., & Njoku, E. G. (2013). Assimilation of remotely sensed soil moisture and vegetation with a crop simulation model for maize yield prediction. *Remote Sensing of Environment, 138*, 149–164.

Jackson, R. D., Idso, S. B., & Reginato, R. J. (1976). Calculation of evaporation rates during the transition from energy-limiting to soil-limiting phases using albedo data. *Water Resources Research, 12*(1), 23–26.

Kaingo, J., Tumbo, S. D., Kihupi, N. I., & Mbilinyi, B. P. (2018). Prediction of soil moisture-holding capacity with support vector machines in dry subhumid tropics. *Applied and Environmental Soil Science, 2018*.

Kalkhajeh, Y. K., Arshad, R. R., Amerikhah, H., & Sami, M. (2012). Multiple linear regression, artificial neural network (MLP, RBF) and anfis models for modeling the saturated hydraulic conductivity (a case study: Khuzestan province, Southwest Iran). *International Journal of Agriculture, 2*(3), 255.

Karandish, F., & Šimůnek, J. (2016). A comparison of numerical and machine-learning modeling of soil water content with limited input data. *Journal of Hydrology, 543*, 892–909.

Keller, S., Riese, F. M., Stötzer, J., Maier, P. M., & Hinz, S. (2018). Developing a machine learning framework for estimating soil moisture with VNIR hyperspectral data. *arXiv.* preprint arXiv:1804.09046.

Khalil, A., Gill, M. K., & McKee, M. (2005, July). New applications for information fusion and soil moisture forecasting. In *2005 7th International Conference on Information Fusion: Vol. 2.* IEEE. 7-pp.

Kogan, F. N. (1995). Application of vegetation index and brightness temperature for drought detection. *Advances in Space Research, 15*(11), 91–100.

Koren, V., Smith, M., Wang, D., & Zhang, Z. (2000). 2.16 Use of soil property data in the derivation of conceptual rainfall-runoff model parameters. In *Proceedings of the 15th conference on hydrology* (pp. 103–106). Long Beach, California: American Meteorological Society.

Koster, R. D., Dirmeyer, P. A., Guo, Z., Bonan, G., Chan, E., Cox, P., … Liu, P. (2004). Regions of strong coupling between soil moisture and precipitation. *Science, 305*(5687), 1138–1140.

Lakhankar, T., Ghedira, H., Temimi, M., Sengupta, M., Khanbilvardi, R., & Blake, R. (2009). Non-parametric methods for soil moisture retrieval from satellite remote sensing data. *Remote Sensing, 1*(1), 3–21.

Liu, W., Baret, F., Gu, X., Zhang, B., Tong, Q., & Zheng, L. (2003). Evaluation of methods for soil surface moisture estimation from reflectance data. *International Journal of Remote Sensing, 24* (10), 2069–2083.

Liu, Y., Yang, Y., Jing, W., & Yue, X. (2018). Comparison of different machine learning approaches for monthly satellite-based soil moisture downscaling over Northeast China. *Remote Sensing, 10*(1), 31.

Long, D., Bai, L., Yan, L., Zhang, C., Yang, W., Lei, H., … Shi, C. (2019). Generation of spatially complete and daily continuous surface soil moisture of high spatial resolution. *Remote Sensing of Environment, 233*, 111364.

Lørup, J. K., & Styczen, M. (1990). Soil erosion modelling. In *Distributed hydrological modelling* (pp. 93–120). Dordrecht: Springer.

Maltese, A., Capodici, F., Ciraolo, G., & La Loggia, G. (2013). Mapping soil water content under sparse vegetation and changeable sky conditions: Comparison of two thermal inertia approaches. *Journal of Applied Remote Sensing, 7*(1), 073548.

Massari, C., Brocca, L., Barbetta, S., Papathanasiou, C., Mimikou, M., & Moramarco, T. (2014). Using globally available soil moisture indicators for flood modelling in Mediterranean catchments. *Hydrology and Earth System Sciences, 18*(2), 839.

McCulloch, W. S., & Pitts, W. (1943). A logical calculus of the ideas immanent in nervous activity. *The Bulletin of Mathematical Biophysics, 5*(4), 115–133.

Minacapilli, M., Iovino, M., & Blanda, F. (2009). High resolution remote estimation of soil surface water content by a thermal inertia approach. *Journal of Hydrology, 379*(3–4), 229–238.

Mitchell, T. M. (1997). *Machine learning* (pp. 870–877). Burr Ridge, IL: McGraw Hill. 45(37).

Moyano, F. E., Manzoni, S., & Chenu, C. (2013). Responses of soil heterotrophic respiration to moisture availability: An exploration of processes and models. *Soil Biology and Biochemistry, 59*, 72–85.

Nasta, P., Schönbrodt-Stitt, S., Bogena, H., Kurtenbach, M., Ahmadian, N., Vereecken, H., … Romano, N. (2019, October). Integrating ground-based and remote sensing-based monitoring of near-surface soil moisture in a Mediterranean environment. In *2019 IEEE international workshop on metrology for agriculture and forestry (MetroAgriFor)* (pp. 274–279). IEEE.

Orchard, V. A., & Cook, F. J. (1983). Relationship between soil respiration and soil moisture. *Soil Biology and Biochemistry, 15*(4), 447–453.

Pachepsky, Y., & Van Genuchten, M. (2011). Pedotransfer functions. In *Encyclopedia of agrophysics*. Berlin: Springer.

Padarian, J., Minasny, B., & McBratney, A. B. (2020). Machine learning and soil sciences: A review aided by machine learning tools. *The Soil, 6*(1), 35–52.

Pekel, E. (2020). Estimation of soil moisture using decision tree regression. *Theoretical and Applied Climatology, 139*(3), 1111–1119.

Peng, J., Loew, A., Merlin, O., & Verhoest, N. E. (2017). A review of spatial downscaling of satellite remotely sensed soil moisture. *Reviews of Geophysics, 55*(2), 341–366.

Prasad, R., Deo, R. C., Li, Y., & Maraseni, T. (2018). Ensemble committee-based data intelligent approach for generating soil moisture forecasts with multivariate hydro-meteorological predictors. *Soil and Tillage Research, 181*, 63–81.

Raclot, D., & Albergel, J. (2006). Runoff and water erosion modelling using WEPP on a Mediterranean cultivated catchment. *Physics and Chemistry of the Earth, Parts A/B/C, 31*(17), 1038–1047.

Rahmani, A., Golian, S., & Brocca, L. (2016). Multiyear monitoring of soil moisture over Iran through satellite and reanalysis soil moisture products. *International Journal of Applied Earth Observation and Geoinformation, 48*, 85–95.

Rodríguez-Iturbe, I., & Porporato, A. (2007). *Ecohydrology of water-controlled ecosystems: Soil moisture and plant dynamics*. Cambridge University Press.

Sánchez-Ruiz, S., Piles, M., Sánchez, N., Martínez-Fernández, J., Vall-llossera, M., & Camps, A. (2014). Combining SMOS with visible and near/shortwave/thermal infrared satellite data for high resolution soil moisture estimates. *Journal of Hydrology, 516*, 273–283.

Sarmadian, F., & Mehrjardi, R. T. (2010, August). Development of pedotransfer functions to predict soil hydraulic properties in Golestan Province, Iran. In *19th World congress of soil science, soil solutions for a changing world* (pp. 1–6).

Seneviratne, S. I., Corti, T., Davin, E. L., Hirschi, M., Jaeger, E. B., Lehner, I., … Teuling, A.J. (2010). Investigating soil moisture–climate interactions in a changing climate: A review. *Earth-Science Reviews, 99*(3–4), 125–161.

Senyurek, V., Lei, F., Boyd, D., Kurum, M., Gurbuz, A. C., & Moorhead, R. (2020). Machine learning-based CYGNSS soil moisture estimates over ISMN sites in CONUS. *Remote Sensing, 12*(7), 1168.

Shekhar, Y., Dagur, E., Mishra, S., & Sankaranarayanan, S. (2017). Intelligent IoT based automated irrigation system. *International Journal of Applied Engineering Research, 12*(18), 7306–7320.

Srivastava, P. K., Han, D., Ramirez, M. R., & Islam, T. (2013). Machine learning techniques for downscaling SMOS satellite soil moisture using MODIS land surface temperature for hydrological application. *Water Resources Management, 27*(8), 3127–3144.

Topp, G. C. (2003). State of the art of measuring soil water content. *Hydrological Processes, 17*(14), 2993–2996.

Torres-Rua, A. F., Ticlavilca, A. M., Bachour, R., & McKee, M. (2016). Estimation of surface soil moisture in irrigated lands by assimilation of landsat vegetation indices, surface energy balance products, and relevance vector machines. *Water, 8*(4), 167.

Verhoef, A. (2004). Remote estimation of thermal inertia and soil heat flux for bare soil. *Agricultural and Forest Meteorology, 123*(3–4), 221–236.

Wanders, N., Pan, M., & Wood, E. F. (2015). Correction of real-time satellite precipitation with multi-sensor satellite observations of land surface variables. *Remote Sensing of Environment, 160*, 206–221.

Weitz, A. M., Linder, E., Frolking, S., Crill, P. M., & Keller, M. (2001). N2O emissions from humid tropical agricultural soils: Effects of soil moisture, texture and nitrogen availability. *Soil Biology and Biochemistry, 33*(7–8), 1077–1093.

Willmott, C. J., Rowe, C. M., & Mintz, Y. (1985). Climatology of the terrestrial seasonal water cycle. *Journal of Climatology, 5*(6), 589–606.

Wu, W., Wang, X., Xie, D., & Liu, H. (2007, August). Soil water content forecasting by support vector machine in purple hilly region. In *International conference on computer and computing technologies in agriculture* (pp. 223–230). Boston, MA: Springer.

Zaman, B., & McKee, M. (2014). Spatio-temporal prediction of root zone soil moisture using multivariate relevance vector machines. *Open Journal of Modern Hydrology, 4*, 80.

Zappa, L., Forkel, M., Xaver, A., & Dorigo, W. (2019). Deriving field scale soil moisture from satellite observations and ground measurements in a hilly agricultural region. *Remote Sensing, 11* (22), 2596.

Zhang, Y., Wei, H., & Nearing, M. A. (2011). Effects of antecedent soil moisture on runoff modeling in small semiarid watersheds of southeastern Arizona. *Hydrology and Earth System Sciences, 15*(10), 3171–3179.

Chapter 7

Automated real-time forecasting of agriculture using chlorophyll content and its impact on climate change

K. Sujatha[a], R.S. Ponmagal[b], K. Senthil Kumar[c], Rajeswary Hari[d], A. Kalaivani[e], K. Thivya[c], and M. Anand[c]

[a]Department of Electrical and Electronics Engineering, Dr. MGR Educational and Research Institute, Chennai, Tamil Nadu, India, [b]Department of Computer Science Engineering, SRM Institute of Science and Technology, Chennai, Tamil Nadu, India, [c]Department of Electronics and Communication Engineering, Dr. MGR Educational and Research Institute, Chennai, Tamil Nadu, India, [d]Department of Bio-Technology, Dr. MGR Educational and Research Institute, Chennai, Tamil Nadu, India, [e]Department of Computer Science Engineering, Saveetha School of Engineering, Saveetha Institute of Medical and Technical Sciences, Chennai, Tamil Nadu, India

1 Introduction

Automated testing is similar to a programmer using a coding language to create programs so as to automate the manual process. In real time, testing very large systems is beyond the scope of the manual team. Hence, an automated software package or a simulation tool can be used to computerize the real-time system. The number of test beds available is less in number, so the depth of coverage is not sufficient to handle the real-time task. Increasing the size of the team for testing also complicates the situation because it increases the work overhead. Hence, an optimal solution to solve this problem is to automate the real-time environment without loss of quality, as it will expand the capacity enormously while sustaining the focus on testing considering the critical elements. Certain factors facilitate the choice of modeling using automated testing tools. They include the presently used testing scheme and its capacity to adjust with the automated test tools and also to accommodate with the current trends in testing. It also initiates to indulge experts who will be using the simulated environment to design the automated testing process for a real-time system. This automated system will provide a way to create a set of performance measures used for evaluation of the real-time system automated using the software package. They

Deep Learning for Sustainable Agriculture. https://doi.org/10.1016/B978-0-323-85214-2.00004-5

169

include repeatability in testing schemes, criticality or risk involved in real-time applications, simplicity in operations, easiness in automation, documentation standards, and requirements. It also involves training the personnel to work with the existing set of test cases and test scripts to infer the most applicable simulation package for test automation.

The testing of software can be classified into three types. They include complete manual testing, partially manual or partially automated testing, and completely automated testing. The complete manual testing is cost-effective, and large-scale testing becomes difficult as it is prone to test errors and causes fatigue. The completely automated testing scheme is reliable and permits the repetition of similar tests at an economical cost. The installation and primitive setup cost is high, but it can adapt to the changing application environment. A partially automated or a partially manual system involves a portion to be tested manually and offers redundancy by backing up automation with manual testing. The disadvantage is that it obviously does not provide as extensive benefits as either extreme solution.

Recently, US economists used a group of data to analyze the year-to-year variations in weather conditions across US countries to forecast the effect of weather, greenhouse gas emissions on agricultural output in a random fashion. This approach has an advantage of controlling the parameters, such as farmer quality, soil quality, climatic conditions, and greenhouse gas emissions (Mall et al., 2016; Sujatha et al., 2018b). This panel of data with data analytics would guide farmers to adapt themselves so that they change the inputs or cultivation techniques to increase the yield, thereby offering a remedial measure against the natural calamities. This assessment approach would prove to be a value-added approach because the impact of the climate change on the Indian people would be extremely terrible, as paucity and agriculture are two salient features of the Indian economy. However, by measuring the effects of annual fluctuations, the artificial neural network-based (ANN-based) approach provides few features for adaptations in the long run, like seasonal crop rotation rather than exit farming (Elza & Balai, 2018; Gondali & Bose, 2019)

One needs to understand the difference between natural and enhanced greenhouse effects. In nature, the Earth experiences natural greenhouse effects because of the traces of water vapor (H_2O), carbon dioxide (CO_2), methane (CH_4), and nitrous oxide (N_2O) present in the atmosphere (Ainsworth & Long, 2005; Bosello & Zhang, 2006; Clement Atzberger, 2013; Foley et al., 2011; Gattinger et al., 2011; Holden, 2008; Meroni et al., 2012; Nelson et al., 2009; Wreford et al., 2010; Zecha et al., 2013). These gases absorb the heat energy emitted by the sun from the surface of the Earth, thereby preventing excessive solar radiation from reaching the Earth's surface. If the natural greenhouse effect is absent, the Earth's surface would be 33°C cooler. On the contrary, the enhanced greenhouse effect induces excessive amounts of radiation resulting from increased concentrations of greenhouse gases induced by human activities, thereby heating the surface of the planet excessively (Hansen et al., 2006; Long et al., 2006; Parry et al., 2004; Zavala et al., 2008).

India being a developing country needs to battle against the effects of climate change, which causes significant fall in crop yield; 15% of India's groundwater resources are damaged and sea levels are rising. In 2016, our nation recorded its hottest day with a temperature of 51°C at Phalodi, Rajasthan. The fossil fuel generation causes depletion of the ozone layer leading to increased pollution levels (Gunda et al., 2017; Runtunuwu & Kondoh, 2016). The Ministry of Environment, Forest and Climate Change has suggested that a few alterations made to combat the pollution from coal-based thermal power plants is bound to adversely impact Tamil Nadu Generation and Distribution Corporation (Tangedco) financially. Neyveli Lignite Corporation (NLC) located at Neyveli, Tamil Nadu, India, contributes to one-third of power generation and liberates greenhouse gases, which affects the agricultural produce.

Coal is desired fuel for power generation in nations like India and China. Coal is available locally in abundance, and continual increase in prices for natural gas and oil, which are imported, makes coal-fired generation of electrical power convenient. The constituents of coal have 60% of carbon content with remaining 30% of moisture content (MC) and impurities. Hence, this impure coal needs to be processed by the coal mills and electrostatic precipitator before it is used as a fuel in the thermal power plants. The fuels normally used for generation includes natural gas, diesel, nuclear, solar, hydro power, and biomass power in urban and industrial areas. Nearly 54.42% of the total electric power is generated by burning coal and lignite in India. The emission of greenhouse gases is aggravated because of relatively lower calorific value, combined with high ash content due to incomplete combustion from thermal power plants in India (Guiteras, 2007; Hansen et al., 2006).

The emissions include CO_2, oxides of nitrogen (NO_x), oxides of sulfur (SO_x), airborne inorganic particles (fly ash, carbonaceous material [soot], suspended particulate matter [SPM]), and small traces of gas species from thermal power plants. Thermal power plants, using about 70% of total coal in India, are among the large point sources (LPS) having significant contribution (47% each for CO_2 and sulfur dioxide [SO_2]) in the total LPS emissions in India (Elza & Balai, 2018; Gondali & Bose, 2019). There arises a need to transform the thermal power plants in India to reduce the usage of coal per unit electricity generation (kg/kWh). Renovation with reduced coal consumption (kg/kWh) will help reduce greenhouse emissions. Though the quality of coal in our country remains the same, the advances in combustion technologies will lead to a reduction in greenhouse gas emissions. It is approximated that a 1%–2% increase in heat transfer rate leading to increase in efficiency in the range of 1%–2% decreases the greenhouse gas emissions per unit electricity.

Carbon content present in the coal results as carbon monoxide (CO) and CO_2 emissions obtained during the combustion of coal in the presence of excess air at power plants. Factors like reactivity of the coal particles, milling, air–fuel ratio, flame turbulence, and fuel residence time cause small amounts of carbon to be left out when coal is burned. This unburned carbon is called as fly ash,and the remaining goes to the bottom ash.

2 Current status

Coal, the prime fuel for electricity production in India and its consumption is continually facing energy demands. Emissions of CO_2, SO_2, and nitric oxide (NO) from coal-fired power plants increased from 2001 to 2002 to 2009 to 2010 in India. The flue gas emission estimation is modeled theoretically by calculating the mass emission factors dependent on combustion and operating conditions of power plants. The period from 2020 to 2021 gives the future values of greenhouse gas generation from 2001 to 2002 and 2009 to 2010. Different qualities of coal and combustion technologies/operating conditions are used by power plants in India (Clement Atzberger, 2013; Gattinger et al., 2011; Nelson et al., 2009; Wreford et al., 2010). The emissions from power plants have increased the total CO_2 emissions from 323 474.85 Gg in 2001–02 to 498 655.78 Gg in 2009–10. SO_2 emissions increased from 2519.93 Gg in 2001–02 to 3840.44 Gg in 2009–10, while NO emissions increased from 1502.07 to 2314.95 Gg. The emissions per unit of electricity ranges from 0.91 to 0.95 kg/kWh for CO_2, from 6.94 to 7.20 g/kWh for SO_2, and from 4.22 to 4.38 g/kWh for NO. In Indian power plants, the future emissions will be 714,976–914 680 Gg for CO_2, 4734–6051 Gg for SO_2, and 366–469 Gg for NO in 2020–21. As estimated by the Planning Commission of India under Business-as-Usual and Best-case-Scenario, an increase in efficiency of electricity generation by coal-fired power plants considerably decreases the greenhouse emissions. This proves to be a constructive tool for catalog preparation for emission factors in sparse.

Investigation of temperature measurement from the flame color in thermal and gas turbine power plants is of enormous significance in the realm of vision machine technology. The primary objective for this work relies on detection, recognition, and understanding of color image processing for flame color analysis. In this effort, soft-computing methods using an ANN model with a backpropagation algorithm (BPA) and ant colony optimization are used for this purpose. Human resources is a great asset, as it is the gift of nature. Exploitation of human resources should strictly be monitored on health aspects. The power generation sectors in view to increase the combustion quality for enhancing the power production contribute to greenhouse gases, which is a threat to human health. The flue gas containing NO_x and SO_x has mammoth impact in the dominion of human health. Hence, a secluded screening scheme using image processing, ANN, and Internet of Things to powerfully curtail the flue gas emissions is enforced (https://www.manage.gov.in/studymaterial/CCA-E.pdf).

This research work includes a combination of Fisher's linear discriminant (FLD) analysis and a radial basis network (RBN) for monitoring the combustion conditions for a coal-fired boiler to allow control of air–fuel ratio. The features of the images—such as average intensity, area, brightness, and orientation of the flame—are extracted after preprocessing the images. Three classes of images corresponding to different burning conditions of the flames have been extracted from continuous video processing. The corresponding temperatures, CO emissions, and other flue gases were obtained through measurement using FLDRBN (Sujatha et al., 2020). The color of the flame indicates whether the combustion taking place is complete, partial, or incomplete. When complete combustion takes place, the flue gases released are within the permissible limits. By analyzing the flame color captured using infrared, the quality of combustion is estimated. If combustion is incomplete, then flue gases will create air pollution. The features are extracted from the flame images, such as average intensity, area, brightness, and orientation. Further training, testing, and validation with the data collected was carried out, and performance of the various intelligent algorithms is presented (Sujatha et al., 2018a).

The aim is to monitor the furnace flame using infrared cameras. To automate this combustion, artificially intelligent algorithms are used to determine the features of the furnace flame that correlate with air–fuel ratio, NO_x, CO, and CO_2 emission levels and temperature. A 3D temperature profiler is designed to provide control furnace and flame temperature, which reduces flue gas emissions. The system provides guidance for balancing the air–fuel ratio so as to ensure complete combustion. This will ensure a safe and secured combustion for addressing the escalating demands to attain high thermal efficiency at the furnace level and improve combustion quality.

In this research work, the primary production along the Bay of Bengal is estimated from the field data collected from 21 stations, between 2013 and 2015 from different algorithms, and compared with primary production determined experimentally in laboratory. Other important oceanographic parameters such as chlorophyll a, nutrients, SPM, dissolved oxygen, and salinity are also evaluated in the water samples. The study resulted with observed primary production values of 339.94 or 225.16 g C m^3 $year^{-1}$ by averaging five different algorithms.

Maritime environment is subjected to an extensive variety of anthropogenic effects related to the advancement of beachfront zones, the contributions of toxins, and excess utilization. Marine photosynthetic life comprises of single-celled phytoplankton, which incorporates less than 1% of worldwide biomass and represents 40% of aggregate worldwide carbon fixation. Centralization of chlorophyll a (principle phytoplankton pigment) is frequently taken as a record of phytoplankton biomass. Available energy flow from primary production during food chain sustenance will ultimately limit fishery yields in the upper trophic stage. From the inputs of field-measured chlorophyll a, average primary production rates were computed from five distinct algorithms throughout the study area (Al-Ghzawi et al., 2018). Pollution of maritime environment is critical throughout the world due to increasing human activity along the coastal boundaries, inputs of pollutants, and depletion of maritime resources due to exploitation. A considerable amount of research was entailed on marine pollution; there is a need to quantify the productivity of oceans and to measure water quality, nutrients, and the resultant effect on littoral habitats. The study appraises various physico-chemical and biological parameters of chlorophyll a, primary productivity at 21 stations to gauge the water quality, and its impact upon marine habitats. The average primary production estimated for the study region is 252.53 g C m^2 year^{-1} (Sharmila & Narayanan, 2018).

Water Quality Index (WQI) is a useful tool for assessing water quality. Nine related parameters were integrated toward evaluation of specific oceanographic parameters through the development of the Marine Water Quality Index in geographic information system for surface water quality 1 (salt pans, shell fishing, mari-culture, and ecologically sensitive zone) and surface water quality2 (bathing, contact water sports, and commercial fishing). The WQI calculated for the post-monsoon and monsoon season using the developed equation. Results were categorized into five different classes from "very good" to "very poor" to indicate the overall quality of marine surface water. Untrammeled human activity along coastal region results in threats to biodiversity and disruption to the coastal ecosystem. SPM comprising organic and inorganic material is one of the major problems in aquatic ecosystems around the world. Ratios of normalized water leaving radiance were correlated with coincident in situ measurements through multiple linear regressions and statistically analyzed toward the development of regional algorithm for estimating suspended sediment load in coastal waters. A developed algorithm is best suited for deriving total suspended matter (TSM) for SeaWiFS and MODIS satellite data for Cuddalore and Pondicherry coastal waters and has a better accuracy than TSM-Clark algorithm provided in the Seadas 5.1.6 (NASA) (Sharmila & Narayanan, 2018).

2.1 National Status

On predicting the potential changes, it is estimated that the agricultural produce will decrease by 10%–30%. All variety of crops may be decreased by 1%, and wheat and barley may decrease by 7%. The growth of vegetables may be decreased by 5%–6% and cashew nuts by 3% (Jolánkai & Csete, 2019; Eitzinger et al., 2019; Frías et al., 2018; Iswoyo et al., 2019; Khan & Wakeel, 2018; Sarker, 2014; Sarvina, 2018; Soglo et al., 2019). The cultivation of jackfruits may be decreased by 2%–3%. At initial stages, water is needed for crops to grow. Seed germination levels are also lowered because of increased temperature levels, which cause precipitation, thereby decreasing the germination of the seeds. The other consequences of climate change are heavy drought conditions, occurrence, and rigorousness of dust storms, and all result in decreased production of crops.

The agricultural set up in India makes up roughly 20% of gross domestic product and provides 52% of employment. Hence, diversification in the farming with varied techniques can reduce the losses due to climate change and also reduce the poverty rate. The changes in crop mixes and other activities could lead to a new variety of exports. Other parts of the economy, such as agribusiness, transportation, and wholesale and retail trade, could increase in value and result in new jobs (Ali & Erenstein, 2017; Eriksen & Brown, 2011; Gornall et al., 2010).

2.2 International status

In 2009, nearly 81.5% of total greenhouse gas emissions, according to the Energy Information Administration, were due to the burning of coal for the operation of power plants. United States and other industrial countries experience continual increase in carbon emissions, and much more rapid increase is expected for countries in Asia, the Middle East, Africa, and Central and South America (Tarnawa et al., 2010; Sirotenko & Romanenkov, 2009; Wamsler et al., 2013). The increase in the average annual rate of carbon emissions is 1.7% starting from 2007 until 2035, reaching 42.38 billion metric tons, to which the United States alone would contribute about 14.9%.

For developing nations, agro-based development plays an important role that impacts the economical status of farmers by creating awareness and incorporating newer techniques in agriculture to adapt to climate change because of various constraints or less access to adaptation technology (Cetner et al., 2014; Jolánkai et al., 2019; Li, 2019; Parmar et al., 2019). In the majority of countries, it is highly difficult. However, if the developed countries are considered for incorporating new schemes in agriculture to fight against the climate change, it poses a challenge because it requires various statistical data regarding the region under development. Particularly, in the United States, the topic of climate change and its impact on agriculture has become the center of attention to the government and researchers because forecasting the outcomes of climate change is a Herculean task. Considering Brazil, it has also experienced significant negative impacts due to climate change, which has increased the atmospheric temperature by 2°C with a 7% rise in precipitation leading to loss in production of agro-based products (https://www.manage. gov.in/studymaterial/CCA-E.pdf; Al-Ghzawi et al., 2018; Sujatha et al., 2018a, 2020).

3 Problem statement

Agriculture is dependent on changes in climate for the crops to be grown in a healthy manner. Research on crop yields with respect to climate change has established important awareness on varied scientific conditions. Plant and soil research indicates the maximum yield is possible from agriculture for the given conditions. Really, it is intricate to estimate the crop yields based on varied weather conditions, which occur as a result of greenhouse gas emissions from thermal power plants at Neyveli. Some studies state that an increase in CO_2 enriches the crops like rice, wheat, soybeans, potatoes, and vegetables. But in reality it is not so, and their growth and yield is affected drastically by greenhouse gas emissions (CO, SO_x, CH_4, and NO_x) from the thermal power plants. A wide increase in temperature as a result of greenhouse gases extends the growing season of the crops and changes the entire life cycle of the crops; for example, it extends the growing season for paddy and causes earlier maturity of the grains, which makes it lose the quality of rice grains.

The core aim of this project is to offer a solution to farmers in the nearby regions of Neyveli to adapt and sustain the agricultural yield for the changes in the climate and environment as a result of global warming by using the forecasting technique. Flue gases from thermal power plants constitute greenhouse gases that results in climate change in the region of Neyveli. Hence, the agricultural yield in and around this region is seriously affected. Thus, forecasting the greenhouse gases and increase in atmospheric temperature along with variations in weather conditions directs farmers to choose seasonal crop rotation or multiple crop raising dependent on weather conditions.

Neyveli (Tamil Nadu, India), being one of the important generating power plants, taking care of one-third of the power generation, emits greenhouse gases that cause climate change. This variation in climate destroys the agricultural lands and vegetation drastically in and around the region. Hence to combat the situation, an optimal forecast of the greenhouse gases causing air pollution, increased atmospheric temperature, and decreased rainfall may help farmers choose seasonal crop rotation or even multiple crop growing that would give better yield dependent on the weather conditions with the help of the directions given.

4 Objective of the proposed work

India being a country whose focus is on agriculture, the researchers have been pondering solutions to combat the effects of climate change. Neyveli, one important region in power generation, is affected drastically by climate change due to emission of greenhouse gases, which cause an increase in atmospheric temperature and decrease in rainfall. This change in nature has affected the biodiversity, which creates a challenging environment for the farmers to fight against these changes and increase crop productivity. After an extensive survey, it was decided to monitor the farmlands using a drone, which captures the images of the farmland. From these images, based on the histogram of oriented gradients (HoG) of the green intensity available pertaining to the crops along with soil moisture data, the three conditions—namely, highly productive (HP), medium productive (MP), and low productive (LP)—are predicted using ANN, this information is assimilated, and appropriate action is taken in the form of applying pesticides, undergoing crop rotation, or suggesting multiple cropping, or storing rainwater for future. The HoG features are fused with the soil moisture data to improve the forecasting efficiency.

This method helps forecast the various greenhouse gases like CO_2, CO, CH_4, SO_x, NO_x, atmospheric temperature, and rainfall by capturing the images of agricultural fields using a drone or by incorporating cameras in farmlands at Neyveli, where NLC is located. Images captured are preprocessed for noise removal followed by HoG feature extraction fused with soil moisture data helps determine the green colored pixels indicating the vegetation. These features are reduced from n-dimensions to two dimensions using PCA. Thereafter, the reduced feature set is used for training and testing the feed-forward neural network trained with BPA. The ANN will now be able to forecast the various parameters (already mentioned) contributing to climate change and pass on the information to farmers to take the appropriate action that would save the farmlands, which is the backbone of the Indian economy. This automated software-based scheme will serve as a guide to farmers, students, and researchers in the field of agriculture.

5 Research highlights

- To assess the impact of climate change on agricultural yield (Neyveli, where the thermal power plant is located)
- To forecast the greenhouse gas emissions from the images of the agricultural lands
- To forecast the impact of climate change on increased atmospheric temperature from the images of the agricultural lands by fusing the HoG features with soil moisture data
- To analyze the images of the agricultural lands with soil MC in three categories (HP, MP, and LP) greenhouse gases, increase in atmospheric temperature, and decrease or excessive rainfall based on chlorophyll content
- To implement algorithms like HoG, PCA, and BPA for feature extraction, feature reduction, and forecasting climate change
- To automate the entire system using standard simulation software package

6 Scientific significance of the proposed work

This work focuses on the design and implementation of a new automated strategy using a standard simulation package for forecasting the impact of climate change. Changes in climate pose a lot of problems for farmers and affects agricultural produce. The farmlands in and around Neyveli are affected drastically because of greenhouse gas emissions from NLC due to the burning of coal to generate electricity. The atmospheric concentration of greenhouse gases has increased by 30% in the last 10 years. Presently, there is no well-defined method to forecast greenhouses gas emissions or their impact on farmlands in the region of Neyveli. Hence, through this scheme, a novel forecasting set up to monitor the agricultural fields based on the chlorophyll content (green colored pixels) present in the image, the amount of greenhouse gases, temperature, rainfall, and the remedial actions farmers need to take to save the crops in order to maximize their yield can be intimated well in advance, thereby creating an awareness to the farmers.

7 Materials and methods

This section comprises of the mathematical formulas for feature extraction, which includes standard deviation, variance, fusion technique (mentioned in Section 8), and algorithm for PCA along with the BPA for forecasting the emissions. The greenhouse gas emissions are computed by processing the images of the agricultural lands under three different categories, and the same is analyzed using the mathematical formulas. This method offers a bottom-up approach for emission inventory development. This software-based automated process will offer emission inventory for CO_2, SOx, CO, CH_4, and NO_x, which are designed exclusively for thermal power plants in Neyveli, India, with respect to the coal characteristics and operational conditions established at the plant. The entire code for the scheme is developed using MATLAB®.

The features include standard deviation and variance for which the formulas is given in Eqs. (1) and (2), respectively.

$$\text{Standard Deviation} \text{``}\sigma\text{''} = \sqrt{1/N \sum (x_i - \mu)^2} \tag{1}$$

$$\text{Variance } (V) = \sigma^2 \tag{2}$$

where "N" denotes the total number of samples, "x_i" denotes the pixels in the original image and "μ" denotes the mean.

7.1 Histogram of oriented gradients

Object detection is done using the HoG feature descriptor. The orientation along with the gradient in the localized regions of the image splits the image into smaller blocks called cells, and finally, the normalized histogram is calculated. The computation of HoG involves the following steps:

Step1: Calculate the gradient by finding I_x and I_y and their central differences. Use the Eq. (3)

$$I_x(r, c) = I(r, c+1) - I(r, c-1) \text{ and } I_y = I(r-1, c) - I(r+1, c) \tag{3}$$

Step 2: Obtain the cell orientation histogram by dividing the window into adjacent and nonoverlapping sections.
Step 3: Apply block normalization.
Step 4: Concatenate the normalized block features into a single HoG feature vector "h" using Eq. (4).

$$h = h / \left(\sqrt{\|h\|^2 + \varepsilon} \right) \tag{4}$$

with "h_n" to be min (h_n, T).

7.2   Principal component analysis

Principal component analysis (PCA) is used to identify the patterns in data, expressing the information so as to emphasize their differences and similarities. In the case of multidimensional data, it is difficult to find the patterns and cast a graphical representation. To solve this problem, PCA, a powerful tool, is used for analyzing the data. The other major advantage of PCA is that once these patterns are found in the data, the data can be compressed in a meaningful way, thereby reducing the number of dimensions without loss of information. This technique is used for data compression and dimension reductionality. The algorithm follows:

Step 1: Read the intensity values in the images (Input data).
Step 2: Subtract the data from the mean values.
Step 3: Compute the covariance using Eq. (5).

$$\text{Cov}(X, Y) = \sum_{i=1}^{n} \left\{ (E_i - \tilde{E})(I_i - \hat{I}) \right\} / (n-1) \qquad (5)$$

Step 4: Compute the Eigen vectors and Eigen values of the covariance matrix.
Step 5: Form the feature vector using Eq. (6).

$$\text{Feature Vector} = \{\text{eig}_1, \text{eig}_2, \text{eig}_3, \ldots\} \qquad (6)$$

Step 6: Form the new data set as in Eqs. (7) and (8).

$$\text{Final data} = \text{Row vector} \times \text{Row data adjust} \qquad (7)$$

$$\text{Image Matrix} = [\text{Image Vec}_1; \text{Image Vec}_2; \text{Image Vec}_3; \ldots] \qquad (8)$$

7.3   Backpropagation algorithm

A neural networks (NN) is a significant data mining tool for classification and clustering. It is a software automated process where the algorithm is designed to mimic the activities of the brain and be able to learn. NNs usually learns from samples. If a NN is given the input data, classification is performed, and a new trend of data pattern is generated. Basically, NN is composed of three layers— input, output, and hidden—as in Fig. 1. Each layer has the processing elements called nodes, and nodes from the input layer are connected to the nodes of the hidden layer, and the nodes of the hidden layer are connected to nodes in the output layer. These connections are represented by random numbers called weights. The BPA is used for training the ANN. The idea behind BPA is simple: the output of ANN is estimated against required output. If the output does not match the set point value, then weights between layers are modified and the process repeats itself till the deviation is negligible.

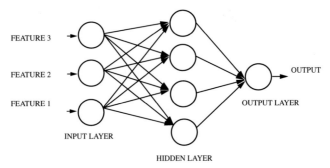

FIG. 1 ANN Architecture

The number of nodes in the input layer is fixed depending on the number of features taken for training the ANN. The number of nodes in the hidden layer can be determined using a well-defined formula or even on a trial and error basis. If the number of nodes in the hidden layer is more, then it increases the computational complexity, which affects the convergence of the network work. An improper number of nodes in the hidden layer can prevent the BPA of its learning ability. The correct balance needs to be maintained. Hence, it is important to monitor the progress of ANN during the training in order to achieve optimal results.

ANN can be controlled by setting and adjusting the weights between nodes of the input and hidden layers and also between the nodes of the hidden and output layers. Initial weights are usually random numbers between 0 and 1, which is adjusted automatically during the training process. The logic for tuning the weights is quite simple. When training the ANN, the weights are updated after iterations. If the results of ANN obtained after weights update are optimal than the previous set of weights, then the new weight values are used for further iteration. The final set of weights should be inferred in such a way that the tuned weights will help reduce the error. This process is also enhanced by using a suitable learning rate: momentum values.

Activation function is an important factor that controls the convergence of the network. The various types are linear, threshold, unipolar sigmoid, and bipolar sigmoid functions. The hidden layer combines the linear and nonlinear characteristics; hence, sigmoid activation function is used typically for hidden layer nodes. SUM is a collection of the outputs from hidden layer that have been multiplied by connection weights, added to get a single number, and put through sigmoid function (activation function). Input to sigmoid is any value between negative infinity and positive infinity number while the output can only be a number between 0 and 1.

Running the ANN consists of a forward and a backward pass. Outputs are calculated and compared with desired outputs in the forward pass. The mean squared error (MSE) between the target and actual outputs are calculated. In the backward pass, this error value is used to change the weights in the network in order to reduce the MSE. Forward and backward passes are repeated until the MSE value is minimum. When training the ANN, the inputs and target values are presented to the network. If the samples total 100, then 70% of the data are used for training, 25% for testing, and the remaining 5% for validation. Choosing the learning rate and momentum will help with weight adjustment.

Finalizing the learning rate is difficult because a wrong value of the learning rate may prolong the convergence process. If a large value is chosen, then the algorithm will diverge. The value of a learning rate can be chosen to be any random number between 0 and 1 depending on the proper choice when training the ANN. Next, the value of momentum plays an important role in network convergence. This term represents inertia. Large values of momentum term will influence the adjustment in the current weight to move in same direction as the previous adjustment.

8 Detailed work plan to achieve the objectives

The color images are generally processed in Red (R), Green (G), and Blue (B) planes to extract useful information based on the intensity of the pixels. Since the captured images of the agricultural lands are all color images, this topic is of a great importance. The color of agricultural lands depends on the quality and quantity of chlorophyll content of the vegetation. This color variation with respect to the farmland category is segregated as HP, MP, and LP lands. The productivity is affected by climate change, which occurs due to an accumulation of greenhouse gases, increased atmospheric temperature, and variation in rainfall at Neyveli, where NLC is located (Sujatha et al., 2018b). As a result, a novel strategy is proposed to forecast the information regarding the greenhouse gas emissions, increased atmospheric temperature, and variation in rainfall from the images of the farmlands, and with this prior knowledge, farmers can take appropriate action to maintain or increase the agricultural yield by adopting sophisticated irrigation techniques, suitable organic pesticides, crop rotation, seasonal farming, or even multiple crop raising. This message is propagated to the agricultural society using an Indigenous integrated system (https://www.manage.gov.in/studymaterial/CCA-E.pdf; Al-Ghzawi et al., 2018; Sujatha et al., 2018a, 2020).

The creation of this proposed real-time application using MATLAB® involves the stages like bugging, error, defect, failure, quality assurance and control, verification, and validation.

Software Bug: The unexpected error in the MATLAB® code, which produces a defect in the output, is called a bug.

Error: The disparity with respect to the specification causes an error in the program.

Defect: The variation in the actual output and the target output is called a defect. The defect can take place due to a flaw, which impacts the customer and systematic operations of a system.

Failure: The flaw that produces a counter-effect paralyzing the operation of a system is called as failure.

Quality Assurance: It is done to prevent flaws by cross-verification with standards and procedures.

Quality Control: It is a measure taken to avoid the production of defective products and also to check if the performance meets the standards.

Verification: It is done to check the functionality of the proposed system, so that it satisfies the customer needs.

Validation: Validation is the actual testing that takes place after verification is completed.

8.1 Methodology

A camera attached to the drone or at various points of the agricultural land keeps monitoring the agricultural fields in and around Neyveli. These images are preprocessed for noise removal. If the images are corrupted with salt and pepper noise, they can be removed using median filter. Then the noise removal is followed by feature extraction, which includes extraction of HoG features. These features are fused with soil moisture data and reduced using PCA. These features are then used for training and testing the ANN trained with BPA to forecast the emission of greenhouse gases like CO_2, CO, NO_x, CH_4, and SO_x and the atmospheric temperature and decrease or increase in rainfall, as shown in Fig. 2A. Additionally the outputs of PCA (Fig. 2B) are also used as inputs for training the ANN. The sample feature set in shown in Table 2.

The data for the greenhouse gas emissions was obtained from NLC, and images of the agricultural lands in and around NLC were captured. The corresponding atmospheric temperature and rainfall data are obtained from http://satellite.imd.gov.in/ and recorded, and these values are tabulated in Table 1a Similarly, using the soil moisture sensor, the MC in the farmlands is recorded, as given in Table 1b. The percentage MC in the soil is calculated using the formula in Eq. (9).

$$\%MC = \{(\text{Moisture content in the wet soil} - \text{moisture content in the dry soil})/$$
$$\text{Moisture content in the dry soil}\} \times 100 \qquad (9)$$

The images of the agricultural lands (HP, MP, and LP) can be obtained by fixing cameras in the agricultural lands or by using the satellite images. The images are preprocessed and HoG features are extracted, fused with the soil moisture data, and reduced using PCA. Then these real-time values are normalized using the formula in Eq. (10).

$$X_i/X_{max} \qquad (10)$$

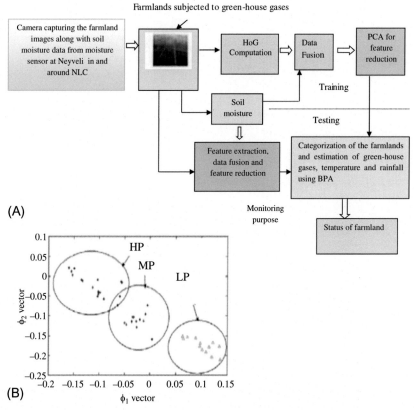

(A)

(B)

FIG. 2 (A) Block diagram for using image processing to detect the greenhouse gases and other related parameters. (B) Output for PCA.

Then a set of weights are chosen, which are random numbers generated using a randomize function along with an appropriate architecture for ANN. Then training and testing is done with nearly 80 and 51 samples of the agricultural land images corresponding to HP, MP, and LP and with greenhouse gases, increased atmospheric temperature, and rainfall values.

9 Results and discussion

A total of nearly 233 samples relating to the images of the agricultural fields categorized under three categories—HP, MP, and LP—which are affected by greenhouse gas emissions with corresponding increase in temperature and subsequent decrease in rainfall are collected. Nearly 173 samples are used for training, and the remaining 60 samples are used for testing. These images may or may not be corrupted by noise. If a sample is corrupted by noise, then it is eliminated using a median filter. Then, using PCA, the intensity values corresponding to green color alone is extracted and reduced. This reduced feature set is

TABLE 1A Greenhouse gases from NLC and weather-related data with images of farmlands.

S. No	Images of agricultural lands	Type of productivity	CO$_2$ emissions (Nm^3/hour)	CO emissions (ppm)	SO$_x$ emissions (mg/Nm^3)	NO$_x$ emissions (mg/Nm^3)	CH$_4$ emissions (mg/Nm^3)	Atmospheric temperature (°C)	Rain fall (mm)	Proposed corrective action by farmers
1.		HP	400	100	400	70	10	27	4	No corrective action required
2.		MP	700	200	600	120	30	32	0.5	Supply extra water for irrigation and manure
3.		LP	1000	300	900	200	40	43	0	Seasonal crop raising can be preferred

TABLE 1B Soil moisture sensor data related with images of farmlands.

S. No	Images of agricultural lands	Type of productivity	Soil moisture (MC) (%)	Proposed corrective action by farmers
1.		HP	98	No corrective action required
2.		MP	63	Supply extra water for irrigation and manure
3.		LP	9	Seasonal crop raising can be preferred

used to train and test BPA so as to predict the greenhouse gas emissions, atmospheric temperature, and decrease in rainfall. Based on these parameters sent to farmers on their mobile, they can choose some remedial measure to save the crops and increase the productivity by combating the effects of climate change. This experimentation is done using MATLAB® software. From Fig. 3A it is inferred that for the agricultural lands in HP category, the green intensity pixels in G-plane has a histogram count of 277. Similarly, from Fig. 3B and C, it is inferred that for the agricultural lands in MP and LP categories, the green intensity pixels in G-plane has a histogram count of 42 and 0, respectively. Let this value be considered as "X." This states that the chlorophyll content is present in less quantity or totally absent in the images corresponding to MP and LP. To support this concept strongly, the soil moisture data (denoted by the variable "Y") obtained from three categories of farmlands are modified using the additive rule in Eq. (11). The extracted feature samples are illustrated in Table 2

$$\text{Fused value} = (X + Y) \qquad (11)$$

In this analysis, there are 60 images for testing. Each image is 414×285 pixels. For each image, an image vector is formed using the Eq. (6). This combines all the images together into a single image matrix used for PCA analysis. Then PCA is performed, and the original image from the transformed image is

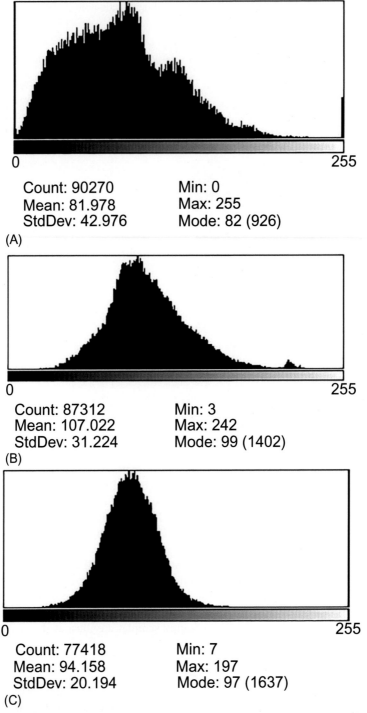

Count: 90270   Min: 0
Mean: 81.978   Max: 255
StdDev: 42.976   Mode: 82 (926)

(A)

Count: 87312   Min: 3
Mean: 107.022   Max: 242
StdDev: 31.224   Mode: 99 (1402)

(B)

Count: 77418   Min: 7
Mean: 94.158   Max: 197
StdDev: 20.194   Mode: 97 (1637)

(C)

FIG. 3 (A) Histogram for agricultural lands in HP. (B) Histogram for agricultural lands in MP. (C) Histogram for agricultural lands in LP.

TABLE 2 Sample feature set used for training and testing.

S. No	Samples of features extracted from farmlands	HP farmlands	MP farmlands	LP farmlands
1.	Histogram count for green intensity pixels from HoG	277	42	0
2.	% MC	98	63	9
3.	Fused value of green intensity with % MC	375	105	9
4.	Standard deviation	42.97	31.22	20.19
5.	Variance	1846.42	974.68	407.64

obtained. This software approach measures the deviation between the transformed image and the original images along the new axes obtained from PCA analysis. Thus the PCA has recognized the statistical patterns in the data set. Since all the vectors are "N" dimensional, "N" eigenvectors are obtained. In practice, some of the less significant eigenvectors are left out so that the identification task is performed well with reduced computational complexity, as shown in Fig. 2B.

To verify the success rate of this fusion logic, the sensitivity is calculated, and its output is validated by finding the True Positive (TP), False Positive (FP), True Negative (TN), and False Negative (FN). In general, positive is identified and negative is rejected. Therefore:

- TP indicates correctly identified as chlorophyll content.
- FP indicates incorrectly identified as chlorophyll content.
- TN indicates correctly rejected as it is not the chlorophyll content.
- FN indicates incorrectly rejected as it is chlorophyll content.

Sensitivity, which is also called True Positive Rate (TPR) is defined as TP/(TP + FN), and its values are shown in Table 3.

The objective functions for training the ANN, which is formulated as in Eq. (12).

$$\text{Objective function for MSE (proposed)} = f\left(T_a, G, M, R\right) \qquad (12)$$

where "T_a" represents increased atmospheric temperature, "G" represents the composition of various greenhouse gases, "M" represents the soil MC, and "R" represents the decreased rainfall. In the long run, for maximizing the agricultural yield, this objective function is to be minimized.

TABLE 3 Validation for chlorophyll content identification using sensor data fusion.

S. No	Agricultural Land category	TP	FP	TN	FN	Calculation for Sensitivity	Sensitivity (%)
1.	HP	17	0	0	1	17/(17 + 1) = 17/18	94.44
2.	MP	19	0	0	2	19/(19 + 2) = 19/21	90.47
3.	LP	11	0	0	1	11/(11 + 1) = 11/12	91.66

A comparative analysis is done using by fixing the optimal value of MSE using the conventional formula as in Eq. (13).

$$MSE\,(conventional) = (A + T)^2/2 \tag{13}$$

where "A" denotes the actual output values, and "T" denotes the target values of the output.

The forecasting by ANN is shown in Fig. 4A–G (results using proposed objective function) for greenhouse gases, atmospheric temperature, and rainfall, and the training parameters are mentioned in Table 4. The forecasting efficiency (which is defined as the ratio of number of parameters forecasted correctly from images to the total number of images in that category) is finally presented in Tables 5a and 5b using proposed and conventional objective functions.

10 Conclusion

The chlorophyll content estimated from the vegetation by extracting green colored pixels from the satellite images of the Indian agricultural area and the soil moisture level for each type of vegetation will then be analyzed for the impact on climate change for agriculture. The analysis will be done by introducing the chlorophyll content and the soil moisture level as the inputs to the ANN using feed-forward with BPA. Hence, the proposed system will incorporate the data analytics and its different regression models to bring out various correlations and trends in the agriculture with respect to the climate change. Based on this analysis, the farmers will be notified via short message service about the type of crops that are favorable for yielding at a particular period of the year. Hence, the

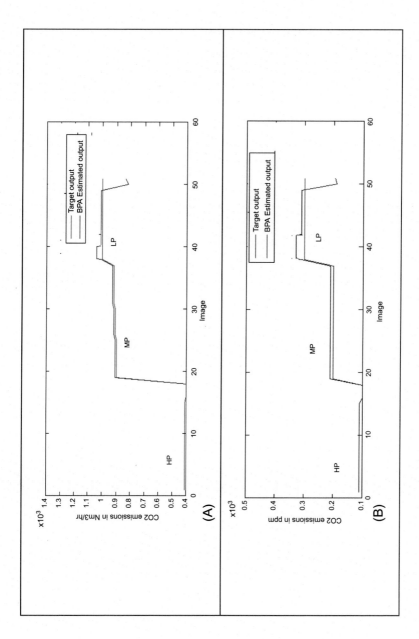

FIG. 4 Testing results for prediction by BPA. (A) Forecasting the CO$_2$ emissions. (B) Forecasting the CO emissions.

(Continued)

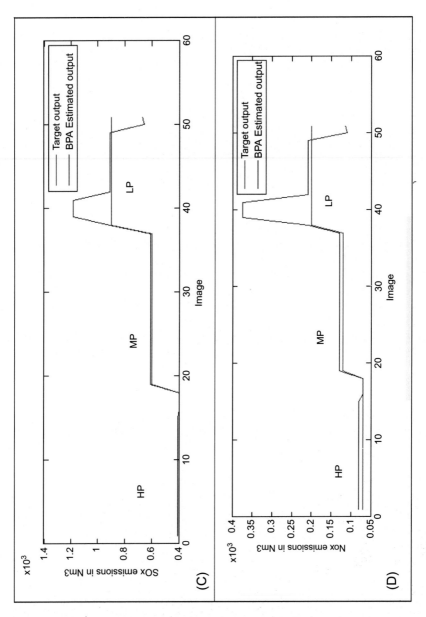

FIG. 4, CONT'D (C) Forecasting the SO$_x$ emissions. (D) Forecasting the NO$_x$ emissions.

(Continued)

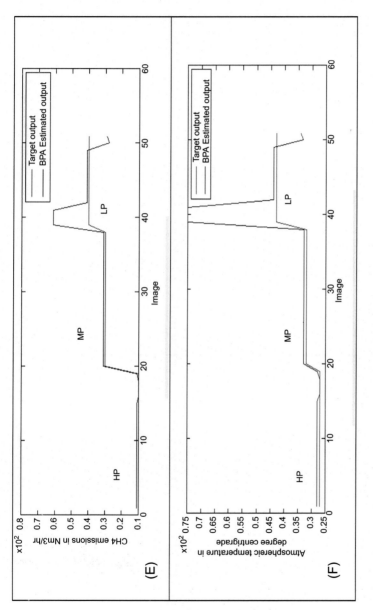

FIG. 4, CONT'D (E) Forecasting the CH₄ emissions. (F) Forecasting the atmospheric temperature.

(Continued)

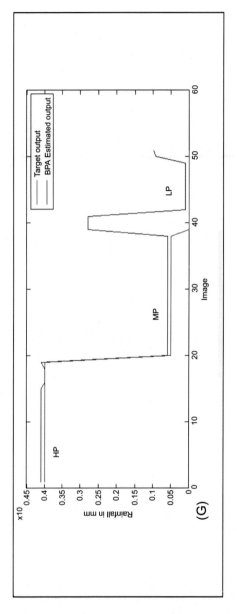

FIG. 4, CONT'D (G) Forecasting the rainfall.

TABLE 4 ANN parameters.

S. No	ANN parameters	Values	Justification for ANN parameters (proposed)	Justification for ANN parameters (conventional)
1.	No. of nodes in input layer	44	S·D, Variance, Fused inputs, and PCA values from the input images corresponding to HP, MP, LP	S·D, Variance, Fused inputs, and PCA values from the input images corresponding to HP, MP, LP
2.	No. of nodes in hidden layer	23	$(N/2) + 1$; where "N" is the no. of nodes in input layer	$(N/2) + 1$; where "N" is the no. of nodes in input layer
3.	No. of nodes in output layer	01	CO_2, CO, NO_x, CH_4 and SO_x along with the atmospheric temperature and decrease or increase in rainfall	CO_2, CO, NO_x, CH_4, and SO_x along with the atmospheric temperature and decrease or increase in rainfall
4.	Activation function	sigmoid	To reach convergence at faster rate	To reach convergence at faster rate
5.	MSE	0.0012	Optimal value is chosen using $f(T_a, G, M, R)$	$(A + T)^2/2$
6.	Learning factor	0.8	Forces the ANN to convergence	Forces the ANN to convergence
7.	Momentum	0.8	Forces the ANN to convergence	Forces the ANN to convergence

TABLE 5A Forecasting efficiency by ANN using proposed objective function.

S. No	Parameters	Forecasting efficiency (%)								
		HP			MP			LP		
		Total no. of images	No. of images correctly identified	% Efficiency	Total no. of images	No. of images correctly identified	% Efficiency	Total no. of images	No. of images correctly identified	% Efficiency
1.	CO_2	18	17	94	21	20	95	12	11	92
2.	CO	18	17	94	21	20	95	12	11	92
3.	SO_x	18	17	94	21	20	95	12	11	92
4.	NO_x	18	17	94	21	20	95	12	11	92
5.	CH_4	18	17	94	21	20	95	12	11	92
6.	Temperature	18	17	94	21	20	95	12	11	92
7.	Rainfall	18	17	94	21	20	95	12	11	92

TABLE 5B Forecasting efficiency by ANN using conventional objective function.

S. No	Parameters	HP			MP			LP		
		Total no. of images	No. of images correctly identified	% Efficiency	Total no. of images	No. of images correctly identified	% Efficiency	Total no. of images	No. of images correctly identified	% Efficiency
1.	CO_2	18	13	72.2	21	15	71	12	09	75
2.	CO	18	13	72.2	21	15	71	12	09	75
3.	SO_x	18	13	72.2	21	15	71	12	09	75
4.	NO_x	18	13	72.2	21	15	71	12	09	75
5.	CH_4	18	13	72.2	21	15	71	12	09	75
6.	Temperature	18	13	72.2	21	15	71	12	09	75
7.	Rainfall	18	13	72.2	21	15	71	12	09	75

Forecasting Efficiency (%)

revenue generated from the Indian agriculture will be more, as the crop selected for farming will be forecasted based on the climate change. Forecasting greenhouse gas emissions from thermal power plants will be helpful not only to the government of Tamil Nadu but also all over the nation and world, wherever coal-fired power plants are operated. These thermal power plants being the generating source of greenhouse gases spoil the agricultural farms, reducing their productivity. So, in order to maintain stability in agro-based production and to fight against the challenging climate change caused due to the emission of greenhouse gases, information from a novel forecasting technique with a hardware set up, if installed in such areas, can be sent to farmers regarding the changes in climate, which will be helpful for them. Hence, this automated software-based system will be utilized by all farmers, thermal power plants, and students and people involved in agricultural research.

References

Ainsworth, E. A., & Long, S. P. (2005). What have we learned from 15 years of free-air CO2 enrichment (FACE)? A meta analysis of the responses of photosynthesis, canopy properties and plant production to rising CO2. *New Phytologist*, *165*, 351–372.

Al-Ghzawi, A. L. A., Khalaf, Y. B., Al-Ajlouni, Z. I., AL-Quraan, N. A., Musallam, I., & Hani, N. B. (2018). The effect of supplemental irrigation on canopy temperature depression, chlorophyll content, and water use efficiency in three wheat (Triticum aestivum L. and *T. durum* Desf.) varieties grown in dry regions of Jordan. *Agriculture*, *8*, 67.

Ali, A., & Erenstein, O. (2017). Assessing farmer use of climate change adaptation practices and impacts on food security and poverty in Pakistan. *Climate Risk Management*, *16*, 183–194.

Bosello, F., & Zhang, J. (March 2006). *The effects of climate change on agriculture*. RePEc.

Cetner, M. D., Pietkiewicz, S., Podlaski, S., Wiśniewski, G., Chołuj, D., Łukasikb, I., & Kalaji, H. M. (2014). Photosynthetic efficiency of Virginia Mallow (Sida Hermaphrodita (L.) Rusby) under differentiated soil moisture conditions. *International Journal of Sustainable Water and Environmental Systems*, *6*(2), 89–95.

Clement Atzberger, C. (2013). Advances in remote sensing of agriculture: Context description, existing operational monitoring systems and major information needs. *Remote Sensing*, *5*, 949–981.

Eitzinger, J., Utset, A., & Trnka, M. (May 2019). Adaptation of methods and technologies in agriculture under climate change conditions. In *International Climate Protection* (pp. 73–82). Springer.

Elza, Y. S., & Balai, S. (July 2018). The use of seasonal climate forecast for agriculture in Indonesia: Current status and future challenge. *Jurnal Sumberdaya Lahan*, *12*(1), 33–48.

Eriksen, S., & Brown, K. (2011). Sustainable adaptation to climate change. *Climate and Development*, *3*(1).

Foley, J. A., Ramankutty, N., Brauman, K. A., Cassidy, E. S., Gerber, J. S., Johnston, M., ... et al. (2011). Solutions of a cultivated planet. *Nature*, *478*, 337–342.

Frías, M. D., Iturbide, M., Manzanas, R., & Gutiérrez, J. M. (January 2018). *An R package to visualize and communicate uncertainty in seasonal climate prediction*. Elsevier.

Gattinger, A., Jawtusch, J., & Muller, A. (November, 2011). (FIBL). *Mitigating greenhouse gases in agriculture—A challenge and opportunity for agriculture policies*. DiakonischesWerk der EKD e.V.

Gondali, H., & Bose, D. K. (March 2019). Effect of climate change on agricultural operations in Dharwad District of Karnataka, India. *International Journal of Current Microbiology and Applied Sciences*.

Gornall, J., Betts, R., Burke, E., Clark, R., Camp, J., Willett, K., & Wiltshire, A. (December 2010). Implications of climate change for agricultural productivity in the early twenty-first century. *Philosophical Transactions of the Royal Society B, Biological Sciences, 365*(1554).

Guiteras, R. (December 2007). *The impact of climate change on Indian agriculture*. Elsevier.

Gunda, T., Bazuin, J., Nay, J., & Yeung, K. L. (February 2017). Impact of seasonal forecast use on agricultural income in a system with varying crop costs and returns: An empirically-grounded simulation. *Environmental Research Letters*. IOP Publishing.

Hansen, J. W., Challinor, A., Ines, A., Wheeler, T., & Moron, V. (December 21, 2006). *Translating climate forecasts into agricultural terms: advances and challenges*. Published in CR Vol. 33, No. 1. Online publication date. Print ISSN: 0936-577X; Online ISSN: 1616-1572.

Holden, N. M. (2008). *Effects of climate change on agriculture*. Taylor & Francis, Ltd.

Iswoyo, H., Stoeber, S., & Ramba, K. T. (February, 2019). Empowering upland farmers to become more resilient towards climate change – Experiences from Toraja, Indonesia. *IOP Conference Series Earth and Environmental Science, 235*, 012039.

Jolánkai, M., Birkás, M., Tarnawa, Á., & Kassai, K. M. (2019). Agriculture and climate change. In *International climate protection* Springer International Publishing.

Jolánkai, M, & Csete, L. L. (2019). Effects of global climate change on agriculture. *International Climate Protection*. Springer.

Khan, F., & Wakeel, A. (March 2018). *"Crop production and climate change: Challenges and solutions", innovations in agriculture: Nourishing Pakistan in changing climate*. Food and Agriculture Organization of the United Nations.

Li, Y. (2019). China's actions on adaption to climate change. In *International Climate Protection* (pp. 129–138). Springer.

Long, S. P., Ainsworth, E. A., Leakey, A. D. B., Nosberger, J., & Ort, D. R. (2006). Food for thought: Lower-than expected crop yield stimulation with rising CO_2 concentrations. *Science, 312*(5782).

Mall, R. K., Sonkar, G., Sharma, N. K., & Singh, N. (January 2016). *Impacts of climate change on agriculture sector in Madhya Pradesh*. Association of Agrometeorologists.

Meroni, M., Atberger, C., Vancutsem, C., Gobron, N., Baret, F., Lacaze, R., ... Leo, O. (2012). Evaluation of agreement between space remote sensing SPOT-VEGETATION fAPAR time series. *IEEE Transactions on Geoscience and Remote Sensing, 41*(4), 1951–1961.

Nelson, G. C., Rosegrant, M. W., Koo, J., Robertson, R., Sulser, T., Zhu, T., ... Lee, D. (2009). *Climate change: Impact on agriculture and costs of adaptation*. Washington, D.C.: International Food Policy Research Institute.

Parmar, M., Shukla, S., & Kalubarme, M. H. (March 2019). Impact of climate change and drought analysis on agriculture in Sabarkantha District using Geoinformatics Technology. *Global Journal of Engineering Science and Researches*, 2348-8034.

Parry, M. L., Rosenzweig, C., Iglesias, A., Livermore, M., & Fischer, G. (2004). Effects of climate change on global food production under SRES emissions and socio-economic scenarios. *Global Environmental Change, 14*(1), 53–67.

Runtunuwu, E., & Kondoh, A. (October 2016). Assessing global climate variability under coldest and warmest periods at different latitudinal regions. *IJAS, 9*(1), 7–18.

Sarker, A. M. (March, 2014). Climate change and farm-level adaptation decisions and strategies in drought-prone and groundwater-depleted areas of Bangladesh: An empirical investigation. *Ecological Economics, 106*, 204–213.

Sarvina, Y. (January 2018). The use of seasonal climate forecast for agriculture in Indonesia: Current status and future challenge. *Environmental Modelling & Software, 99*, 101–110. December 2018.

Sharmila, K. J., & Narayanan, R. M. (2018). Assessment of various oceanographic parameters and inter comparison of primary production estimates around Chennai coast—Tamilnadu, India. *Applied Ocean Research, 72*(1), 3.

Sirotenko, O. D., & Romanenkov, V. A. (2009). *Mathematical models of agricultural supply, Mathematical models of life support systems: Vol. II*. Encyclopedia of Life Support Systems (EOLSS).

Soglo, Y. Y., Melaine, G., & Nonvide, A. (May 2019). Climate change perceptions and responsive strategies in Benin: The case of maize farmers. *Climatic Change, 155*(2), 245–256. Springer.

Sujatha, K., Bhavani, N. P. G., Cao, S.-Q., & Ram Kumar, K. S. (2018a). Soft sensor for flame temperature measurement and IoT based monitoring in power plants. *Materials Today: Proceedings, 2018*, 37–47. Elsevier.

Sujatha, K., Bhavani, N. P. G., & Ponmagal, R. S. (2018b). In *Impact of NOx emissions on climate and monitoring using smart sensor technology*. IEEE.

Sujatha, K., Bhavani, N. P. G., Srividhya, V., Karthikeyan, V., & Jayachitra, N. (2020). *Soft sensor with shape descriptors for flame quality, prediction based on LSTM regression, Real-Time Data Analytics for Large Scale Sensor Data*. https://doi.org/10.1016/B978-0-12-818014-3.00006-1.

Tarnawa, Á, Klupács, H, Sallai, A, Szalay, K, Kassai, M K, Nyárai, H F, & Jolánkai, M. (2010). *Study on the impact of main climatic factors of crop production in a mathematical model*. Elsevier.

Wamsler, C., Brink, E., & Rivera, C. (July 2013). Planning for climate change in urban areas: From theory to practice. *Journal of Cleaner Production, 50*(1), 68–81.

Wreford, A., Moran, D., & Adger, N. (2010). *Climate change and agriculture—Impacts, adaptation and mitigation*. OECD.

Zavala, J. A., Casteel, C. L., DeLucia, E. H., & Berenbaum, M. R. (2008). Anthropogenic increase in carbon dioxide compromises plant defense against invasive insects. *Proceedings of the National Academy of Sciences of the United States of America, 105*.

Zecha, C. W., Link, J., & Claupein, W. (2013). Sensor platforms in precision farming: Categorization and research applications. *Remote Sensing, 12*, 31–36.

Chapter 8

Transformations of urban agroecology landscape in territory transition

José G. Vargas-Hernández

University Center for Economic and Managerial Sciences, University of Guadalajara, Zapopan, Jalisco, Mexico

1 Introduction

Agroecological transition requires a goal-seeking approach to operate the changes projected and targeted on environmental sustainability and ecosystem services. The economic assessments in terms of positive or negative externalities and environmental costs and benefits of the ecosystem services in agroecological transitions are very limited. Steering the agroecological transition involves all the stakeholders concerned on a collaborative learning process through which the capacities and capabilities of communities and individuals propose the planning of change and implementation of actions.

The agroecological transition is complex and interdependent between ecological, economic, social, and technological components and a multilaterally power-driven interplay on stakeholders. Technical knowledge is relevant for the agroecological transition, as the resources dedicated to monitor the changes on the ecosystem service bundles and valuations and the agroecological transition, proxies, social perceptions of changes, and so forth. Stakeholders have to identify the technical knowledge, acceptability, regulatory and administrative issues, and external economic, institutional, and cultural dynamics of the agroecological transition.

As a contemporary, scientific perspective on agroecological transition, permaculture is an agroecological-related discipline grouped within life sciences and has a minority of scholarly literature and work. The scholarly work on permaculture design systems has a high level of abstraction engaged in topics beyond biophysical and agricultural but has weak ties to agroecology.

Agroecology as the key element in the construction of food system sovereignty requires the transformation of social and political power structures moving away from corporate control toward community governance.

This analysis of transformations of urban agroecology landscape in territory transition begins with a section on the agroecological landscapes to continue with the agroecological practices and the implications on the urban territorial transformation and transition of agroecology. Finally, there advanced some relevant conclusions.

2 Agroecological landscapes

The agroecological rationale of small-scale farming represents community-based, local agriculture to continue feeding people in most rural and urban landscapes. Urban agroecology is related to the growing, processing, distributing, and marketing of organic food through intensive plant cultivation and animal husbandry in cities. Urban agroecology is a broad term to describe grassroots and institution-led projects of food cultivation and animal husbandry on urban land, which creates alternatives of commons to capitalist organization reshaping urban landscapes.

Urban sustainable agroecology refers to food cultivation and animal husbandry on urban and peri-urban land, reshaping city landscapes and forms of recreation of commons as an alternative of urban life organization. Urban agroecological actors and stakeholders can open their lands and build socioeconomic communities for mutual support to build more natural, open green spaces in the rural and urban interfaces.

Urban agroecology is a feature of the urban economy that is not integrated into the urban land use system and remains outside, contributing to income, employment, and healthy food supply. Urban agroecology is growing or producing healthy food in urban land used for this purpose in heavily populated settlements. Feeding the world's growing population while caring for public health and the environment, urban agroecology can be the answer to solve the problems if land use, financial incentives, infrastructure, and support systems are properly planned and implemented. Urban agroecology and animal production occurring within inner cities and peripheries is a productive process linked to the feeding of urban population.

Urban agroecology is integrated and embedded into the urban socioeconomic and ecological system, managing the use of natural resources, competing with other uses of land and water, and connecting with urban food systems based on the needs of healthy nutrition of resident consumers.

Agroecology produces food by restoring degraded landscapes of smallholder producers to maximize biodiversity and ecosystem services provided by natural resources. Ecosystems are shaped by the benefits of agroecological landscapes involving different interests of various stakeholders and actors. Some stakeholders' agroecological initiatives, practices, and policies to improve biodiversity and natural resource management in natural landscape elements embedded in food systems are the territorialized agro-environmental measures (Hart et al., 2015). Agroecology demands changes in specific policies and practices to transform socially unjust structures, behaviors, and cultures.

From a large landscape perspective, biodiversity conservation moves agroecology toward sustainable priority more than food crisis. The impacts of climatic changes on food production creating a food crisis requires solutions that have a sustainable agroecology approach. Climate change has an impact on agriculture that increases uncertainty of production, land use degradation, floods, and droughts and affects the management of sustainable natural resources and their contributions to food insecurity. Establishing economically sustainable urban agroecology farming and gardening to make a living by creating urban productive landscapes ensures access to nutrients and increases the food security and self-reliance of the city.

The social component in agroecological contexts goes beyond food production and includes the demand for quality of consumers guided by ethics (Boogaard et al., 2010) and the landscapes valued as aesthetic and educational resources (Lindemann-Matthies et al., 2010). Agroecology has multiple dimensions in policy development supporting climate change, organic food production and practices, ecosystems services resilience, and more.

3 Agroecological practices

Agroecology applies ecological concepts, principles, and practices to the design and management framework for sustainable agricultural ecosystems. Numerous farms around the world are following organic and agroecological practices. Agroecological farms base their production on innovative methods not using chemical inputs such as fertilizers. Agroecology refers to a scientific discipline, a social movement, and agricultural practices (Wezel et al., 2009).

Urban agroecology is a promising concept and practice to foster food production while enhancing resilience and sustainability of urban ecosystems. Small farms adopting agroecological farming techniques and practices increase the ecosystem resilience to irregular weather patterns and are better keepers of environmental sustainability (Cohn et al., 2006). Urban agroecology is engaged in food production and other related activities practiced by various stakeholders with different socioeconomic backgrounds and motivations (Mougeot, 2006; FAO, 2007; Duží et al., 2014; Simon Rojo et al., 2014).

New concepts, trends, and practices in urban agroecology for food production are permeating into multiple disciplines reflecting new, alternative, sustainable, and environmentally supportive models of production, distribution, supply, and consumption. These new models establish new forms of relationships among agroecological food producers and consumers in urban geographical proximity sharing responsibilities for inputs and outputs in supply chains (Mundler & Laughrea, 2016), food systems (Holloway et al., 2007;

Kirwan et al., 2013; Hiroki et al., 2016; Kneafsey et al., 2013), community-supported agriculture CSA (Hvitsand, 2016), and alternative food networks (Maye, 2013; Renting et al., 2003).

Efforts to combat malnutrition and hunger, improve livelihoods for small-scale farmers, upgrade urban ecosystems, and transition to low-carbon and natural resource practices require achieving higher levels of urban agroecological food production.

Development of urban agroecology food policies focuses on replacing conventional practices for food production and food waste with community-supported participation for food sovereignty through major structural change. Agroecology practices contribute to challenge and tackle the causes of existing power structures. The biggest agroecological challenge is that access to land and water is not always affordable in efficient irrigation practices. Besides policies and investments, agroecology practices require fiscal incentives, payment of ecosystem services, market opportunities, supply management mechanisms, other institutional support, and more to enable farmers to acquire long-term resources.

Agroecology is considered a science, a practice, and a social movement. Agroecology is a science that focus on the mechanisms, technologies, processes, practices, and socioeconomic, ecological, and environmental dynamics of diversified agricultural systems. Agroecology is a science-based transformative movement to radically counter ideologies, strategies, policies, and practices aimed at maximizing agricultural yields over other economic, socioecological, environmental, and biocultural objectives.

Agroecology is related in a dialectical process to alternative agro-food movements engaged in coproduction of knowledge and practice, shaping each other, identifying opportunities, and developing policy. Agroecology develops an extensive knowledge about food security, adaptation to local practices, and climate mitigation. Agroecology is a social movement, a practice, and scientific knowledge combined with local knowledge and experience for a more just and sustainable world.

There is enthusiasm for agroecology science, practices, and movements among scientists and academics, farmers and agricultural producers, farmers' organizations, alliances between farmers and nonfarmers, food justice organizations, food system actors, and consumers in general to achieve socioeconomic and environmental transformations through changing policies to food system governance. Agroecological practices produce food integrating ecosystem services as fundamental elements (Wezel et al., 2014). Agroecology is an alternative to conventional agriculture and refers to a science, practices, and a social movement (Wezel et al., 2009) with the objective of developing healthy and sustainable production systems from socioeconomic and ecological dimensions (Altieri, 1989).

Agroecology has resurged as place-based knowledge excluded from dominant industrial land use practices as a response of the degradation left by the agricultural production model. The agroecological knowledge and practices are created, acquired, and altered continuously by farmers. Agroecology is knowledge-intensive and innovative using participatory methods and exchange networks focusing on farmer knowledge to share practices, expertise, techniques, ideas, ecosystem resilience, weather patterns, and management schemes to minimize dependence on agro-chemical inputs.

Knowledge and practical expertise of agroecological farming offer insights to scientists. The integrated agroecological systems include diverse forms of scientific, technological, and Indigenous knowledge learning, experiences, and practices connected to the food sovereignty movement through transparent and democratic governance. Developing agroecology in any context is based on sustainable alternative agricultural practices sustained by traditional Indigenous knowledge systems for food provisioning practices. Food provisioning activities involves fisheries, foraging, and other forms besides agriculture practices aligned with agroecological principles.

Radical urban agroecological politics is a critical space of dialogue, education, and practice aimed at transforming the lives of people through collective work experiences by creating potentially material changes in self-valorizing dynamics of more natural ecosystem spaces in the inner city and peri-urban areas. Urban and peri-urban agroecology studies are focused on the role of intensive agroecological practices in providing food to urban inhabitants. Agroecology has moved beyond self-sufficiency subsistence-based traditional systems using dynamic practices on natural resources, technology, and other sources of income, sometimes driven by cash crop business. Agroecology practices have increased in urban and peri-urban contexts with a potential promotion of food justice and the advancement of environmental sustainability.

Natural resources supporting agroecology practices based on knowledge and experimentation developed by small-scale farmers tend to be more effective at enhancing biodiversity, sustainability of soils and water, and climate change reduction. Small-scale owners and producers of urban agroecological land help break production, commercial, and business monopolies and transform the food system.

Certain urban agroecology practices are healthier and have more positive effects than others considering other factors such as regulations, management practices, population density, ecological sensitivity, potential risks, and so on. Ecological methods to reduce risks related to agrochemicals are the use of animal wastes management, proper use of wastewater, and irrigation practices. Urban agroecological growers adopt the same agroecological concepts that already accepted other movements for food justice and security, despite the risks associated with agroecological practices. Agroecological soil and land management practices can overcome identified constraints and enhance farm yields and contribute significantly to food security. For example, shade cover of coffee agroecosystems is directly related to the mitigation of variability in soil moisture and microclimate for the coffee crop.

The agroecological food movement needs new approaches to agricultural production aimed at solving the political confrontations to the economic system while scaling out the perpetuation of land speculation, corporate control, market practices that preclude poor consumers from accessing sustainable food goods, labor injustices, and so on. Urban food movements embrace agroecology as a base principle at international and local contexts but also at a grassroots non-profit by incorporating agroecological practices to address urban hunger.

Agroecology practices protect and maintain biodiversity and ecosystem services through processes, such as erosion control and pollination, soil organic matter, and water quality and quantity. Stakeholders propose to drive soil erosion control by increasing hedge density and the no-till option. Stakeholders wanting to control erosion may turn to no-till agroecological practices or increase the density of hedges. The agroecosystem intensive in permaculture requires management of water through a network of surface impoundments, contour ditches, berms, and basins (Holmgren, 2004; Lancaster & Marshall, 2008).

Any agricultural and agroecological system is a set of a belief system, knowledge, and normative framework, practices, and land use goals (Berkes et al., 2000; Norgaard, 1984). Agroecological practices by small producers can be scaled up to achieve optimal levels of quality compliance and meet the higher standards of production. Some of the agroecological practices include improving the biodiversity and ecosystem services, minimizing environmental impacts, and increasing the efficiency of input use in processes and products (Duru & Thérond, 2015).

Agroecology is a holistic approach that uses principles that can be applied globally to appropriate local practices based on specific economic, social, cultural, and environmental contexts. A holistic perspective of agroecology is practiced by Indigenous peoples. A holistic approach to agroecology can be treated in dimension to explain the potentials for a sense of living in harmony with other people and nature leading to human rights and the right of food. The agroecology practice is a whole-systems approach focused on agriculture and the development of local food systems based on traditional knowledge and practices and alternative agriculture experiences.

The closest proxy of agroecology is certified organic agricultural production. This fails to explain some dimensions of agroecological practices. Agroecology is characterized by the integration of crops and livestock of pasture-raised animals relying on organic inputs such as cattle and other ruminants using grazing practices as a form of agroecological practices. The urban collective agroecological gardens and orchards can be used as cultural and educative contexts with activities that provide elements to define theoretical principles, methods, and objectives connecting with practices. Agroecology education is an integral concept with different dimensions to foster sustainable and educative practices supported by theories and methods of natural and social knowledge framed by a complex understanding of complex socioecological systems.

Agroecology practices have scaled up extensive benefits, such as crop rotation, intercropping, organic fertilizers and composting, biological controls, and more, and promoting new techniques, making them more accessible and affordable. Agroecological practices improve the agro-system sustainability based on ecosystem services and biodiversity conservation. Agroecological practices influence the flows of the ecosystem services, which have an impact on productivity (Dale & Polasky, 2007; Duru & Thérond, 2015). The influence of agroecological practices at existing farm scale on the ecosystem services are critically needed (Porter et al., 2009; Sandhu et al., 2010) to develop a holistic approach of the socioecological components of agroecological systems.

Urban agroecological practices foster ecosystem services at the urban landscape. Urban space landscape supporting urban agroecology practices favor patterns of urban economic sustainable development. Small-intensive urban agroecological crops and farming may be practiced in land and housing states, public spaces, schoolyard greenhouses, rooftop gardens and beehives, restaurant-supported salad gardens, allotments, balcony and windowsill vegetable growing, guerrilla gardening, and other initiatives (Hou et al., 2009; Mougeot, 2005; Nordahl, 2009; Redwood, 2008).

The concept of agroecology designates future farming systems in science and practice strongly connected to the principle of the right to adequate and healthy food achieved when every human being has physical and economic access or means for procurement. Urban small-scale agroecological farm practices, in their own or leased land, more than a business should meet the ecological principles to realize the long-term benefits. Agroecology contributes to urban economic development and sustainable development because it is most effectively practiced in small urban plots of land, and it is also more labor intensive. Agroecological production methods and practices are facilitated by the labor of local and migrant farm workers.

Ecological principles integrated into agroecological practices increase healthy food production and ecosystem services (Garbach et al., 2017; Ponisio et al., 2014; Seufert et al., 2012). Agroecological practices are based on principles of sustainability that result from the transition away from unsustainable agricultural practices depending on the ecological system and the local conditions (Altieri & Nicolls, 2005; Reijntjes et al., 1992). Agroecological practices have to be implemented to reduce leaching of nutrients and pesticides to the groundwater or surface water and to control contamination. The evolving agroecological principles have to be revised in practice, which eventually leads to updating and building a practical guide as the basis for a dialogue on what agroecology means and its practices within the different stakeholders involved in the agroecology movement.

Agroecology addresses economic, environmental, and social dimensions with new conceptual frameworks and operational tools to be used in sustainable land use planning and policy making decisions, which can be used in agroecological contexts (Zhang et al., 2007; Power, 2010; Duru & Thérond, 2015;

Landis, 2017, etc.) and practices (Barral et al., 2015; Rapidel et al., 2015; Sandhu et al., 2010). Agroecological policy in some regulatory frameworks is shortsighted to integrate science, practices, and movements without recognizing its transformative potential. Policies and regulations are implemented to force the stakeholders to change agroecological practices toward an agroecological transition and conservation of natural resources and agro-biodiversity.

Urban agroecology is related to urban land use planning integrated into urban sustainable development to regulate and stimulate economic growth, social equity and inclusion, and ecological and environmental sustainability. Testing of soil and water quality where contamination and pollution occur in urban agroecological plots and aquaculture is a practice to continue the viability subject to the city planning abilities to develop strategies for effective monitoring and treatment to separate toxic wastes from sewages.

Agroecological extension and nongovernmental organizations may introduce ecological space-intensive and risk-reducing practices, water- and energy-saving technologies, development and assessment technology processes, and more. Agroecological research has developed considerable technologies, inputs, and practices, such as organic improvement of seeds, optimal use of water, and planting density, which are helping the small farmers increase production and reduce the negative effects of industrial agriculture. Some debates surrounding agroecological research based on policy and practice concerns with provision of ecosystem services or yield maximization, conventional or organic production, and intensification or intensification.

Agroecological scientific research in urban contexts may focus on productivity of agroecological practices and environmental services. Research projects focusing on transformative agroecological practices and sustainable agriculture are a low proportion of all agricultural research funding, which provide an insight of the research priorities. Urban agroecology research and extension institutions together with and to small-scale urban farmers have to develop and disseminate technologies and agroecological methods of food production that do not harm the environment, such as water saving, irrigation systems, cultivars, and production practices.

Government policy framework for small farming should encourage agroecological practices more than industrial agriculture systems through an incentive structure. Agroecological practices are adapted by local stakeholders to be involved, engaged, and embedded in agroecological socio-technical networks and regimes (Geels, 2004). A multistakeholder planning approach is applied to policy design and programming to integrate urban land uses planning to develop multifunctional sustainable urban agroecology. Urban agroecological producers are informally organized, and their power and voices are weak with poor participation in urban policymaking and planning in development plans and programs.

Environmental services require different agroecological management scenarios and trajectories to design change strategies and trace the outcomes of landscape evolution. Agroecological management in urban and peri-urban areas should be linked to local authorities with projects aimed and protecting the landscape. A concentric model of land use planning is the zones of use intended to determine the distances and the required management to maximize agroecological labor productivity (Bane, 2012; Bell, 2005; Hemenway, 2009; Holmgren, 2004; Mars, 2005; Mollison, 1988; Mollison & Holmgren, 1978).

Vacant land in open spaces is a critical asset for urban agroecology, its availability, suitability and accessibility for urban producers through the demarcation of urban areas of land use, protecting urban green areas, creating buffer zones between areas of land use conflicts, and so on. Urban vacant land in urban areas can be inventoried using a geographic information system or community mapping to analyze suitability to be used for agroecology and stimulate the landowners to give longer lease land terms to local producers. This stimulus can be tax reductions, creating allotment gardens, and so forth.

Human geography takes into consideration landscape planning of urban agroecology supported by cultural studies to sustainable and healthy urban agroecology. Urban agroecology remains a marginal field of human geography beyond sustainability, food, and health issues.

Keyline planning is an innovative design applied to agricultural landscapes and adopted into the developing permaculture framework (Mulligan & Hill, 2001, p. 202; Mollison & Holmgren, 1978; Mollison, 1979). The keyline system of landscape planning, the biochar, the aerobic compost tea, and the herb spiral are alternative agroecological techniques adopted by permaculture practices (Avis, 2012; Mollison, 1988; Mollison & Holmgren, 1978; Soleil, 2012; Yeomans, 1954).

Despite the relevance of urban farming and gardening for provisioning of food to urban populations, local landscape diversity, and land use features of agro-ecosystems are very vulnerable to natural predatory practices and pests that require biological control services.

4 Agroecological territorial transformation and transition

Agroecology is a radical transformation of agriculture guided by ecological change and promoted with economic, social, political, and cultural changes. The geographical-spatial urban and peri-urban territoriality is an essential component of urban agroecology taking into consideration the development pressures of these spaces experiencing conflicts of land use that leads to new synergies (Wästfelt & Zhang, 2016; Fanfani, 2006 in Fanfani, 2013). An agroecology territory is defined as the place engaged in a transition process toward sustainable agroecological food systems.

Agroecology has a transformative vision cocreated by social movements and demonstrated in platforms and mechanisms. A new ecosystem-based paradigm is emerging for territorial food system complementing the global food supply chains aimed at creating a sustainable food system, improving its local management, and providing food security (FAO, 2011). The food shed as a strategy is a broad definition of local food, the geographical and territorial area in which the urban conglomerate is located and loosely delineating the boundaries from where the food can be sourced (Thompson Jr. et al., 2008, 4). Agroecology links together theoretical and practical approaches to transform local food systems into environmental sustainability, human health, and wellbeing.

Food system transformation takes place in an economic and cultural context able to support transitions to more sustainable practices of development. Traditional and local agroecological knowledge and practice of farmers converge with technological applications contested by social movements supported by principles of participation, equity, and justice and create a process of transformation toward sustainable food systems. Transformation of food systems based on agroecology mitigate climate change. Agroecological social movements have in common a commitment to economic and social transformation by different discursive and practice processes to develop alternative food systems framed as political agroecology.

A critical geography of urban agroecology has started to explain that the contemporary urban forms are connected to the spheres of land tenure regimes, such as land privatization, commons, rural-to-urban migrations (Bradley, 2009; Fairlie, 2009), the transformations of local agroecological systems, the provision and commodification of urban food, and the development planning systems of urban living spaces and environments (Van der Schans & Wiskerke, 2012). Changes of thinking and action in the global food system has a high impact on agroecology providing farm-driven change processes building on the transformation nature of human development, ethical systems, and culture.

A more holistic territorial food system may support healthy livelihoods, wellbeing, and environmental sustainability. Agroecology as a driver in a local-scale territory interconnects relationships of stakeholders (Sebillotte, 2000) toward a transition to sustainable agroecological food systems. A local regime transformation in agroecology can be supported by participatory action research approaches constructed between society, policy, and science to facilitate the transition through inclusive, integrative ecosystem services assessments.

Agroecology is seen as a resistance to an economic model of food system in forms of the green revolution and bioeconomics to transform and repair food system materials devastated by industrial food production. Mainstream agroecology is being coopted by the industrial food system to justify the environmental discourse linked to social transformation through the use of terms, such as sustainable, climate-smart agriculture, and ecological intensification.

Transnational corporate agribusiness and institutions are consolidating unprecedented power in food production, distribution, and marketing, which represent a threat to small food producers, agribusiness, food social movements, and consumers. Agroecology may transform inequitable power and dynamics in the agro-food system. Climate-smart agroecology address the challenges of adaptation, mitigation, and food security through policy tools to facilitate transformative transitions supported by science-based practices.

Incentives to support and protect agroecological practices require a strategy for building policy to transform the existing industrial agricultural model of production and develop institutional capacities involving private, public, academic, and social sectors. Gliessman (2015a, 2015b) propose a framework for food system change based on five levels. The first three levels are aimed at transforming the industrial and conventional agroecosystems and the following two levels to deepen a broader food system.

The task of agroecological transition requires the integration of different sectors in a research program based on rigorous analysis or permaculture theory and practice aimed at designing agro-systems. Agroecological transition requires a context to make meaningful practices using new knowledge and techniques (Sanford, 2011).

A territorial agroecological transition requires the implementation of agroecological practices aimed at integrating ecosystem services to the landscape scales favored by exchanges of knowledge, extension services delivered, sharing of resources, inputs, machinery, technology, and incentive provisions. Agroecological practices derived from a wide range of methodological and subject approaches. The action research methodology identifies agroecological stakeholders' actions in an agroecological territory scale as the relevant space for action (Dalgaard et al., 2003).

Agroecology is a science embedded with practice to struggle for food sovereignty. Agroecology is at a crossroads in the global struggle for food sovereignty strengthened by food providers and social movements that require a transformation of practice, policy, and research. Agroecology is politically focused to transform control structures of power in society, such as the global markets for self-governance by communities. Urban food strategies have a common element in the governance context of the food system transformation as the stake that cities have to produce food in connection with the urban environment (Unger & Wooten, 2006, 11). Development of sustainable agroecology requires structural changes, technological innovation, institutional transformations and regulations, farmer-to-farmer and to consumer networks, and so forth.

The collapse of the Soviet Union in 1991 brought an immediate decline in Cuban agricultural production, forcing small farmers to transform practices. Cuba had to design and implement a model of agricultural development not using heavy machinery and chemical fertilizers, technicians' and farmers' shared experiences, or expertise and innovative practices supported by networks and organizations to achieve an increase in food production. Cuban agriculture, which was highly dependent on Soviet Union input, faced a challenge in providing food security when suddenly confronted with reduction by responding to alternative agroecological technologies to sustain productivity (Rosset, 1997a, 1997b).

Organizations and individual farmers involved on the food sovereignty approach have adopted agroecological practices. The adoption of agroecology by institutions is considered and treated as a technical matter more than the transformative economic and political change of the system, easily coopted, such as has happened with organic agriculture and sustainable development.

Urban ecology requires practical and political engagement for social transformation. Urban agroecology linked to food sovereignty projects are material, political, and cultural engagements, dialogue and action in the context of political and practical social transformation. In the struggles for food sovereignty, engaged actors together have to remake meaning in a common political project of urban ecology across the different levels, scales, and places for social transformation. Agroecology provides a radical space for social and ecological transformation. Local-level initiatives engaged in urban agroecology are connected to transformative political thinking and action. When this connection is weak, the transformative potential of urban agroecology is weak and marginal.

Territories, collective rights, and access to the commons are fundamental pillars of agroecology. Urban sprawl, widespread urbanization, and urban decentralization are some factors that have contributed to territory break-up, fragmenting the city into networks, eroding the natural and agroecological spaces, and enlarging the urban footprint.

Addressing agro-environmental issues through innovative approaches at different territorial scales provides potential integration of agroecological principles into policy. Designing agroecological transitions should be based on shared concepts from various knowledge sources and learning supported by participatory implementation and coconstructed feedback and assessment processes aimed at building a territorial perspective.

An agroecological transition to complex and sustainable agroecosystems is required to achieve the transformation of conventional farming systems (Gliessman, 2009) based on practices that connects the social and ecological environment. Transformation of agroecosystems imply collective engagements in ecosystem services assessments from a more holistic perspective (Mills, 2012).

The territorial agroecological transition results in stakeholder and individual decisions and actions that integrate landscape environmental protection. The expectations of the stakeholders regarding the agroecology management of the territory to steer the agroecological transition implies the tradeoffs among the ecosystem services. Stakeholder agroecological actions have to be well-organized in agroecology territories using participative and transdisciplinary action-oriented methodology (Méndez et al., 2013).

To assure transition, improving the territorial agroecological biodiversity and natural resource management are supported on the initiatives from the cooperation between stakeholders and local authorities in charge, nongovernmental organizations, nature conservation organizations, and more. The stakeholders' community combines decisions and actions to adapt agricultural practices, biodiversity, natural resources conservation, and embedded food systems in an agroecology territory.

Community-supported agroecology is involved in transformative actions of producers and other stakeholders toward sharing common values and building bridges in forging a new global food economy and strong local food sovereignty movement. Development of sustainable agroecological food systems at local territorial scales is an alternative to feed the growing world population, considering quantitative production, environmental, economic, and social issues.

The geographical-spatial urban and peri-urban territoriality is an essential component of urban agroecology taking into consideration the development pressures of these spaces experiencing conflicts of land uses that leads to new synergies (Wästfelt & Zhang, 2016; Fanfani, 2006 in Fanfani, 2013). Changing from natural agroecological landscape into urban agroecological landscape in a spatial-temporal dominated with artificial spatial structures is related to an evolutional transformation that has created landscape fragmentations and ecological declination. Spatial analysis of land use is applied for urban agroecology as a component of multifunctional urban green infrastructures. Urban land use transformations are related with the processes of economic diversification and proportionally increasing around alternative agricultural and agroecological land.

Natural resources and improvement of biodiversity conservation and management at landscape scale is a relevant issue in the transition process to agroecology territories. Applying agroecological practices enhance resources conservation and biodiversity based on the specialization and diversification of agroecological farming systems. Conservation of natural resources and biodiversity in crops, livestock, soil, and land are the basis for an ecosystem services in established agroecological territories.

Crop diversification techniques and practices, along irrigation technology systems, aim to strengthen agroecology-based productive systems. Agroecology promotes diversification of crop production and use of biodiversity, farming practices and methods, preservation and efficient use of natural resources, minimum employment of artificial and chemical inputs, and so on. Agroecology is innovative, knowledge-intensive science and practices converging from agronomy and ecology, organized and participative. Agroecology is knowledge-intensive and requires investment in knowledge creation, dissemination, and sharing trough networks as a know-how practice between farmers.

An agroecology territory exists in a transition toward sustainable agroecological practices and where biodiversity and resource conservation is linked to territory with an embedded food system supported by stakeholders. The stakeholders in an agroecological territory are responsible for adapting the agroecological practices, conservation of natural resources, and biodiversity for the transition toward an agroecological food system. The land-sharing model is based on agroecology and biodiversity conservation on the same territory (Perfecto & Vandermeer, 2010; Vandermeer & Perfecto, 2007).

Agroecology territories establish natural landscape elements to serve as ecological corridors in and around cities to fulfill ecological functions and services while they also have a relevant function for producers of food and to protect against soil erosion, reduction of nutrients, and biological agroecological conservation control. Urban landscape performance can be improved by integrating design principles of urban agroecology and urban forestry.

All the stakeholders involved in urban agroecology may collaborate to create an inventory of all land uses that can be dedicated to urban agroecology and map urban agroecology initiatives to identify the areas in a database. Technical and social dimensions of agroecology require political struggles to be transformed. In any transition toward agroecology territories, the scale of embedded food systems are socio-technical networks to facilitate the links and interactions between stakeholders, natural resources, and artifacts, encompassing the landscapes scales, such as the terroir products, geographical labels, and more. The resilient system is diverse at multiple scales where the elements have different but complementary roles in the agroecological landscape contributing to diverse ecosystem services and ecological functions provided to society at large.

Urban agroforestry cultivates perennial woody fruit- and nut-producing species and provides food while offering environmental, cultural, and recreational services in urban landscapes (Nordahl, 2009). The net benefit of agroforestry practices is higher to nonfertilized production and yields higher returns in areas where infrastructure is poor (Ajayi, 1987). Urban agroforestry ecology remains separate in their science and practice without integrated ecological multifunctional concepts to improve urban landscape sustainability for urban food forestry. Urban agroforestry, the cultivation of perennial woody plants and crop or animal farming serving multiple purposes, such as food security and the alleviation poverty (Garrity, 2004), has been rarely practiced in cities (Lelle & Gold, 1994; Sachez, 1995; Smith, 1929a, 1929b) to provide ecosystem services, soil regeneration, and biodiversity habitats (Belsky, 1993; Blanco & Lal, 2010; Kumar, 2006; Nair, 1993).

Integrating scientific principles from agroecology and urban agroforestry into urban forestry may improve nutrition and health. Urban food forestry is defined as the strategic use of woody perennial food-producing species in urban landscapes to improve the sustainability and resilience of urban communities (Clark & Nicholas, 2013). Urban food agroforestry integrates ecosystem services into landscapes through the strategic use of multifunctional species that embody services of urban forestry and urban agroecology, including biodiversity habitat, climate regulation, oxygen production, air and water quality, erosion control (Konijnendijk, 2003; Nowak, 2006; Nowak & Dwyer, 2007), community involvement and social capital, food security, public health, and microenterprising opportunities (Brown & Jameton, 2000; FAO/WB, 2008; Dubbeling et al., 2009; Lovell, 2010; De Zeeuw et al., 2011). Food agroforestry planting in mutistory designs consider the plant heights (Crawford, 2010; Jacke & Toensmeier, 2005).

Agroecology principles are related to the permaculture principles that have corollaries articulated at high abstract level (Holmgren, 2004; Mollison, 1988; Mollison & Slay, 1997). Extrapolation from ecological knowledge and principles, current land use may be replaced with permaculture systems in any context (Mollison & Slay, 1997, p. 1). Access to public and community land use for local agroecology to produce sustainable food in urban and peri-urban areas and promote integration with urban development planning and policymaking. Policy on urban agroecology based on different scenarios are a specific mix of the perspectives and give emphasis according to the locations, actors, and populations in the different territories.

Permaculture is defined as "consciously designed landscapes which mimic the patterns and relationships found in nature, while yielding an abundance of food, fiber and energy for provision of local needs" (Holmgren, 2004, p. xix). Permaculture is the harmonious integration of landscape and people providing their food, energy, shelter, and other material and nonmaterial needs in a sustainable way (Mollison, 1988). Permaculture contributes to agroecological transition design and practice enhanced by exchanging knowledge with related disciplines, such as agroecology, ecological engineering, agroforestry, and more.

Permaculture is a conscious design and maintenance of agroecological productive ecosystems maintaining the diversity, stability, and resilience of natural ecosystems. The agroecological social movements connected to current practices of the science of agroecology and its role in research have policy landscape on the agenda. Agroecology and permaculture design and practice overlap in the agroecological transition and calls for collaborative research to assess the impacts in sites and field trials through comparative analysis of agroecosystems.

Ecosystem services valuation may lead to sustainable agroecological landscapes by improving the quality of the environment and reducing inequalities. Permaculture is an international movement that refers to a design system and a set of associated practices. Permaculture's movement is a conceptual framework for integrating knowledge and practice to design the agroecological system transition supported by collaboration between the different stakeholders involved with land users and researchers.

Permaculture is movement that disseminates and practices a design system framework adapted for the application (Guitart et al., 2012; Wezel & Soldat, 2009). Permaculture contributions incorporate the principles of agroecologist frameworks for the agro-system design of the transition project toward an agroecosystem configuration. Agroecosystem design oriented by permaculture practices is based on site specificity and spatial configurations of microclimate and interactive components from field-scale polycultures and multiple functions to agroecosystem-scale land use diversity. Permaculture practices are adopted, traditional agroecological systems, tropical home gardens, and food forests (Mollison & Holmgren, 1978).

Permaculture is an active movement in food sovereignty that has the potential to provide solutions to the complexity of food systems by involving residents in suburban landscapes with access to soil with nutrients, water, and sunlight and by making efficient use of urban infrastructure and energy to grow vegetables, fruit, and livestock.

Food sovereignty in local communities provides political linkages between regional and local authorities, and farmers aim to redesign the food system, secure land tenure, provide water access, detoxify from use of chemicals in agroecological food production, and meet the demands for healthy food.

Land use diversity in the permaculture scientific literature includes integrated terrestrial and aquatic systems, perennial and annual plant and animal production, and synergistic benefits (Bane, 2012; Berg, 2002; Dalsgaard & Oficial, 1997; Devendra & Thomas, 2002; Dey et al., 2010; Frei & Becker, 2005; Gomiero et al., 1999; Jamu & Piedrahita, 2002; Kadir Alsagoff et al., 1990; Mollison, 1988; Mollison & Holmgren, 1978; Pant et al., 2005; Rukera & Mutanga, 2012; Talpaz & Tsur, 1982).

Changes in the design of food system process may guide the policies and strategies for the transformation of a sustainable environment based on agroecology. Urban food strategies and policies aimed to interrelate the food chain and the food cycle and develop synergies and transformative innovations between food producers and consumers and between urban and rural areas, focusing on a systemic approach of spatial, socioeconomic, and ecological perspectives (Lang & Barling, 2012, 318; Sonnino, 2009; Viljoen & Wiskerke, 2012; Marsden & Sonnino, 2012).

5 Conclusion

Urban agroecology projects must be articulated in the food sovereignty and sustainable food system movements for social transformation reached through innovative practices but organized through shifts of power relationships for economic, social, political, cultural, and institutional change. Agroecology must transform rather than conform to the industrial food system supported by agro-businesses and institutions. Generation and transfer of agroecological knowledge and practices must be facilitated by government institutions, nonprofits, and grassroots organizations.

The transition toward agroecology territory practices must take into consideration the territorial conservation of natural resources and biodiversity and the development of a food system. An integrated land use planning and management collaboration for urban agroecological practices between local and city governments must apply a holistic and ecosystem approach on natural resources and landscape features. Participative management is a strategy to accomplish transformation of the local food system. The stakeholders involved in the agroecological transition must have a shared knowledge and understanding of a multilevel system framework to make decisions on the biophysical-economic-socio-environmental implications embedded in the social valuation. Transition to agroecology sustainable systems should be designed for biodiversity, resilience, and autonomy of local stakeholders and actors with disparate interests, expectations, and values but integrated under the ecosystem services valuation aimed to develop shared knowledge for a concerted action.

Local-based agroecological practices must take into account the stakeholder's capacity considering the global regulations and forces to undertake local changes at specific agroecology territories (Pimbert et al., 2001). Plot agroecology practice must not be contentious in nature to be practiced within institutional frameworks governing and regulating farming activities and access to available and vacant land and water, framed by conflict resolution and interaction among the stakeholders.

Urban agroecological transformation requires public awareness of how it can benefit cities, even though agro-food production practices have been present. Integrated ecosystem services valuations monitor the agroecological transition, although the policy and governance can be targeted in issues such as the equity in a context of power imbalances.

References

Ajayi, M. T. (1987). Effects of spacing/number of plants per stand and fertilizer placement on performance of two maize varieties intercropped with cowpea in the forest zone of Nigeria. *Ghana Journal of Agricultural Science, 20*, 39–46.

Altieri, M. A. (1989). Agroecology: A new research and development paradigm for world agriculture. *Agriculture, Ecosystems and Environment, 27*(1–4), 37–46. https://doi.org/10.1016/B978-0-444-88610-1.50006-1.

Altieri, M. A., & Nicolls, C. (2005). *Agroecology and the search for a truly sustainable agriculture.* Mexico City: UNEP. www.agroeco.org/doc/agroecology-engl-PNUMA.pdf. (Accessed 15 July 2015).

Avis, R. (2012). Compost teas and extracts: brewin' and bubblin' basics. In *Permaculture research institute – Permaculture forums, courses, information.* http://permaculturenews.org/2012/07/11/compost-teas-and-extracts-brewin-and-bubblin-basics/. (Accessed 28 May 2013).

Bane, P. (2012). *The permaculture handbook: Garden farming for town and country.* New York: New Society.

Barral, M. P., Rey Benayas, J. M., Meli, P., & Maceira, N. O. (2015). Quantifying the impacts of ecological restoration on biodiversity and ecosystem services in agroecosystems: A global meta-analysis. *Agriculture, Ecosystems and Environment, 202*, 223–231. https://doi.org/10.1016/j.agee.2015.01.009.

Bell, G. (2005). *The permaculture garden.* White River Junction: Chelsea Green.

Belsky, J. M. (1993). Household food security, farm trees, and agroforestry: A comparative study in Indonesia and the Philippines. *Human Organization, 52*(2), 130–141.

Berg, H. (2002). Rice monoculture and integrated rice-fish farming in the Mekong Delta, Vietnam—Economic and ecological considerations. *Ecological Economics, 41*, 95–107. https://doi.org/10.1016/S0921-8009(02)00027-7.

Berkes, F., Colding, J., & Folke, C. (2000). Rediscovery of traditional ecological knowledge as adaptive management. *Ecological Applications, 10*, 1251–1262. https://doi.org/10.1890/1051-0761(2000)010[1251:ROTEKA]2.0.CO;2.

Boogaard, B. K., Bock, B. B., Oosting, S. J., Wiskerke, J. S. C., & Zijpp, A. J. (2010). Social acceptance of dairy farming: The ambivalence between the two faces of modernity. *Journal of Agricultural and Environmental Ethics, 24*(3), 259–282.

Blanco, H., & Lal, R. (2010). *Principles of soil conservation and management* (pp. 261–263).

Bradley, M. (2009). *Down with the fences: Battles for the commons in South London*. The Land.

Brown, K. H., & Jameton, A. L. (2000). Public health implications of urban agriculture. *Journal of Public Health Policy, 21*(1), 20–39.

Clark, K. H., & Nicholas, K. A. (2013). Introducing urban food forestry: A multifunctional approach to increase food security and provide ecosystem services. *Landscape Ecology, 28*, 1649. https://doi.org/10.1007/s10980-013-9903-z.

Cohn, A., Cook, J., Fernandez, M., Reider, R., & Steward, C. (2006). *Agroecology and the struggle for food sovereignty in the Americas*. International Institute for Environment and Development (IIED), the Yale School of Forestry and the Environmental Studies (Yale F&ES) and the IUCN Commission on Environmental, Economic and Social Policy (CEESP).

Crawford, M. (2010). *Creating a forest garden: Working with nature to grow edible crops*. UK: Green Books.

Dale, V. H., & Polasky, S. (2007). Measures of the effects of agricultural practices on ecosystem services. *Ecological Economics, 64*(2), 286–296. https://doi.org/10.1016/j. ecolecon.2007.05.009.

Dalgaard, T., Hutchings, N. J., & Porter, J. R. (2003). Agro ecology, scaling and interdisciplinarity. *Agriculture, Ecosystems and Environment, 100*(1), 39–51. https://doi.org/10.1016/S0167-8809 (03)00152-X.

Dalsgaard, J. P. T., & Oficial, R. T. (1997). A quantitative approach for assessing the productive performance and ecological contributions of smallholder farms. *Agricultural Systems, 55*, 503–533. https://doi.org/10.1016/S0308-521X(97)00022-X.

Devendra, D., & Thomas, T. (2002). Crop–animal interactions in mixed farming systems in Asia. *Agricultural Systems, 71*, 27–40. https://doi.org/10.1016/S0308-521X(01)00034-8.

De Zeeuw, H., Van Veenhuizen, R., & Dubbeling, M. (2011). The role of urban agriculture in building resilient cities in developing countries. *The Journal of Agricultural Science, 149*, 153–163.

Dey, M. M., Paraguas, F. J., Kambewa, P., & Pemsl, D. E. (2010). The impact of integrated aquaculture–agriculture on small-scale farms in SouthernMalawi. *Agricultural Economics, 41*, 67–79. https://doi.org/10.1111/j.1574-0862.2009.00426.x.

Duru, M., & Thérond, O. (2015). Designing agroecological transitions: A review. *Agronomy for Sustainable Development, 35*(4), 1237–1257. https://doi.org/10.1007/s13593-015-0318-x.

Duží, B., Tóth, A., Bihuňová, M., & Stojanov, R. (2014). Challenges of urban agriculture. Highlights on Czech and Slovak experience. In J. Vávra, M. Lapka, & E. Cudlínová (Eds.), *Current challenges of Central Europe: Society and environment* (pp. 82–107). Prague: Charles University.

Dubbeling, M., Campbell, M. C., Hoekstra, F., & van Veenhuizen, R. (2009). Building resilient cities. *Urban Agriculture Magazine, 22*, 3–11.

Fairlie, S. (2009). A short history of enclosure in Britain. *The Land, 7*, 16–31.

Fanfani, D. (2013). Local development and "Agri-urban" domain: Agricultural Park as promotion of an "active Ruralship". *Planum. The Journal of Urbanism, 27*(2), 38–47.

Fanfani, D. (2006). Il governo del territorio e del paesagio rurale nello spazio "terzo" periurbano. Il parco agricolo come strumento di politiche e di progetto. In *Ri-Vista Ricerche per la progettazione del paessagio, Semestrale on line del Dotorato di Ricerca in progettazione pae-sística* DUPT, Facolta di Architettura di Firenze. N. 6 Lugio-Dicembre.

FAO. (2011). *Food, agro ecology and cities: Challenges of food and nutrition security, agro ecology and ecosystem management in an urbanizing world.* http://www.fao.org/fileadmin/templates/FCIT/PDF/FoodAgriCities_Oct2011.pdf. (Accessed March 2012).

FAO. (2007). *Profitability and sustainability of urban and peri-urban agriculture.* FAO: Rome.

FAO/WB. (2008). *Urban agriculture for sustainable poverty alleviation and food security.* Rome: Food and Agriculture Organization of the United Nations. http://www.fao.org/fileadmin/templates/FCIT/PDF/UPA_-WBpaper-Final_October_2008.pdf. (Accessed December 2012).

Frei, M., & Becker, K. (2005). Integrated rice-fish culture: Coupled production saves resources. *Natural Resources Forum, 29*, 135–143. https://doi.org/10.1111/j.1477-8947.2005.00122.x.

Garbach, K., Milder, J., DeClerck, F., de Wit, M. M., Driscoll, L., & Gemmill-Herren, B. (2017). Examining multifunctionality for crop yield and ecosystem services in five systems of agroecological intensification. *International Journal of Agricultural Sustainability, 15*(1), 11–28. https://doi.org/10.1080/14735903.2016.1174810.

Garrity, D. P. (2004). Agroforestry and the achievement of the millennium development goals. *Agroforestry Systems, 61*, 5–17.

Geels, F. (2004). From sectoral systems of innovation to socio-technical systems. Insights about dynamics and change from sociology and institutional theory. *Research Policy, 33*(6–7), 897–920. https://doi.org/10.1016/j.respol.2004.01.015.

Gliessman, S. R. (2015a). *Agroecology: The ecology of sustainable food systems* (3rd ed.). Boca Raton, FL: CRC Press/Taylor and Francis Group.

Gliessman, S. R. (2015b). Agroecology: A growing field. *Agroecology and Sustainable Food Systems, 39*, 1–2. https://doi.org/10.1080/21683565.2014.965869.

Gliessman, S. R. (2009). The framework for conversion. In S. R. Gliessman, & M. Rosemeyer (Eds.), *The conversion to sustainable agriculture: Principles, processes, and practices* (pp. 3–16). Boca Raton, Florida, USA: CRC Press. https://doi.org/10.1201/9781420003598-c1.

Gomiero, T., Giampietro, M., Bukkens, S. G., & Paoletti, M. G. (1999). Environmental and socio-economic constraints to the development of freshwater fish aquaculture in China. *Critical Reviews in Plant Sciences, 18*, 359–371.

Guitart, D., Pickering, C., & Byrne, J. (2012). Past results and future directions in urban community gardens research. *Urban Forestry & Urban Greening, 11*, 364–373. https://doi.org/10.1016/j.ufug.2012.06.007.

Hart, A. K., McMichael, P., Milder, J. C., & Scherr, S. J. (2015). Multi-functional landscapes from the grassroots? The role of rural producer movements. *Agriculture and Human Values, 33*, 305–322. https://doi.org/10.1007/s10460-015-9611-1.

Hemenway, T. (2009). *Gaia's garden: A guide to home-scale permaculture* (2nd ed.). White River Junction: Chelsea Green.

Hiroki, S., Garnevska, E., & Mclaren, S. (2016). Consumer perceptions about local food in New Zealand, and the role of life cycle-based environmental sustainability. *Journal of Agricultural and Environmental Ethics, 29*(3), 479–505.

Holloway, L., Kneafsey, M., Venn, L., Cox, R., Dowler, E., & Tuomainen, H. (2007). Possible food economies: A methodological framework for exploring food production–consumption relationships. *Sociologia Ruralis, 47*(1), 1–19.

Holmgren, D. (2004). *Permaculture: Principles and pathways beyond sustainability.* Hepburn: Holmgren Design.

Hou, J., Johnson, J. M., & Lawson, L. J. (2009). *Greening cities, growing communities: Learning from Seattle's urban community gardens.* Seattle, WA: University of Washington Press.

Hvitsand, C. (2016). Community supported agriculture (CSA) as a transformational act-distinct values and multiple motivations among farmers and consumers. *Agroecology and Sustainable Food Systems, 40*(4), 333–351.

Jacke, D., & Toensmeier, E. (2005). *Edible forest gardens: Ecological design and practice for temperate climate permaculture. Vol. 2.* Vermont: Chelsea Green Publishing Company.

Jamu, D. M., & Piedrahita, R. H. (2002). An organic matter and nitrogen dynamics model for the ecological analysis of integrated aquaculture/agriculture systems: II. Model evaluation and application. *Environmental Modelling & Software, 17,* 583–592. https://doi.org/10.1016/S1364-8152(02)00017-8.

Kadir Alsagoff, S. A., Clonts, H. A., & Jolly, C. M. (1990). An integrated poultry, multi-species aquaculture for Malaysian rice farmers: A mixed integer programming approach. *Agricultural Systems, 32,* 207–231. https://doi.org/10.1016/0308-521X(90)90002-8.

Kirwan, J., Ilbery, B., Naye, D., & Carey, J. (2013). Grassroots social innovations and food localization: An investigation of the local food programme in England. *Global Environmental Change, 23*(5), 830–837.

Kneafsey, M., Venn, L., Schmutz, U., Balázs, B., Trenchard, L., Eyden-wood, T., & Blackett, M. (2013). Short food supply chains and local food systems in the EU. A state of play of their socio-economic characteristics. In *JRC scientific and policy reports* Joint Research Centre Institute for Prospective Technological Studies, European Commission.

Konijnendijk, C. C. (2003). A decade of urban forestry in Europe. *Forest Policy and Economics, 5* (2), 173–186.

Kumar, B. M. (2006). Agroforestry: The new old paradigm for Asian food security. *Journal of Tropical Agriculture, 44,* 1–14.

Lancaster, B., & Marshall, J. (2008). *Water-harvesting earthworks.* Tucson: Rainsource.

Landis, D. A. (2017). Designing agricultural landscapes for biodiversity-based ecosystem services. *Basic and Applied Ecology, 18,* 1–12. https://doi.org/10.1016/j.baae.2016.07.005.

Lang, T., & Barling, D. (2012). Food security and food sustainability: Reformulating the debate. *The Geographical Journal, 178,* 4313–4326.

Lelle, M. A., & Gold, M. A. (1994). Agroforestry systems for temperate climates: Lessons from Roman Italy. *Forest & Conservation History, 38*(3), 118–126.

Lindemann-Matthies, P. R., Briegel, B., Schüpbach, B., & Junge, X. (2010). Aesthetic preference for a Swiss alpine landscape: The impact of different agricultural land-use with different biodiversity. *Landscape and Urban Planning, 98*(2), 99–109.

Lovell, S. (2010). Multifunctional urban agro ecology for sustainable land use planning in the United States. *Sustainability, 2*(8), 2499–2522. https://doi.org/10.3390/su2082499.

Mars, R. (2005). *The basics of permaculture design.* White River Junction: Chelsea Green.

Marsden, T., & Sonnino, R. (2012). Human health and wellbeing and the sustainability of urban-regional food systems. *Current Opinion in Environmental Sustainability, 4,* 427–430.

Maye, D. (2013). Moving alternative food networks beyond the niche. *International Journal of Sociology of Agriculture and Food, 20*(3), 383–389.

Méndez, V. E., Bacon, C. M., & Cohen, R. (2013). Agroecology as a transdisciplinary, participatory, and action-oriented approach. *Agroecology and Sustainable Food Systems, 37*(1), 3–18.

Mills, J. (2012). Exploring the social benefits of agri-environment schemes in England. *Journal of Rural Studies, 28*(4), 612–621. https://doi.org/10.1016/j.jrurstud.2012.08.001.

Mollison, B. (1988). *Permaculture: A designer's manual.* Tasmania: Tagari.

Mollison, B. (1979). *Permaculture: A designer's manual.* Tagari Publications.

Mollison, B., & Holmgren, D. (1978). *Permaculture one: A perennial agricultural system for human settlements.* Tyalgum: Tagari.

Mollison, B. C., & Slay, R. M. (1997). *Introduction to permaculture* (2nd ed.). Tasmania: Tagari.

Mougeot, L. J. A. (2006). *Growing better cities: Urban agriculture for sustainable development.* Ottawa: International Development Research Centre.

Mougeot, L. (Ed.). (2005). *Agropolis: The social, political and environmental dimensions of urban agriculture.* London: Earthscan.

Mulligan, M., & Hill, S. (2001). *Ecological pioneers: A social history of Australian ecological thought and action.* Cambridge: Cambridge University Press.

Mundler, P., & Laughrea, S. (2016). The contribution of short supply chains to territorial development: A study of three Quebec territories. *Journal of Rural Studies, 45*, 218–229.

Nair, P. K. R. (1993). *An introduction to agroforestry.* The Netherlands: Kluwer Academic Publishers.

Nordahl, D. (2009). *Public produce: The new urban agriculture.* Washington, DC: Island Press.

Norgaard, R. B. (1984). Traditional agricultural knowledge: Past performance, future prospects, and institutional implications. *American Journal of Agricultural Economics, 66*, 874–878. https://doi.org/10.2307/1241018.

Nowak, D. J. (2006). Institutionalizing urban forestry as a "biotechnology" to improve environmental quality. *Urban Forestry and Urban Greening, 5*, 93–100.

Nowak, D. J., & Dwyer, J. F. (2007). Benefits and costs of urban forest ecosystems. In J. E. Kuser (Ed.), *Urban and community forestry in the northeast* (pp. 25–46). Netherlands: Springer.

Pant, J., Demaine, H., & Edwards, P. (2005). Bio-resource flow in integrated agriculture–aquaculture systems in a tropical monsoonal climate: A case study in Northeast Thailand. *Agricultural Systems, 83*, 203–219. https://doi.org/10.1016/j.agsy.2004.04.001.

Perfecto, I., & Vandermeer, J. (2010). The agro ecological matrix as alternative to the land-sparing/agriculture intensification model. *Proceedings of the National Academy of Sciences, 107*(13)), 5786–5791. https://doi.org/10.1073/pnas.0905455107.

Pimbert, M. P., Thompson, J., Vorley, W. T., Fox, T., Kanji, N., & Tacoli, C. (2001). *Global restructuring, agri-food systems and livelihoods. Gatekeeper series 100.* London: International Institute for Environment and Development.

Ponisio, L., M'Gonigle, L. K., Mace, K. C., Palomino, J., de Valpine, P., & Kremen, C. (2014). Diversification practices reduce organic to conventional yield gap. *Proceedings of the Royal Society B, 282*, 20141396. https://doi.org/10.1098/rspb.2014.1396.

Porter, J., Costanza, R., Sandhu, H., Sigsgaard, L., & Wratten, S. (2009). The value of producing food, energy, and ecosystem services within an agroecosystem. *AMBIO: A Journal of the Human Environment, 38*(4), 186–193. https://doi.org/10.1579/0044-7447-38.4.186.

Power, A. G. (2010). Ecosystem services and agriculture: Tradeoffs and synergies. *Philosophical Transactions of the Royal Society of London B: Biological Sciences, 365*(1554), 2959–2971. https://doi.org/10.1098/rstb.2010.0143.

Rapidel, B., Ripoche, A., Allinne, C., Metay, A., Deheuvels, O., Lamanda, N., … Gary, C. (2015). Analysis of ecosystem services trade-offs to design agroecosystems with perennial crops. *Agronomy for Sustainable Development, 34*(4), 1373–1390. https://doi.org/10.1007/s13593-015-0317y.

Redwood, M. (2008). *Agriculture in urban planning: Generating livelihoods and food security.* London: Earthscan.

Reijntjes, C. B., Haverkort, B., & Waters-Bayer, A. (1992). *Farming for the future. An introduction to low-external input and sustainable agriculture.* London: Macmillian Press.

Renting, H., Marseden, T. K., & Banks, J. (2003). Understanding alternative food networks: Exploring the role of short food supply chains in rural development. *Environment and Planning A, 35*, 393–411.

Rosset, P. M. (1997a). Cuba: Ethics, biological control, and crisis. *Agriculture and Human Values*, *14*, 291–302.

Rosset, P. M. (1997b). Alternative agriculture and crisis in Cuba. *Technology and Society*, *16*(2), 19–25.

Rukera, S. T., Mutanga, O., & Micha, J.-C. (2012). Optimization of an integrated rabbit-fish-rice system for sustainable production in Rwanda. *Rwanda Journal*, *24*.

Sachez, P. A. (1995). Science in agroforestry. *Agroforestry Systems*, *30*, 5–55.

Sandhu, H. S., Wratten, S. D., & Cullen, R. (2010). Organic agriculture and ecosystem services. *Environmental Science and Policy*, *13*(1), 1–7. https://doi.org/10.1016/j.envsci.2009.11.002.

Sanford, A. W. (2011). Ethics, narrative, and agriculture: Transforming agricultural practice through ecological imagination. *Journal of Agricultural and Environmental Ethics*, *24*, 283–303. https://doi.org/10.1007/s10806-010-9246-6.

Sebillotte, M. (2000). Territoires: De l'espace physique au construit social. Les enjeux pourdemain et les apports de la recherche. *OCL Oléagineux Corps Gras Lipides*, *7*, 474–479. https://doi.org/10.1051/ocl.2000.0474.

Seufert, V., Ramankutty, N., & Foley, J. A. (2012). Comparing the yields of organic and conventional agriculture. *Nature*, *485*, 229–232. https://doi.org/10.1038/nature11069.

Simon Rojo, M., Moratalla, A. Z., Alonso, N. M., & Jimenez, V. H. (2014). Pathways towards the integration of peri-urban agrarian ecosystems into the spatial planning system. *Ecological Processes*, *3*(13), 16.

Smith, J. R. (1929a). *Tree crops: A permanent agriculture*. Rahway: Quinn and Boden Company, Inc.

Smith, J. R. (1929b). *Tree crops: A permanent agriculture*. New York: New York Brace & Co.

Soleil, S. (2012). The biochar miracle. In *Permaculture research institute - permaculture forums, courses, information, news*. http://permaculturenews.org/2012/02/03/the-biochar-miracle/. (Accessed 28 May 2013).

Sonnino, R. (2009). Feeding the city: Towards a new research and planning agenda. *International Planning Studies*, *14*, 425–435.

Talpaz, H., & Tsur, Y. (1982). Optimising aquaculture management of a single-species fish population. *Agricultural Systems*, *9*, 127–142. https://doi.org/10.1016/0308-521X(82)90027-0.

Thompson, E., Jr., Harper, A. M., & Kraus, S. (2008). *Think globally—Eat locally: San Francisco Foodshed Assessment, American Farmland Trust*. http://www.farmland.org/programs/states/ca/Feature%20Stories/San-Francisco-Foodshed-Report.asp. (Accessed 23 June 2009).

Unger, S., & Wooten, H. (2006). *A food systems assessment for Oakland, CA: Toward a sustainable food plan*. Oakland, CA: Mayor's Office of Sustainability.

Van der Schans, J. W., & Wiskerke, J. S. C. (2012). Urban agriculture in developed economies. In A. Viljoen, & W. JSC (Eds.), *Sustainable food planning: Evolving theory and practice* (pp. 245–258). Wageningen: Wageningen Academic Publishers.

Vandermeer, J., & Perfecto, I. (2007). The agricultural matrix and a future paradigm for conservation. *Conservation Biology*, *21*(1), 274–277. https://doi.org/10.1111/cbi.2007.21.issue-1.

Viljoen, A., & Wiskerke, J. S. C. (Eds.). (2012). *Sustainable food planning: Evolving theory and practice* (pp. 349–364). Wageningen: Wageningen Academic Publishers.

Wästfelt, A., & Zhang, Q. (2016). Reclaiming localization and revitalising agriculture: A case study of peri-urban agricultural change in Gotheburg, Sweden. *Journal of Rural Studies*, *47*, 172–185.

Wezel, A., Casagrande, M., Celette, F., Vian, J. V., Ferrer, A., & Peigné, A. (2014). Agroecological practices for sustainable agriculture. A review. *Agronomy for Sustainable Development*, *34*(1), 1–20. https://doi.org/10.1007/s13593-013-0180-7.

Wezel, A., Bellon, S., Doré, T., Francis, C., Vallod, D., & David, C. (2009). Agroecology as a science, a movement and a practice. A review. *Agronomy for Sustainable Development, 29*, 503–515. https://doi.org/10.1051/agro/2009004.

Wezel, A., & Soldat, V. (2009). A quantitative and qualitative historical analysis of the scientific discipline agroecology. *International Journal of Agricultural Sustainability, 7*(1), 3–18. https://doi.org/10.3763/ijas.2009.0400.

Yeomans, P. A. (1954). *The Keyline plan.* Sydney: PA Yeomans.

Zhang, W., Ricketts, T. H., Kremen, C., Carney, K., & Swinton, S. M. (2007). Ecosystem services and dis-services to agriculture. *Ecological Economics, 64*, 253–260. https://doi.org/10.1016/j.ecolecon.2007.02.024.

Chapter 9

Weednet: A deep neural net for weed identification

Shashi Prakash Tripathi, Rahul Kumar Yadav, and Harshita Rai
Analytics and Insights Unit, Tata Consultancy Services, Pune, Maharashtra, India

1 Introduction

Sustainable agriculture is an approach where the profits generated are measured both in terms of financial gain and the impact these processes have on our environment. The key being to maintain a balance between the two. With the adverse impact of the unsustainable agricultural practices on the global environment, it has become crucial that we move away from these practices to a more responsible approach where the agricultural sector as a whole looks beyond their immediate gain. The advancements in artificial intelligence has provided various methods that could help us in achieving them without a very high financial burden on farmers or the agriculture sector. The use of machines and robots to automate various agricultural processes has been going on for a while now; this, when combined with some intelligence on the part of the machine or robot, could help bridge the gap between productivity and cost.

One stream of artificial intelligence that has a lot of application in agricultural processes is computer vision, starting with soil preparation and profiling, to help perform various tasks like planting, weeding, harvesting, detecting plant health, and assessing the quality of the end product.

Targeted weed removal systems are capable of reducing labor cost while also potentially reducing herbicide usage with more efficient selective application to weed targets. Improving the efficacy of weed control would have enormous economic impact. The task of targeted weed removal has three parts: capturing the image of the weed in real time, identifying whether it is a weed or a crop, and removing the identified weeds. The part where computer vision can help in this complete process is the identification of the weed in its natural surroundings. Weed identification is a classification problem where the captured images of the plants are to be classified either as weed or crop.

The introduction of machines has increased agricultural productivity (Fernández-Quintanilla et al., 2018; Gonzalez-de-Santos et al., 2017). The main advantage of using machines for the weeding process is minimizing the use of weedicides and herbicides tremendously. The cost associated with manual labor required is also reduced. An efficient weeding process not only decreases the production cost but also has a huge impact on the economy. Billions of dollars are spent by farmers around the world for weed control. These expenses can be reduced by improving the use of machines in agriculture.

Autonomous weed control systems have four core technologies: detection and identification, mapping, guidance, and precision in-row weed control (Slaughter et al., 2008). The development of detection and identification technology is a major impediment in commercializing autonomous weed control systems (Shaner & Beckie, 2014; Slaughter et al., 2008). Primarily, methods based on different light spectrum representations are used for detection and identification. Photographs of weeds obtained from ground views and aerial views are used for detection and identifications using methods such as image-based (Bakhshipour & Jafari, 2018; Dyrmann et al., 2017; dos Santos Ferreira et al., 2017; Wu et al., 2007; Carranza-Rojas et al., 2017; Hall et al., 2015; Kalyoncu & Toygar, 2015; Kumar et al., 2012; Lee et al., 2017; Lee et al., 2015), spectrum-based (Li et al., 2017; Shirzadifar et al., 2018), and spectral image-based (Lin et al., 2017; Louargant et al., 2018). If high control is required for a certain environment, then spectral and spectrum-based methods are used. Whereas, image-based methods are easier to implement in a wide variety of environments, mostly when they are employed in a moving vehicle (Mahesh et al., 2015). And the implementation of image-based methods in real-time is much cheaper than the spectral and spectrum-based methods. That is why, in this work, an image-based technique is developed for automatic weed control.

Detecting a particular area of interest in an image is a popular problem in computer science(Olsen et al., 2015). And in this chapter, our area of interest is recognizing the weed plants among the crop plants. Leaf images of weed plants are used for solving this problem. Now the detection and identification problem can be solved using different leaf-classification methods that are based on deep learning models. Convolution neural networks (CNNs) (dos Santos Ferreira et al., 2017; LeCun et al., 2015; Lee et al., 2015; Lee et al., 2017) and their different versions are used for detection, identification, and classifications of weed plants. These deep learning models can efficiently and accurately detect and identify the species of weed from other plant species.

The quality of the dataset determines the accuracy and performance of the implemented model. Generally, leaf images of weed plants are taken in a standard environment with suitable lighting conditions and cognate vegetation. But in the proposed work, we have used images from a dataset that contains leaf images of weed species that are collected from a real-world environment that has uneven and rough terrain, extensive and remote, and has complicated target backgrounds. By using this DeepWeeds (Olsen et al., 2019) dataset, the proposed model was able to learn the real-world scenarios and was able to classify leaf images of weed species more precisely and accurately.

2   Related work

The research work presented by Olsen et al. (2019) provides the data set that we have used to train and validate the proposed approach and provides a baseline for the comparison of classification result. Their classification model has an average accuracy of 95%.

Another study (He et al., 2016) presented a residual learning framework presented that decreases the complexity in training networks that are deeper than the previous network. They have reformulated the layers as learning remaining capacities regarding the layer contributions, rather than learning unreferenced works, and give complete, exact proof demonstrating that these leftover connections are simpler to improve and can pick up exactness from impressively expanded profundity. The assessment was performed on the ImageNet dataset for ResNet with 152 layers—$8 \times$ more depth than VGG neural architecture yet having lower intricacy. Ensembling these neural architecture results in 3.57% error against ImageNet testset.

One study (Zhang et al., 2015) attempts to accelerate the test-time computation of deep CNNs, taking nonlinear units into account. They built up a powerful solution for the subsequent nonlinear optimization issue without stochastic gradient descent (SGD).

Another study (Szegedy et al., 2017) worked on understanding the benefit in combining the Inception architecture with residual connections. The results suggest that training with residual connections accelerates the training of Inception networks significantly, and residual Inception networks outperform similarly expensive Inception networks without residual connections. They further present several framework architecture for residual and nonresidual Inception networks. These flavors performed really well in ILSVRC 2012 classification category. They also demonstrated the Impact of activation scaling on stabilizing the training of very wide residual Inception networks. With assembling Inception-v4 and three residual achieved 3.08% top-5 error in the ImageNet Classification Challenge (CLS) against the testset.

In another study, researchers (McCool et al., 2017) presented a three-step approach wherein the first step is to utilize a pretrained model (DCNN with 25 M parameters [Inception-v3]) that helps them achieve state-of-the art performance but with a very high computation cost in terms of complexity. In the second step, they have used model compression to reduce the parameter magnitude and learn a lightweight DCNN, which is less accurate than the pretrained model. In the third step, they utilized K lightweight models that combine to form a mixture model and improve the accuracy of the final model. They were able to achieve an accurate of 90% on their weed dataset while using considerably fewer parameters capable of processing between 1.07 and 1.83 fps.

One study (Dyrmann et al., 2017) presented a fully connected convolutional neural network based on a modified version of the GoogleNet architecture for detecting weeds in highly occluded cereal fields. The dataset for the training of the network has thousands of annotated images to help the network in identifying single weed instances in cereal fields despite heavy leaf occlusion. The algorithm accuracy is 46% in detecting weeds in a field, despite weeds overlapping with wheat plants. The algorithm has limitations when it is trying to identify very small weeds or grass due to high overlap and also in marking boundaries for the complete plant when dealing with large plants.

A different study (Milioto et al., 2017) developed a classification system based on CNN. This system focuses mainly on vision-based parameters utilizing four channels and does not require prior geometrics. The CNN is implemented using prebuilt libraries (Tensorflow) that helps in quicker replication of the model. The system works with blobs of vegetation and provides output as blobs as well after the classification, making a faster and applicable real-time processing.

The authors of one study (Bi et al., 2020) present a low-cost, scalable, and high-accuracy mobile-based CNN architecture to identify diseased leaves. They based the architecture on depth-wise separable convolution, which helps in factorizing the complexity of the model depth-wise. They used two hyperparameters, width multiplier and resolution multiplier, to manage the model complexity depending on the problem size. The authors in another study (Hsieh & Kiang, 2020) drew comparisons between various CNN versions, including 1D-CNN with pixel wise spectral data, 1D-CNN with selected bands, 1D-CNN with spectral-spatial features, and 2D-CNN with principal components. These CNNs are used for the classification of hyperspectral images (HSIs) of agricultural lands. The HSI data from two varying areas were used to measure the performances of the CNNs. The average accuracy for the two data sets is between 98% and 99% applying 1D-CNN with augmented input vectors, which includes both spectral and spatial features embedded in the image data. Another paper (Sethy et al., 2020) presents a 5932-image dataset of four varieties of rice leaf disease. It also draws a performance comparison and evaluation between 11 CNN models in transfer learning approach and deep feature plus support vector machine (SVM) was carried out. The classification results in the case of deep feature and SVM approach is better when compared to the transfer learning approach.

3 WeedNet

The proposed approach utilizes the residual learning concept and used ResNet for transfer learning. The intuition behind this is to use the feature map generated in the pretrained model. In this section, we will discuss the detailed model architecture that helps us achieve the state-of-the-art solution.

3.1 Model architecture

The proposed architecture is a deep convolution neural architecture that starts with ResNet (Fig. 1) with 18 layers as the initial building block then a combination of hidden linear units and activation function with fully connected networks. The basic building block of the proposed architecture is residual and scaled permuted block (Fig. 2).

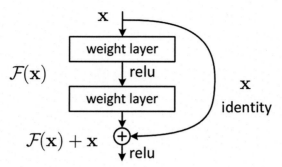

FIG. 1 Residual block.

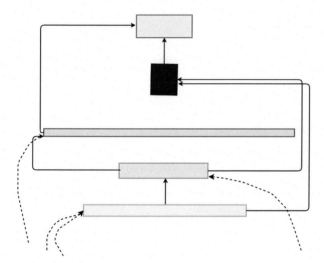

FIG. 2 Scaled permuter architecture.

For residual block, let us contemplate $R(x)$ as fundamental planning to be fit by a couple of stacked layers, with x indicating the contributions to the initial layers. If one theorizes that various nonlinear layers can asymptotically be estimated as convoluted functions, at that point it is comparable to theorize that they can asymptotically estimate the remaining capacities, that is, $R(x) - x$ (accepting that the information and yield are of similar shape). So, as opposed to envisioning that stacked layers should reward $R(x)$, we unequivocally let these layers gather an extra limit $F(x): = R(x) - x$. Then the initial formulation would become $F(x) + x$. while the two structures ought to have the option to asymptotically surmise the ideal capacities (as assumed), the proficiency of learning may be nonidentical. The resultant equation of the block:

$$y = F(x, \{W_i\}) + x. \tag{1}$$

The representation of F and x must be equivalent in Eq. (1). If this assertion is not true (e.g., while changing the information/yield channels), then we can play out a straight projection Wp to match the resultant dimension:

$$y = F(x, \{W_i\}) + W_p x. \qquad (2)$$

The scaled permuted architecture consists of reordering the neurons setup, concatenation of layers, and the block scaling. The orderings of the layer are significant because each neuron must be worked from those that preexist. We characterize the pursuit space of scale changes by modifying initial and final layers, separately.

We initialize a two-weight matrix for each layer in the search space. The parent layer can be any layer with a lower dimension. The scaling of layers is optional.

The initial block of the proposed architecture is the ResNet block made of modified residual block, and later blocks are a combination of linear and activation function to achieve the output as per requirement. The proposed neural architecture mentioned in Fig. 3 is annotated with the shape.

The last layer is nothing but a softmax layer to find the output class. The shape is set to 9 because the total number of classes in the DeepWeeds dataset is 9,8 with class labels as weed name and 1 for others category.

3.2 Complexity analysis

Here we are utilizing the transfer learning, hence the model is more complex than baseline methods like ResNet, VGG, and others mentioned in the Deep-Weeds literature. But one advantage of the transfer learning is you can utilize

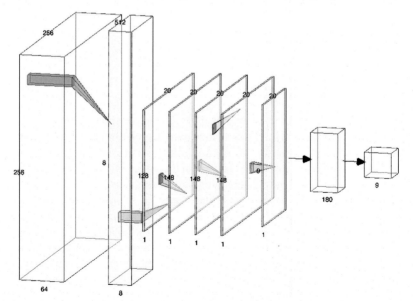

FIG. 3 WeedNet model architecture.

TABLE 1 Block/layer-wise parameters.

Block/layer	Parameters
ResNet Block	1,11,76,512
Linear	5140
ReLU	0
Linear	5540
ReLU	0
Linear	5540
ReLU	0
Linear	5540
ReLU	0
Linear	729
Softmax	0

a pretrained model, meaning you do not need to update weights for all the hidden layers. You only need to manipulate the weights of the last few layers. This helps us reduce the training time also because the number of trainable parameters is less, hence the convergence rate is also high. The baseline literature is showing 95% accuracy for top 1% in 110 epochs, but the proposed approach is getting 97% accuracy in 10 epochs only. For the parameters at each layer, please refer to Table 1.

As explained earlier in the section, ResNet block parameters are set to false for trainability, hence very few parameters are trainable here that result in fast training.

4 Evaluation strategy

As the problem is defined as a multiclass problem, we can use the following metrics to evaluate the results. We split our dataset into two distributions based on the class balance: the train and test dataset. The model is trained on training dataset and tested against unseen test dataset. The split was 70:30.

4.1 Performance metrics

The performance metrics used to evaluate the performance of proposed and compared methods are defined in this section. For a multiclass problem, the commonly used metrics are accuracy, precision, recall and area under curve

(AUC). Accuracy is a good measure but depends on thresholding value, hence we are using AUC to mitigate that issue.

4.1.1 AUC

This metric is used to plot the model performance based on the confidence of every prediction. The resultant graphical representation is called the receiver operating curve and the area covered by the curve is the actual metric AUC. This plot utilizes true positive rate (TPR) and false positive rate (FPR) for every data point.

$$TPR = \frac{t_p}{t_p + f_n}$$

$$FPR = \frac{f_p}{f_p + t_n}$$

The value of AUC varies from 0 to 1 where 0 corresponds to the predicted value and is not the expected value and 1 corresponds to the predicted value as expected value.

4.1.2 Precision

Precision refers to the fraction of positive prediction from total predicted value, meaning the proportion of correct value predicted. For multiclass, we take weightage average precision to measure the performance of the model.

$$P = \frac{t_p}{t_p + f_p}$$

4.1.3 Recall

In any system, precision and recall as a performance metric helped us understand all the sides of prediction. For perfect systems, precision and recall should be equal to 1. Sensitivity, TPR, or probability of detection are also terms for recall.

Recall is a fraction of true positive and condition positive. For this problem, we are taking weightage average to measure the performance.

$$R = \frac{t_p}{t_p + f_n}$$

4.1.4 Accuracy

Accuracy or Rand Index, introduce by William M. Rand, is more suitable for binary classification, but we can also utilize this metric for multiclass classification using the average. Accuracy is a complement value of error rate, meaning that the lower the error rate, the higher the accuracy.

$$Accuracy = \frac{t_p + t_n}{t_p + t_n + f_p + f_n}$$

4.2 Data set

The DeepWeeds (Olsen et al., 2019) dataset contains 17,509 leaf images of weed species of eight different classes. These images are manually labeled to give accurate information to the model at the time of learning. These images contain leaf images of weed plants that are local to pastoral grasslands of the state of Queensland. Weed species that are covered in this dataset are: Chinee apple, Snakeweed, Lantana, Prickly acacia, Siam weed, Parthenium, Rubber vine, and Parkinsonia. These images are collected from different sites all over Queensland such as: Black River, Charters Towers, Cluden, Douglas, Hervey Range, Kelso, McKinlay, and Paluma. Table 2 contains the statistical information of the DeepWeeds (Olsen et al., 2019) dataset.

5 Experimental setup

The proposed and other mentioned neural architectures are designed in Python language only. Neural architecture was written in Python 3.7 with PyTorch library. The development environment was a hybrid system of CPU and GPU. Intel(R) Xeon(R) CPU @ 2.00GHz 2 vCPU with 13 GB RAM and Nvidia Tesla P100 with 16 GB RAM and 1480 MHz processor.

6 Experimental evaluation

In Table 3, we contrast the past best single-model outcomes with proposed model. Our WeedNet, proposed architecture accomplished exceptionally serious precision. Our transfer learning-induced model has a solitary model and weighted accuracy is 97.032%. This single-model outcome outflanks all past outfit results. We join three models of various profundity to shape an outfit (mentioned in the DeepWeeds dataset baseline). This prompts with 1.96% FPR on test set.

In Table 3, it is clearly visible that our proposed algorithm outperforms the available methods in the DeepWeeds dataset. The evaluation recorded an average of 20 runs of each algorithm. We used a first order SGD-based Adam optimizer for convergence, and the output was based on 20 epochs only whereas the ResNet-50 and Inception-v3 requires 100 epochs to achieve the mentioned results as explained by Alex et al.

The proposed deep neural architecture outperforms in terms of accuracy and time. The accuracy for some the classes were through the roof, but some of the class models suffered to beat the accuracy of preexisting methods. However, the overall result was faster and better than the preexisting methods (Fig. 4).

7 Conclusion

This chapter means to introduce the idea and structure of a novel deep neural network (DNN) model called WeedNet focused on agri datasets. The proposed

TABLE 2 Dataset distribution of DeepWeeds.

Species					Locations				
	Black river	Charters towers	Cluden	Douglas	Hervey range	Kelso	McKinlay	Paluma	Total
Chinee Apple	0	0	0	718	340	20	0	47	1125
Lantana	0	0	0	9	0	0	0	1055	1064
Parkinsonia	0	0	1031	0	0	0	0	0	1031
Parthenium	0	246	0	0	0	776	0	0	1022
Prickly Acacia	0	0	132	1	0	0	929	0	1062
Rubber Vine	0	188	1	815	0	5	0	0	1009
Siam Weed	1072	0	0	0	0	0	0	2	1074
Snake Weed	10	0	0	928	1	34	0	43	1016
Negatives	1200	605	1234	2606	471	893	943	1154	9106
Total	2282	1039	2398	5077	812	1728	1872	2301	17,509

TABLE 3 Comparative analysis of WeedNet, Inception-V3, and ResNet-50.

Species	Top-1 accuracy (%)			Precision (%)			FPR (%)		
	WeedNet	Inception-v3	ResNet-50	WeedNet	Inception-v3	ResNet-50	WeedNet	Inception-v3	ResNet-50
Chinee Apple	**92.12**	85.3	88.5	**93.8**	92.7	91	**0.43**	0.48	0.61
Lantana	94.56	94.4	**95**	90.2	90.9	**91.7**	0.58	0.62	**0.55**
Parkinsonia	**98.7**	96.8	97.2	**98.2**	95.6	97.9	**0.12**	0.29	0.13
Parthenium	**96.5**	94.9	95.8	96.5	95.8	**96.7**	**0.19**	0.26	0.21
Prickly Acacia	**95.8**	92.8	95.5	**93.5**	93.4	93	**0.42**	0.43	0.46
Rubber Vine	**94.34**	93.1	92.5	99.19	**99.2**	99.1	**0.05**	0.05	0.05
Siam Weed	**97.8**	97.6	96.5	**98.1**	94.4	97.2	0.21	0.38	**0.18**
Snake Weed	**91.2**	88	88.8	**91.3**	86.9	90.9	**0.48**	0.82	0.55
Negatives	**98.8**	97.2	97.6	**96.87**	96.5	96.7	**3.48**	3.77	3.59
Weighted average	**97.032**	95.1	95.7	**96.0056**	95.1	95.7	**1.96**	2.16	2.04

Boldness depicts the best value in that the category.

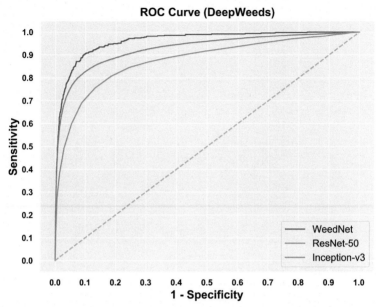

FIG. 4 Receiver operating characteristic curve for WeedNet, Inception-V3, and ResNet-50.

neural architecture has a novel method of uniquely detecting data and taking neighborhood choices. The primary downside of the ongoing proposed DNNs is in their computational escalation because of large input dimensions. In this chapter, we present the viability of WeedNet on a DeepWeeds benchmark dataset, prompting the improvement of the characterization exactness. Besides, the WeedNet involves less computation than other available methods. Consolidating with transfer learning and VGG, the WeedNet has accomplished a state-of-the-art execution in dataset. In future examinations, we will attempt to improve the precision of the proposed WeedNet and afterward apply the improved WeedNet to a wide scope of true situations.

References

Bakhshipour, A., & Jafari, A. (2018). Evaluation of support vector machine and artificial neural networks in weed detection using shape features. *Computers and Electronics in Agriculture*, *145*, 153–160.

Bi, C., Wang, J., Duan, Y., Fu, B., Kang, J. R., & Shi, Y. (2020). Mobilenet based apple leaf diseases identification. *Mobile Networks and Applications*, 1–9. https://doi.org/10.1007/s11036-020-01640-1.

Carranza-Rojas, J., Goeau, H., Bonnet, P., Mata-Montero, E., & Joly, A. (2017). Going deeper in the automated identification of Herbarium specimens. *BMC Evolutionary Biology*, *17*(1), 1–14.

dos Santos Ferreira, A., Freitas, D. M., da Silva, G. G., Pistori, H., & Folhes, M. T. (2017). Weed detection in soybean crops using ConvNets. *Computers and Electronics in Agriculture*, *143*, 314–324.

Dyrmann, M., Jørgensen, R. N., & Midtiby, H. S. (2017). RoboWeedSupport-detection of weed locations in leaf occluded cereal crops using a fully convolutional neural network. *Advances in Animal Biosciences, 8*(2), 842–847.

Fernández-Quintanilla, C., Peña, J. M., Andújar, D., Dorado, J., Ribeiro, A., & López-Granados, F. (2018). Is the current state of the art of weed monitoring suitable for site-specific weed management in arable crops? *Weed Research, 58*(4), 259–272.

Gonzalez-de-Santos, P., Ribeiro, A., Fernandez-Quintanilla, C., Lopez-Granados, F., Brandstoetter, M., Tomic, S., ... Perez-Ruiz, M. (2017). Fleets of robots for environmentally-safe pest control in agriculture. *Precision Agriculture, 18*(4), 574–614.

Hall, D., McCool, C., Dayoub, F., Sunderhauf, N., & Upcroft, B. (2015). Evaluation of features for leaf classification in challenging conditions. In *2015 IEEE winter conference on applications of computer vision, January* (pp. 797–804). IEEE.

He, K., Zhang, X., Ren, S., & Sun, J. (2016). Deep residual learning for image recognition. In *Proceedings of the IEEE conference on computer vision and pattern recognition* (pp. 770–778).

Hsieh, T. H., & Kiang, J. F. (2020). Comparison of CNN algorithms on hyperspectral image classification in agricultural lands. *Sensors, 20*(6), 1734.

Kalyoncu, C., & Toygar, Ö. (2015). Geometric leaf classification. *Computer Vision and Image Understanding, 133*, 102–109.

Kumar, N., Belhumeur, P. N., Biswas, A., Jacobs, D. W., Kress, W. J., Lopez, I. C., & Soares, J. V. (2012). Leafsnap: A computer vision system for automatic plant species identification. In *European conference on computer vision, October* (pp. 502–516). Berlin, Heidelberg: Springer.

LeCun, Y., Bengio, Y., & Hinton, G. (2015). No title. *Deep Learning. Nature, 521*(7553), 436–444.

Lee, S. H., Chan, C. S., Mayo, S. J., & Remagnino, P. (2017). How deep learning extracts and learns leaf features for plant classification. *Pattern Recognition, 71*, 1–13.

Lee, S. H., Chan, C. S., Wilkin, P., & Remagnino, P. (2015). Deep-plant: Plant identification with convolutional neural networks. In *2015 IEEE international conference on image processing (ICIP), September* (pp. 452–456). IEEE.

Li, L., Wei, X., Mao, H., & Wu, S. (2017). Design and application of spectrum sensor for weed detection used in winter rape field. *Transactions of the Chinese Society of Agricultural Engineering, 33*(18), 127–133.

Lin, F., Zhang, D., Huang, Y., Wang, X., & Chen, X. (2017). Detection of corn and weed species by the combination of spectral, shape and textural features. *Sustainability, 9*(8), 1335.

Louargant, M., Jones, G., Faroux, R., Paoli, J. N., Maillot, T., Gée, C., & Villette, S. (2018). Unsupervised classification algorithm for early weed detection in row-crops by combining spatial and spectral information. *Remote Sensing, 10*(5), 761.

Mahesh, S., Jayas, D. S., Paliwal, J., & White, N. D. G. (2015). Hyperspectral imaging to classify and monitor quality of agricultural materials. *Journal of Stored Products Research, 61*, 17–26.

McCool, C., Perez, T., & Upcroft, B. (2017). Mixtures of lightweight deep convolutional neural networks: Applied to agricultural robotics. *IEEE Robotics and Automation Letters, 2*(3), 1344–1351.

Milioto, A., Lottes, P., & Stachniss, C. (2017). Real-time blob-wise sugar beets vs weeds classification for monitoring fields using convolutional neural networks. *ISPRS Annals of the Photogrammetry, Remote Sensing and Spatial Information Sciences, 4*, 41.

Olsen, A., Han, S., Calvert, B., Ridd, P., & Kenny, O. (2015). In situ leaf classification using histograms of oriented gradients. In *2015 international conference on digital image computing: Techniques and applications (DICTA), November* (pp. 1–8). IEEE.

Olsen, A., Konovalov, D. A., Philippa, B., Ridd, P., Wood, J. C., Johns, J., ... Calvert, B. (2019). DeepWeeds: A multiclass weed species image dataset for deep learning. *Scientific Reports, 9*(1), 1–12.

Sethy, P. K., Barpanda, N. K., Rath, A. K., & Behera, S. K. (2020). Deep feature based rice leaf disease identification using support vector machine. *Computers and Electronics in Agriculture, 175*, 105527.

Shaner, D. L., & Beckie, H. J. (2014). The future for weed control and technology. *Pest Management Science, 70*(9), 1329–1339.

Shirzadifar, A., Bajwa, S., Mireei, S. A., Howatt, K., & Nowatzki, J. (2018). Weed species discrimination based on SIMCA analysis of plant canopy spectral data. *Biosystems Engineering, 171*, 143–154.

Slaughter, D. C., Giles, D. K., & Downey, D. (2008). Autonomous robotic weed control systems: A review. *Computers and Electronics in Agriculture, 61*(1), 63–78.

Szegedy, C., Ioffe, S., Vanhoucke, V., & Alemi, A. (2017). Inception-v4, inception-resnet and the impact of residual connections on learning. In *Vol. 31. Proceedings of the AAAI conference on artificial intelligence, February*.

Wu, S. G., Bao, F. S., Xu, E. Y., Wang, Y. X., Chang, Y. F., & Xiang, Q. L. (2007). A leaf recognition algorithm for plant classification using probabilistic neural network. In *2007 IEEE international symposium on signal processing and information technology, December* (pp. 11–16). IEEE.

Zhang, X., Zou, J., He, K., & Sun, J. (2015). Accelerating very deep convolutional networks for classification and detection. *IEEE Transactions on Pattern Analysis and Machine Intelligence, 38*(10), 1943–1955.

Chapter 10

Sensors make sense: Functional genomics, deep learning, and agriculture

Ross McDougal Henderson, Claudia Rossi, and Michelle Burgess
CAREM, LLC, Falls Church, VA, United States

1 Introduction

The National Agricultural Statistics Service (NASS) is the primary data collection agency within the US Department of Agriculture and collaborates extensively with international agencies such as the international Organisation for Economic Cooperation and Development (OECD) Agriculture and Food Division. Both NASS and OECD collect agricultural data using an integrated multimodality, multiplatform approach, from human inspectors on the ground to satellite imagery from space. Yet satellite imagery is becoming increasingly difficult to analyze via conventional pattern detection algorithms, with petabytes of Earth imagery data collected every month. Furthermore, there is a limit to the benefits that imagery and visual crop inspection alone can provide. Crops and other vegetation inhabit an ecosystem that is far more extensive than their growth patterns, land use, yield, robustness, hyperspectral signatures, and other physical properties can characterize.

From a systems perspective, plant physiology is more or less an inversion of human physiology. Whereas we humans have most of our supportive metabolome on the inside—in our gut—plants have most of their metabolome on the outside—at their roots. Whereas most of our oxygen-carbon dioxide exchange takes place in our lungs, most of a plant's O_2—CO_2 exchange occurs in its leaves. Furthermore, most of our movement is over a wide spatial range, and that movement and structural support is provided mainly by our musculoskeletal system. Plants, in contrast, move on relatively miniscule yet potentially consequential spatial scales, and that movement results mostly from their outer vascular structures. Therefore, in order to gather comprehensive metrics for agricultural dynamics, diverse crop sustainability, food security, and overall improvements in utilitarian farming practices for the latter half of this century

Deep Learning for Sustainable Agriculture. https://doi.org/10.1016/B978-0-323-85214-2.00014-8

and beyond, agronomists will find it necessary to get to the root of the matter. And functional genomic investigations of the entire plant-carbon and plant-silicon life cycle dynamics, using deep learning (DL) algorithms and related agent-based adaptive learning techniques, have the potential to be one of the key drivers for prediction and control of agricultural yield, pest and blight mitigation, land use optimization, and environmental restoration of agricultural spaces.

In a consensus study report released by the US National Academies of Sciences, Engineering, and Medicine (Bock & Kirkendall, 2017), four approaches for improvement of agricultural modeling and integration of agricultural simulations are identified:

(1) composite indications derived from direct surveys, remote sensing data, administrative data, and prior models and estimates;
(2) the NASS Cropland Data Layer (CDL), a machine learning tool using remote sensing data obtained at various spectral scales to find best-fit linear models that predict a continuous outcome variable;
(3) an empirical rule-based cash rents model, using economic indicators as primary predictors for agricultural land use and crop yield; and
(4) a Bayesian model using a priori end-of-season yields to predict future outcomes.

This chapter will provide a fifth approach, using the recently developed worldwide distributed acoustic sensing (DAS) network, which to date has been used primarily to characterize seismic and geodesic measurements. We will review an open source DL toolbox, Ludwig. We will show how Ludwig can be used in an agricultural and aquacultural context, and we will also introduce a new and comprehensive agent-based algorithm, GRANITE (Genetic Regulatory Analysis for Investigational Tools Environment), to model and predict the functional genomics of agricultural crops.

Major contribution of this chapter: this chapter highlights the role of functional genomics in agriculture and aquaculture and shows how high-resolution multicomponent DAS, DAS networks with helical optical fiber, can be combined with DL architectures, including the open source software toolbox Ludwig. In so doing, we present an augmented toolbox for network discovery and systems medicine, GRANITE NDT, which incorporates adaptive learning simulations and predictive learning models beneficial to crop surveillance, food safety, health, and sustainability under adverse conditions.

The chapter is organized as follows:

Section I. Functional genomics
    A. The emerging applications of soil microbial metabolites
    B. Agricultural-based metabolites to advance nutraceutical production and drug discovery

C. Marine microalgae, aquaculture, and the DL toolbox Ludwig
D. Pollinators, Ludwig combiners, and the carbon-energy cycle
Section II. DAS networks
E. Agricultural factors in the plant-silicon cycle: Genomic regulation of blight, drought, and invasive species
F. Helically wound DAS
Section III. GRANITE and the agent-based GRANITE Network Discovery Tool
Conclusions
References

2   Section I. Functional genomics

2.1   The emerging applications of soil microbial metabolites

With the advent of functional genomics, widely credited to 1990 and the 13-year effort to map the human genome, there have been an increasing number of emerging concurrent applications to agriculture, specifically to the understanding of the role of soil microbial metabolites and environmental metabolomics. Environmental metabolomics allow researchers to measure and calculate the effects of genetic potential in situ and to directly correlate the chemical and biological properties of the microbial cellular biology of soil. However, these measurements are confined to static and discrete samples, and there is at present no comprehensive way to measure the dynamic activity of these soil microbiomes. One reason for this is the significant variation of plant-soil community level phenotypes across microbial extents, due the localizations, expressions, and population densities of genes in various and changing environmental and biogeochemical conditions. This interactome, as it is sometimes called, can be thought of as not only the protein-protein interactions (PPIs) among a single organism but also PPIs between organisms, such as between soil microbial metabolites and plants, which for the purposes here represent agricultural products.

Complementing static biogeochemical measurements with continuous monitoring of soil and plant activity at the molecular level is theoretically possible. Moreover, it is becoming increasingly practical using sophisticated sensing techniques and computational algorithms. Genes and their functions can be characterized and evaluated for near optimal crop health, yield, and sustainability. Several variables directly involved in these sensing techniques and algorithms include the composition and concentration of organic soil nutrients, their bioavailability with respect to the plant, competing factors for nutrients at both the cellular and systems level, and environmental conditions. As such, the spatial distribution of the soil microbes and metabolites is not only at surface level but also three-dimensional and represents yet another computational layer necessary for linking plant-soil metabolomics and metagenomics to soil biogeochemistry.

The potential payoff for the ability to link global plant-soil metagenomic profiles with their local agrochemistry and statistical sampling of crop yield and variation is enormous (McGrew et al., 2014). For one, comprehensive agricultural metagenomic profiles allow researchers to more precisely identify carbon-depleted marginal soils and to restore the amount of bioavailable carbon in targeted locations. This practice could substantially decrease atmospheric CO_2 while simultaneously improving water and micronutrient retention, increasing biodiversity, protecting the Earth's carbon sink, and provisioning for an increasing global population. In addition, a broader understanding of plant-soil genomic interactions will lead to new sources of bioenergy crops with customizable and controllable microbiomes useful for synthesis of carbon containing soil-based biofuels. Evidence indicates that an additional 0.4–1.2 GT of carbon per year can be stored in the Earth's soils, which represents an approximate 5%–15% offset of global fossil-fuel emissions (Lal, 2004).

Additionally, a comprehensive computational model of agricultural exometabolomics, that is, the functional genomics of soil microbes and their metabolites, will increase the understanding of the relationship between crop genotype and phenotype. This relationship can be conceptualized by an initial high-level recurrent neural network (RNN) model for DL applied to agricultural dynamics: soil microbiome sampling ➔ soil biochemistry ➔ plant interface/root system ➔ plant biochemistry ➔ crop-sensor detection/bioinformatic evaluation and interventional tools, including genomic sequencing and editing ➔ then full circle to soil microbiome sampling and updates to the recursively iterative algorithm.

2.2 Agricultural-based metabolites to advance nutraceutical production and drug discovery

Life on Earth is metabolically diverse, yet all life shares a well-established biochemical basis. This basis is characterized by several common biochemical properties, broadly: energy intake, energy stasis, energy outflow, and energy regeneration. More succinctly this summarizes to: eat, sleep, excrete, die. These basis vectors are not necessarily orthogonal across species, and may, in fact, overlap. For instance, regeneration may be modeled as a part of stasis, and for organisms that reproduce, this reproduction may be modeled as a part of regeneration. For the purposes of developing a practical DL RNN for agriculture, we will assume that four basis vectors will be sufficient: nutrient uptake, plant growth and stasis, waste release, and harvest.

The chemical potential of organisms arises from four basic strategies, likely developed long ago in the evolutionary timeline. These strategies are: photoautotrophic, photoheterotrophic, chemoautotrophic, and chemoheterotrophic (Wolf-Simon, 2012). Studies at the molecular level in regenerative medicine and functional genomics have shown that while usually a few specialized sentinel molecules do most of the gatekeeper functions, rarely if ever does a single metabolic pathway depend on a unique microbe or even a single genetic regulatory signal transduction pathway (Petkova et al., 2019).

Genomic information is encoded at the functional level in the pluripotent stem cells, whereby the emergence of precise and reproducible mappings of the genetic program is encoded. In biological cellular networks, neural networks included, input stimuli signals are transformed to output responses that can be measured as readouts. These readouts provide an explicit test of hypotheses as to what degree the stimulus modulates the response and how biologically meaningful information is stored inside the network. However, the mathematical representation of this model is a very high dimensional vector space, as there are many dendritic inputs converging on one synapse and many axon outputs conveying the action potentials along the network. Each input dendrite itself is represented by many genetic signatures, and there are thermodynamic thresholds and biochemical kinetic activation potentials which must be considered. The problem becomes a black box problem with Kolmogorov complexity, and due to hidden entropies within the genetic signature propagations over time, the computing problem is NP-complete, is not very well suited to biophysical closed form sets of equations, and is therefore very well suited to DL algorithms.

It becomes apparent that to account for changing environmental conditions within even the simplest agricultural interactomes, sophisticated and complex algorithmic frameworks are required. Although exceptions may exist, such as with the GFAJ-1 microbe found in high-arsenic soda lakes in Nevada and California, nearly all life on Earth requires six critical elements—hydrogen, carbon, nitrogen, oxygen, phosphorus, and sulfur—and these six elements are used to form DNA, RNA, proteins, and lipids. Thus, a robust computational tool to optimize plant-soil functional genomics should include controls for modifying not only crop-environment strategies but also molecular concentrations of H, C, N, O, P, and S and their uptake at the DNA and RNA level.

As in humans, microorganisms living inside plants can promote and sustain host growth and health. A recent study highlights that endophytic root microbiomes contain a multitude of functional traits that work in concert to protect plants from the inside out. Using network inference and metagenomics, bacterial consortia and functional gene clusters were identified in a soil sample that is suppressive to disease caused by *Rhizoctonia solani*, a soil-borne pathogenic fungus with a worldwide distribution and a wide range of target plant species, including rice, wheat, and sugar beet. Using strain-level genome reconstruction, plant root endospheres of chitinase genes and other gene clusters were enriched for Chitinophagaceae and Flavobacteriaceae, and an inoculant was developed that consistently suppressed fungal root disease in sugar beet plants (Carrión et al., 2019).

The implications of interventional functional genomic techniques to foster crop growth, development, and health are not confined to the root endosphere but also include the plant's rhizosphere, phyllosphere, and spermosphere. Much information in the form of plant crop sequence data and descriptive chemistry has been collected, though few studies have been conducted to show how this information can be reconstructed to form a comprehensive and dynamic interactome model. To this end, new modalities for sensing and imaging plant cellular dynamics on a functional level have been recruited. Using nanoimaging, the process by which plant cells expand and reshape has been elucidated. Previous studies postulated that plant cell expansion for nutrient intake and waste outflow was largely a function of turgor acting on the cell wall. Nanoimaging sensors reveal a finer control mechanism, one containing pectin nanofilaments possessing an intrinsic expansion capacity, and suggest that extracellular matrix function may guide cell shape and signaling in plants and animals alike (Haas et al., 2020).

For proof of concept, Homogalacturonan (HG) polysaccharides containing exclusively linear chains of 1,4-linked α-D-galactosyluronic acid (GalpA) were imaged, though HG glycan domains also exist in branched and cyclic heteroglycan structures, including rhamnogalacturonan type I and type II, and in glycoconjugates, which can be used in pharmaceutical and nutraceutical design and synthesis. Examining plant cell dynamics in muro can lead to techniques that will not only improve plant growth and health but also inform researchers as to how best to modify these dynamics to enhance seed germination. Advanced imaging modalities, including superresolution three-dimensional direct stochastic optical reconstruction microscopy (3D-dSTORM) and cryoscanning electron microscopy (cryo-SEM), can provide ∼40–50 nm lateral resolution, ∼80 nm axial resolution, and depth reconstruction of ∼800 nm on 4 μm-thick plant tissue sections.

3D-dSTORM and cyro-SEM show how the cell wall and extracellular matrix respond to extra- and intracellular stimuli to effect cell shape, size, and division. These optical measurements can then be used as input for mathematical constructs, such as a 3D nonlinear finite element model (FEM) analysis, used for simulations and hypothesis testing of plant tissue topology, cell wall tension, thickness, and growth. High-resolution sensor capability provides the FEM model to precisely determine metabolomic exchanges at the anticlinal and periclinal cell walls and has the potential for modeling similar self-expansion and self-organizing structures of extracellular matrix polymers. Furthermore, biochemical processes similar to those that act upon pectins might also describe growth patterns and protection mechanisms of plant organisms that have cell walls but do not have HG.

Nanoimaging of plants in an agricultural environment, as opposed to a laboratory workspace, is challenging and perhaps at present impractical considering the many genomic pathways needed to be modeled and analyzed for pharmaceutical and nutraceutical discovery. Therefore, an intermediate platform—one between farm and lab—is proposed. This platform would mirror the NIH NCATS (National Center for Advancing Translational Sciences) Tissue-on-Chips initiative (Ginsberg et al., 2016). Tissue chips are integrated

3D platforms engineered to support living human tissues and cells, embedded in modular and reconfigurable chips, in order to evaluate the specificity, safety, efficacy, and toxicity of potential drug candidates. The project encompasses 10 human physiological systems—circulatory, endocrine, gastrointestinal, immune, integumentary, musculoskeletal, nervous, reproductive, respiratory, and urinary. The pathology and physiology of these various systems is instantiated so as to replicate the microvasculature, innervation, and bioreactors necessary for tissue response, and spatial and temporal patterning motifs necessary for realistic immune response, perfusion, structure, cell type, scaffolding, and functional readouts.

Tissue chip technology currently focuses on human physiological systems and pharmacogenomic signal transduction pathways, yet this technology is amenable to plant physiology with minimal modifications. This is because the functional genomics of agricultural products, as with human physiological processes, involve several comparable technological approaches and produce several correspondingly similar applications. In particular, loss-of-function analysis, including gene silencing and gene editing, are established technologies in human genome studies, while microRNA targeting for gene function analysis is an emerging application of functional pharmacogenomics (Hunsberger et al., 2015).

The ability to profile on a genome-wide transcriptome basis and to ascertain gene expressions in the form of DNA copy numbers, variations in sequence, and DNA and chromatin modifications have produced increasingly precise models of the molecular biology of agricultural products. At the same time, the ability to measure and collect data at such small scales and narrow bandwidths has led to the formation of very large datasets requiring increasingly greater computational power and algorithmic complexity. For the purposes of ascertaining which, if any, genetic variations are associated with a specific trait, and then incorporating those variations into an RNN, a genome-wide association study can be conducted. In agent-based evolutionary learning RNNs, the agents are the variations of the gene activities and the proteins they encode and the signals between gene activity and cellular function on a genomic spanning basis. It should be noted that this technique is markedly different than collective learning systems, for example, swarm models of gene-protein networks where reactants are considered the "agents" randomly interacting in a static environment. Rather, in agent-based evolutionary learning RNNs, it is the reactions, and not the reactants, which are the agents. Furthermore, signal transduction is modeled not as a one-to-one correspondence between reactants but as a perturbation to the entire interactome. This distinction will be expounded upon in Section 4.

For now, the first step in developing an agent-based DL RNN for functional genomics is to identify the amino acids necessary for plant growth and development. The amino acid profile of apples, for instance, contains nine amino acids: tryptophan, threonine, isoleucine, leucine, lysine, methionine, phenylalanine, valine, and histidine. Grains such as rice and wheat, on the other hand, generally contain 17 of the 20 essential amino acids required by humans—tryptophan, isoleucine, lysine, methionine, phenylalanine, valine, arginine, asparagine, aspartic acid, cysteine, glutamine, glutamic acid, glycine, proline, serine, and tyrosine—lacking only in threonine, leucine, and histidine. Since there are 20 amino acids essential for proteomic signal transduction pathways, the first question to be answered when coding an agent-based learning RNN for functional genomics becomes: how is the coding information relayed from the gene strands along the DNA molecule to the final protein molecule?

In a DNA molecule, the static variable components are the four base nucleotides: adenine (A), cytosine (C), guanine (G), and thymine (T). These four nucleotides code for 20 amino acids as follows:

1. If one base nucleotide coded for one amino acid, then $4^1 = 4$ would be the greatest upper bound, or maximum number, of amino acids that could be coded. This base nucleotide is called a codon.
2. If two codons were required to code for one amino acid, then $4^2 = 16$ would be the maximum number of amino acids that could be coded.
3. If three codons were required to code for one amino acid, then $4^3 = 64$ would be the maximum number of amino acids that could be coded.

Hence, to code for all 20 amino acids essential to humans, the minimum number of base nucleotides that are required is 3. Yet three nucleotides can combinatorially produce as many as 64 possible amino acids, and there exist four nucleotides in a DNA molecule. Therefore, it stands to reason that some amino acids are coded for by different codons. It is the goal of functional genomics to ascertain what codons will signal which proteomic pathways, what are the essential pathways, which are redundant, and which of the nonredundant pathways might produce insight for potential pathway candidates for drug targeting and nutraceutical discovery.

2.3 Marine microalgae, aquaculture, and the DL toolbox Ludwig

Most of the current understanding of microbial metabolites and the chemistry of microbiomes stems from laboratory-induced strains grown in nutrient rich cultures. In nearly all widely investigated environments, however diverse—be they soil or the human gut—bacteria are surrounded by a dense and varied spectra of other microbes and exhibit classic competitive/cooperative mechanisms for access to nutrients in order to maximize their likelihood for survival. For agricultural diversity, sustainability, and overall crop health, it is vital to understand these competitive/cooperative strategies in the soil, the crop plant, and the surrounding environment. Yet soil and the microbes therein comprise a relatively small part of the Earth, and older, more evolved, and perhaps simpler symbiotic relationships between microalgae and bacteria exist in the world's oceans.

One such microalgae species is *Emiliania huxleyi*, a single-celled microorganism 5–10 μm in length and so abundant that its colonies of seasonal blooms are readily seen from Earth-orbiting satellites. These blooms cover areas as large as 3×10^5 km^2 which, by generating massive amounts of O_2 during photosynthesis, and by synthesizing large amounts of dimethylsulfoniopropionate (DMSP), play a significant role in the Earth's biogeochemical cycles. *E. huxleyi* interacts with marine bacteria, roseobacter, which are abundant in all oceans, principally in the coastal zones where they constitute approximately 20% of bacterial communities, increasing to 60% during algae blooms. A representative roseobacter *Phaeobacter inhibens* has been shown to facilitate a mutual symbiosis with *E. huxleyi*, whereby *E. huxleyi* provides DMSP to *P. inhibens*, which *P. inhibens* can then use as a sole source of carbon and sulfur (Seyedsayamdost, 2017). In exchange, *P. inhibens* produces auxin phenylacetic acid (PAA), providing growth and health to *E. huxleyi* while also producing tropodithietic acid (TDA). TDA protects the *E. huxleyi-P. inhibens* assembly from environmental marine pathogens. In the laboratory, this symbiosis has been found to be controlled by two phases—a mutualistic build-up phase and a parasitic break-down phase. In the build-up phase, PAA provides a precursor to TDA, and both metabolites function as nutrients to *E. huxleyi*. The algae, in turn, provide *P. inhibens* with nutrients via DMSP. To keep this balance in check, the *E. huxleyi-P. inhibens* symbiotic system has developed a bacterial mutualistic-to-parasitic switch, which in DL algorithms can be considered as an inclusion set of cross-validation and parameter sweeps from hyperparameter optimization. With increasing cell densities, *E. huxleyi* produces p-coumaric acid (pCA), and the *P. inhibens* respond by combining fragments of DMSP, PAA, and pCA to produce a new metabolite, roseobacticide (RSB). RSB possesses potent algaecidal activities specific to *E. huxleyi*. However, this model has been derived only in controlled laboratory confines, as no sensor system has yet to be devised that can capture the *E. huxleyi-P. inhibens* relationship at the very large scale that is found in marine environments.

If such a sensor system were to be devised, then the amounts of data would be massive. Yet the variation of that data would be manageable, given the relatively straightforward biochemical exchange mechanisms between algae and bacteria. Using the DL toolbox Ludwig as an example, a working model for the algal-bacterial symbiosis between *E. huxleyi* and *P. inhibens* can be constructed. Ludwig is a software toolbox based on TensorFlow that allows researchers to train and validate DL architectures. Ludwig is particularly good for hypothesis generation and experimentation because it provides a seamless way to swap in and out many DL modules. The level of abstraction is based on data types, so that metabolites can map to many types of machine learning strategies, utilizing DL training and prediction algorithms. Typical Ludwig constructs for training and prediction are shown in Figs. 1 and 2.

To instantiate a Ludwig DL session, a model definition is specified. The Ludwig definition is straightforward: a model is named, an input data file is identified, and the model definition input parameters and output features are indicated as shown in Fig. 3.

Training

Field mappings, model hyper-parameters and weights are saved during training

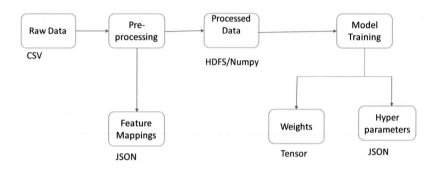

Source: Piero Molino, Ph.D. AI Summer School 2020

FIG. 1 Ludwig training construct.

Prediction

The same field mappings obtained during training are used to pre-process each datapoint and to post-process each prediction of the model in order to map back to labels

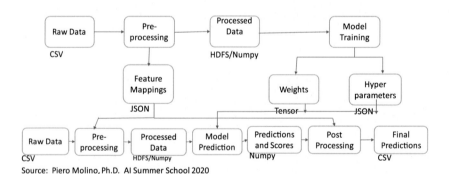

Source: Piero Molino, Ph.D. AI Summer School 2020

FIG. 2 Ludwig prediction construct.

Once the model definition is given, a Ludwig experiment is run as in Fig. 4. Ludwig can utilize one or several DL paradigms, or feature encoders, including stacked convolution neural network (CNN), parallel CNN, stacked parallel CNN, RNN, CNN RNN, and Transformer/BERT (Bidirectional Encoder Representations from Transformers). An example of a Ludwig module using both stacked CNN and ResNet (Residual Network) is shown in Fig. 5.

Model Definition

```
ludwig experiment
--dataset_symbiosis.csv
--config "{input_features: [name: algal_conc, type: numerical}],
   output_features: [name: class, type: category}]}"
```
FIG. 3   A Ludwig model definition.

Running Experiments

The experiment trains the model on a training set and predicts the model on a test set.
Prediction outputs, test statistics, and training statistics are inputs to the Visualization module.

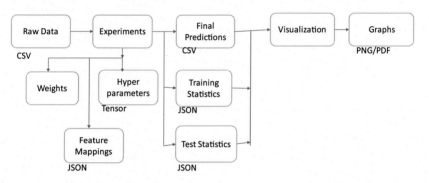

Source: Piero Molino, Ph.D. AI Summer School 2020

FIG. 4   A Ludwig experiment.

Ludwig is based on an adaptive business machine learning process for model evaluation and tuning. Datasets are collected, integrated into the model, prepared for processing, and then processed via training and hyperparameter tuning. A schematic of this DL process is shown in Fig. 6.

Hyperparameter tuning allows the Ludwig user to make informed decisions about the experiment as exemplified in Fig. 7.

Ludwig is also extensible, so that mutualist-to-parasite switches can be finely tuned as new metabolic pathways similar to *E. huxleyi-P. inhibens* interactions are discovered.

As an example, a table is constructed that contains two columns. The first column is labeled Uninfected, and contains mixed signal measurements of the cell density of *E. huxleyi* and the concentration of *P. inhibens* in a given sample. The second column is called Parasitized, the entries of which are discretized gradient levels. These gradient levels correspond directly to biochemical

Image Feature Encoders

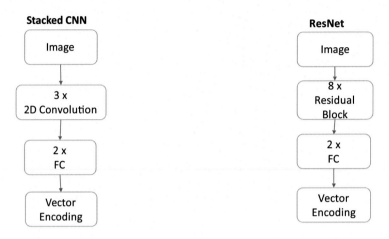

Source: Piero Molino, Ph.D. AI Summer School 2020

FIG. 5   Feature encoders for a Ludwig experiment.

The Machine Learning Process as Characterized by Ludwig

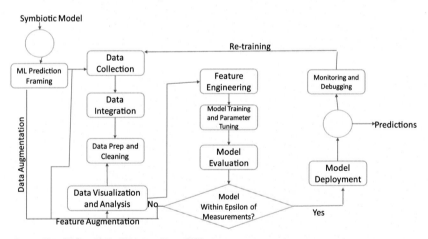

Source: Piero Molino, Ph.D. AI Summer Camp 2020

FIG. 6   The Ludwig machine learning process.

exchanges between *E. huxleyi* and *P. inhibens* and vary in degree from symbiotic and beneficial for *E. huxleyi* growth to neutral to parasitic and lethal. This construct is a form of principal component analysis, and the objective is to train a model that will learn to separate the cell density of *E. huxleyi* from the

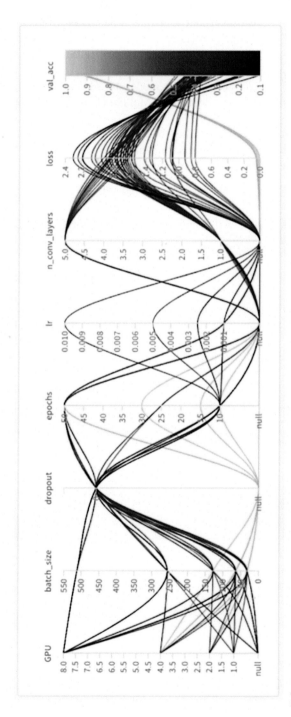

FIG. 7 A representation of hyperparameter visualization in Ludwig (Molino et al., 2019).

concentration of *P. inhibens* and to recognize which Parasitized classes, that is, which gradient levels, are associated with which uninfected concentrations. New additions to the table in the form of sample measurements will produce new symbiotic/parasitic predictions.

Snippets of Ludwig code for this model, based on a generalization of a parasitized-uninfected host organism (Molino et al., 2019) are shown in Figs. 8 and 9.

The model definition delineating the input features and output features, or keys, is first specified. To train such a model in Ludwig, the Ludwig experiment command is then invoked. The experiment command:

1. splits the Concentration data into training, validation, and test sets;
2. trains the model on the training set;
3. validates the model on the validation set, with Early Stopping if peak performance is achieved; and
4. makes predictions on the test set.

Basically, when Ludwig is given an input Concentration, it will produce a symbiotic/parasitic prediction Class.

After the first epoch of training, Ludwig produces a table showing the performance of the model, which contains the loss, the accuracy, and a metric called hits-at-k on all the split sets—training, validation, and test. Loss is cross-entropy loss, which indicates the distance between what the model

Mutualist Parasite

Uninfected	Parasitized	Beneficial
algal_conc_gradient_01_01	algal_conc_gradient_01_02	True
algal_conc_gradient_01_02	algal_conc_gradient_02_01	False
algal_conc_gradient_02_01	algal_conc_gradient_02_02	False

```
ludwig experiment
--datset symbiosis.csv
--config "{input_features: [{name: algal_path_1, type: numerical}
                           [{name: algal_path_1, type: numerical,
                             tied_weights: algal_path_1}]
           output_features[{name: same, type: binary}]}"
```

FIG. 8   Working directory for symbiotic/parasitic predictions (snippet of code).

```
#Delete all the default files
rm –rf Parasitized/default.db
rm –rf Uninfected/default.db

#Rename directories
mv Parasitized Parasitized_all
mv Uninfected Uninfected_all

#Create the new directories
for i in _train _test _validate

#Transfer the data into the specified directories
cd Parasitized_all
cp 'ls Parasitized_all.db | Parasitized_all
cd Uninfected_all
cp 'ls Uninfected_all.db | Uninfected_all
```

FIG. 9   Data integration process for Ludwig run of symbiotic/parasitic prediction.

calculates the output distribution to be and what the output distribution really is. Cross-entropy measure is a widely used alternative of least squares error and is used when the probability that each hypothesis might be true, that is, when the output is a hypothesized probability distribution. Hits-at-k is the accuracy calculated when any prediction in the first k predictive models is correct and is useful if the model generates more than one prediction, as might be the case when predicting gradient values.

After a few epochs of training, if performance increases and peak accuracy is achieved, Ludwig continues to run until no further gain in performance is noted. When this occurs, Ludwig returns the DL model, which provides the highest accuracy on the validation set. At the end of this process, a full evaluation is performed on the test set, and statistics are returned that show accuracy, hits-at-k, a confusion matrix, and statistics that are specific for each class that are contained in the classification problem: precision, recall, sensitivity, specificity, hit rate, miss rate, and many others, including informedness, which is the probability that a test will return an informed prediction, as opposed to a guess. It is calculated by adding the sensitivity to the specificity and then subtracting the sum by 1.

In Ludwig, field mappings, model hyperparameters, and weights are saved during training. The raw data input, which can be sensor data, is input to a preprocessing module, which takes that data, creates some feature mappings, and saves them in JSON format. These mappings are used for transforming data into tensors and are important as they are subsequently used for mapping new input data into the same tensor sets. If a new set of sensor Concentration data has a high degree of similarity to a previously processed set of Concentration data, then that new dataset will map into the same processed data, based on congruence of their corresponding tensors. These tensors are then provided to the training module, which ultimately produces a model with its tuned weights and hyperparameters.

During the prediction run of Ludwig, new data are introduced into the model, and the same mappings, weights, and hyperparameters that were developed during the training phase are loaded and used for obtaining new preprocessed data for model prediction. If real-time sensor datasets are available, then the Ludwig training set can be taken to the agricultural crop field—or marine aquacultural environment—where signals can be collected and then fed directly into the trained dataset in order to produce a DL predictive model of the metabolomic interactions. This process is standard in unsupervised learning systems, statistical pattern recognition, and intelligent control systems involving computer vision, navigational guidance, chemical processing, nuclear generation, natural language processing, and many other applications. What makes Ludwig attractive to modeling the functional genomics of agricultural plant-soil dynamics is that it facilitates the interface of sensor input with the DL architecture by its innate ability to handle data type abstraction, its use of a declarative model definition, YAML, which is human readable and easily modifiable, and its smart use of **kwargs. **kwargs is a Python construct of keyword arguments that allows the declaration of variables and their amount within the calls to the function arguments directly.

The final predictions and scores are produced in raw numerical format, and these data are processed using the same mappings produced during training. The result, for this functional genomic DL model, is the final prediction of mutualist vs parasite switch, and the degree of symbiosis or lethality.

Once the processing of the training and prediction modules is finished, Ludwig is ready for hypothesis testing and experimental runs. The experiment trains a model on the training set and predicts on the test set, providing output predictions, and training and test statistics in JSON format, used by the visualization component of Ludwig to obtain graphs. Massively parallel processors, such as the AN/UYS-2, using the Processing Graph Method 2, and other symbolic signal processing algorithms, use a somewhat similar technique to obtain navigational and guidance optics and acoustics but at significantly greater complexity and cost (Little, 1991). Ludwig allows the user to declare only the specific code necessary to modify the arguments that are pertinent to the model hypothesis. This hypothesis is used to provide parameters to a function that are collected in a dictionary with their names and their values and then merged with the Ludwig defaults, allowing full inspection of all parameters at the machine language level.

The Ludwig default model is divided into five sections: input features, output features, a combiner, a training component, and a preprocessing component.

The training and preprocessing components allow the user to modify the behavior of the training loop and change the side-channel leaks or change the learning rate. The input and output feature types—and there can be many besides Concentration and gradient Class—include text, category, date, numerical, binary, bag, image, audio/speech, waveform, time series, set, sequence, (geophysical) map, and H3, which is a geospatial index. Each input feature interfaces with an encoder specific for its feature type, and each output feature interfaces with a decoder specific for its feature type, yet there may be multiple encoders associated with a specific input data type, as there may also be multiple decoders associated with a specific output data type. In other words, each input type has multiple encoders to choose from, and each output type has multiple decoders to choose from.

Central to the encoder ➔ decoder routing is a Ludwig component called a combiner. The combiner is a mechanism for taking one or more inputs and producing one single output. Combiners encapsulate many-to-one mappings, and they are necessary because often, and almost always with functional genomics, multiple inputs of different types produce a single output. As a result, different instantiations of this input ➔ encoder ➔ combiner ➔ decoder ➔ output architecture allow a variety of machine learning problems to be solved. For example, the architecture: image ➔ encoder ➔ combiner ➔ decoder ➔ text will produce an image classification system as is depicted in Fig. 10, while the three-to-one mapping:

numerical input ➔ encoder1 \
binary input ➔ encoder2—combiner ➔ decoder ➔ numerical output
category input ➔ encoder3 /

will produce a classical regression system as depicted in Fig. 11.

The encoders are functions that take raw tensors and manipulate them into a latent representation; the decoders then take the latent representations and generate outputs. To reiterate, the encoders for input features that are currently

Image Object Classification

image_path_concentration	class
imagenet/image00000x	mutualist
imagenet/image00000y	parasite
Imagenet/image00000z	neutral

ludwig experiment
--data_csv imagenet_csv
--model_definition "{input_features:
[{name: image_path_: stacked_cnn}],
output_features: [{name: class, type: category}]}"

FIG. 10   Image classification in Ludwig.

Classic Regression

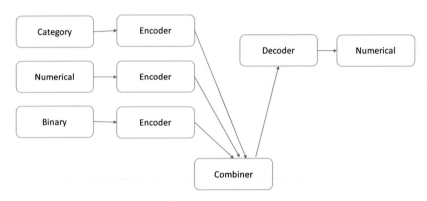

Source: Piero Molino, Ph.D. AI Summer School 2020

FIG. 11   Classical regression in Ludwig; predictive yet nonretrodictive.

available in Ludwig are stacked CNN, parallel CNN, stacked parallel CNN, RNN, CNN RNN, and Transformer/BERT. Regardless of the input feature type and the tensors that they represent, after internal computations by the encoder, the result is a vector encoding. For instance, the stacked CNN uses several 1D convolutions followed by several fully connected layers, while the parallel CNN uses several 1D convolutions of varying kernel widths in parallel, followed by several fully connected layers.

Each encoder has its own hyperparameters that can be tuned, and so for high order systems, or even for low order ensemble systems with great variability like the *E. huxleyi-P. inhibens* metabolite/pathogen switch, many hypotheses can be tested given adequate access to sensor input. In the laboratory, where factors are more easily controlled, rosepbacticide diversity has been explored, and their opportunistic symbiont interactions with algal cells other than *E. huxleyi* has also been investigated. Because different phenylpropanoids are produced by different algal hosts, many variations on the *E. huxleyi-P. inhibens* metabolite/pathogen switch are possible. In a Ludwig encapsulation of a more general *Emiliania*-roseobacter clade model, *Emiliania* is characterized by input feature types, and the variable characteristics of the roseobacter clade as a whole comprise the output feature types. This study is now within the capability of most modern molecular biology labs yet to date remains to be undertaken because of inadequate sensing platforms.

Seyedsayamdost (2017) and colleagues have examined the effects of sinapic acid, ferulic acid, cinnamic acid, and caffeic acid on RSB production in *P. inhibens*. The effects of cinnamic acid and caffeic acid on the secondary metabolome of RSB production were negligible, but the introduction of sinapic acid and ferulic acid to the environment led to the discovery of 10 additional analogs of RSB. From these results, the conclusion is reached that roseobacter such as *P. inhibens* may biochemically match their RSB output to the host with which they are interacting. This conclusion could be verified and expanded upon by Ludwig simulations. Further studies are required, and *Emiliania*-roseobacter interactions in their marine environments would be amenable to machine learning algorithms, given metabolomic biochemical sensor input at the cellular level.

2.4   Pollinators, Ludwig combiners, and the carbon-energy cycle

The Ludwig combiner is a powerful DL construct, and is elucidated in Fig. 12.

The combiner aggregates input types, and after a series of deep dive feature detections, statistical pattern classifications and simulated annealing produce a predictive model output. In an agricultural context, this ability to combine inputs coherently and with reproducibility is vital to understanding the entire soil-plant microbiome, which is in turn very advantageous for gaining a clear understanding of sustainable crop management, food safety, and environmental protection.

Advanced plant-soil metabolomic introgression models also are emerging. In the past 10 years, the field of functional genomics has progressed from shot-gun approaches of DNA sequencing to RNA velocity studies to transient cell states characterized by activation barriers and basins of attraction to dynamic modeling of not only genes but also gene signatures, that is, simulations of genetic functional changes over time. In the process, it has become clear that

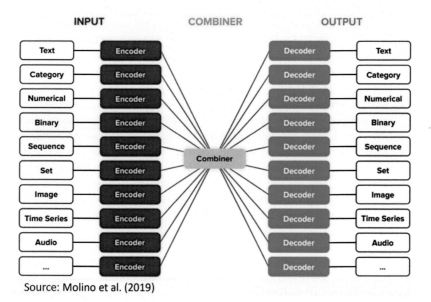

Source: Molino et al. (2019)

FIG. 12   The Ludwig combiner.

not only are full descriptions of single cell genomics necessary to elucidate genome function but connections of genes and their interactions are crucial as well. Genes are regulated in a bistable manner, so that transfer learning relies not on single genes but on several key genes whose signatures are modulated across signal transcription bridges and which can be used for multiple cellular functions. Stein-O'Brien et al. (2019) postulate that biochemical cell signals, at their fundamental level, exhibit multiscale dimensionality that propagate in a hierarchy of dimensions. Modeling the interactome thus becomes a matter of determining to what dimensions this hierarchy collapses, so that the pertinent dimensions can be characterized.

Cellular level measurements indicate that the propagation of the gene signatures is not linear but follows a jump from one basin of energy attraction to another. Signal transduction occurs in a latent space, via fractional order processes, from one sequential attractor state to another (Damarla & Kundu, 2019; Dracopoulos, 1997; Mehta & Henderson, 1991). These attractor states need not be spin states, as is the case with magnetic dipole moments of hydrogen in a magnetic field (spin up or down). Szu and Henderson (1993) have shown that using lattice embedding, attractor states can follow a specific trajectory. It remains an open question as to which trajectories genetic signatures traverse.

Regardless of the latent space, the hierarchy of collapsible dimension space necessary for Ludwig frameworks need not be overly complex for hypothesis generation. Ludwig relies on an iterative process to determine nearly optimal system behaviors and does not require perfect retrogression tracebacks to an initial state for validation of encoder choices. Reductionism does not imply constructionism.

Even if it were physically possible to identify all genes and all of their interactions in a genome, it would not necessarily mean that a way can be identified to put those building blocks back together. Recombination alone cannot account for differential introgression. Therefore, the ability to incorporate multiple encoders into a DL algorithm, as Ludwig is able to do with its combiners, provides a computational bridge from theoretical biophysics to systems engineering when modeling agricultural genomics. Just as sexual reproduction results in gene flow, which facilitates adaptation within species, gene flow via introgression and recombination among species has been observed in natural processes and can have long-term effects on the genus. Such introgression, called adaptive radiation in evolutionary biology, could—if properly understood and controlled—result in crop variations that foster rapid divergence, particularly when changes to the environment make new resources available, restrict access to existing resources, or open new niches for crop propagation.

As with the *E. huxleyi-P. inhibens* metabolite/pathogen switch, which exhibits a symbiotic-to-pathogenic trigger under excess algal density and perhaps other environmental conditions, it has been shown that bumble bees damage plant leaves and accelerate flower production when pollen is scarce (Pashalidou et al., 2020). Many bees, including the western honey bee

Apis mellifera, face harm by multiple pest and pathogen stressors, despite ineffective interventional strategies, which are short-term, expensive, or impractical. One solution for bee health and survival is to feed or inject the host bee with RNA interference (RNAi) to silence essential parasite genes (Leonard et al., 2020). Honey bees possess the genetic mechanisms for RNAi, a eukaryotic antiviral immune system in which double-stranded RNA molecules (dsRNA) trigger degradation of other RNA molecules with similar nucleotide sequences. This dsRNA provides protection against RNA viruses, as well as *Varroa destructor*—a species of parasitic mite. Yet there are complications. For one, direct administration of dsRNA yields patchy and transient effects. For another, there are off-target effects. Also, this method is problematic at large scale when defending a hive, as dsRNA is expensive to produce and degrades rapidly in the environment.

One promising alternative to direct injection of dsRNA is to genetically modify a symbiotic bee gut bacteria, *Snodgrassella alvi*. The modified *S. alvi* is designed to release specific dsRNA that initiates an immune response in the host bee. Because of the modular nature of the Ludwig DL toolbox, Ludwig offers a good platform for testing optimal immunization strategies involving *S. alvi*. Importantly, Ludwig uses the declarative model definition language YAML to serialize data and does so by modifying only a small subset of the input feature variables. Very precise immunoresponse pathways can be simulated while merging these modifications with most of the remaining input feature defaults. Also, because there is a many-to-one mapping between input features and output features via Ludwig's combiner, RNAi targeting pathways can be fine-tuned in order to ascertain which genetic triggers silence essential parasite genes while minimizing off-target effects. It remains an open question as to whether or not this RNAi-based defense can be passed from adult to larvae or from adult to adult via flowering plants.

One initial experimental design to test the null hypothesis that RNAi-based defense strategies cannot be inherited or obtained metabolically is to model the best predictive RNAi silencing pathway of *S. alvi* pathway using a systematic combination of CNN and RNN encoders. As previously mentioned, with DL agent-based adaptive learning algorithms—as opposed to more traditional combinatoric methods—agents are represented not by components, such as reactants or genes, but rather by actions of those components, such as kinetic reactions or genetic expressions. Within this framework, an experiment using Ludwig is designed where a CNN encoder encapsulates the *S. alvi* RNAi metabolic production and pathogen silencing genetic pathways, while an RNN encoder encapsulates the introgression genomic pathways from host to flowering plant, and the inheritable genomic pathways from adult honey bee to larvae. Because of the modular and parallelizable capabilities of Ludwig, evolutionary programming using the seminal techniques of genetic algorithms and the optimal allocation of trials pioneered by Holland (1973) can be readily performed at the parallelizable matrix level with rapid updates and feedback checks rather than over long-term linear one-dimensional time series profiles. Models for hypothesis testing using causal networks and probabilistic simulations are underway, using conventional computing platforms and quantum computing platforms alike (Mehta, 2020).

Although bee health is a relatively small component of the Earth's ecosystem, it is an essential one, especially with respect to many of the world's agricultural crops and thus to the entire carbon-energy cycle. Models of the carbon-energy cycle abound. At an overarching level, when organisms use matter for metabolism, energy is produced. Energy not used by the organism is cycled back to the ecosystem, usually as heat. Changes in this cycle can be beneficial, and they can be detrimental. Regardless of their impact, knowing how these cycles behave is important for keeping the detrimental impacts low, while at the same time maximizing both the local and the global beneficial impacts within the ecosystem. The carbon-energy exchange process is a living process, necessary for life and a part of life. As most models of living processes are complex, iterative, branching, and multilayered, they are ideal candidates for implementation by DL neural networks. The intricacies of the carbon-energy cycle can be studied at a very detailed scale, yet they can also be explained on a system-wide scale, whereby CO_2 is used by green plants during photosynthesis and oxygen is released as a by-product.

The fixed carbon enters the food chain, where it is used as an energy source directly by herbivores and omnivores and decomposers and indirectly by carnivores. Production of CO_2 occurs by, among other things, respiration of animals, burning of wood and fossil fuels, volcanic eruptions, and release from hot springs and fissures. Carbon reservoirs include CO_2 in the atmosphere, CO_2 in water, fossil fuels such as coal and petroleum, and carbonates in the Earth's crust—the 40-km outermost shell of the planet, containing 1% of the Earth's mass and, to date, all known life in the universe. These processes can be measured by chemical and thermal sensors as inputs for Ludwig and other advanced DL architectures. Ludwig can then, in turn, be used to model the measured chemical and thermal processes and generate epigenetic landscapes for genomic editing on an intraspecies basis and progressively on an cross-species basis. This ability to dynamically test hypotheses in silico and then use the results of these tests for best agrochemical practices, from genomic editing to crop selection and rotation, is a powerful tool for beneficially monitoring and improving agricultural crop resources and products.

Moreover, cross-kingdom gene transfer has been shown to be possible with genetic engineering and has the potential to alleviate some of the global impediments to agricultural crop health and sustainability. As one example, the fungus *Fusarium graminearum* is a major pathogen of wheat, and infections by *F. graminearum* on wheat crops result in annual losses of ~28 million metric tons, valued at $5.6 billion USD. *F. graminearum* not only reduces harvest yield but also infects wheat with trichothecene toxins including deoxynivalenol (DON) that render harvested wheat too poisonous for consumption. Perhaps more alarming, *F. graminearum* is becoming increasingly prevalent because of the increased production of maize, which is also a host for the fungus. The global trend in the decreased practice of plowing, that is, no-till farming, also plays a role in the spread of *F. graminearum*. Plowing, or tillage, is detrimental to *F. graminearum* as it renders the fungus less capable of survival on the previous year's fallow.

Recently Wang et al. (2020) have isolated the *Fusarium* head blight 7 gene (Fhb7). Fhb7 encodes a glutathione *S*-transferase that decodes and disrupts DON production. The Fhb7 gene was acquired via a natural fungus-to-wheat transfer in a wild wheat analog. Although lateral gene transfer events, that is, the transfer of genetic material between agricultural plant species and their pathogens, is rare, occurrences have been studied in the lab, albeit with no practical agricultural crop applications to date. Genetic transfer between sweet potato and its parasitic Agrobacteria, and also between sorghum and its parasitic *Striga*, have been engineered using bioinformatically informed next generation sequencing (NGS) tools (Golosova et al., 2014). It is quite possible that many other cross-species gene transfers are not only experimentally feasible but also agriculturally beneficial. It stands to reason that DL toolboxes like Ludwig, used to model predictive genomic defense mechanisms in agricultural crops, help make such possibilities promising.

3   Section II. DAS networks

3.1   Agricultural factors in the plant-silicon cycle: Genomic regulation of blight, drought, and invasive species

Silicon is an important regulator of the Earth's carbon-energy cycle. Silicon is the second most abundant element in the Earth's crust and influences diatom microalgae metabolomic pathways in oceans. The weathering of silicate materials on land provides beneficial plant nutrients and also provides resistance to herbivory and plant pathogens. Furthermore, the plant retention of silicon by plants during ecosystem retrogression, such as drought (De Vries et al., 2020; Gupta et al., 2020), blight, and invasive species competition (Weiss, 2020) suggest potential agricultural reclamation in nutrient-poor and nutrient-depleted environments (Carey, 2020; De Tombeur et al., 2020).

Intelligent management of nutrient-poor soils is a growing area of interest, particularly in extreme environments where haloarchea exist (Kunka et al., 2020). Using Raman spectroscopy in the purple portion of the visible spectrum, it is possible to detect this third kingdom on Earth. In future applications of off-Earth agricultural platforms, including the International Space Station, this is important in that haloarchea provide a link for identifying and studying potential agricultural environments in hostile environments, such as off-Earth bases and the Earth's polar regions (Henderson, 2021).

Over the past 50 years, optical fiber-based sensing devices have become increasingly prevalent and are used in both terrestrial and marine environments for measuring thermal climes, reservoir contours, and other geodesic phenomena. Fiber-based sensors are a viable alternative to point-based electronic sensors and consist of an optical interrogator that sends visible light through the core of an optical fiber. As the light propagates through the fiber, it passes through a fiber Bragg gradient (FBG), which contains a series of optical filters that can reflect specified wavelengths back the traversed portion of the fiber while letting other wavelengths proceed. This gating ability is accomplished by periodically altering the refractive index of the fibers in much the same way that a kaleidoscope operates, yet in a more precise and purposeful way. External factors including heat, vibration, pressure variation, and acceleration cause a shift of the wavelength of the reflected light, which in turn can be measured and translated into physical units such as temperature, amplitude, and strain. FBG sensors are designed to measure within a specified range of wavelength, and so it is relatively straightforward to link multiple sensors on a single optical fiber. Since FBG sensors are nonconductive, electrically passive, and impervious to electromagnetic interference, they are able to operate in environments where noise, corrosion, or high voltage could disrupt or damage electronic or chemical sensors. Nevertheless, these optical sensors have drawbacks, namely that they are only quasidistributed and hence not entirely satisfactory for sensing continuous gradient conditions at the detailed levels that would be necessary in plant-soil microbiomes, marine aquacultural regions, or agricultural plant-silicon cycle environments.

3.2   Helically wound DAS

DAS uses inhomogeneities in the fiber that scatter—via Raleigh scattering—laser pulses emanating from the light source, which is then captured and measured. Thus, the fiber itself is the sensor, and in unperturbed environments, the signal emanating along the fiber will be uniform. That is, the shape and the strength of the electromagnetic wave propagating along the top and the bottom of the sensor fiber will be the same, as shown in Fig. 13.

However, where there is a disturbance to the fiber caused by some dynamic activity, the distance between the inhomogeneities will change, albeit slightly, as shown in Fig. 14.

A disturbance, which might be caused by subsurface seismic events, extreme and sudden weather disruptions, or agricultural crop sabotage, can be detected. The disruption will result in a slight change of the optical path lengths, which can be detected and measured with an interrogating unit. The precision of the measurement is limited only by the strength of the signal and the sensitivity of the detector. With DAS technology, vertical displacement and curvature of the scattered and reflected signal are measured as Figs. 15 and 16 indicate.

shape sensing   helical fiber

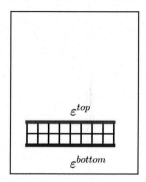

$$\varepsilon^{top} = \varepsilon^{bottom}$$

Source: Paul Sava, Ph.D.
Colorado School of Mines
Private Correspondence June 2021

FIG. 13   A uniform signal along an unperturbed DAS fiber.

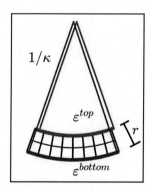

$$\varepsilon^{top} < \varepsilon^{bottom}$$

$$\kappa = \frac{\varepsilon^{bottom} - \varepsilon^{top}}{r}$$

Source: Paul Sava, Ph.D.
Colorado School of Mines
Private Correspondence June 2021

FIG. 14   A perturbed DAS fiber.

vertical displacement

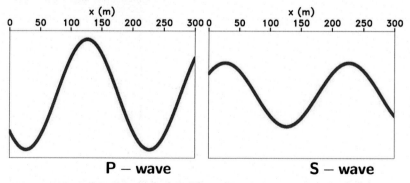

Source: Paul Sava, Ph.D.   Colorado School of Mines   Private Correspondence June 2021

FIG. 15   Vertical displacement along a perturbed DAS fiber.

curvature

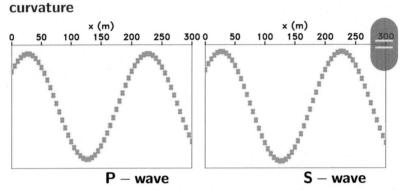

Source: Paul Sava, Ph.D. Colorado School of Mines   Private Correspondence June 2021

FIG. 16   Curvature change along a perturbed DAS fiber.

This is a simple yet powerful design, as demonstrated by Ning and Sava (2018). Channel spacing is determined by the laser source and the measurement instruments, not in the manufacturing specifications of the fiber cable. Even so, there are downsides. Primarily, such fiber sources are sensitive to strains in the axial direction, that is, along the fiber. For vertical seismic profiling this is non-problematic, since laser pulses impinge on the cable almost in line with the fiber. DAS is also used in hydraulic fracture monitoring, where microseismic events occur very close to the fiber, and thus there is always a partial waveform that is parallel to the fiber and can be detected by the interrogating unit.

Yet DAS, when used with a single straight fiber, does not work very well for remote dynamic events, which occur at approximately the same depth as the fiber. When this is the case, the waveforms arrive at the fiber wall in an isoplanar cross pattern, and there is no in-line side component to measure. The same situation applies for surface seismic events and ground perturbations, including crop monitoring for pest swarms, soil degradation caused by long-term climate change, and other scenarios important for crop protection and food security. In these situations, the source is at or near the soil surface. Therefore the laser pulse source travels vertically down to the fiber, hits the horizontal cable, and then is reflected so that the angle between the reflected pulse the fiber is nearly 90 degrees and there is no sensitivity in that direction. The signal is stealth, as shown in Fig. 17.

For agricultural soil-microbiome sensing and marine aquacultural sensing, quasidistributed fiber optic sensors are an improvement over point-based electronic sensors. Likewise, single straight fiber Raleigh scattering DAS is an improvement over Bragg gradient fiber optical sensors. Yet for measurements requiring the sensitivity and precision necessary for agricultural microbiome sensing, even further improvements are required. Presently, one such

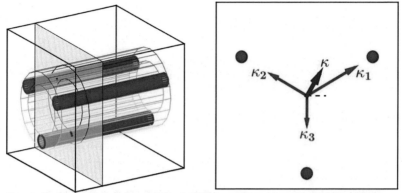

Source: Paul Sava, Ph.D. Colorado School of Mines   Private correspondence June 2021

FIG. 17   A DAS single straight fiber measuring isoplanar wave forms.

improvement exists and has been field tested: the helically wound fiber cable. Fig. 18 shows a schematic of such a DAS cable.

For a relatively rigid DAS helically wound cable, a single event in (x, y, z) spatial dimensions can be detected. Such a scenario is depicted in Fig. 19. A localized agricultural crop disruption is accurately identified.

With single straight fiber cable, the cable is cylindrical and sheaths a straight central linear fiber. With helically wound fiber cable, the cable is cylindrical and sheaths a helical fiber. If the cable were to be cut and opened along its surface of length AB and the sheathed fiber within this portion were to be unwound, then with some high degree of probability, P, the fiber would form the diagonal of a rectangle with sides of length AB with a wrapping angle α. The accuracy or specificity of the measurement of A, B, and α depend on P, and P approaches unity as the compactness of the winding of the fiber is increased. As the rigidity of the helically wound cable decreases, the sensitivity of the cable to the environmental signal increases. This increased sensitivity results in a chirping signal as the period of the helix is varied, and is illustrated in Fig. 20.

When chirping occurs in a helix, DAS can detect multiple disruptive events in the agricultural field. Such a scenario is depicted in Fig. 21.

If the displacement of the helical DAS cable, its density, its stress tensor, and its stiffness tensor are known, then the equation of motion and the stress-strain relationship are calculated by the formulas in Fig. 22.

Fig. 23 shows the downward displacement of a DAS cable when a localized signal burst such as an explosive force propagator impinges upon it.

When a DAS cable senses multiple agricultural crop disruptions, such as might be encountered by a locust swarm convergence, the helical displacement and chirping frequency is an amalgamation of the resulting signal strengths as shown in Fig. 24.

shape sensing
helical fiber

Source: Paul Sava, Ph.D. Colorado School of Mines
Private Correspondence June 2021

helix

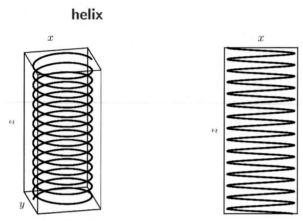

FIG. 18 A DAS helically wound cable.

helix

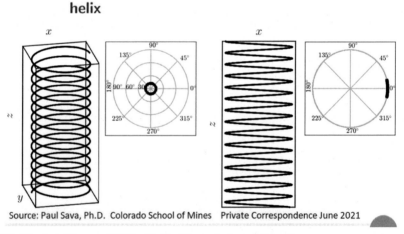

Source: Paul Sava, Ph.D. Colorado School of Mines   Private Correspondence June 2021

FIG. 19 A rigidly wound DAS cable identifies a single crop disruption.

Therefore, if a dynamic change to the soil is propagated as multiple waves, no matter how slow or how small, they will impact a helically wound DAS cable with some degree of broadside compression. That is, the waves will hit the fiber at a side. In theory, the precision or sensitivity of the measurement is dependent only on the wavelength and precision of the laser source at the interrogator of

chirping helix

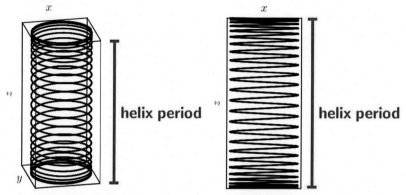

Source: Paul Sava, Ph.D. Colorado School of Mines   Private Correspondence June 2021

FIG. 20   A chirping signal resulting from a dynamic helical period.

chirping helix

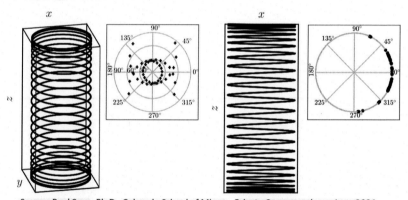

Source: Paul Sava, Ph.D. Colorado School of Mines   Private Correspondence June 2021

FIG. 21   Localized spatial signals from a chirping helix.

equation of motion	stress-strain relation
$\rho\ddot{\mathbf{u}} - \nabla \cdot \underline{\sigma} = \mathbf{f}$	$-\underline{\sigma} + \underline{c} : \underline{\varepsilon} = \underline{h}$

$\mathbf{u}$ = displacement	ρ = density
$\underline{\sigma}$ = stress tensor	$\underline{c}$ = stiffness tensor

Source: Paul Sava, Ph.D. Colorado School of Mines   Private Correspondence June 2021

6

FIG.22   Equations for helical motion and stress-strain relationship.

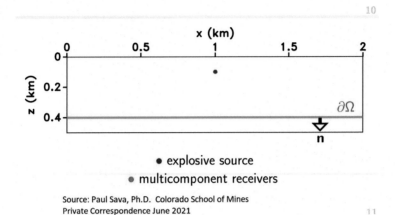

FIG. 23   An explosive source impinging on a DAS cable.

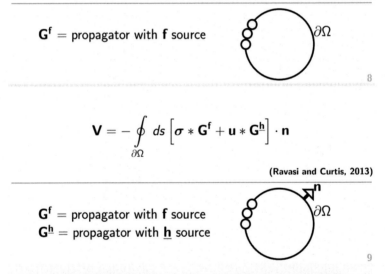

FIG. 24   Characterization of two disruptive signal sources.

the DAS fiber. The problem remains how to analyze this repeated back propagation of signal. DAS with machine learning algorithms provide one such solution. Machine learning was first applied to DAS data in 2015, and the first CNN applied to DAS data followed shortly thereafter in 2017. Currently there is much interest in generalized adversarial networks using DAS data, and because data sources may be physically distant from data storage locations, concurrent projects are underway using high-performance computing, CUDA, GPU, and TPUs. Applications using data lakes that minimize the need for data downloads and facilitate edge computing are also being developed. Such applications allow processing alongside the sensor where only relevant information is extracted from very large data streams. Furthermore, sensors within sensors using capillary-electrophoresis applied to mass spectrometry (CESI-MS) sheathed with DAS fiber currently exist for precise measurements of soil metabolomics, the local soil-crop environment, and key elements of the Earth's hydrologic cycle (Kafader et al., 2020). All such DL and computational developments are applicable for measuring soil signals to inform and enhance practices for sustainable agriculture.

4   Section III. GRANITE and the agent-based GRANITE Network Discovery Tool

GRANITE is an agent-based modeling (ABM) software suite for simulating large, complex, and dynamical systems, particularly biological networks and their communication motifs. We have validated and verified GRANITE on metabolic networks, specifically on the mycolic acid biosynthesis pathway of *Mycobacterium tuberculosis* (Henderson, 2012) where 197 metabolites participate in 219 reactions catalyzed by 28 proteins. This is a relatively uncomplicated pathway as there are 28 exchanges regulated by 197 agents. An interactive demonstration of this pathway can be found at https://youtu.be/c_38zCuDuPU. Further experiments using GRANITE are being conducted using DNA encoding libraries for drug and natural pesticide discovery and for quickly and informatically targeting hit molecules where RNase L (latent) activates viruses acting on RNA molecules.

GRANITE is a scalable and computationally efficient tool for DL that allows researchers to interact with dynamically evolving simulations, propose and test systems-level hypotheses, and make predictions to substantiate, augment, or reject these hypotheses. GRANITE uses environmental feedback and unsupervised learning algorithms to model biological pathways, allowing researchers to perturb those pathways, make predictions, and formulate hypotheses based upon those perturbations. GRANITE is expressive enough to capture many important biological networks, GRANITE can modularly use different interaction models, and GRANITE is computationally tractable.

To illustrate, consider a trivial network where repression of A activates B, which then activates C and D, and the activation of D represses E. Other biological pathway analysis tools offer no way for researchers to easily measure the effect of A upon E without tracing the entire network. In this example, only five nodes are represented; the solution space grows exponentially as the number of nodes increases linearly. Calculations of results become increasingly complicated when analyzing networks that consist of millions or more components.

Furthermore, by using Flux Balance Analysis, GRANITE provides a solution space to study genomic networks when specific concentrations of nodes or factors such as temperature and pH vary within the network.

GRANITE accounts for these conditions by the way in which agents are represented and by the way in which these agents interact. In GRANITE, agents are represented not by components such as reactants or genes but rather by actions of components such as kinetic reactions or genetic expressions. In GRANITE, interactions are based not on agent-agent interchanges but rather by agent-environment couplings. Because the effect of the environment is global, local perturbations can be measured throughout the simulated biological network almost instantaneously, limited only by hardware processing time and any incorporated time delays designed to track observed biological processes. Consequently, GRANITE is able to simulate the effects of A upon E without tracing through the entire network, a process known as stigmergy.

Implementation of GRANITE is based on three subsystems:

(1) a simulation framework where agents are organized into dynamic models;
(2) a domain specific language (DSL) for expressing genomic functions; and
(3) a graphical user interface (GUI) called glimpseGRANITE for visualizing and interacting with simulations.

The GUI is implemented in Java, while all other components are implemented in Scala.

A system model is created for an experiment in the GRANITE context by instantiating a biological network from systems biology markup language representational format, or from GRANITE DSL. A set of reaction agents and their supporting entities are created by parsing the model, initializing the agents and their environments, and populating the environment with metabolites or genetic components. The agents are then placed in the simulated framework where they interact with one another indirectly, using the environment as the mediator. GRANITE employs an expressive modular ABM to express units of metabolomic function. An enzymatic reaction, for instance, is represented by an agent that embodies its dynamics. There are no limits placed on the techniques for expressing a functional response to environmental conditions, so alternative assumptions and models can be modularly swapped into the GRANITE framework where they can then be simulated and tested.

We use a multiagent simulation with choice of scheduling strategies to create computationally tractable and scalable models and simulations. Agents compete with one another to achieve their goals in one or more environments. The simulation framework uses a standard BDI (belief-desire-intent) model to regulate changes in the environments, resulting from agent activities scheduled in the system's agent-environment specifications. In the context of metabolic regulatory networks, the agent is a reaction. The belief that the agent may have about its environment is that there are substrates available for metabolizing. The desire that the agent may have about those substrates is to metabolize as many as possible in a given time increment, either fixed or variable. The intent that the agent may have about metabolizing those substrates may be to do so as efficiently as possible, given the biophysical constraints of the system. The BDI formulation is characteristic in ABM; GRANITE's advantage is that a specific agent's beliefs are decoupled from another agent's beliefs. In other words, an agent is dependent solely on the environment and the way in which it interacts and is coupled to the environment. It is not dependent on another agent's beliefs or interactions with the environment.

In real-world biological communications networks, the environment is a necessary component for signal transmission. The environmental conditions are established in the DSL, allowing the experimenter to define concepts and simulations using a straightforward human understandable syntax. An extension of Scala, the GRANITE DSL expresses state, coordination, and activity for all dynamics of the system. Creating simulations requires instantiating environments and associating interaction models to those environments.

Below is a DSL sample defining a simulation context where memes, that is, reactants a, b, and c and product p are associated with concentration properties. It should be noted that all contexts are encapsulated within the DSL; that is, the GRANITE user does not need to have prior knowledge of the semantics of the code in order for the DSL to be properly parsed. Moreover, units of measure guardrails are built into the code to prevent mismatch of properties, as would happen if one species' concentration were given in molality and another species' concentration were given in molarity.

```
val sc1 = SimulationContext called "sc1"
containing(
a where ConcentrationIs(1000.0)
b where ConcentrationIs(2000.0)
c where ConcentrationIs(50.0)
p where ConcentrationIs(60.0)
) using metabolicNetwork
```

Using the following construct, a model is instantiated by defining which simulation contexts are part of the simulation:

```
Simulation of sc1
```

This one line of DSL code encapsulates the entire simulation context, providing for economy of program execution. Processor level instructions are fetched efficiently, and execution is scalable across memes, bounded only by physical memory constraints, facilitating metabolic and genomic models for hypothesis testing.

Although these hypotheses are now able to be tested in the lab, and sometimes in the field, there are many problems that remain in agronomy, agriculture and machine learning, and we still have much to learn about crop health and sustainability, and much to learn about DL. GRANITE continues to be developed, with a new focus on agricultural sustainability and crop production and protection.

5 Conclusions

New ways to measure agricultural environments are a key objective of the United Nations Food and Agriculture Organization. The world's crop space is limited, and new approaches to crop sustainability, crop surveillance, food safety, and environmental protection are required as the Earth's population grows and its resources become stressed or shifted. Functional genomic modeling of plant-soil interactions provide a path to understanding the complex relationships between agricultural products and the environment, and DL toolboxes such as Ludwig provide an architectural framework for hypothesis testing with respect to these relationships. The current limitations are the nature and strength of the signals that measure the soil-plant interactions, and their platforms. DAS, which for much of the Earth's land cover is shovel-ready in the form of existing fiber, provides a platform for collecting encoder variables to Ludwig, and the resulting hypotheses that are generated can then be used as inputs to agent-based network discovery tools such as GRANITE NDT for further evaluation on a multiscalar, multivector, multitensor, multi-Hamiltonian level for simulation and evaluation, with the goal of sustaining the Earth's agricultural heritage for generations to come.

Acknowledgments

The authors would like to acknowledge Jamie Lawson and Rajdeep Singh of S3 Data Science, San Diego, CA and Price Kagey, Ph.D. of KG Science Associates LLC, San Diego, CA for their work in developing the GRANITE toolbox.

References

Bock, M., & Kirkendall, N. (Eds.). (2017). *Improving crop estimates by integrating multiple data sources: A consensus study report of the National Academies of Sciences, Engineering, and Medicine* (pp. 26–33). The National Academies Press. https://doi.org/10.17226/24892.

Carey, J. (2020). Soil age alters the global silicon cycle. *Science, 369*, 1161–1162.

Carrión, V., Perez-Jaramillo, J., et al. (2019). Pathogen-induced activation of disease-suppressive functions in the endophytic root microbiome. *Science, 366*, 606–612.

Damarla, S., & Kundu, M. (2019). *Fractional order processes: Simulation, identification, and control.* Taylor & Francis Group, LLC Boca Raton, Florida: CRC Press. ISBN: 9781138586741.

De Tombeur, F., Turner, B., Laliberté, E., Lambers, H., Mahy, G., Faucon, M.-P., et al. (2020). Plants sustain the terrestrial silicon cycle during ecosystem retrogression. *Science, 369*, 1245–1248.

De Vries, F., Griffiths, R., Knight, C., Nicolitch, O., & Williams, A. (2020). Harnessing rhizosphere microbiomes for drought-resilient crop production. *Science, 368*, 270–274.

Dracopoulos, D. (1997). *Evolutionary learning algorithms for neural adaptive control.* Springer-Verlag London Ltd. ISBN: 3-540-76161-6.

Ginsberg, G., Terry, S., et al. (2016). Potential next steps in using genomics to advance drug discovery. The National Academies of Sciences, Engineering, and Medicine In *Deriving drug discovery value from large-scale genetic resources: Proceedings of a workshop* (pp. 49–58). Washington, DC: The National Academies Press. 71–84 10.17226/23601.

Golosova, O., Henderson, R., Vaskin, Y., Gabrielian, A., Grekhov, G., Nagarajan, V., et al. (2014). Unipro UGENE NGS pipelines and components for variant calling, RNA-seq and ChIP-seq data analyses. *PeerJ, 2*. https://doi.org/10.7717/peerj.644, e644.

Gupta, A., Rico-Medina, A., & Caño-Delgado, A. (2020). The physiology of plant responses to drought. *Science, 368*, 266–269.

Haas, K., Wightman, R., Meyerowitz, E., & Peaucelle, A. (2020). Pectin homogalacturonan nanofilament expansion drives morphogenesis in plant epidermal cells. *Science, 367*, 1003–1007.

Henderson, R. (2012). Modeling emergent properties of biological systems with an agent-based simulation suite. In *The eighth international conference on bioinformatics of genome regulation and structure\systems biology. BGRS\SB'12, Novosibirsk, Russia, June 25–29, 2012* Russian Academy of Sciences, Siberian Branch. Institute of Cytology and Genetics.

Henderson, R. (2021). From files to vials: A framework for a tissue-on-chips facility aboard the International Space Station. *Bulletin of the American Astronomical Society, 53*(4). https://doi.org/10.3847/25c2cfeb.f3dd9d4b (Planetary/Astrobiology Decadal Survey Whitepapers).

Holland, J. (1973). Genetic algorithms and the optimal allocation of trials. *SIAM Journal on Computing, 2*(2), 88–105. https://doi.org/10.1137/0202009.

Hunsberger, J., Chibane, F., Elkahloun, A., Henderson, R., Singh, R., Lawson, J., et al. (2015). Novel integrative genomic tool for interrogating lithium response in bipolar disorder. *Translational Psychiatry, 5*(2). https://doi.org/10.1038/tp.2014.139, e504.

Kafader, J., Melani, R., Durbin, K., et al. (2020). Multiplexed mass spectrometry of individual ions improves measurement of proteoforms and their complexes. *Nature Methods, 17*(4), 391–394. https://doi.org/10.1038/s41592-020-0764-5.

Kunka, K., Griffith, J., Holdener, C., Bischof, K., Li, H., DasSarma, P., et al. (2020). Experimental evolution of the Haloarchaeon Halobacterium sp. NRC-1 selects mutations affecting arginine transport and catabolis. *Frontiers in Microbiology, 11*. https://doi.org/10.3389/fmicb.2020.00535.

Lal, R. (2004). Soil carbon sequestration impacts on global climate change and food security. *Science, 304*, 1623–1627.

Leonard, S., Powell, J., Perutka, J., Geng, P., Heckmann, L., et al. (2020). Engineered symbionts activate honey bee immunity and limit pathogens. *Science, 367*, 573–576.

Little, B. (1991). *A technique for predictable real-time execution in the AN/UYS-2 parallel signal processing architecture*. Naval Postgraduate School. Theses and Dissertations. http://hdl.handle.net/10945/26805.

McGrew, J. C., Lembo, A. J., & Monroe, C. B. (2014). *An introduction to statistical problem solving in geography*. Waveland Press. ISBN: 978-1-47861-119-6.

Mehta, N. (2020). In B. MacDonald (Ed.), *Quantum computing: Program Next-Gen computers for hard, real-world applications* The Pragmatic Programmers LLC. ISBN-13: 978-1-68050-720-1.

Mehta, N., & Henderson, R. (1991). Controlling chaos to generate aperiodic orbits. *Physical Review A, 44*(8), 4861. https://doi.org/10.1103/PhysRevA.44.4861.

Molino, P., Dudin, Y., & Miryala, S. S. (2019). *Ludwig: A type-based declarative deep learning toolbox*. arXiv:1909.07930.

Ning, I., & Sava, P. (2018). High-resolution multi-component distributed acoustic sensing. *Geophysical Prospecting, 66*(6). https://doi.org/10.1111/1365-2478.12634.

Pashalidou, F., Lambert, H., Peybernes, T., Mescher, M., & Moraes, C. (2020). Bumble bees damage plant leaves and accelerate flower production when pollen is scarce. *Science, 368*, 881–884.

Petkova, M., Tkacik, G., Bialek, W., Wieschaus, E., & Gregor, T. (2019). Optical decoding of cellular identities in a genetic network. *Cell, 176*(4), 844–855. e15.

Seyedsayamdost, M. (2017). Talking with molecules: Marine bacteria and microalgae. The National Academies of Sciences, Engineering, and Medicine In *The chemistry of microbiomes, proceedings of a seminar series* (pp. 77–84). Washington, DC: The National Academies Press. https://doi.org/10.17226/24751.

Stein-O'Brien, G., Clark, B., Sherman, T., Zibetti, C., Hu, Q., Sealfon, R., et al. (2019). Decomposing cell identity for transfer learning across cellular measurements, platforms, tissues, and species. *Cell Systems, 8*(5), 395–411. https://doi.org/10.1016/j.cels.2019.04.004.

Szu, H., & Henderson, R. (1993). Control of chaos using neural networks. In *Proceedings of 1993 international joint conference on neural networks, Volume 2, IJCNN '93-Nagoya, Japan* (pp. 1781–1784).

Wang, H., Sun, S., Ge, W., Zhao, L., Hou, B., et al. (2020). Horizontal gene transfer of *Fhb7* from fungus underlies *Fusarium* head blight resistance in wheat. *Science, 368*, 844–850.

Weiss, K. (2020). On Pacific Islands, coconut palms are an aggressive invader. Biologists are trying to eradicate millions of palms from one atoll. *Science, 369*, 1047–1049.

Wolf-Simon, F. (2012). Microbes and the four basic strategies for life on Earth. The National Research Council of the National Academies In *Research frontiers in bioinspired energy: Molecular-level learning from natural systems. Report of a workshop* (pp. 26–28). Washington, DC: The National Academies Press. ISBN-10: 0-309-22044-0.

Chapter 11

Crop management: Wheat yield prediction and disease detection using an intelligent predictive algorithms and metrological parameters

Nandini Babbar[a], Ashish Kumar[a], and Vivek Kumar Verma[b]

[a]*Department of Computer Science & Engineering, Manipal University Jaipur, Jaipur, Rajasthan, India,* [b]*Department of Information Technology, Manipal University Jaipur, Jaipur, Rajasthan, India*

1 Introduction

Agricultural automation is a major and emerging concern of all countries. Machine learning (ML) is providing a new opportunity for data-intensive science with working on big data technology and high-performance computing (Liakos et al., 2018). Agricultural technology and precision agriculture are now called "digital agriculture" and come from a variety of science disciplines that use powerful approaches to increase agricultural productivity while minimizing negative environmental impacts. Nowadays, biotechnology and digital technologies, like remote sensing (Bastiaanssen et al., 2000), cloud computing, and the Internet of Things (Hashem et al., 2015), are supporting agricultural practices, which leads to the concept of "smart farming" (Kamilaris et al., 2017). The development of new ideas and technologies for better crop production and a better life for farmers attracts the idea of precision agriculture, which includes enhanced present contextual management and administrative tasks, situations, and location awareness.

Typically, ML is a kind of automatic learning process with the experience to achieve a particular task. By using ML algorithms, machines will be capable to automatically do the same task a human can. At the end of learning processes, the model trained with ML is able to predict, categorize, or cluster new examples.

Deep Learning for Sustainable Agriculture. https://doi.org/10.1016/B978-0-323-85214-2.00006-9
273

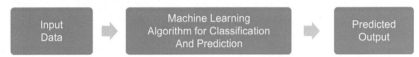

FIG. 1   Machine learning approach.

Basically, ML tasks are categorized into two main types, according to the scheme or pattern of learning system. One of the learning processes is known as supervised learning and the other is unsupervised learning. In supervised learning, the data is presented with examples of inputs and outputs, and the corresponding rules for obtaining a specific output from each input. There is difference between training a data set and a test set in supervised learning. For unsupervised learning, a data set is not provided to the user. There is no difference between a training data set and a test set in unsupervised learning. Agents learn from experience itself by performing tasks many times (Fig. 1).

Generally, there are four fields in agriculture: crop management, livestock management, soil management, and water management. In this chapter, we will concentrate only on a broad field of crop management dealing with subfields, that is, yield prediction and disease detection for the wheat crop (Fig. 2).

Wheat is the main crop in India and the country is the second largest producer of wheat worldwide with a total of 29.7 million hectares for wheat production, and this production is increasing significantly. The main boost in wheat productivity has been observed in Haryana, Punjab, Uttar Pradesh, and also now a day's high production in the state of Madhya Pradesh. Wheat is rich in carbohydrates, vitamins, proteins, minerals, fat, and many more, thus their quality and quantity determination is most important (Guha et al., 2017). Many techniques are introduced to know the yield prediction and disease detection, but at the present time, many farmers are unaware about how to grow and nurture the crops at right place and at right time. Many resources, such as water, air, soil,

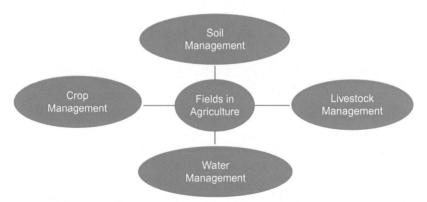

FIG. 2   Fields in Indian agriculture.

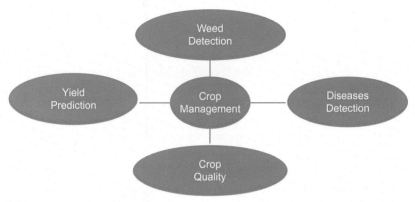

FIG. 3   Areas in crop management.

temperature, and weather, play significant roles in production (Kaur & Kaur, 2019) (Fig. 3).

In this chapter, we will discuss what techniques farmers can use to find the accurate wheat yield production and diseases detection in wheat crop in order to get sufficient and healthy wheat for everyone (Table 1).

TABLE 1 List of abbreviations for machine learning algorithms.

SIF	Sun-Induced Chlorophyll Fluorescence
LASSO	Least Absolute Shrinkage And Selection Operator
WOFOST	World Food Studies
NDVI	Normalized Difference Vegetation Index
RMSE	Root Mean Square Error
DSSAT	Decision Support System for Agro technology Transfer
CWP	Crop Water Productivity
IWP	Irrigation Water Productivity
EVI	Enhanced Vegetation Index
SRI	Spectral Reflectance Indices
NDNI	Normalized Difference Nitrogen Index
NDVI	Normalized Difference Water Index
SAVI	Soil Adjusted Vegetation Index
MODIS	Moderate Resolution Imaging Spectroradiometer

2 Literature review

Since wheat is the most required crop for everyone's survival, it is necessary for us to produce more wheat yield, and while producing, one should take care that it contain a small amount of pesticides and chemicals in order to make a person healthy, One must take care about wheat disease detection so that the wheat produced does not harm anyone in any manner.

Here, we are discussing techniques used in wheat yield prediction and wheat diseases detection with their merits and demerits of every used technique. The conclusion of each paper is determined and what we can enhance in current technique in order to get better results in wheat yield prediction and in diseases detection is discussed.

2.1 Wheat yield prediction

Yield predicting in precision agriculture is considered very important for improving crop management, fruit advertising, and marketing planning. With specially predicted yields, farm inputs in conjunction with fertilizers are applied differently depending on the estimated crop and soil needs.

2.1.1 Genotype × environment interaction for wheat yield prediction

Gene-environment (GE) interactions are states in which different environmental factors have different effects on individuals depending on their genotype, and genetic factors have different effects on different environmental attributes, clustering genotype × surroundings. GE interactions and significant motives of GE interactions are important in crop breeding programs. To look at the reasons for GE interactions, numerous genotypic and environmental covariables have been used (Mohammadi et al., 2015). Two dissimilar genotypes can react to environmental variations in dissimilar ways. A graph can demonstrate the relationship between genes and environment factors. Wheat genotype is evaluated for yield prediction by genotype interaction. A cluster with a high mean genetic correlation was found. These represent the major places where a large number of entries may increase in future seasons (Trethowan et al., 2018) (Table 2).

2.1.2 Machine learning algorithms for wheat yield prediction

Decision support system (DSS): A DSS is a system that provides information and maintains the administrative activities of a business or organization. A DSS addresses organizational administration, operations, and development levels to help in making the decisions about quickly changing issues that may not be easily identified in advance. A DSS can be fully automatic, human-powered, or a combination of each. A DSS has inputs, such as factors, numbers, and characteristics for analyzing user information and proficiency. Users need to analyze the inputs and outputs manually. Transformed data produces a DSS "decision."

TABLE 2 Wheat yield prediction by genotype.

Technique used	Merits	Demerits	Conclusion	Future scope
• Factor analytics model for genotype × environment interaction (Mohammadi et al., 2015)	Predicate accurate result by considering: • Zonal classification • Sowing time • Latitude • Irrigation factor	• Can be more efficient by ML algorithm	• Relationship between genes & environment factors is shown • Yield of wheat genotype evaluated by genotype interaction	• Large correlation can be found with more number of entries in future

Outcomes produced by DSS are built on specific criteria. DSSs that bring out certain cognitive decision-making functions are assembled with artificial intelligence (AI) or intelligent agent technology and known as intelligent DSS. The DSS for harvesting high superiority wheat holds the idea of the united method in making multidisciplinary DSSs. This DSS is taken into account and provides selection provision for all key elements of the production chain, from strategic selection to tactical operations (Rossi et al., 2010).

Regression method: Regression evaluation is a hard and fast statistical technique for estimating the relationships among a based variable and one or more independent variables. If there is no reasonable dependency among variables, one can attempt mathematical equations in order to find a link between them (Niedbała, 2018). The maximum common regression evaluation is linear regression in which a researcher reveals the line that most intently fits the statistics in step with a precise mathematical criterion. Regression evaluation is normally used for two conceptual functions. Initially, regression evaluation is broadly used for predicting and forecasting, where its use has considerable overlap with the field of ML. Then, in some conditions, regression analysis can be used to conclude a fundamental relationship between the independent and dependent variables.

Random forest (RF): Random decision forest is a collaborative learning method that works by constructing a huge number of decision trees during training and outputting classes that are the modes of sorting and grouping or mean prediction (regression), for classification, regression, and other tasks. RF corrects the tendency of overfitting a training set of decision trees. The RF classifier is a collective method that trains numerous decision trees similar with bootstrap, which is collectively called bagging, and subsequent aggregation. RF is an effective and flexible ML technique for crop yield predictions on both a regional and a global scale for its excessive accuracy and exactness, accessibility, and effectiveness in facts analysis. For classification and regression purpose, RF can be used, and when needed, it can be used as regression model also (Jeong et al., 2016).

Support vector machine (SVM): SVM is a set of ML rules developed by way of Vapnik and is primarily based at the principles of statistical learning theory. SVM uses an introduced feature of structural and experimental threat reduction. It has the capability to do the mapping of the functions in high dimensional space though translating the difficult problems to a linearly separable event (Kumar et al., 2019). The determination of the SVM algorithm is to find that the RF classifier (i.e., ensemble method) that trains numerous decision trees in parallel with bootstrap. If you have a set of training samples, each one is marked as association to one of two groupings and the SVM algorithm generates a model that allocates the new example to one of the groups and a nonstochastic binary linear classification. The SVM model represents the examples as points in space, that is, it maps the individual categories into the widest possible gaps. The new examples are then mapped to that identical area and expected to fit to a group primarily built on the aspect of the distance on which they fall.

Neural network: A neural network includes neurons, organized in layers, which translate an input vector into an output vector. Input is taken at each unit after applying numerous features on it, and at that moment passes output to the next layer. Artificial neural networks (ANNs) are extraordinarily crude electronic networks of neurons created on the basis of neural structure of the brain. They learn by analyzing the records one by one and comparing the record's classification with the identified actual classification of the document. The faults from the preliminary class of the first record is fed lower back into the network and conditioned to adjust to the network's set of rules. A group of input values (xi) and related weights (wi) and a characteristic function (g) does the summation of weights and draws the result to the output (y). A neural community includes neurons organized in layers and transforms an enter vector into several outputs. Every unit proceeds with an input, puts a function to it, and passes its output to the succeeding layer (Training an Artificial Neural Network, 2020).

Multilayer perceptron neural network (MLP): MLP is a category of feed-forward ANN, or networks consist of several layers of perceptron. MLP are as often colloquially known as "vanilla" neural networks, specifically when they are having a hidden layer. An MLP contains an input layer, a hidden layer, and an output layer. Through the exclusion of input nodes, every node is a neuron that uses a nonlinear activation function. The input layer gets the parameters to control the neurons of the hidden layer(s) and the output layer method and the weighted indicators from the neurons of its preceding layer and calculate an output cost, making use of an activation feature (Kross et al., 2018). MLP makes use of a supervised learning method referred to as backpropagation (BP) for training. It is a combination of layers and nonlinear activation that differentiate MLP from a linear perceptron and can make a distinction of data that is not linearly separable.

Adaptive network-based fuzzy inference system (ANFIS): ANFIS refers to synthetic neural community based on the Takagi-Sugeno fuzzy inference device. By integrating neural networks in addition with fuzzy logic principles, it is possible to combine the advantages of both into a particular framework. The inference system supports a series of fuzzy IF-THEN rules with a learning function that approximates nonlinear functions. One can identify two parts of the network structure: the premise and consequence. In detail, the architecture consists of five layers. The first layer contains input fuzzy rules, the second layer contains input membership functions, the third layer contains fuzzy neurons, the fourth layer contains output membership functions, and the fifth layer contains a summation of all operations (Rusgiyono, 2019).

Self-organizing map (SOM): A SOM is a form of ANN that uses unsupervised learning to provide a two-dimensional discretized view of the input space of a training sample called a map, and it is a way to reduce dimensions. Unlike other synthetic neural networks, SOMs follow competitive learning rather than error-correcting learning, so we have experience using neighborhood features to hold topological assets in the input space. It is common to think of this type of network structure associated to a feed-forward network in which the nodes are imagined as connected, but this kind of structure varies in arrangement and motivation. The SOM models involve input nodes demonstrating the principle features in wheat crop manufacturing, including biomass signs, organic carbon (OC), pH, Mg, Total N, Ca, cation exchange capacity, moisture content (MC), and the output weights characterized the class labels similar to the anticipated wheat yield (Pantazi et al., 2014).

Supervised Kohonen networks (SKNs): SKN models are supervised neural networks, rising from SOMs used for sorting and grouping. In the case of SKNs, the SOM and output layers are amassed collectively to provide a joint layer trained in keeping within the regime of SOMs. In the SKN network, the input map Xmap and the output map Ymap are "combined" to form the joint input/output map (XYmap) as a result of the unsupervised Kohonen network training scheme. (Melssen et al., 2006) (Table 3).

2.1.3 Remote and satellite data for wheat yield prediction

World Food Studies (WOFOST) Crop Simulation Model: The WOFOST simulation model is implemented to study the progress and production of field crops underneath a vast variety of climate and soil situations. This study is significant initially to evaluate to what degree crop production is inadequate by the features of light, moisture, and macro-nutrients, and additionally estimates what enhancements are possible. It describes the hypothetical idea of production status modeled by WOFOST, and the hierarchy of potential production and water limited restriction production status in the study (Van Diepen et al., 1989).

Normalized Difference Vegetation Index (NDVI): NDVI is the most frequently used vegetation index in ecosystem monitoring. NDVI is a vegetation productiveness proxy based totally on estimates of absorbed photosynthetic active radiation; however, it is also used to estimate different functions consisting of leaf location index, plant life biomass, and water availability. NDVI is

TABLE 3 Wheat yield prediction summary by machine learning algorithms.

Technique used	Merits	Demerits	Conclusion	Future scope
• DSS (Timsina et al., 2008)	• Estimated yield forecast using; Climatically driven potential yield • From water balance component • DSSAT software showed how the yield prediction can be enhanced with increases in CWP and IWP	• Has certain assumptions • Input parameters have some uncertainty	• Dynamic model simulates crop growth and yield prediction • Throughout the planting period sowing can be done • On the basis of atmospheric demand stimulus can be applied	• Effect of weed and pests were not included in the input parameters • Can add them as they also effect the yield prediction
• Regression method • RF • SVM • Neural network (Dadhwal et al., 2003)	• Predict wheat yield before two months of their maturity	• Assumptions in the results presented • Uncertainty in the input parameters • Used static wheat growing areas that leads to error	• Input EVI perform better yield prediction that SIF • Mix of satellite data and climate provides high-performance yield forecast	• Soil information can be taken in order to increase yield production
• MLP (Bhojani & Bhatt, 2020)	• Newly generated algorithms of MLP proves improved output using low RMSE and RAPE	• Recommendation of activation functions for small network structure only	• Activation function provides the results with more accuracy • DharaSig, DharaSigm, and SHBSig, activation functions was created • Increase the performance of neural network	• Can also add weather dataset and soil dataset for crop yield prediction
• Regression model • SVM • RF • Neural network (Cai et al., 2019)	• EVI • achieved better performance than SIF • Combining climate data with satellite data provides high-performance yield forecasts	• Climate data cannot be captured by satellite data, so unable to get 100% accurate result	• Improvement of vegetation index from MODIS and solar-induced chlorophyll fluorescence	• Can add soil factor with temperature, water, and satellite data

• ANN • Multilayer perceptron (Kadir et al., 2014)	• MLP • Networks have been proven to be effective with linear and nonlinear data	• Pesticides effect • Soil conditions • Diseases Affect wheat yield but these parameters were not considered	• Seven input parameters were there • MLP could predict wheat yield with 98% accuracy	• Can reduce the input parameter to increase efficiency
• ANFIS • Used to simulate the hydration properties of wheat grain (Shafaei et al., 2016)	• The simple structure ANN simulation framework was easier to use as compared with the three different structures of ANFIS	• To attain higher moisture content • Usage of longer hydration times instead of higher hydration temperatures	• Water absorption rate is drastically increased with increasing hydration time with temperature	• Higher hydration temperatures can be used with this procedure to measure water content in a short time.
• Supervised SOM and crop sensors • Were used to predict soil properties for yield prediction (Pantazi et al., 2016)	• Reduced labor • Time costs required for soil sampling and analysis • The output shows that cross-validation-based yield predictions for the low-yield class SKN model surpassed 91%	• Being unable to model continuous output relationship	• The resulting nodes consisted of predicted yield equal frequency classes from three trained networks such as CP-ANN, XY-F, and SKN	• Proposed architecture can be enhanced with smooth interpolating kernels to deals with inability of continuous output kernel

considered a qualitative parameter for two reasons. First, it is not a biophysical quantity in itself. Somewhat, it offers an indirect indicator of vegetation range besides health and is polluted by nonvegetation-related features. Second, Advanced Very-High-Resolution Radiometer usually does not incorporate the calibration installed in the observable and NIR bands (Acker et al., 2014).

Soil Adjusted Vegetation Index (SAVI): SAVI is generally used to modify NDVI for the impact of soil brightness in regions wherein vegetative cover is low. Empirically resulted NDVI products have been exposed to be volatile, varying with soil color, soil moisture, and saturation effects from immoderate density vegetation. To improve NDVI, we have evolved a vegetation index that explains the difference between red and near-infrared (NIR) destruction through plant canopies. The index is a conversion approach that reduces soil brightness affects from spectral flora indices associated with red and NIR wavelengths. The index is given as SAVI. The SAVI is an essential step in describing a dynamic soil-vegetation system from remote sensing data (Huete, 1988).

Normalized Difference Nitrogen Index (NDNI): NDNI is intended to evaluate the relative amount of nitrogen contained in vegetation canopies. Reflectance at 1510 nm is determined by means of nitrogen concentration of leaves and the overall foliage biomass of the cover. Multiple scattered signals from the vegetation background can significantly reduce the accuracy of nitrogen prediction. To reduce contextual noise interference, we did two steps to fix the novel NDNI. Initially, the red band within the SAVI was changed through the 1510 nm band. After that, the authentic NDNI is separated using the reviewed SAVI (Xue & Su, 2017).

Normalized Difference Water Index (NDWI): NDWI is one of the indexes derived from at least two remote sensors related to liquid water. One is used to analyze variations in content of water in leaves, the usage of NIR and quick-wave infrared (SWIR) wavelengths. The other is used to check the updates associated with the amount of water in water bodies by means of green and NIR wavelengths defined by McFeeters. The aggregate of the NIR with the SWIR removes versions triggered via leaf inner shape and leaf dryness counted as content material, enhancing the accurateness in recovering the vegetation moisture water content material. NDWI is a measurement of liquid water particles in a vegetation canopy and is associated with incident solar radiation and is primarily considered for soil moisture and canopy soil moisture and cover moisture estimation (Serrano et al., 2019).

Landset-8: Landsat satellites have been in continuous operation since the first Landsat satellite, Earth Resources Technology Satellite 1, was launched in 1972 (Leslie et al., 2017). Landsat 8 is an American Earth observation satellite propelled on February 11, 2013. It is the eighth satellite in the Landsat program; the seventh to reach orbit successfully. Formerly known as the Landsat Data Continuity Mission, this is an association between NASA and the United States Geological Survey. Landsat 8's Operational Land Imager (OLI) is an improved version of the Landsat sensor of the past, built by Ball

Aerospace under a contract with NASA. OLI uses a technical method established by the Advanced Land Imager sensor onboard NASA's experimental EO-1 satellite.

Moderate Resolution Imaging Spectroradiometer (MODIS): MODIS is a payload imaging sensor constructed by Santa Barbara Remote Sensing launched into Earth orbit by NASA. MODIS makes use of four onboard calibrators similar to the distance vision acceptable to offer in-flight calibration: solar diffuser (SD), sun diffuser stability reveal (SDSM), spectral radiometric calibration meeting (SRCA), and a v-groove black frame. MODIS statistics also contribute significantly to decades of continuity. Recording satellite data has made great strides in the field of remote sensing on Earth. Long-term data records from MODIS observations have been extended by visible infrared. The MODIS description help group (MCST) is devoted to the manufacturing of a brilliant MODIS standardized product that is a predecessor to each geophysical product. A certain explanation of the MCST mission declaration and other information can be determined at MCST Web (Xiong et al., 2020).

Metrological simulation model: Meteorological grid fashions use logical and arithmetical formulations that simulate atmospheric approaches consisting of the change of winds and temperature in time. These meteorological parameters are calculated at a discrete spatially equidistant points on an area of interest referred to as a grid. Agro-meteorology deals with all-weather sensitive additives of chains leading from manufacturing to the intake of agriculture products, in particular together with animals and plant life (Gommes, 2001) (Table 4).

2.1.4 CERES-Wheat model for wheat yield prediction

CERES-Wheat V3.5 Model: CERES-Wheat is a system-oriented management model for wheat and is commonly applied worldwide with suitable data available as input. The genetic coefficients essential to run the CERES-Wheat v4.6 model were derived for commonly cultivated varieties. The main additives of the model are nutrition and generative expansion, carbon balance, water balance, and nitrogen balance modules. The model describes vegetative and reproductive development, photosynthesis, respiration, division, leaf, stem, root, shell, seed growth, transpiration, root water uptake, soil evaporation, soil water flow; penetration, and drainage (Lai et al., 2018) (Table 5).

2.1.5 Evapotranspiration and soil moisture content for wheat yield prediction

Crop RS-Met model is remote sensing and climatological model of crop real evapotranspiration (ET) and soil water content (SWC), which is a familiar form of the RS-Met ET model to find daily approximations of ET and root zone area SWC. Crop RS-Met uses the crop factor (Kc), which is distinct as the ratio of ET to reference from the crop and soil surface, using the dual crop FAO56 formula ET (ET0) derived from meteorological data. Together RS-Met and crop RS-Met

TABLE 4 Wheat yield prediction summary by remote and satellite data.

Technique used	Merits	Demerits	Conclusion	Future scope
• WOFST model • To remotely detect input data (Tripathy et al., 2013)	• From satellite data, planting dates can be derived	• The sowing date was estimated by remotely sensed data and climate data, but it can be varied according to situation	• The output shown that with RMSE of <0.4 ton ha-1 at state level • And it can be used for spatial yield prediction	• Accuracy can be improved in spatial yield estimation
• SRI, NDVI, NDNI, NDWI, SAVI	• Find the best representative stage of yield prediction among four stages (i.e., tillering, booting, heading, and milking)	• Rough estimation of yield in booting stage	• With the use of NDVI, yield can be estimated in heading stage • With NDWI yield prediction, milking stage can be estimated	• Can improve the estimation technique in tillering and booting stage
• Multitemporal satellite data (Landset-8 & MODIS) (Chandel et al., 2019)	• Satellite-derived acreage valuation can be chosen as a substitute of the traditional-based CCE survey • 80% accuracy of wheat assessment was observed	• Indian farmer's plot is small compared to the pixel size of the satellite data, making an accurate area mapping of the satellite data at a coarser resolution impossible	• The accuracy of the yield forecast depends on the accuracy of the wheat acreage map resulting from the remote sensing	• Can consider the field data in such a way so that accurate acreage mapping be performed
• Metrological simulation model (Parida & Ranjan, 2019)	• Focus more on reliability and efficient production	• Fuzzy regression sensed data was not considered	• Forecasting techniques such as multiple linear • Regression used for weather prediction and presence and absence of diseases	• We can add satellite data to the existing model and, with AI, can predict better output
• WOFOST model • For maturity date prediction (Lamba & Dhaka, 2014)	• Accuracy of this method was a correlation coefficient R2 of 0.90 and an RMSE of 1.93d	• As this forecast was done for winter wheat maturity date • But some sites did not have winter wheat pixel	• LAI-derived framework was used as input for future meteorological data	• Can add algorithm for wheat health like disease if any at the stage of maturity date
• Landset time integrated NDVI model (Gao et al., 2018)	• Help out farmers to make decisions about particular site-soil and nutrient management • Accuracy within field is average RMSE is 0.79 Mg/ha	• Accuracy of the model is low and there is a large difference between the training and validation datasets	• The model describes a general relationship between wheat yield and NDVI and takes into account spatial and temporal differences between farms, yields, and years	• Homogenous dataset can be used for better prediction

TABLE 5 Wheat yield prediction summary by CERES-Wheat model.

Technique used	Merits	Demerits	Conclusion	Future scope
• CERES-Wheat V3.5 model (Baxla et al., 2018)	• Accuracy of weather prediction was also tested	• Since weather conditions vary greatly, another static factor may be also added into it	• Yield prediction with the assessment of medium range weather forecast, and then value of perfect conditions were predicted	• Can add live data through remote sensing in order to be the more accurate system

TABLE 6 Wheat yield prediction summary by evapotranspiration and soil moisture content.

Technique	Merits	Demerits	Conclusion	Future scope
• Proximal-based biophysical model (Attri & Rathore, 2003)	• Forecast GYEOS available to farmers for decision-making during critical wheat growth stages	• Conclusion can be only based on soil content, no other parameter used	• The consequences show that the crop RS-Met precisely reproduces the seasonal variation of SWC	• Here wheat yield forecasts were made in areas with limited water supplies. We can add more data to it

models use daily NDVI to experience maximum Kc (Kcmax) on specific crops and soil surfaces obtained by empirical means to seasonal changes. When testing with a proximal-based biophysical model of actual ET and soil MC can help predict early grain yields in dry land wheat yields. NDVI is used to regulate Kcmax through the developing stages of various crops as a substitute for vegetation cover and leaf development (Attri & Rathore, 2003) (Table 6).

2.2 Wheat diseases detection

Wheat is one of the most crucial and extensively used vegetation in the world, so rapid detection and identification of the causative agent was required. The significant factor in reducing crop quality and quantity is plant disease. Recognizing plant diseases is the key to preventing agricultural losses. Traditional methods for diagnosing crop diseases depend on expertise. A group of scientists have introduced new technologies that make it feasible. If the infection is found in the early stages of the crop, the effects can be reduced and a healthy crop can be obtained. This section describes the techniques used to detect wheat diseases and their merits, demerits, and how to enhance them for better use in the future.

2.2.1 Machine learning algorithms for wheat diseases detection

Support Vector Regression (SVR): SVR makes use of the identical precept as SVM but for regression problems. SVMs are widely used for grouping and sorting the problems. The usage of SVMs in regression is not always well-documented. Such models are SVRs. The difficulty with regression is finding a function that approaches the mapping from the input domain to the actual number in the training sample idea. SVR is primarily about considering points within the boundaries of a decision. SVR is a prevailing algorithm that provides flexibility and permits you to choose tolerance for errors through both a satisfactory error margin (ϵ) and an acceptance adjustment that exceeds the acceptable error rate (Helman et al., 2019).

Gaussian process regression (GPR): GPR is a nonparametric Bayesian methodology to regression, which is booming in the field of ML. GPR was constructed for the approximation of disease severity (DS) stages on a canopy scale and the reflectance data was measured in the particular area by the use of spectroradiometer. GPR has numerous advantages, including the ability to work well with small data sets and provide predictive uncertainty measures. In the theory of probability and statistics, the Gaussian process is a stochastic process, and all finite sets of these stochastic (random) variables have a multivariate normal distribution. To be precise, all those finite linear combinations are usually scattered. The Gaussian process distribution is a joint distribution of all these random variables, so we can say that it is a distribution of functions with continuous sections (An Introduction to Support Vector Regression (SVR), 2020).

Convolutional neural network (CNN): In deep learning, CNN, or ConvNet, is a class of deep neural network, generally applied to visual image analysis. CNNs can extract learned features in an interpretable format that can identify test images and their disorders, ensuring reliability and validating model reliability and training datasets with human intervention. CNN is a normalized form of the MLP. MLP is typically a fully connected network. Such that, every neuron in one layer is connected to every neuron in the next layer. These networks are "fully connected," which makes it easier for the data to overfit. A general technique of regularization is done by the addition of a specific form of weight quantity to the loss function. CNN takes a different approach to regularization. Taking advantage of hierarchical patterns in data and building smaller and simpler patterns into more complex patterns. Therefore, on the scale of connectivity and complexity, the CNN is extremely low (Azadbakht et al., 2019).

BP neural network: A BP network is a multilayer feed-forward network, with an input layer, a hidden layer (which might have multiple layers), and an output layer. Once a pair of training samples is referred to the network, initially the activated values of the neural node are sent through the input layer, the hidden layer, and finally the output layer. After that the gathered weights are changed from the output, hidden layer, and input layer based on the output error. This is termed as error BP. The procedure makes the network more responsive to input modes. The learning rule in this is to use BP to adjust network weights and thresholds to assume the steepest descent technique to achieve the sum of squares of the minimum error (Toda & Okura, 2019) (Table 7).

2.2.2 Web-based system with multiple regression for wheat disease detection

The Web GIS platform is the browser/server (B/S) architecture of choice, accessing the system interface via a simple, fast, and easy-to-use web browser. It also analyzes information regarding crop pests and disease outbreaks with time, efficiency, and with quantitative measures, and it provides thematic maps and scientific reports of pests and diseases. Crop pest and disease monitoring and prediction systems provide real information of pests and diseases that occur in the agricultural region, providing the scientific origin for developing pest and disease prevention and control measures of crops and provide a records basis and technical guide for the crop network control. Web-based GIS results allow end users to detect disease patterns and contribute to administrators and decision makers by selecting domain and spatial test parameters. End users are healthcare professionals, instructors, local societies, healthcare sector establishments, and decision makers (Wang & Ma, 2011) (Table 8).

2.2.3 Image-processing techniques for wheat disease detection

Most farmers used the naked eye to observe plants that required continuous monitoring and expertise. This method is very time consuming, vast, and impossible in large-scale agriculture. Therefore, it is important to have an automated solution to identify these diseases. Therefore, image-processing techniques must be used for detection and classification. It deals with image formation, initial image acquisition. and processing to achieve the goal (Dong et al., 2019). It includes subsequent steps (Dixit & Nema, 2018):

Image acquisition: This is the preliminary step for starting image operations. Acquiring a digital image is the creation of a digitally encoded representation of an object's visual characteristics, such as a physical scene or the internal structure of the object. This includes preprocessing, for instance, scaling and color conversion.

Image filtering: In image processing, after capturing the image, filters are primarily used to suppress one of the high frequencies of an image, smoothing the image, or the enhancement or detection of edges in the image, in order to improve the rating so as to get a more attractive and relevant image in the output.

Images can be filtered by either frequency or spatial domain.

Colored image processing: Today, digital image processing includes pseudo-color and full-color processing models that systematically and

TABLE 7 Wheat diseases detection summary by machine learning algorithms.

Technique used	Merits	Demerits	Conclusion	Future scope
SVR RF GPR (Li et al., 2012)	• Identification of subcanopy wheat leaf rust • The performance of ML methods improved as LAI value	• Only data collected by spectroradiometer was taken as input	• Result showed that v-SVR outperformed to all three LAI levels with ML method $R^2 \sim 0.99$	• Various remote sensing • Sensors will be used with different LAI levels • in order to extract more efficient wavelength
CNN (Azadbakht et al., 2019)	• Produce more nonlinear mappings and improve expressiveness	• Calculation burden penalty often occurs in parallel networks	• M-bCNN brought improvements and achieved 96.5% data set accuracy and 90.1% test accuracy	• Focus on architecture and hyperparameter optimization and use of M-b CNN for other challenging fine grained classification task
Supervised deep learning framework (Lin et al., 2019)	• The proposed system is embedded in a real-time mobile application for the diagnosis of agricultural diseases	• No suitable dataset	• VGG-FCNVD16 and VGG-FCNS, achieved average recognition accuracy of 97.95% and 95.12% respectively	• Can add more channels to deep learning architecture and via fine tuning find more diseases classes
Neural network (Lu et al., 2017)	• Helping in predicting DON toxin • This mycotoxin in wheat samples is a hypothetically valuable tool to avoid fungus from entering the food chain	• Fusarium head blight (FHB) epidemic causes serious losses by directly reducing grain yields and increasing grain cleaning costs	• Precisely forecast prevalence and nonprevalence of FHB in fungal diseases with a probability of approximately 80%	• Soil and water factors can be used with temperature
BP prediction models (Klem et al., 2007)	• Predictive model shows that its accuracy is better than stepwise regression	• A catastrophic climate and widespread disaster causes a big loss	• Mean square deviation between all predicted outcomes and actual values for test samples within the range of 0.1 to 0.4 level for modified BP	• With the spread and application of rust preventives, it is necessary to investigate the role of planted area and antidisease properties in detail, we can further verify the prediction model
SVM (Mo, 2010)	• SVM technique can attain high fitting and prediction accuracy • Applying this method to predict wheat rust is feasible and efficient	• Predicting wheat rust using a regression model established on small data can increase the prediction error	• Appropriate accuracy varies with each of 3 model, 100% fitting accuracy and 75% prediction accuracy for data set 1, for dataset 2, accuracies are 80.77% and 100% respectively and for data set 3, accuracies are 40.91% and 50%	• Data can be normalized for further processing

TABLE 8 Wheat diseases detection summary by web-based system.

Technique used	Merits	Demerits	Conclusion	Future scope
• Web-based system (Bui & Pham, 2016)	• Web-based forecasting system developed for wheat rust, provided a suitable and fast way to predict wheat rust	• Collection of regression forecasting models for wheat rust is partial, maximum models can only be used locally	• Wheat stripe prediction results that rust may appear in different colors on web maps by predicted value of disease prevalence	• As the assumptions change, we must improve the accuracy of the model even further
• Web GIS platform (Kuang et al., 2012)	• The system quantitatively monitors and predicts crop pest and disease outbreaks	• Since client layer collects data, due to disturbance, data may be inappropriate	• It improves the calculation speed and efficiency, reduces the quantity of data storage, realizes the automation process, and makes the system easy and comfortable to use	• Can add security and validation algorithms while collecting data

completely color images. Color images have three values (or channels) per pixel, which quantify light intensity and chrominance. The real data stored in the digital image data is the luminance information for each spectrum prohibited.

Image compression: One can do the compression of the actual image and encode that real image into less bits. The application or procedure of compression is considered image compression. The purpose of image compression is to decrease image redundancy and collect or send data in an efficient design. It consists of the methods that carry out operations to decrease the image with the aid of reducing its size while maintaining the high quality of the photo (Table 9).

3   Discussion

This chapter compiles research work of various authors written in 58 articles. It begins with the importance of argi-technology in traditional agriculture and moves on to subcategories with its importance in yield prediction and disease detection for the most required crop to survive, that is, wheat. The main diseases that occur in wheat crop are fungal diseases, and most of them are leaf rust, stem rust, and stripe rust. From the studied articles, tables are created based on the techniques used in them, including their merits, demerits, conclusions, and future scope. Here, in this chapter, sections are mainly divided in two parts: yield prediction and disease detection. The first section begins genotype interaction for finding yield prediction and moves on to various ML algorithms and how remote and satellite data help in better yield prediction. Then a CERES-Wheat model without using ML is used; after that how evaporation and SWC can determine yield prediction is discussed. Next, in the second section for wheat disease detection, different tables start from how ML algorithms can detect diseases, how web-based systems can help in diseases detection, and how the main detection is done by performing various operation on images of the particular crop. Image processing is examined.

4   Conclusion and future scope

From the analysis of these articles, it is concluded that, typically, supervised learning methods are used. Fig. 4 contains a pie chart showing the techniques that are frequently used and how we can combine multiple techniques.

Most work for wheat yield prediction is done with consideration of either remote-sensed data for weather or soil characteristics. Future techniques can integrate satellite and climate data using various regression and ML methods, root zone soil water, and other multilayer soil data with satellite imagery crop growth features in order to make an efficient algorithm for better wheat yield prediction.

TABLE 9 Wheat diseases detection summary by image-processing techniques.

Technique used	Merits	Demerits	Conclusion	Future scope
• Image-processing technology to automatically detect and classify plant diseases (Gaikwad & Musande, 2017)	• Efficient way to detects and classify fungal diseases in wheat plants	• The database had very little data to evaluate; it consisted of 120 images; 35% of the images were used for training purposes	• By using a neural network, the accuracy was 80.21% and with SVM accuracy was 89.23%	• Suggested improvements in algorithms for reducing classification errors
• Image-processing techniques to find diseases in agriculture/horticulture crops (Pujari et al., 2014)	• 80.83% accuracy for all image types that use color features • 5% accuracy for all image types using shape features • All image types using color texture functions have an accuracy of 85.33%	• There was no calculation details of accuracies prediction	• The outcomes show that the color texture feature using the SVM classifier is better suited for identifying and classifying symptoms of fungal diseases that affect grain leaves	• Further, we can increase the efficacy of the model

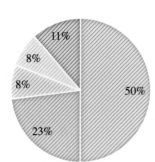

- Machine Learning Algorithms
- Remote and Satellite Data
- Web Based System
- Image Processing Techniques
- Other Models

FIG. 4   Representation of techniques used in the articles.

And from the second section it is observed that image processing does a good job for disease detection, but we can combine a CNN framework (i.e., VGG-FCN-VD16 and VGG- FCN-S) with increased efficiency by enhancing the current algorithm with an image-processing technique using SVM based on the features of color, shape, and texture. By combining these two, we can improve disease detection.

References

Acker, J., Williams, R., Chiu, L., Ardanuy, P., Miller, S., Schueler, C., et al. (2014). *Remote sensing from satellites.*

An Introduction to Support Vector Regression (SVR). (2020). 29 September. Retrieved from https://towardsdatascience.com/an-introduction-to-support-vector-regression-svra3ebc1672c2.

Attri, S. D., & Rathore, L. S. (2003). Pre-harvest estimation of wheat yield for NW India using climate and weather forecast. *Mausam, 54*(3), 729–738.

Azadbakht, M., Ashourloo, D., Aghighi, H., Radiom, S., & Alimohammadi, A. (2019). Wheat leaf rust detection at canopy scale under different LAI levels using machine learning techniques. *Computers and Electronics in Agriculture, 156,* 119–128.

Bastiaanssen, W., Molden, D., & Makin, I. (2000). Remote sensing for irrigated agriculture: Examples from research and possible applications. *Agricultural Water Management, 46*(2), 137–155.

Baxla, A. K., Singh, K. K., Mall, R. K., Singh, P. K., Gohain, G. B., & Rana, M. (2018). Wheat yield prediction using CERES-wheat V4. 6 an operational approach for Uttar Pradesh, India. *Journal of Pharmacognosy and Phytochemistry, SP1,* 2494–2497.

Bhojani, S. H., & Bhatt, N. (2020). Wheat crop yield prediction using new activation functions in neural network. *Neural Computing and Applications, 32,* 13941–13951.

Bui, T. Q., & Pham, H. M. (2016). Web-based GIS for spatial pattern detection: Application to malaria incidence in Vietnam. *Springerplus, 5*(1), 1–14.

Cai, Y., Guan, K., Lobell, D., Potgieter, A. B., Wang, S., Peng, J., et al. (2019). Integrating satellite and climate data to predict wheat yield in Australia using machine learning approaches. *Agricultural and Forest Meteorology, 274,* 144–159.

Chandel, N. S., Tiwari, P. S., Singh, K. P., Jat, D., Gaikwad, B. B., Tripathi, H., et al. (2019). Yield prediction in wheat using spectral reflectance indices. *Current Science, 116*(2), 272.

Dadhwal, V. K., Sehgal, V. K., Singh, R. P., & Rajak, D. R. (2003). Wheat yield modelling using satellite remote sensing with weather data: Recent Indian experience. *Mausam, 54*(1), 253–262.

Dixit, A., & Nema, S. (2018). Wheat leaf disease detection using machine learning method-a review. *International Journal of Computer Science and Mobile Computing, 7*, 124–129.

Dong, Y., Xu, F., Liu, L., Du, X., Ye, H., Huang, W., et al. (2019). Monitoring and forecasting for disease and pest in crop based on WebGIS system. In *2019 8th international conference on agro-geoinformatics (agro-geoinformatics), July* (pp. 1–5). IEEE.

Gaikwad, V. P., & Musande, V. (2017). Wheat disease detection using image processing. In *2017 1st International conference on intelligent systems and information management (ICISIM), October* (pp. 110–112). IEEE.

Gao, X., Huang, J., Ma, H., Zhuo, W., & Zhu, D. (2018). *Regional winter wheat maturity date prediction using remote sensing-crop model data assimilation and numerical weather prediction.* August.

Gommes, R. (2001). Agrometeorological models and remote sensing for crop monitoring and forecasting. In *Vol. 1215. Proceedings of the report of the Asia-Pacific conference on early warning, preparedness, prevention and management of disasters, Chiang-Mai, Thailand, June.*

Guha, P., Bhatnagar, T., Pal, I., Kamboj, U., & Mishra, S. (2017). Prediction of properties of wheat dough using intelligent deep belief networks. *Journal of Experimental & Theoretical Artificial Intelligence, 29*(6), 1283–1296.

Hashem, I., Yaqoob, I., Anuar, N., Mokhtar, S., Gani, A., & Ullah Khan, S. (2015). The rise of "big data" on cloud computing: Review and open research issues. *Information Systems, 47*, 98–115.

Helman, D., Lensky, I. M., & Bonfil, D. J. (2019). Early prediction of wheat grain yield production from root-zone soil water content at heading using crop RS-Met. *Field Crops Research, 232*, 11–23.

Huete, A. (1988). A soil-adjusted vegetation index (SAVI). *Remote Sensing of Environment, 25*, 295–309.

Jeong, J. H., Resop, J. P., Mueller, N. D., Fleisher, D. H., Yun, K., Butler, E. E., et al. (2016). Random forests for global and regional crop yield predictions. *PLoS One, 11*(6), e0156571.

Kadir, M. K. A., Ayob, M. Z., & Miniappan, N. (2014). Wheat yield prediction: Artificial neural network based approach. In *2014 4th international conference on engineering technology and technopreneuship (ICE2T), August* (pp. 161–165). IEEE.

Kamilaris, A., Kartakoullis, A., & Prenafeta-Boldu´, F. (2017). A review on the practice of big data analysis in agriculture. *Computers and Electronics in Agriculture, 143*, 23–37.

Kaur, N., & Kaur, A. (2019). *Analysis of wheat production techniques.*

Klem, K., Vanova, M., Hajslova, J., Lancová, K., & Sehnalová, M. (2007). A neural network model for prediction of deoxynivalenol content in wheat grain based on weather data and preceding crop. *Plant Soil and Environment, 53*(10), 421.

Kross, A., Znoj, E., Callegari, D., Kaur, G., Sunohara, M., van Vliet, L., et al. (2018). Evaluation of an artificial neural network approach for prediction of corn and soybean yield. In *Proceedings of the 14th International Conference on Precision Agriculture, Montreal, QC, Canada, June* (pp. 24–27).

Kuang, W., Liu, W., Ma, Z., & Wang, H. (2012). Development of a web-based prediction system for wheat stripe rust. In *International conference on computer and computing Technologies in Agriculture, October* (pp. 324–335). Berlin, Heidelberg: Springer.

Kumar, S., Kumar, V., & Sharma, R. K. (2019). Rice yield forecasting using support vector machine. *International Journal of Recent Technology and Engineering, 8*, 2588–2593.

Lai, Y. R., Pringle, M. J., Kopittke, P. M., Menzies, N. W., Orton, T. G., & Dang, Y. P. (2018). An empirical model for prediction of wheat yield, using time-integrated Landsat NDVI. *International Journal of Applied Earth Observation and Geoinformation, 72*, 99–108.

Lamba, V., & Dhaka, V. S. (2014). Wheat yield prediction using artificial neural network and crop prediction techniques (a survey). *International Journal for Research in Applied Science and Engineering Technology, 2*, 330–341.

Leslie, C. R., Servina, L. O., & Miller, H. M. (2017). *Landsat and agriculture: case studies on the uses and benefits of Landsat imagery in agricultural monitoring and production.* US Department of the Interior, US Geological Survey.

Li, J., Cheng, J. H., Shi, J. Y., & Huang, F. (2012). Brief introduction of back propagation (BP) neural network algorithm and its improvement. In *Advances in computer science and information engineering* (pp. 553–558). Berlin, Heidelberg: Springer.

Liakos, K., Busato, P., Moshou, D., Pearson, S., & Bochtis, D. (2018). Machine learning in agriculture: A review. *Sensors, 18*(8), 2674.

Lin, Z., Mu, S., Huang, F., Mateen, K. A., Wang, M., Gao, W., et al. (2019). A unified matrix- based convolutional neural network for fine-grained image classification of wheat leaf diseases. *IEEE Access, 7*, 11570–11590.

Lu, J., Hu, J., Zhao, G., Mei, F., & Zhang, C. (2017). An in-field automatic wheat disease diagnosis system. *Computers and Electronics in Agriculture, 142*, 369–379.

Melssen, W., Wehrens, R., & Buydens, L. (2006). Supervised Kohonen networks for classification problems. *Chemometrics and Intelligent Laboratory Systems, 83*(2), 99–113.

Mo, L. (2010). Prediction of wheat stripe rust using neural network. In *Vol. 3. 2010 IEEE international conference on intelligent computing and intelligent systems, October* (pp. 475–479). IEEE.

Mohammadi, R., Farshadfar, E., & Amri, A. (2015). Interpreting genotype × environment interactions for grain yield of rainfed durum wheat in Iran. *The Crop Journal, 3*(6), 526–535.

Niedbała, G. (2018). Application of multiple linear regression for multi-criteria yield prediction of winter wheat. *Journal of Research and Applications in Agricultural Engineering, 63*(4), 125–131.

Pantazi, X. E., Moshou, D., Alexandridis, T., Whetton, R. L., & Mouazen, A. M. (2016). Wheat yield prediction using machine learning and advanced sensing techniques. *Computers and Electronics in Agriculture, 121*, 57–65.

Pantazi, X. E., Moshou, D., Mouazen, A. M., Kuang, B., & Alexandridis, T. (2014). Application of supervised self organising models for wheat yield prediction. In *IFIP international conference on artificial intelligence applications and innovations, September* (pp. 556–565). Berlin, Heidelberg: Springer.

Parida, B. R., & Ranjan, A. K. (2019). Wheat acreage mapping and yield prediction using Landsat-8 OLI satellite data: A case study in Sahibganj Province, Jharkhand (India). *Remote Sensing in Earth Systems Sciences, 2*(2–3), 96–107.

Pujari, J. D., Yakkundimath, R., & Byadgi, A. S. (2014). Identification and classification of fungal disease affected on agriculture/horticulture crops using image processing techniques. In *2014 IEEE international conference on computational intelligence and computing research, December* (pp. 1–4). IEEE.

Rossi, V., et al. (2010). A web-based decision support system for managing durum wheat crops. In *Decision support systems, advances in.*

Rusgiyono, A. (2019). Adaptive neuro fuzzy inference system (ANFIS) approach for modeling paddy production data in central Java. *Journal of Physics: Conference Series, 1217*(1), 012083.

Serrano, J., Shahidian, S., & Marques da Silva, J. (2019). Evaluation of normalized difference water index as a tool for monitoring pasture seasonal and inter-annual variability in a Mediterranean agro-silvo-pastoral system. *Water, 11*(1), 62.

Shafaei, S. M., Nourmohamadi-Moghadami, A., & Kamgar, S. (2016). Development of artificial intelligence based systems for prediction of hydration characteristics of wheat. *Computers and Electronics in Agriculture, 128*, 34–45.

Timsina, J., Godwin, D., Humphreys, E., Kukal, S. S., & Smith, D. (2008). Evaluation of options for increasing yield and water productivity of wheat in Punjab, India using the DSSAT-CSM-CERES-wheat model. *Agricultural Water Management, 95*(9), 1099–1110.

Toda, Y., & Okura, F. (2019). How convolutional neural networks diagnose plant disease. *Plant Phenomics, 2019*, 9237136.

Training an Artificial Neural Network. (2020, August 8). Retrieved from https://www.solver.com/training-artifical-neural-network-intro.

Trethowan, R., Chatrath, R., Tiwari, R., Kumar, S., Saharan, M. S., Bains, N., et al. (2018). An analysis of wheat yield and adaptation in India. *Field Crops Research, 219*, 192–213.

Tripathy, R., Chaudhari, K. N., Mukherjee, J., Ray, S. S., Patel, N. K., Panigrahy, S., et al. (2013). Forecasting wheat yield in Punjab state of India by combining crop simulation model WOFOST and remotely sensed inputs. *Remote Sensing Letters, 4*(1), 19–28.

Van Diepen, C. V., Wolf, J., Van Keulen, H., & Rappoldt, C. (1989). WOFOST: A simulation model of crop production. *Soil Use and Management, 5*(1), 16–24.

Wang, H., & Ma, Z. (2011). Prediction of wheat stripe rust based on support vector machine. In *Vol. 1. 2011 Seventh international conference on natural computation, July* (pp. 378–382). IEEE.

Xiong, X., Angal, A., Chang, T., Chiang, K., Lei, N., Li, Y., et al. (2020). MODIS and VIIRS calibration and characterization in support of producing long-term high-quality data products. *Remote Sensing, 12*, 3167.

Xue, J., & Su, B. (2017). Significant remote sensing vegetation indices: A review of developments and applications. *Journal of Sensors, 2017*. https://doi.org/10.1155/2017/1353691, 1353691.

Chapter 12

Sugarcane leaf disease detection through deep learning

N.K. Hemalatha[a], R.N. Brunda[a], G.S. Prakruthi[a], B.V. Balaji Prabhu[b,c], Arpit Shukla[d], and Omkar Subbaram Jois Narasipura[c]

[a]*Dr. Ambedkar Institute of Technology, Bangalore, Karnataka, India,* [b]*Malnad College of Engineering, Hassan, Karnataka, India,* [c]*Indian Institute of Science, Bangalore, Karnataka, India,* [d]*National Institute of Technology Srinagar, Srinagar, Jammu and Kashmir, India*

1 Introduction

Agriculture contributes about 6.4% to the world's economy. Among the world's 226 countries, 9 countries hold agriculture as its dominant sector of economy contributor. China is the largest contributor, then comes India, and the United States takes third place. Among the commercial agricultural crops, sugarcane is one of the major commercial crops as it is used for the production of various by-products like sugar, fermented liquids like syrups and capsules, bagasse used for fuel, fiberboard and molasses used in distilleries for the manufacture of ethyl alcohol, butyl alcohol, citric acid, and so on.

Sugarcane is an ancient crop of the Austronesian and Papuan people. It was introduced to Polynesia, Island Melanesia, and Madagascar in prehistoric times via Austronesian sailors. It was also introduced to India and Southern China by Austronesian traders at around 1200–1000 BCE. It is the world's largest crop by production quantity, with 1.9 billion tons produced in 2015, with Brazil accounting for 41% of the world total. In 2012, the Food and Agriculture Organization estimated that it was cultivated on around 26 million hectares (64 million acres) in more than 90 countries. Sugarcane is a tropical, perennial grass that produces multiple stems by forming lateral shoots at the base, typically 3–4 m (10–13 ft) high and about 5 cm (2 in) in diameter. These stems grow into a cane stalk, which constitutes about 75% of the entire mature plant. A mature stalk is typically composed of 12%–16% soluble sugars, 2%–3% nonsugars, 11%–16% fiber, and 63%–73% water. The sugarcane crop is sensitive to climate, soil type, irrigation, disease control, fertilizers, insects, varieties, and the harvest period. The average yield of cane stalk is around 60–70 tons per hectare (24–28 long ton/acre; 27–31 short ton/acre) per year. However, this figure can vary between 30 and 180 tons per hectare depending on the knowledge and crop management approach used in sugarcane cultivation. Sugarcane is a cash crop but is also used as livestock fodder.

Though sugarcane is spread vast across the world, it is a painstaking job for farmers all over when the crops are subjected to unforeseeable climatic fluctuations and menacing pests and diseases. Production quantities are affected by pests and diseases that occur in sugarcane plants. Immense commercialization in the agricultural field is also a contributing factor for plant diseases. There are multifarious diseases that affect the crop in yield and quality. Some of these are detected by farmers when they visually inspect the leaves. However, most of the diseases go undetected, leading to huge losses to farmers. Therefore, it is crucial to identify the type of infestation to aid in controlling its damage. To prevent these diseases, costly methods and various pesticides are used in the agriculture. The widespread use of these chemical methods harm plant health and human health and affects the environment negatively. Also, these methods, increases production costs. In such cases, farmers are suggested for precise agricultural applications, where medicines are sprayed only to the affected area. It is necessary to determine the regions where the plant diseases occur and spread. Deep learning (DL) is widely used in precision agriculture. It is helpful for image-based plant disease recognition. DL is the state-of-the-art machine learning (ML) method that utilizes artificial neural networks (ANNs) with hidden layers.

In the literature, various researchers have worked on detection of plant diseases to help farmers in identifying diseases at an early stage and take necessary actions to deal with the same.

Sladojevic et al. (2016) developed a leaf disease detection (LDD) system to automatically classify and detect 13 different classes of plant diseases from leaf images using a deep convolution neural network approach consisting of five convolution and three fully connected layers. Even though the system achieves a good performance, improper implementation of the system for use by farmers, like a globally hosted website, makes it difficult to for farmers. Maniyath et al. (2018) developed a LDD system using a ML algorithm "random forest" in order to differentiate between healthy and diseased. But the major drawback in this implementation is that they used a ML approach instead of DL, which gives more efficient training results by effective feature learning. Kulkarni (2018) proposed a crop disease detection system that included 38 different classes of diseases and the image dataset consisted of 54,306 images. The detecting model was prepared using the pretrained model named MobileNet. There is no proper description of the crops and diseases Kulkarni considered for training the model, and the implementation of the system as a smartphone application is one among his future enhancements. Toda and Okura (2019) proposed a convolution neural network-based (CNN-based) approach to diagnose plant diseases. They considered 38 varieties of plants, classifying them into two classes, namely, diseased and healthy. They used an InceptionV3 pretrained model for training the dataset and visualized the results based on output, features, semantic dictionary, and Padilla et al. (2019) came up with the main objectives of producing a system capable of identifying a yellow spot diseased leaf among sugarcane leaves using a support vector machine algorithm. The system was designed with a Noir camera integrated with a Raspberry Pi and an LCD monitor that helped for observation and classification. Saleem, Potgieter, and Arif (2019) developed DL architectures along with visualization techniques for plant disease classification. They implemented the dataset on various algorithms from LeNet until the latest VGG inception. Mohanty et al. (2016) developed a model using a DL approach using a public image dataset of 54,306 images of diseased and healthy plant leaves under controlled conditions. They trained for 14 varieties and 26 classes of diseases. They achieved an accuracy of 99.35%. Patil and Pawar (2017) developed an Android application that identifies a plant species based on a photo captured through a mobile camera. The morphological features of the leaves that computes the angle code histogram, and then the classification is done based on a novel combination of the computed metrices.

The literature reveals that works carried by various researchers focused on developing an improved accurate model. But the works do not reach farmers to take the advantage of the same. So, it is very important to develop a system that can easily accessed and used by any farmer. To address this issue, we propose a DL neural network architecture in which the type of disease afflicting the sugarcane crop is predicted by training the model on images of affected leaves. The advancements in telecommunication and its technology made smartphone affordable. So, the proposed work majorly involves the smartphone as an end device to made it possible for the research to reach the farming community.

This chapter discusses the methodologies used, which includes dataset, proposed system architecture, and the proposed Android application. Then there is a discussion about the experimentation conducted, the results are discussed, and conclusions are presented.

2 Methodology

This section discusses the dataset, system architecture and network model used and also the proposed SAFAL-FASAL Android application.

2.1 Dataset

The quality, relevancy, and availability of the data directly affects the goals of DL model. Incomplete or inaccurate data sets will train the model like an illiterate human who cannot understand the environment better. Hence, choosing the right data for the model will also help achieve accurate results. Therefore, a model deserves the best data that are precisely labeled, which can only help the model achieve the best level of accuracy at an affordable cost.

In this work, we have used a dataset containing 2940 images of sugarcane leaves belonging to 6 different classes (5 diseases and 1 healthy), as shown in Fig. 1. All these images were taken in natural environments with numerous variations. The images were taken at various cultivation fields, including the University of Agricultural Sciences and nearby farms in Bangalore and Mandya. All the images were taken using phone cameras at various angles, orientations, and backgrounds accounting for most of the variations that can appear for images taken in the real world. The dataset was collected with the company of experienced pathologists. The distribution of the images into different classes is detailed in Table 1.

2.2 Leaf disease detection system architecture

Fig. 2 shows the architecture of the proposed LDD system for detection of sugarcane leaf diseases. The system architecture brief about the sequence of

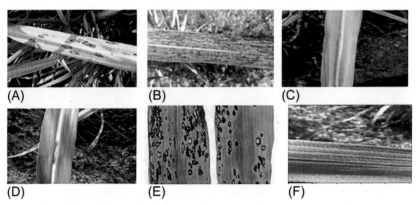

FIG. 1 Sugarcane leaf disease classes along with healthy class, (A) Helminthospora, (B) rust, (C) yellow leaf, (D) red rot, (E) Cercospora leaf spot, and (F) healthy leaf.

TABLE 1 Distribution of images into different classes.

Sl. No	Class	Count
1	Cercospora Leaf Spot	346
2	Helmanthospura Leaf Spot	410
3	Rust	382
4	Red Rot	454
5	Yellow Leaf Disease	420
6	Healthy	928

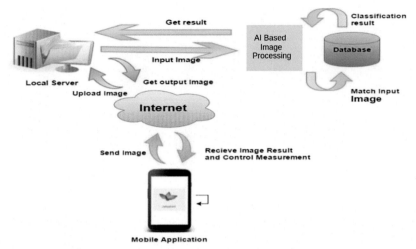

FIG. 2 LDD system architecture.

operations need to be followed in detecting the leaf disease. The SAFAL-FASAL mobile application is developed to provide information to farmers about the diseases affecting their crop so that they can take necessary measures to avoid losses. Any user with the SAFAL-FASAL app installed on their mobile can capture images of the sugarcane leaf through the camera or by selecting an existing leaf image from the phone's gallery and upload the image to detect the type of disease affecting the sugarcane plant. Upon uploading the leaf image through the mobile, SAFAL-FASAL will send the image to the server for analysis. At the server end, the image is processed by the developed LDD model to detect the corresponding disease. The LDD model predicts the class of the disease infected by that sugarcane plant. The predicted class is displayed on the mobile screen. The user can either view the class of the disease affecting the leaf or view that the leaf is healthy.

2.3 Leaf disease detection model architecture

CNNs are an evolution of traditional ANNs, focused mainly on applications with repeating patterns in different areas of the modeling space, especially image recognition. For image recognition applications, several baseline architectures of CNNs have been developed, which have been successfully applied to complicated tasks of visual imagery. Some of the well-known CNN architectures used for the task of classification are LeNet-5, AlexNet, VGG-16, Inception-v1, Inception-v3, ResNet-50, Xception, Inception-v4, Inception-ResNets, and ResNeXt-50. The studies prove that LeNet-5 outperforms other network models in the task of image classification. So, LeNet-5 architecture is used as a network

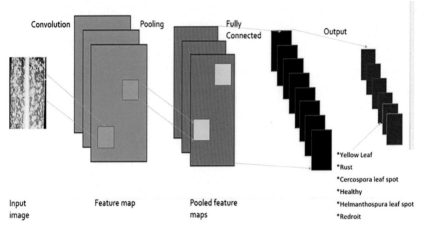

FIG. 3 LDD model network architecture.

architecture to develop LDD model. Fig. 3 shows the network architecture of LDD model, which uses LeNet-5 as a base model.

The proposed LDD model architecture consists of nine layers, including three convolutional layers (C1, C3, and C5), two subsampling (pooling) layers (S2 and S4), and two fully connected layer (F6), followed by the output layer. The input layer is built to take in $255 \times 255 \times 3$, and these are the dimensions of images that are passed into the next layer.

The official first layer, convolutional layer C1, produces as output 32 feature maps and has a kernel size of 5×5. The kernel/filter is the name given to the window that contains the weight values that are utilized during the convolution of the weight values with the input values.

A subsampling (pooling) layer S2 follows the C1 layer. The S2 layer halves the dimension of the feature maps it receives from the previous layer to $127 \times 127 \times 32$ with the filter size 2×2; this is known commonly as downsampling. This is to decrease the computational power required to process data through dimensionality reduction. Furthermore, it is useful for extracting the dominant features that are rotational and positional invariant. The S2 layer also produces 32 feature maps, each one corresponding to the feature maps passed as input from the previous layer. There are two types of pooling:

(1) Max pooling returns the maximum value from the portion of the image covered by the kernel.
(2) Average pooling returns the average of all the values from the portion of the image covered by the kernel.

Pooling is followed by the convolutional layer C3 with 64 filters applied on the feature maps, which are the output of the previous layer S2. The fourth layer (S4) is again a pooling layer with filter size 2×2. This layer is the same as the second layer (S2) except it has 64 feature maps so the output will be reduced to 63x63x64. The fifth layer (C5) is a fully connected convolutional layer for output mapping and for producing the predictions.

The sixth layer is the dense layer, which had a specified number of units or neurons within each layer, while the output layer has six units.

The last layer has six units that correspond to the number of classes that are used in the dataset. The activation function for the output layer is a softmax activation function.

Softmax is an activation function that is utilized to derive the probability distribution of a set of numbers within an input vector. The output of a softmax activation function is a vector in which its set of values represents the probability of an occurrence of a class/event. These values within the vector all add up to 1.

2.4   SAFAL-FASAL android application

The system design for the proposed SAFAL-FASAL application is given in Fig. 4. The user has to capture the image of the sugarcane leaf and upload it. This image is fed as input to the trained TensorFlow Lite (TFLite) model for processing; after processing, the model outputs the predicted class. The predicted disease will then be displayed in the application for the user to learn about the disease affecting the crop.

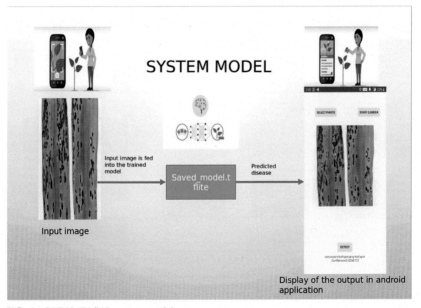

FIG. 4   SAFAL-FASAL system model.

The proposed LDD model is deployed in the Android platform for classifying the image on the phone to provide it as an end system for users. For deployment to the Android system, the tensorflow or keras model is converted to TFLite format, which is fit to be used in Android or iOS platform. Inference is performed using TFLite Android Support Library and TFLite Java API. TFLite Task Library contains a set of powerful and easy-to-use task-specific libraries for the app developers to create a ML experience with TFLite. It supports the common data formats for inputs and outputs, including images and arrays. It also provides pre- and post-processing units that perform tasks such as image cropping and resizing.

TFLite is comprised of a runtime on which any preexisting models can be run and a suite of tools used to prepare the models for use on mobile and embedded devices. Fig. 5 shows the architecture of TFLite API. A trained TensorFlow model is fed into the TFLite converter for conversion from "model.protobuf" to "model.tflite" format. This model.tflite can be deployed easily for use on Android or iOS phones.

After training the model, there are three files generated: Graph Def (.pb), Checkpoints (.ckpt), and the Saved model (.pb). The checkpoint and the graph file are frozen and optimized for inference before conversion. And finally, they are passed through the TFLite converter for conversion. All these processes are clearly represented in the Fig. 6.

2.5   Method of evaluation

Performance of the developed LDD model is evaluated using confusion matrix, precision, accuracy, recall, specificity, and F1-score as an evaluation criterion.

The confusion matrix is the way of visualizing the performance of the prediction model. Each entry in a confusion matrix denotes the number of

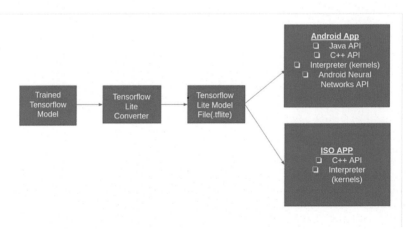

FIG. 5   The architecture of TFLite API.

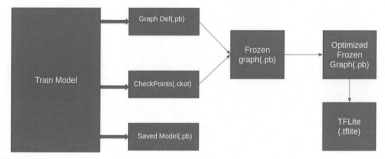

FIG. 6 TFLite converter architecture.

predictions made by the model whether it classified the classes correctly or incorrectly. Confusion matrix uses the values True Positive (TP), True Negative (TN), False Positive (FP), and False Negative (FN) to evaluate the correctly and incorrectly classified classes. A pixel is considered to be TP if its predicted and actual class are positive. TN is when the predicted and actual value are negative. A pixel is considered to be FP if it is wrongly predicted as positive and FN when the predicted value is wrongly predicted as negative. TP, TN, FP, and FN values are used to calculate the performance measures of precision, recall, accuracy, specificity, and F1 score, which enables us to compare the developed model against comparison models and which are computed as follows:

$$Precision = TP/(TP + FP)$$

Recall, commonly called sensitivity, corresponds to the TP rate of the considered class and is computed as:

$$Recall = TP/(TP + FN)$$

Specificity, it corresponds to the TN rate of the considered class:

$$Specificity = TN/(TN + FP)$$

F1-score combines the precision and the recall into a single measure:

$$F1 - score = 2 \times Precision \times Recall$$

$$Precision + Recall$$

The accuracy is calculated as the sum of correct classifications divided by the total number of classifications.

3 Experimentation

The experiment is performed using Python as its scripting language because of its learning simplicity and its huge collection of libraries. The dataset consists of 2490 images; these images were categorized into 6 folders with each folder named with the class name and consisting of images belonging to the respective class. The training image consists of only RGB channels. The images in the dataset are of different resolutions, and it is necessary to convert them into a common resolution before giving it to the network for training. All the images were reduced to 255x255x3 size. The images are then converted into Numpy arrays and given to the network. The network consists of 9 layers, the combination of three convolution, activation, and max pooling layers. The experiment was performed with sparse categorical cross-entropy loss function. We run the network for 15 epochs. Initially, the loss will be high and the accuracy will be less, as the epochs increase, the network learns(extracts) more features and the accuracy increases. At the end of the fifteenth epoch, we achieved (attained) a maximum accuracy of 96% and least loss of 0.289. The corresponding graph representing the variation of loss and accuracy with the number of epochs is shown in Fig. 7. For optimization, we use Adam. The models are implemented using tensorflow-keras API. The model was trained on a system with Nvidia 2080 ti GPU.

A single image is considered to explore the feature maps across the layers, and the same is discussed here. The LDD model uses nine layers to classify the leaf diseases.

The first layer is the convolutional layer and 32 filters being applied on the $255 \times 255 \times 3$ dataset with the kernel size of 5×5. Each filter is independently convolved with the original image, and we end up with 32 feature maps (activation maps) of shape $255 \times 255 \times 3$. Fig. 8 shows the feature extraction of the input sugarcane leaf image.

The second layer is the activation function, which removes every negative value from the filtered images and replaces them with zeros. It is happening to avoid the values from adding up to zero. Rectified Linear unit (ReLU) is used as a activation function, as it only activates a node if the input is above a certain

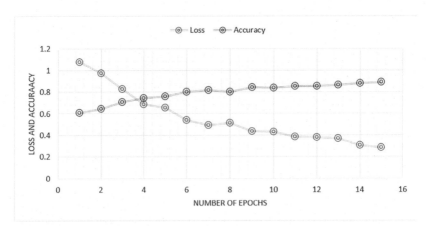

FIG. 7 Loss vs. Accuracy graph.

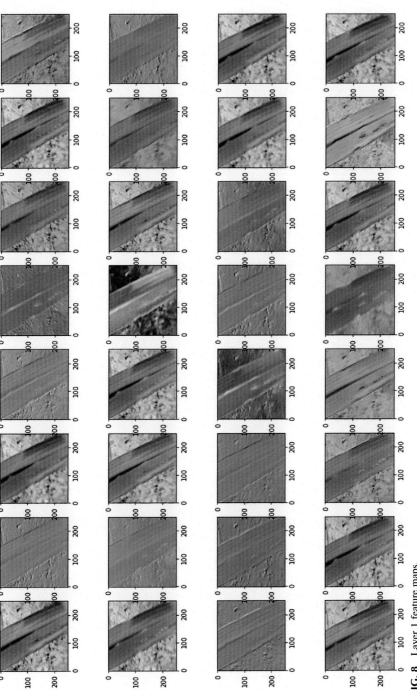

FIG. 8 Layer 1 feature maps.

threshold value. While the data is below zero, the output is zero, but the information rises above a threshold when it is above zero. It has a linear relationship with the dependent variable. The feature maps for layer 2 is given in Fig. 9.

Layer 3 is a max pooling used as a pooling layer. The input for layer 3 is the output of the previous layer (layer 2), feature maps of size $255 \times 255 \times 3$ in a deep CNN and 2×2 filter. Pooling layer operates on each feature map independently. It progressively reduces the $255 \times 255 \times 32$ feature maps to $127 \times 127 \times 32$ feature maps to reduce the number of parameters and computation in the network, as shown in Fig. 10.

In layer 4, the same operations are performed as in layer 1. Here, 64 filters are applied on the feature maps $127 \times 127 \times 32$, which is the output of layer 3 (pooling layer). This again extracts many features left out in the previous process, and we end up with 64 feature maps of shape $2127 \times 127 \times 32$, as shown in Fig. 11.

The resultant convolution feature map is passed through the ReLU activation function in layer 5 to remove the negative values from it. The resultant image of sugarcane leaf after ReLU layer 5 is shown in Fig. 12.

In layer 6, the same operations are performed as in the layer 3. Here the feature maps from the previous layer (ReLU_layer-6) are reduced from $127 \times 127 \times 64$ to $63 \times 63 \times 64$ as shown in Fig. 13.

In layer 7, the reduced image is again passed for the third iteration into the convolution layer with 64 filters and 3×3 kernel size. Now the final convolution feature map generated in the process is shown in Fig. 14.

Layer 8 passes the feature map through ReLU activation function, which takes care of removing the negative values from the feature matrix, and the resultant image is as shown in Fig. 15.

Layer 9 is the max pooling layer, which reduces the feature maps from $63 \times 63 \times 64$ to $32 \times 32 \times 64$, as shown in Fig. 16, suitable for passing through the fully connected layer for output mapping and for producing the predictions.

4   Results and discussion

This section presents and discusses the results obtained from the proposed LDD system. To verify the performance of the proposed system, the network is tested with the unseen leaves. Six images for six considered diseases were given to the network to predict their class. Fig. 17 shows the results obtained from the model along with their actual class.

Fig. 17 shows the results obtained from the trained model for the given input image. The input image of size 255×255 is given to the model as input, and the trained model processes the image and predicts the disease of the leaf in the input image. Fig. 17A depicts that the input image to the model is from the class

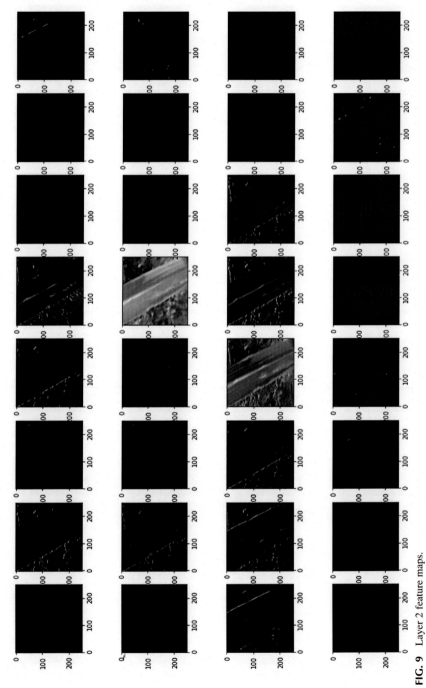

FIG. 9 Layer 2 feature maps.

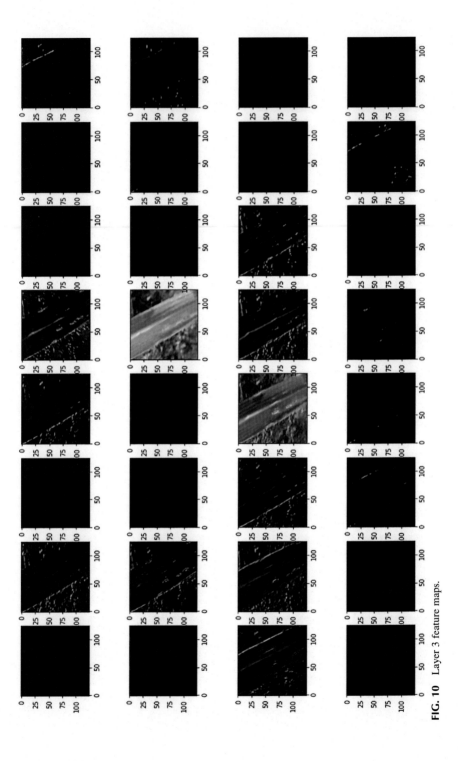

FIG. 10 Layer 3 feature maps.

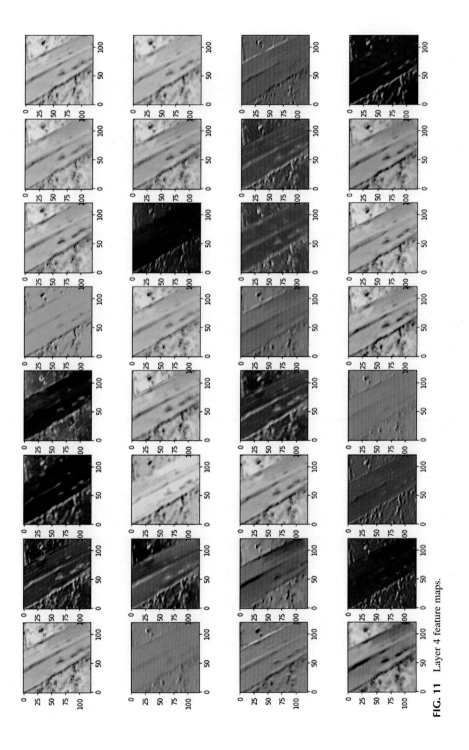

FIG. 11 Layer 4 feature maps.

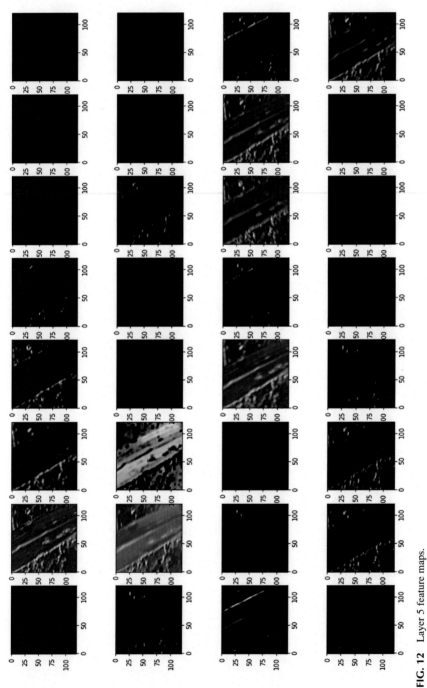

FIG. 12 Layer 5 feature maps.

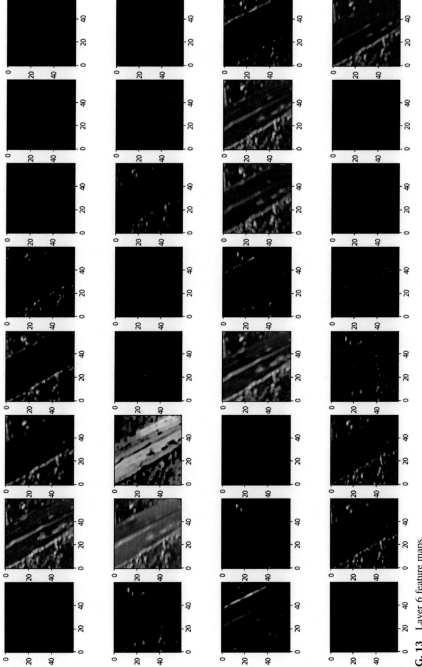

FIG. 13 Layer 6 feature maps.

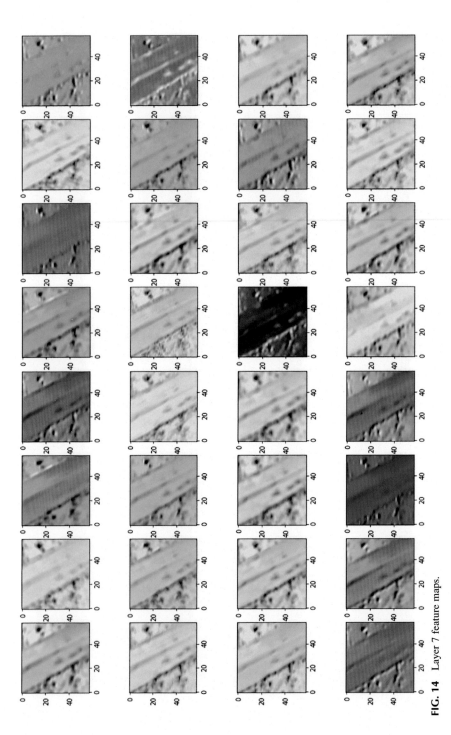

FIG. 14 Layer 7 feature maps.

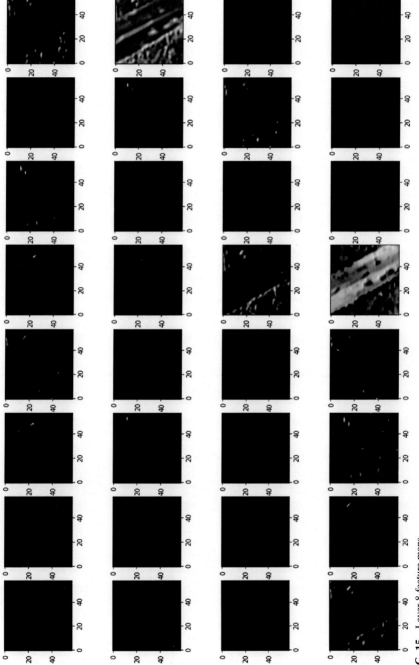

FIG. 15 Layer 8 feature maps.

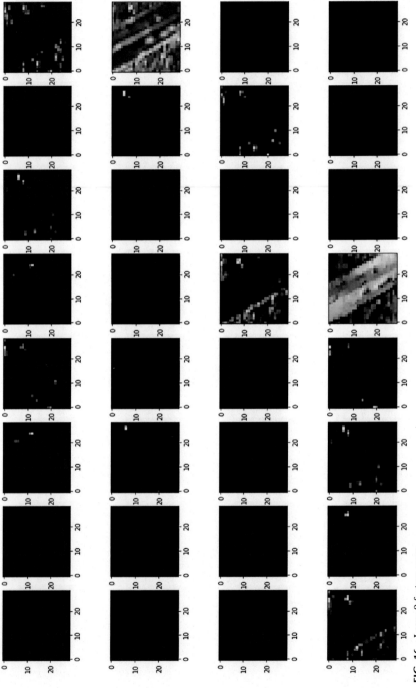

FIG. 16 Layer 9 feature maps.

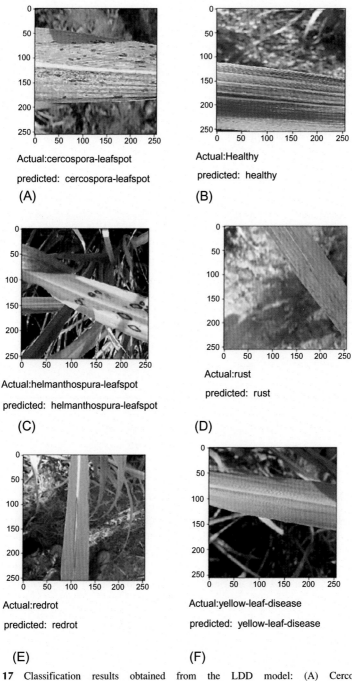

FIG. 17 Classification results obtained from the LDD model: (A) Cercospora, (B) Helmanthospura, (C) rust, (D) red rot, (E) yellow leaf disease, and (F) healthy.

Cercospora leaf spot, and the class predicted by the model is Cercospora leaf spot. Fig. 17B–F show the predictions of class healthy, Helmanthospura leaf spot, rust, red rot, and yellow leaf disease, respectively. It is evident that the model is performing well in predicting the classes for test images. The model is able to predict the classes accurately.

4.1 Performance evaluation

The quantitative analysis of the LDD model is evaluated using quantitative measure. We have a dataset that has six class labels: Cercospora, Helmanthospura, Rust, Red rot, Yellow leaf disease, and Healthy. Table 2 is a possible confusion matrix for these classes.

Consider the class Cercospora, the values of the metrics from the confusion matrix is calculated as follows:

$$TP = 66 \quad FN = (2+1) = 3 \quad FP = (2+2+1) = 5 \quad TN$$
$$= (79+1+73+1+86+1+1+2+2+81+1+2+2+3+177) = 511$$

Similarly, we can calculate the performance measures for the other classes. Table 3 is a table that shows the values of each performance measure for each class.

Since we have all necessary metrics for class Cercospora from the confusion matrix, we can now calculate the performance measures for class Cercospora as:

$$Precision = 66/66 + 5 = 0.92$$

$$Recall = 66/66 + 3 = 0.95$$

$$Specificity = 511/511 + 5 = 0.99$$

$$F1 - score = 2 \times \frac{0.92 \times 0.95}{0.92 + 0.95} = 0.93$$

4.2 SAFAL-FASAL Android application results

The working procedure along with the resultant snapshots for the usage of the SAFAL-FASAL Android application is given in this section. After installing the SAFAL-FASAL application on an Android phone, a user has to open the application and select the Start Camera option to capture the leaf image through the phone camera or select the Select Photo option to select the leaf image from the phone gallery.

The captured image or the selected image will be displayed below the options, as shown in Fig. 18. The user has to select the Detect option, as shown in Fig. 19 to find the disease, which is affecting the sugarcane plant. The image will be given to the trained model for processing, and the model will give the predicted disease class name, which will be displayed below the Detect option along with the confidence. Figs. 20 and 21 are the screenshots of the application showing predictions for two classes.

TABLE 2 Confusion matrix.

Class	Cercospora	Helmanthospura	Rust	Red rot	Yellow leaf disease	Healthy
Cercospora	66	2	1	0	0	0
Helmanthospura	2	79	1	0	0	0
Rust	2	0	73	0	1	0
Red rot	0	1	0	86	1	2
Yellow leaf disease	0	0	2	0	81	1
Healthy	1	0	2	2	3	177

TABLE 3 Precision, recall, specificity, F1 score matrix.

Class	Precision	Recall	Specificity	F1-score
Cercospora	0.92	0.95	0.99	0.93
Helmanthospura	0.96	0.96	0.99	0.96
Rust	0.92	0.96	0.98	0.93
Red rot	0.97	0.95	0.99	0.95
Yellow leaf disease	0.94	0.96	0.99	0.94
Healthy	0.98	0.95	0.99	0.96

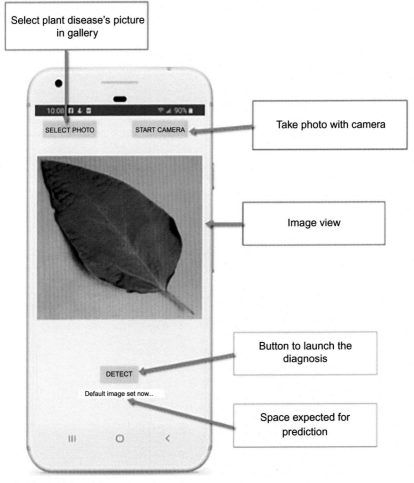

FIG. 18 Selecting an image.

FIG. 19 Uploading the image for disease detection.

FIG. 20 Predicted output 1.

FIG. 21 Predicted Output 2.

5 Conclusion

Many farmers spend money on disease management without adequate technical support. This results in poor disease management and control. The proposed approach helps farmers detect disease more correctly with less effort. It reduces the time required to detect diseases. The proposed LDD model achieves 98% of accuracy in detecting the disease classes. So, this can be used as a cost-effective solution to our farmers to address the issues of sugarcane leaf detection.

References

Kulkarni, O. (2018). Crop disease detection using deep learning. In *Proceedings of 2018 4th International conference on computing communication control and automation ICCUBEA 2018* (pp. 2018–2021). https://doi.org/10.1109/ICCUBEA.2018.8697390.

Maniyath, S. R., et al. (2018). Plant disease detection using machine learning. In *Proceedings of 2018 international conference design innovations for 3Cs compute communicate control ICDI3C 2018* (pp. 41–45). https://doi.org/10.1109/ICDI3C.2018.00017.

Mohanty, S. P., Hughes, D. P., & Salathé, M. (2016). Using deep learning for image-based plant disease detection. *Frontiers in Plant Science, 7*, 1–10. https://doi.org/10.3389/fpls.2016.01419.

Padilla, D. A., Magwili, G. V., Marohom, A. L. A., Co, C. M. G., Gaño, J. C. C., & Tuazon, J. M. U. (2019). Portable yellow spot disease identifier on sugarcane leaf via image processing using support vector machine. In *2019 5th international conference on control, automation, and robotics ICCAR 2019* (pp. 901–905). https://doi.org/10.1109/ICCAR.2019.8813495.

Patil, M. A. N., & Pawar, M. V. (2017). Detection and classification of plant leaf disease. *Iarjset, 4* (4), 72–75. https://doi.org/10.17148/iarjset/nciarcse.2017.20.

Saleem, M. H., Potgieter, J., & Arif, K. M. (2019). Plant disease detection and classification by deep learning. *Plants, 8*(11). https://doi.org/10.3390/plants8110468.

Sladojevic, S., Arsenovic, M., Anderla, A., Culibrk, D., & Stefanovic, D. (2016). Deep neural networks based recognition of plant diseases by leaf image classification. *Computational Intelligence and Neuroscience, 2016*. https://doi.org/10.1155/2016/3289801.

Toda, Y., & Okura, F. (2019). How convolutional neural networks diagnose plant disease. *Plant Phenomics, 2019*, 1–14. https://doi.org/10.34133/2019/9237136.

Chapter 13

Prediction of paddy cultivation using deep learning on land cover variation for sustainable agriculture

D.A. Meedeniya[a], I. Mahakalanda[a], D.S. Lenadora[a], I. Perera[a],
S.G.S. Hewawalpita[a], C. Abeysinghe[a], and Soumya Ranjan Nayak[b]
[a]*University of Moratuwa, Moratuwa, Sri Lanka*, [b]*Amity School of Engineering and Technology,
Amity University Uttar Pradesh, Noida, India*

1 Introduction

Geospatial analytics is often regarded as a promising method of spatial data processing and analysis. Recently, it has been attracting greater attention from the
agricultural research community as a high-quality, informed decision-making
tool. Deep learning-based geospatial land usage monitoring can be both conceptually and practically appealing to efficiently identify and respond to the diverse
needs of agents in the paddy supply chain. The inspiration of this study pertains
to the problem of missing mechanisms for periodical estimating of the land use
for paddy cultivation in Sri Lanka. To date, the Sri Lanka paddy sector has experienced both successes and failures, but failures dominate (Lal, 2011; Menike &
Arachchi, 2016).

In the absence of efficient markets for rice in Sri Lanka, demand and supply
for rice vary based on time of year, and significant mismatches are common. In
recent years, either local paddy farmers were not able to fully meet the demand for
rice throughout the year, on average, resulting in soaring prices for rice or the
price slumped due to oversupply. The current market regime has failed to manage
horizontal and vertical integration issues in rice supply chains to create maximum
social benefits to both producers and consumers (Senanayake & Premaratne,
2016). Politically, "quick and easy" regulatory fixes such as imposing overres-
trictive trading rules and market interventions by the authorities seem more
attractive to some parties. However, how would these measures affect various
agents in the supply chain, including the consumer? This debate over the years

seems focused on the emotive discussion of poor planning and the absence of reliable information for agents in the supply chain to respond to market signals and adverse climate conditions. For example, Sri Lanka recorded about a 44% shortfall in rice demand when the country faced its worst drought in 37 years in 2017 (FAO and WFP, 2017), and soon after, the country was hit by floods.

Our study involves developing a deep learning-based geospatial analytics model to estimate the agricultural land area under paddy cultivation, which varies largely due to adverse climate conditions such as droughts and floods in Sri Lanka. This information will help assess the compensation payable to insurance claims for losses sustained during a particular year, predict paddy yield, estimate subsidies for fertilizer by computing the usage/area, compute methane emissions, estimate annual water allocations, and determine nonpoint source pollutants.

The aspects of market design issues and supply chain management, and the likelihood of exercise of market power and gaming are not considered in this research scope. In our view, there are many significant obstacles to overcome. One such key obstacle would be the likelihood of perverse and inconsistent outcomes in the mapping of paddy farms lands in the country, the assessment of crop losses, and the devising of farmer compensation, and the computing of methane emissions and nonpoint source pollutants in the absence of reliable land use information (e.g., geographical information system (GIS) data and remote sensing (RS) data) that covers the entire country (Rathnayake et al., 2020; Subasinghe et al., 2016). Developing accurate and complete data on land use can be a costly exercise for a small country like Sri Lanka (Jayanetti et al., 2017; Meedeniya et al., 2020). RS and satellite imaging technologies coupled with deep learning (DL) methods can be used to automatically identify and accurately classify land use (Gao et al., 2017; Hansen & Loveland, 2012).

DL-based solutions for paddy classification using RS imagery seems both practically and conceptually appealing for informed decision-making (Gadiraju et al., 2020). This chapter deploys state-of-the-art DL methods such as convolutional neural networks (CNNs) to classify the satellite image datasets collected over a period for the predictive model development. The fine-tuned predictive model will be validated against GIS data, followed by an evaluation scenario of a selected paddy cultivation area validating the forecasts through the analysis model further lead for possible policy implications for sustainable agriculture directives of the Sri Lankan government.

The main objective of this study is to develop a geospatial analytics model to monitor and evaluate land use for paddy cultivation in Sri Lanka. We follow well-known principles of DL techniques to interpret ground referencing data that, surprisingly, have hardly been applied for paddy farming. We use RS images with spectral and spatial resolutions to reflect the land surface under paddy farming. We have combined bands 11, 8, and 2 of Sentinel-2 imagery to construct the base image. The Mask Region-based CNN (Mask RCNN) model uses this base image annotated using an available GIS image as the training and test datasets. Currently available GIS data of some regions of the country will be used to establish the ground through the results of this study.

This chapter is organized in the following ways: Section 2 reviews the previous work related to applications of geospatial analytics for agriculture. It begins by discussing how both RS and GIS technologies can be applied to analyze geospatial data to address important agricultural economic questions on sustainable development of land use. Then, it highlights literature on machine learning in modern agricultural activities in conjunction with GIS and RS. The used datasets are described in Section 3. Section 4 presents the system model proposed in the study, and Section 5 presents the details about the experiment design and data analysis. Section 6 discusses the main contributions, open challenges, and future research directions. Section 7 concludes the chapter.

2   Applications of geospatial analytics for agriculture

Many GIS and RS technologies have been used for analyzing the sustainable development of land use. In this section, we give an overview of how scholars, public organizations, and private agencies are currently using RS and GIS technologies. Agricultural land use accounts for more than one-third of the total land cover in Sri Lanka and paddy cultivation dominates (Näsström & Mattsson, 2011; Rathnayake et al., 2020).

2.1   Importance of remote sensing to estimate paddy area

The literature refers to RS and satellite-based technologies as promising approaches to self-generate statistical information on paddy area. In addition to paddy crop area and rice production estimation, literature also refers to the applications, such as RS technology-based crop damage assessment methods, the assessment of meteorological or climate impacts on rice yield, and agricultural market information systems (Guan et al., 2018). There are several international initiatives, such as the Group of Twenty (G20) Agriculture Ministers summit in 2011 to promote the use of RS technologies and capacity development to support agriculture (Rotairo et al., 2019). Typically, a GIS is designed to capture, store, manipulate, analyze, manage, and visualize spatially referenced data. The remotely sensed image analysis is supported by GIS software applications.

RS is a set of techniques that can be used to derive Earth surface information via images captured by different types of sensors (e.g., visible and reflected infrared, thermal infrared, and microwave) connected to overhead objects such as drones, fixed-wing unmanned aerial vehicles (UAVs), small airplanes, and satellites orbiting several hundred kilometers above the Earth (Campbell & Wynne, 2011). These images are constructed from electromagnetic radiation waves that are either reflected or emitted from the Earth's surface. RS literature refers to spatial (fitness of details), temporal (location precision), spectral (recording intervals of a specific wavelength), and radiometric (accuracy of reflection levels) resolutions of the images (Rotairo et al., 2019).

With the increase of the technology, the acquisition of RS data on an unprecedented scale has become an easy task. The availability of satellite data enables the potential for unlocking previously hard-to-access land-cover information about the Earth's surface. The literature favors satellite imagery acquired through Landsat 8/OLI and Sentinel-2 satellites placed in sun-synchronous orbits to detect land-use cover change (Claverie et al., 2018; Forkuor et al., 2018). However, it is challenging to guarantee that these sensors can capture clear images when there is cloud cover present in the target areas.

2.2 Related studies based on satellite imaginary

There has been greater attention paid in the literature for GIS-based land-use monitoring, analysis and visualization using spatial-temporal data (Barbosa et al., 2020; Bauer et al., 2019; Marj & Meijerink, 2011; Meedeniya et al., 2020; Wang et al., 2018). Digital information on land use for various human activities can be stored in multiple layers (e.g., classified images, topographical maps, soil maps, hydrological maps, land use maps), accurately measured, analyzed, and visualized using GIS (Weng, 2002) with provisions of outputs in different formats (Alqurashi & Kumar, 2013).

2.2.1 Applications with machine learning approaches

As a branch of artificial intelligence (AI) domain, the concepts and tools of machine learning are having dramatic impacts on geospatial related work. The implementations of machine learning can be via supervised and unsupervised learning. Applications of both supervised and unsupervised classification techniques in the area of detection of land-use change have been extensively studied by many researchers.

A support vector machine (SVM) is a supervised nonparametric statistical learning technique. Its fast learning pace and the ability to train using a small dataset have proven a very reliable technique in classifying remotely sensed data (Mountrakis et al., 2011). Ustuner et al. (2015) investigated the use of SVMs for land use classification by using high-resolution, three-meter or lower spatial resolution satellite images captured by RapidEye of a study area in Turkey. Ustuner experimented with 63 different configurations of SVM models and achieved satisfactory results with over 80% accuracy.

Onojeghuo et al. (2018) showed the use of satellite data together with machine learning techniques such as SVMs) and random forest (RF) to map the spatial distribution of paddy rice fields in some parts of Sanjian region, China. However, field-level classification of crop types can be achieved given that the input satellite data has a good quality spatial resolution (Lobell, 2013).

On the other hand, unsupervised classification methods can find a prede-fined number of clusters in a remotely sensed spatial data without having prior knowledge of the land cover/use (Jia & Richards, 2002).

2.2.2 Applications with deep learning approaches

Recently many studies have addressed the field of DL for RS image classifica-tions for land use. Among them, Sidike et al. (2019) developed a novel approach named deep Progressively Expanded Network (dPEN), for mapping heteroge-neous agricultural fields using WorldView-3 imagery. They showed that by using visible/near-infrared and short-wave infrared bands, their model can achieve higher overall accuracy compared to other methods such as SVM and RF.

Wang et al. (2018) proposed DL models to predict soybean crop yield. This study applies a DL technique to predict crop yield using satellite imagery. First, the authors develop a model to predict the soybean harvest in Argentina where the available dataset is sufficient for the purpose. Then the authors utilize trans-fer learning to predict the soybean crop yield in Brazil where the data is limited. They showed the cost-effectiveness of remotely sensed data and the use of transfer learning to successfully predict the crop yield for areas where fewer data are available.

An approach for forecasting the climate indices to identify the impacts of droughts for agriculture was presented by Marj and Meijerink (2011). This study uses an artificial neural network (ANN) to predict the normalized differ-ence vegetation index (NDVI). The predicted NDVI, which is based on climatic signals taken from satellite data, was in turn used to forecast agricultural droughts and its effects in future. This model mainly applies to semiarid conditions. The results were useful for making well-informed decisions on the crops and livestock.

Barbosa et al. (2020) deployed DL techniques to predict crop yield. Their predictions are based on the spatial structure of the farm and the amount of nitrogen fertilizer applied throughout the growing season. A CNN was devel-oped to capture spatial structures of field attributes and model the crop yield response to nutrient and seed rate management. The models are trained from a dataset created from nine cornfields. Since the excessive treatment of nitrogen fertilizer and nutrients can reduce the crop yield and the crop quality, the results were used to understand and control nutrient application.

An automated analytic platform that measures the yield-related phenotypes of lettuce production from ultra-scale aerial imagery is proposed by Bauer et al. (2019). They have used ultra-scale NDVI aerial images to measure yield-related phenotypes. First, a CNN architecture-based model was established for lettuce counting. Then an unsupervised machine learning algorithm was used to classify the detected lettuces into three sizes. Finally, a Global Positioning System-tagged (GPS-tagged) map representing harvest regions based on the let-tuce size category was produced. They showed that facilitating real-time crop monitoring during different growth stages allows for the tweaking of crop management under changeable agricultural conditions to boost production.

Importantly, Mask RCNN is the latest development in the RCNN family of object detectors, and it combines a segmentation network and detection network (Girshick, 2015; Girshick et al., 2014). Mask RCNN can be trained end-to-end directly on RS images, but better performance and faster converging can be achieved by using transfer learning. In transfer learning, the neural network is first trained on a different dataset like COCO (Lin et al., 2014), ImageNet (Deng et al., 2009) to learn basic features of an image. When training the network for RS data, techniques like weights decay or dropouts can be used to make sure that the network uses the minimum number of parameters needed for RS images.

2.3 Related studies based on the Internet of Things

Changes to an object or a phenomenon (e.g., land use, ecosystems) can be assessed using data obtained from classification of RS imagery using edge devices. The application of RS imagery in agricultural activities has been an extensively studied phenomenon in the literature (Franklin et al., 2015; Vincent et al., 2019; Vogelmann et al., 2016). RS refers to the monitoring of the Earth's surface via sensors mounted on space-borne objects such as satellites. As a result, repetitive coverage in RS was identified as one premise approach to capture the biophysical characteristics of land surfaces both in time and space (Weng, 2002).

An interesting approach by integrating sensor networks with AI-based neural networks and multilayer perceptron (MLP) was presented by Vincent et al. (2019) for the assessment of agriculture land suitability. Sensor devices capture some important crop productivity parameters such as pH value, soil moisture content (SMC), and salinity. The system focused on farmers to assess the agricultural land for cultivation in terms of four decision classes, namely, more suitable, suitable, moderately suitable, and unsuitable. This helps address the issue of spatial variation in precision agricultural management systems.

2.4 Related studies with integrated data

With the advancement of computational abilities, more recent literature highlights the use of GIS in conjunction with RS (Song et al., 2016). Integration of GIS and image processing capabilities can provide a better understanding of socioeconomic issues on land use. However, it appears that postclassification and GIS techniques are commonly used in conjunction with RS to monitor land use (Alqurashi & Kumar, 2013). This discussion leads us to review the literature on various classification techniques applied for the analysis of RS image data.

The study presented by Song et al. (2016) addressed a macroscopic cellular automata (MCA) DL model to evaluate the distribution of spatial-temporal distribution of soil moisture. The focus of this study was to analyze the quality of the soil in terms of SMC over an irrigated cornfield. They obtained data using 172 wireless sensors and satellite images. Feature activations were implemented through a restricted Boltzmann machine, which is a generative stochastic ANN. It enabled us to learn the probability distribution over a set of inputs. Moreover, they used deep belief networks (DBNs) architecture for feature learning. The DBN-MCA approach showed better results in highly nonlinear forms.

2.5 Dataset associated with land-use land-cover data

Following are some of the datasets used in related studies for land-use land-cover (LULC) map data:

- Landsat 8: map data with Thermal Infrared Sensor and Operational Land Imager (OLI), acquired from an American Earth observation satellite. This covers global landmass at different spatial resolutions.
- Sentinel-1: contain C-band imaging that operates in different modes, resolution, and coverage acquired from Earth observation satellites and ground-based information.
- Sentinel-2: contain optical imagery with multispectral, high-spatial resolution and coverage acquired from the European Earth observation mission.
- MODIS13Q1: Moderate Resolution Imaging Spectroradiometer (MODIS) Version 6 data that produces every 16 days at 250-m spatial resolution. NDVI is a continuity index to the existing National Oceanic.
- UAV data captured by drones in specific regions.
- Synthetic Aperture Radar (SAR) data acquired from Advanced Land Observing Satellite (ALOS). This data can operate at wavelengths that are least affected by low illumination or cloud cover and can get any time of the day with all weather conditions.
- Satellite data from the Japan Aerospace Exploration Agency (JAXA).
- TerraSAR-X: Spotlight and strip map data obtained by an imaging radar Earth observation satellite.

2.6 Comparison of related studies with satellite imagery and deep learning

According to the literature, most of the recent studies have addressed land-use and land-cover applications, where data acquired from satellite images and several types of sensors have been used to make predictions about the quality of the soil and other features of the land. Table 1 shows a comparison of techniques used by some of the related studies. The following abbreviations are used for the learning models in the related studies: deep neural network (DNN), CNN, ANNs, DBN, RCNN, recurrent neural networks (RNNs), long short-term memory (LSTM), gated recurrent units (GRUs), RF, maximum likelihood estimation (MLE), SVM, Gaussian Fitting Decision Tree (GFDT). Accordingly, it can be

TABLE 1 Summary of techniques used by related studies.

Related work	LSTM	CNN	RCNN	RNN	GRU	ANN	DBN	RF	MLE	SVM	GFDT
Barbosa et al. (2020)		X									
Bauer et al. (2019)		X									
Bazzi et al. (2019)								X			X
Hutt et al. (2016)								X	X		
Knopp et al. (2020)		X									
Marj and Meijerink (2011)						X					
Ndikumana et al. (2018)	X			X	X					X	
Nguyen et al. (2020)	X	X									
Song et al. (2016)							X				
Rahman et al. (2017)		X				X					
Tri et al. (2017)		X									
Steinhausen et al. (2018)								X			
Wambua (2014)						X					
Wang et al. (2018)			X								
Zhang et al. (2009)										X	
Zhang et al. (2018)		X						X		X	

seen that many of the latest related studies used DL-based neural networks. However, there is a research direction to try out different DL techniques for accurate classification of map data.

Table 2 presents a comparison of the related studies in terms of their datasets, features, and limitations. Different classification techniques are used in these studies based on the available data types. However, each study has its features that can account for the usefulness of the model and its limitations. Thus,

TABLE 2 Summary of the dataset, features, and limitations in related studies.

Study	Dataset	Features	Limitations
Bazzi et al. (2019)	SAR Sentinel-1	Rice crops are described by a Gaussian profile; achieve high accuracy with a relatively simple approach	Works on a single type of crop at a time
Hutt et al. (2016)	TerraSAR-X	Pixel level classification; use multiple bands from satellite image	Dataset is limited to certain types of terrain
Knopp et al. (2020)	Sentinel-2	The architecture is trained with fewer data and less trainable parameters; does not use a pretrained model	Only works for burned area segmentation
Nguyen et al. (2020)	Landsat 8	Use a data preprocessing pipeline; use a multitemporal high-spatial-resolution classification to enable a pixel-based mapping at different temporal resolutions	Accuracy degrades for real-time segmentation
Ndikumana et al. (2018)	SAR Sentinel-1	Classical machine learning methods show high accuracy, but RNN based classifier outperformed them	High misclassification rate between some classes
Sirirattanapol et al. (2020)	Satellite data from JAXA	End-to-end DL network; reinforcement learning	Accuracy is affected by noise and back-scattering of radar

Continued

TABLE 2 Summary of the dataset, features, and limitations in related studies—cont'd

Study	Dataset	Features	Limitations
Steinhausen et al. (2018)	Sentinel-1, Sentinel-2	Combine radar and optical imagery; work on small-scale; complex agriculture and with cloud cover	Need extra computational cost to process radar images
Tri et al. (2017)	Drone data	Perform yield assessment using DNNs	Work on UAV images
Zhang et al. (2009)	SAR data from ALOS	Pixel level classification; temporal variation of rice backscatter playa to separate paddy rice from other vegetative land uses	Small and less continuous areas cause noisy and scattered pattern in classification
Zhang et al. (2018)	Landsat 8, MODIS13Q1 NDVI	Combines Landsat 8, phenology data, and land surface temperature	Not classify with only spectral data, paddy rice misclassified as grass

there is a demand to research the most appropriate learning models that produce accurate results for different map data types.

This section discussed different approaches to identify, map, analyze, and store land use for agricultural activities. According to the authors' knowledge, it would appear that no consideration has yet been given to developing paddy cultivation land use data for Sri Lanka. Therefore, the following sections apply a Mask RCNN model to spot paddy cultivation land use in a given period for Sri Lanka.

3 Material analysis

3.1 Data source

This study uses two datasets, namely, satellite imagery and ground truth GIS data.

The satellite images for the selected regions of Sri Lanka are taken from planet.com. These images originated from Sentinel-2 satellite from a period between 2017 and 2018. Later images were used even with the visible difference due to the clarity, considering features such as low cloud coverage, which gave better results from the model. The original dataset consists of 13 Sentinel-2 bands, where the pixel size of each band is 10, 20, or 60 m. For this study, we

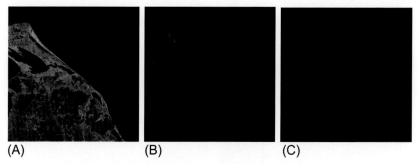

(A)   (B)   (C)

FIG. 1 Satellite image bands: (A) band 11, (B) band 8, and (C) band 2.

FIG. 2 SVG data of map tile 8 and 9.

used the band combinations short-wave infrared-1 (B11), near-infrared (B8), and blue (B2), which represent agriculture-based bands. Since short-wave and near-infrared bands appear as dark green, they are suitable to show dense vegetation; hence, they were used to monitor the health of the crops (GIS Geography, 2020). Fig. 1 shows the original satellite image bands, where the grayscale values were taken from a specific sensor in the satellite. These image combinations are later used to generate the composite RGB (Red, Green, and Blue) image.

Additionally, this study is used GIS data of paddy fields obtained from the currently available GIS-tiled maps published by the Survey Department of Sri Lanka. These data are taken as the ground truth source and later overlapped with the satellite images for processing. Fig. 2 shows two map times of the original data, which was transformed into scalable vector graphics (SVGs) format for processing.

3.2   Analysis of raster data

GIS is designed to capture, store, manipulate, analyze, manage, and visualize spatially referenced data as discussed by Ian (2010). It represents real-world phenomena using raster models and vector models. Generally, raster models are applied to represent remotely sensed continuous geographic images. On the other hand, the vector model is more suitable to map discrete geographic entities.

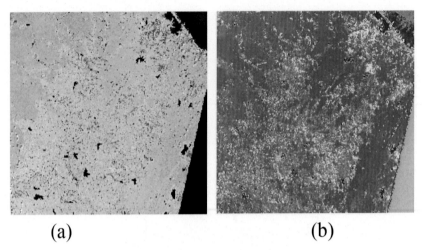

(a)   (b)

FIG. 3   (A) Composite agriculture band and (B) NDVI for Sentinel-2 images.

Fig. 3A and B compares the differences between the agriculture composite band constructed using band 11, band 8, and band 2 together with the NDVI constructed using band 8 and band 4 captured from Sentinel-2, respectively. Fig. 3B provides better visualization on remotely sensed green vegetation biomass (Belgiu & Csillik, 2018).

Fig. 4 constructs the variation of the greenness of vegetation using the NDVI raster image, shown in Fig. 3B. Variation score analogous to color contrast is given by a range from −1 to +1.

The low NDVI values correspond to nonvegetation areas such as bare soil and rock. Shrub and grassland are allocated moderate values (e.g., 0.2–0.4). High values represent forest cover, and negative values are attached to water bodies (Gandhi et al., 2015). Many studies recommended using NDVI to

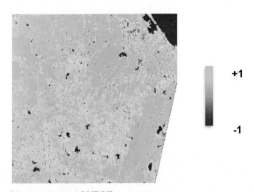

+1

-1

FIG. 4   Variation of the greenness of NDVI.

estimate the vegetation and crop cover, crop growth, drought monitoring, and assessment of drought levels (Gandhi et al., 2015). However, it seems challenging to estimate the paddy cultivation land use and to establish ground truth as paddy areas can provide inconsistent NDVI values at any given period. For example, land use for paddy follows several stages, including bare land, land underwater, early paddy crops, fully grown paddy crops, and reporting both negative and positive NDVI values. While only preliminary, our discussion of the previous raster data analysis suggests that developments along machine learning classification-based land use assessment may be important in creating an informed decision-making model that is acceptable to all stakeholders.

4 System model design and implementation

4.1 Process view

In this research, the objective was set to identify paddy field areas given a satellite image, so that such findings can facilitate accurate decision-making for sustainable paddy cultivation. The process view of the proposed approach of segmenting the areas with paddy field locations is shown in Fig. 5. The system inputs satellite images and the corresponding GIS data. The initial training process uses GIS annotations of paddy fields as the ground truth and the most matching satellite image of the area sourced from the Sentinel-2 satellite. Following the preprocessing of collected data, a transfer learning model is then trained using the aforementioned data and pretrained model weights. Utilizing the predicted areas by the model, this can be used as a backbone for many applications. The details of the process are described in the following subsections.

4.2 Data preprocessing and feature selection

The proposed study utilizes satellite imagery and GIS data with annotated paddy field location data as the ground truth values for the corresponding

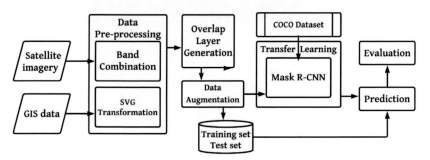

FIG. 5 Process overview of the proposed solution.

regions. The original satellite images were obtained from three bands that represent agricultural data. During the data preprocessing stage, the three-band satellite images were combined to generate a composite image with RGB values that enhances the features of agricultural areas using a System for Automated Geoscientific Analyses tool. The images for band 11 were in a lower resolution compared to bands 8 and 2, thus they had to be upscaled when compositing to RGB format. Fig. 6 shows the resultant RGB image obtained by combining the bands 2, 8, and 11, corresponding to Fig. 1. This helps segment the areas where the paddy fields are located.

Also, the annotated GIS data with shapefiles were transformed into an SVG format for further processing. We used ARCGIS (version 10.7.3) to read the GIS data.

As the next step of data processing, we overlapped the processed satellite image with the corresponding GIS data in SVG format for the better alignment of the satellite and annotated map tile data with the paddy field locations. Fig. 7A and B shows an example of the GIS data and the corresponding satellite image tile, respectively. Fig. 7C shows the resultant image after the integration. Here, the key feature is matching points in the annotations, including country boundaries, such as shoreline and edges of paddy fields, against areas such as rivers, lakes, and roads. In this process, the best match with the areas similar to paddy fields was overlapped with the data annotated as paddy fields. Later, the annotated GIS data in shapefiles were transformed into an SVG format for further processing.

As a solution to get a sufficient number of images, the larger tiles were segmented into subtitles manually, where a given image contains multiple paddy

FIG. 6 The composite image with band combination.

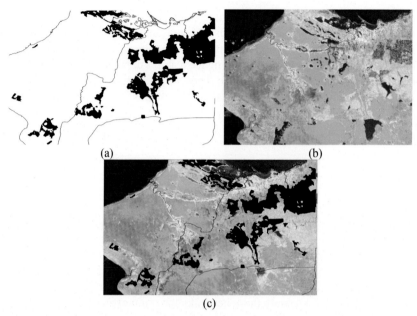

FIG. 7   Overlapping process (A) GIS data, (B) satellite imagery, and (C) overlapped image.

fields and has notable features to recognize them even visibly. Fig. 8 shows a sample of such segmentations.

Thus, we obtained 125 images from the original dataset. In order to further increase the dataset size, data augmentation that changes the orientation and image flipping are applied. Five processes, namely, horizontal flip, vertical flip,

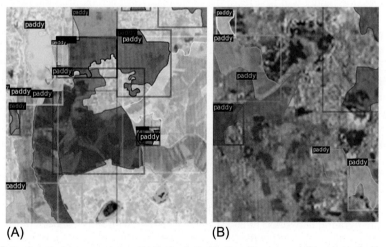

FIG. 8   Sample data segmentation. (A) Region in the Northern Province and (B) region in the North Central Province.

rotation by 90 degrees, rotation by 180 degrees, and rotation by 270 degrees, were applied during the augmentation. We did not apply color changes, as the pixels in the image used from bands combined in the satellite image tended to relay some information. This helps in understanding the features of paddy fields rather than identifying the paddy field in the image. Thus, with the original dataset, the input size of the training dataset is 125×6 images, which is 750 images.

4.3 Transfer learning process

Satellite data classification can be considered as a combination of segmentation and detection problems. Thus, the transfer learning model used for this study is the Mask RCNN model. Mask RCNN network can perform both the segmentation and detection in a single network and train in an end-to-end manner. Mask RCNN is the best performer in RCNN family of multistage object detectors (He et al., 2017). Also, it has a separate branch to predict a mask over the detected object. For computer vision problems, CNNs have shown better performance in benchmark datasets like MNIST. Although there are some networks like Capsule networks, that shows better performance in small datasets like MNIST, it is difficult to train those networks for complex image datasets.

For transfer learning, there are few common options like COCO (COCO, 2020; Lin et al., 2014) and ImageNet (Deng et al., 2009). COCO is a large-scale dataset with features such as object detection, automated captioning, and segmentation. The purpose of training on such a dataset is teaching the network, low-level features of an image. In the first layers of the network, it learns common features like edges, lines, contours, colors, and so on. Those are common for all the images. Then, in later layers, the network creates complex concepts (vehicle, humans, etc.) based on those basic features. By training on common object images, the model will first learn the basic features. Then the training process of the satellite images will allow feature learning corresponding to the proposed dataset. Also, it would be possible to increase the accuracy by keeping the weights of the first layers unchanged during the optimizing stage.

Therefore, as the next step, we have used the Mask RCNN model with pre-trained model weights using the images from the COCO dataset. This was used for the transfer learning process to avoid training the model from scratch, where low-level features would have likely been identified already. This implementation is based on the PyTorch framework with Detectron2. Next, the trained model is used to predict whether the given image contains a paddy area or not by feeding a preprocessed image.

The high-level view of the Mask RCNN is shown in Fig. 9. The backbone used in the implementation of the Mask RCNN model in this research was ResNet-50 + FPN, which is a combination of ResNet (He et al., 2017) and feature pyramid networks (FPNs) (Lin et al., 2017), with fully connected heads and convolution layers for box boundary and mask prediction. Moreover, we experimented with the model and varying learning rates and optimizers such

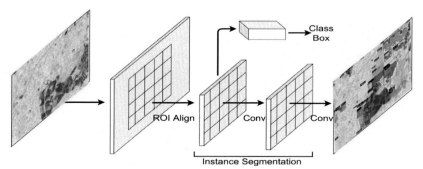

FIG. 9 A high-level diagram of the Mask RCNN model.

as Stochastic gradient descent (SGD) and Adam, where the Adam optimizer showed better results. Further, we used model hyperparameters such that images per batch: 3, base learning rate: 0.00015, maximum iterations: 10,000, and warmup iterations: 500.

Further, we fine-tuned the parameters of the learning model to obtain better accuracy. These parameters include the learning rates and iterations. We increased the learning rate over the epochs until it reached the expected learning rate. Also, we used different optimizers such as SGD and Adam, which is an adaptive learning rate optimization algorithm that showed better results.

5 System evaluation

5.1 Model evaluation

The model is evaluated using the validation set by measuring the average precision (AP), which is a standard procedure when evaluating a trained model based on Mask RCNN with ResNet-50+FPN (Padmasiri et al., 2020). Further, In the process of object detection, the overlap of the prediction and the ground truth is measured by the Intersection over Union (IoU). For instance, when the predicted value for the bounding box is closer to the actual value of the bounding box, then the intersection becomes large and results in a high IoU value. Thus, the IoU threshold indicates the accuracy by classifying whether the predictions are correct or incorrect. Eventually, it calculates the precision based on the values of true positive, false positive, true negative, and false negative.

5.2 Ground truth measurement

The accuracy for the Mask RCNN model is approximately 0.9, as shown in Fig. 10 (with 53.065 and 29.341 AP for bounding boxes and segmentation, respectively). Thus, it can be mentioned that the model can identify the features of paddy fields in the training set. However, from the AP values of the graphs in Figs. 11 and 12, it is possible to identify that the model overfits to the training

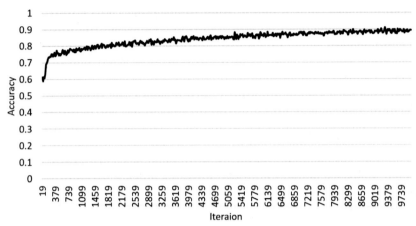

FIG. 10 Mask RCNN accuracy for the test set (with 0.6 smoothening).

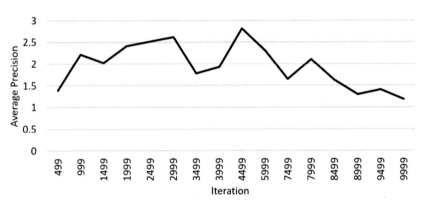

FIG. 11 Bounding box AP score for the validation set (with 0.6 smoothening).

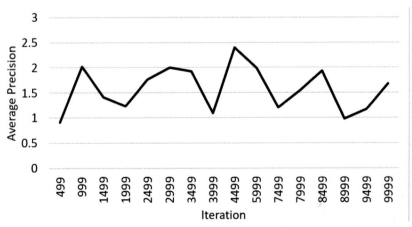

FIG. 12 Segmentation AP score for the validation set (with 0.6 smoothening).

data at a considerably early point (around 4500 iterations), even though the accuracy of the model for the training data is quite high. A possible reason for this would be the lack of data.

Moreover, we used the COCO evaluation method named maximum-detection, as it is a standard method used to evaluate object detection and segmentation models. Further, Figs. 13 and 14 show a sample of image pairs, where image (a) shows the ground truth image data, and image (b) shows the inference image obtained from the learning model.

Further, Table 3 shows the paddy fields detection metrics obtained for large areas, where a given tile contains approximately unprocessed images.

5.3 Model prediction comparison for contextual analysis

We used three scenarios to test the model under different input data quality conditions. In order to preserve the efficacy of the model predictions, these input images were tested with a confidence threshold of 50%; that is, we needed at least 50% confidence from the predictions of the model to consider that as a valid prediction indicating a paddy area. Figs. 15–17 show a sample of map data in the regions Horowpothana, Kilinochchi, and Monaragala, respectively, are used for the testing process. In all those cases, Fig. 15A gives the paddy predictions with confidences, and Fig. 15B gives the actual paddy areas.

(1) Case 1: A land area image with a high degree of feature mapping with the training dataset from Horowpothana region (North Central Province) in Sri Lanka.

(2) Case 2: A land area image with a high degree of feature mapping with the training dataset. This image is from Kilinochchi of North Province. This area of land shares similar terrain and paddy cultivation parameters as in the Horowpothana (North Central Province) land cover.

(3) Case 3: A land area image from a relatively different area of the country. This image is from Monaragala District of Uva Province. This area of land has different terrain and paddy cultivation parameters compared to the training dataset area obtained from Horowpothana (North Central Province) land cover. Mainly the Uva province has uneven terrain with small mountains and plateaus areas. Due to this terrain nature, the paddy areas are also in different sizes and shapes. It can be observed that the distribution of the paddy area is low compared to the land area.

Table 4 summarizes the observed features and accuracy related measurements of the model predations compared to the actual data.

Fig. 15 in Case 1 is from a region, which is characterized by many paddy fields with adjacent land plots. It is also from the same regional area that was considered for model training. One of the challenging features with the selected land area is large and overlapping like paddy fields, which even identified as multiple parts of paddy area at the ground-truth level. Paddy land

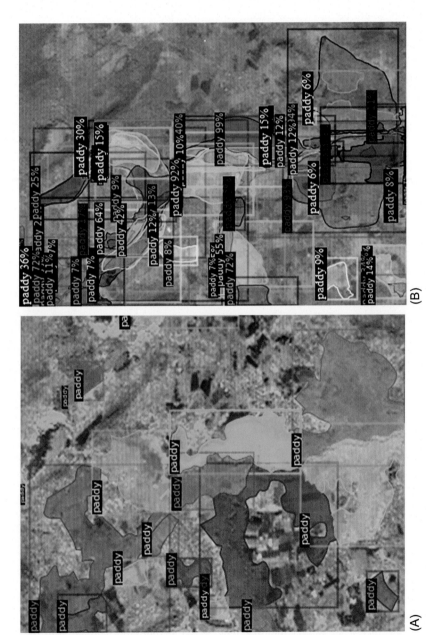

FIG. 13 Sample region 1. (A) Ground truth image and (B) inferences image.

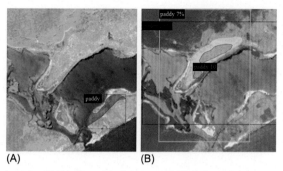

(A)   (B)

FIG. 14   Sample region 2. (A) Ground truth image and (B) inferences image.

TABLE 3 Paddy fields detection metrics.

Title no	Actual paddy field area (ha)	Predicted paddy field area (ha)	Prediction (%)
Tile 12	6304.98	5082.77	80.6
Tile 13	8169.41	3766.98	46.1

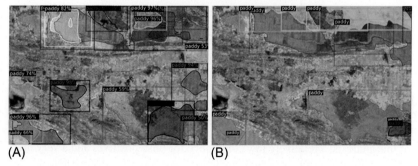

(A)   (B)

FIG. 15   Horowpothana test data: (A) predictions with confidences and (B) reality from data.

lookalike area plots such as barren paddy land and grass planes are also present in high frequency, which resulted in three false positive cases with the model prediction. However, the prediction confidence is high (average %) in this case, as given in Table 4.

In Case 2, Fig. 16 was taken from a relatively similar but different province, a land area known as Kilinochchi. This map image represents a flat land terrain. However, one difference observed between Case 1: Horowpothana area (training

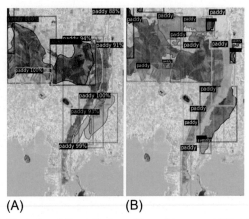

FIG. 16 Kilinochchi test data: (A): predictions with confidences and (B) reality from data.

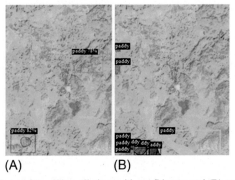

FIG. 17 Monaragala test data: (A) predictions with confidences and (B) reality from data.

data region) and Case 2: Kilinochchi area is the distribution of paddy lands. In Case 2, the paddy land tends to be nonadjacent and relatively smaller, though there are many small-sized paddy lands scattered across the selected land plot. For this analysis, a relatively low confidence for false positives and a very high average confidence for the actual predictions was observed, as in Table 4.

Case 3, Fig. 17, was taken from a land area different from the training data. This data represent a land image from Monaragala district in Uva province (in the southeast region of the island) and contains a high degree of uneven and relatively rough terrain consisting of mountains and valleys. Due to this, it is also apparent that the paddy cultivation traits, including the selection of land areas, paddy field polygon shapes, and relative sizes of the paddy fields, are somewhat unique compared to the North, and North Central region of the country. However, the model did not predict well with the input image, as it could only predict two paddy areas out of which one is a false positive case.

TABLE 4 Summary of case analysis.

Case	Area info	Actual paddy units (ground truth)	Prediction of paddy units	False positive avg. confidence (%)	Actual mapping avg. confidence (%)	Accuracy % (intersection) >50% confidence (%)
1	Horowpothana (NC)	13	16	84.6	89.7	76.9
2	Kilinochchi (North)	51	29	57.3	92.44	49.1
3	Monaragala (Uva)	46	2	78	82	2.2

In overall, subject to model limitations, Cases 1–2 predictive results indicate fairly accurate paddy land instance identification with a high level of average confidence. For Case 1, 76.9% intersection accuracy (>50% confidence) was reported, and for Case 2, 49.1% intersection accuracy (>50% confidence) was observed. For Case 3, which is from a different land condition in the country but used for paddy cultivation, the model prediction accuracy was just over 2% (intersection accuracy, >50% confidence).

This low reliability of the model prediction in Case 3 is expected for obvious ground truth variations across the country and paddy field management practices specific to local regions. This also highlights the unwarranted complexity of building a countrywide or national scale DL model to help support decision-making toward sustainable paddy field management. While the trained model and its predictive ability are acceptable for practical use as a first attempt model for the Sri Lankan context, it is essential to note that localized variants of the model are required when different parts of the country have different paddy cultivation parameters. As such, one high level of the model providing the predictive framework and a few parameterized localized models can be explored for a higher level of accuracy of paddy land identification and for deriving paddy management-related decision support information with high confidence.

Moreover, the following reasons can be pointed out specific to this evaluation explaining the limitations of the observed results through the case studies. The test images were taken from a period with vast differences in features to that of data used to train the model. With visible inspection, it is identified that the images used for training had harvested or seeding fields, which both account for brownish and yellow land patches with clear boundaries due to openness. The test image data contained lush fields with vegetation on it, making it difficult to identify the boundaries. Another factor observed is the region-specific average sizes of the paddy lands. Although the used land tile images represented equal sizes of land area, it is observed that paddy field units show different sizes. For example, the size of the paddy fields in Case 3 seems to be quite small. That also indicates a different style of paddy cultivation is done in the area as an adaptation to the available and suitable land plots for the cultivation subject to other terrain conditions.

6 Discussion

6.1 Contribution of the proposed study

The main contribution of this research for sustainable agriculture and sector development is proposing a learning model for informed decision-making using a low-cost, noninvasive approach compared with the existing methods. RS-based machine learning models seem desirable when the outcome sought is multidimensional, adaptable, accurate, and low-cost.

Most paddy cultivation regions in the developing world are sometimes without basic infrastructure. Thus, obtaining real-time data through seamless sensor integration is not a viable option. Most of the focus in the agriculture literature recently has been on precision agriculture using the Internet of Things, but RS-based learning models show a lot of promise as a way to develop institutional arrangements to increase efficient resource use and ultimately put in place policies toward sustainable agriculture. This study explored the related literature and identified the commonly used datasets, DL models, open challenges, and future research directions.

This chapter deploys a state-of-the-art DL method, Mask RCNN, to classify the satellite image datasets collected over a period for the predictive model development. The proposed Mask RCNN DL model allows us to use GIS and RS imagery conjointly to detect the actual land use for paddy farming, although with only mixed success. Data quality and availability issues preclude model developments in some directions such as land-use change detection under hydrological or economic uncertainty.

A DL-based geospatial land usage monitoring can be both conceptually and practically appealing, to efficiently identify and respond to the diverse needs of agents in the paddy supply chain. The proposed analytics model can be used to estimate the agricultural land area under paddy cultivation, which varies largely due to adverse climate conditions such as droughts and floods in Sri Lanka. This information will help assess many aspects such as the compensation payable to insurance claims for losses sustained during a particular year, paddy yield prediction, estimate subsidies for fertilizer by computing the usage/area, compute methane emissions, estimate annual water allocations, determine nonpoint source pollutants, identify future food security, decide government annual budgets allocation for subsidies, and upgrade infrastructure. The information with a fine-tuned predictive analysis model can lead to possible policy implications for sustainable agriculture directives of the Sri Lankan government.

6.2   Limitations of the datasets

Data is the most concerning factor that affected the research throughout. The research is subject to the following limitations, mainly from the datasets used for the model development and testing. Since we have used standard DL techniques and methodologies it can be concluded that overcoming the following limitations for the used dataset can significantly improve the outcome of the research without altering the proposed models or incorporate different analysis techniques.

● The low amount of data points is one of the key challenges affecting this study. There were only approximately 1200 data points in the source. In order to obtain higher accuracies with DL, a larger dataset with many data points is always desired.

- The issues with the time the ground truth annotations were obtained. It was difficult to discern an exact period from satellite images and due to paddy field areas that could be either crop areas or open fields. Thus, the model finds difficulty in properly separating the paddy field areas. The model is identifying open grass areas like paddy fields as they visually may seem the same. Therefore, the time when the satellite images were taken may play a role to get better results. For example, time periods of seeding the land, fully grown paddy, before/after harvesting, and so on. Therefore, it was not possible to verify the accuracy of a combined GIS annotation and satellite imagery pair beyond a certain level.
- Having unreliable data will affect the accuracy of the learning model. When integrating the satellite imaginary with GIS data, both datasets should be consistent to ensure the reliability of data. Also, the overlapping of the aerial images and the annotated GIS map data should be acquired at the same time, and the annotation of GIS data should avoid offsetting points from their real locations. Otherwise, the map data will not be correctly annotated as paddy areas and will lead to a poor training process.
- Certain annotations did not seem to "fit" any satellite images when compared visually. Possible reasons are that the period the data was from was not in the period where the satellite images were considered (2017–2020) or that the annotations had a certain error. Nonetheless, feeding the tiles that "did not fit" properly lowered the accuracy of the model.
- The relatively low resolution of the satellite images. One could try other satellite sources, albeit with sacrificing the multiband images.
- Map image distortions can occur due to environmental impacts such as rain, fog, and clouds. Since rice takes a considerable period to cultivate, when taking a batch of images, there can be images with clouds or fog in certain areas. If at least one image of the same land is identified as a paddy field, then the entire image set can be annotated or referred to as identified land. However, image processing techniques may help identify and remove the cloudy or foggy areas for better classification accuracy.
- Cross-validation from a selected locality with actual paddy area boundaries could not be performed.

6.3   Future research directions

This study provides a unique research exploration in the context of data analysis for agriculture sustainability in Sri Lanka. It can be considered as one of the early attempts to incorporate DL as the technical approach to facilitate the decision-making process relevant to paddy cultivation. Beyond this exploratory study, the following future research avenues can be clearly stated as possible related extensions to the current study.

One of the promising future studies will be to develop a shallow model that is specifically customized for the selected domain rather than a generic model that is used in this research for object detection and segmentation with a high number of layers. This can help fine-tune the specialized model considering domain parameters to gain higher accuracy. Alternatively, one could also consider using trained models that were specialized in solving problems related to satellite imagery (e.g., urban planning) then use those for transfer learning to apply within the paddy cultivation analysis domain.

Moreover, different backbones, such as ResNet 50, ResNet 101, and Inception V2n can be tried with the Mask RCNN transfer learning model to compare the accuracy levels (Padmasiri et al., 2020). Also, the results can be compared with other object detection and segmentation models such as U-Net and YOLO. Also, it might be possible to achieve better accuracy by integrating unsupervised image segmentation with a non-DL classifier, which can be trained using less labeled data.

Another potential future research would be to integrate other features such as other bands from satellite images, imagery from other satellites, and moisture values to obtain a holistic view of the predictive output so that the decisions for agrarian services and tools for achieving sustainability can be further facilitated. The integration of different types of related data would increase the accuracy and reliability of the data (Jayanetti et al., 2017; Meedeniya et al., 2020). Thus, improving the dataset size will improve model performance.

Furthermore, research that focuses on improving RS image quality through machine learning techniques can be another fruitful area to explore. Using stochastic processes to model change detection can also be useful research given that several varying conditions considerably affect the trend and the amount of paddy cultivation area for a given period.

7 Conclusions

Sustainable agriculture in developing countries such as Sri Lanka depends on a range of factors that can be extremely challenging to manage through conventional means. Resource constraints, climate risks, socio-cultural preferences, economic viability, and policy intervention are critical conditions that demand state-of-the-art technology incorporation to overcome. While the technology-enriched agriculture processes are always essential for the sectoral growth and productivity, it is noteworthy that the informed decision-making capability backed with real-time data at any point of intervention in agricultural processes is crucial for gaining consistent yields in volumes throughout the year, irrespective of ground realities.

Through this study, it was quite evident that one of the main limiting factors for utilizing DL techniques to enhance local agriculture is the difficulty in accessing sufficiently accurate data corresponding to ground realities for decision-making. Lack of predictive models, even for fundamental estimates, such as paddy cultivation area within a locality, seriously questions the effectiveness of the administrative and government agrarian service efforts to sustain the agriculture within the local community. Due to economic and other logistical constraints, in situ smart sensing with data collection is still not a viable option for the government even with low-cost solutions. As elaborated previously, relying on satellite imagery-based predictive models can open an opportunity to the decision-makers in the agriculture sector to formulate effectively and update policy directives that promote sustainability in the community and regional agriculture. While there is still room for improvement in obtained estimates through the DL models in this study with more data, the study, among the first of its kind in the context of the Sri Lankan paddy cultivation sector, suggests the necessity of such models for sustainable agriculture.

References

Alqurashi, A., & Kumar, L. (2013). Investigating the use of remote sensing and GIS techniques to detect land use and land cover change: A review. *Advances in Remote Sensing, 2*(2), 193–204.

Barbosa, A., Trevisan, R., Hovakimyan, N., & Martin, N. F. (2020). Modeling yield response to crop management using convolutional neural networks. *Computers and Electronics in Agriculture, 170*, 105197.

Bauer, A., Bostrom, A. G., Ball, J., Applegate, C., Cheng, T., Laycock, S., … Zhou, J. (2019). Combining computer vision and deep learning to enable ultra-scale aerial phenotyping and precision agriculture: A case study of lettuce production. *Horticulture Research, 6*(1), 1–12. 70.

Bazzi, H., Baghdadi, N., Hajj, M. E., Zribi, M., Minh, D. H. T., Ndikumana, E., … Belhouchette, H. (2019). Mapping paddy rice using Sentinel-1 SAR time series in Camargue, France. *Remote Sensing, 11*, 887.

Belgiu, M., & Csillik, O. (2018). Sentinel-2 cropland mapping using pixel-based and object-based time-weighted dynamic time warping analysis. *Remote Sensing of Environment, 204*, 509–523.

Campbell, J. B., & Wynne, R. H. (2011). *Introduction to remote sensing* (5th ed.). Guilford Press.

Claverie, M., Ju, J., Masek, J. G., Dungan, J. L., Vermote, E. F., Roger, J. C., … Justice, C. (2018). The Harmonized Landsat and Sentinel-2 surface reflectance data set. *Remote Sensing of Environment, 219*, 145–161.

COCO. (2020). *Common objects in context dataset.* https://cocodataset.org/#home. (Accessed 1 October 2020).

Deng, J., Dong, W., Socher, R., Li, L., Li, K., & Fei-Fei, L. (2009). ImageNet: A large-scale hierarchical image database. In *IEEE conference on computer vision and pattern recognition, Miami, FL* (pp. 248–255).

FAO and WFP. (2017). *Fao/wfp crop and food security assessment mission to Sri Lanka, Special Report.* http://lk.one.un.org.

Forkuor, G., Dimobe, K., Serme, I., & Tondoh, J. E. (2018). Landsat-8 vs. Sentinel-2: Examining the added value of sentinel-2's red-edge bands to land-use and land-cover mapping in Burkina Faso. *GIScience & Remote Sensing, 55*(3), 331–354.

Franklin, S. E., Ahmed, O. S., Wulder, M. A., White, J. C., Hermosilla, T., & Coops, N. C. (2015). Large area mapping of annual land cover dynamics using multitemporal change detection and classification of Landsat time series data. *Canadian Journal of Remote Sensing, 41*(4), 293–314.

Gadiraju, K. K., Ramachandra, B., Chen, Z., & Vatsavai, R. R. (2020). Multimodal deep learning based crop classification using multispectral and multitemporal satellite imagery. In *26th ACM SIGKDD international conference on knowledge discovery & data mining* (pp. 3234–3242).

Gandhi, G. M., Parthiban, S., Thummalu, N., & Christy, A. (2015). Ndvi: Vegetation change detection using remote sensing and gis—A case study of Vellore District. *Procedia Computer Science*, *57*, 1199–1210.

Gao, F., Anderson, M. C., Zhang, X., Yang, Z., Alfieri, J. G., Kustas, W. P., … Prueger, J.H. (2017). Toward mapping crop progress at field scales through fusion of Landsat and MODIS imagery. *Remote Sensing of Environment*, *188*, 9–25.

Girshick, R. (2015). Fast R-CNN. In *IEEE international conference on computer vision (ICCV)* (pp. 1440–1448).

Girshick, R., Donahue, J., Darrell, T., & Malik, J. (2014). Rich feature hierarchies for accurate object detection and semantic segmentation. In *IEEE conference on computer vision and pattern recognition, Columbus, OH* (pp. 580–587).

GIS Geography. (2020). *Sentinel 2 band combinations.* https://gisgeography.com/. (Accessed 1 October 2020).

Guan, K., Hien, N. T., Li, Z., & Rao, L. N. (2018). Measuring rice yield from space: The case of Thai Binh Province, VietNam. *ADB economics working paper series*. Manila: Asian Development Bank. 541.

Hansen, M. C., & Loveland, T. R. (2012). A review of large area monitoring of land cover change using Landsat data. *Remote Sensing of Environment*, *122*, 66–74.

He, K., Gkioxari, G., Dollár, P., & Girshick, R. (2017). Mask R-CNN. *Computer Vision and Pattern Recognition*. arXiv:1703.06870.

Hutt, C., Koppe, W., Miao, Y. X., & Bareth, G. (2016). Best accuracy land use/land 512Cover (LULC) classification to derive crop types using multitemporal, multi sensor, and multi-polarization SAR satellite images. *Remote Sensing*, *8*(8), 684.

Ian, H. (2010). *An introduction to geographical information systems*. Pearson Education India.

Jayanetti, J. A. A. M., Meedeniya, D. A., Dilini, M. D. N., Wickramapala, M. H., & Madushanka, J. H. (2017). Enhanced land cover and land use information generation from satellite imagery and foursquare data. In *6th International conference on software and computer applications (ICSCA 2017)* (pp. 149–153). ACM.

Jia, X., & Richards, J. A. (2002). Cluster space representation for hyperspectral classification. *IEEE Transactions on Geoscience and Remote Sensing*, *40*(3), 593–598.

Knopp, L., Wieland, M., Rättich, M., & Martinis, S. (2020). A deep learning approach for burned area segmentation with Sentinel-2 data. *Remote Sensing*, *12*(15), 2422.

Lal, M. (2011). Implications of climate change in sustained agricultural productivity in South Asia. *Regional Environmental Change*, *11*(1), 79–94.

Lin, T.-Y., Dollár, P., Girshick, R., He, K., Hariharan, B., & Belongie, S. (2017). Feature pyramid networks for object detection. In *IEEE conference on computer vision and pattern recognition (CVPR), Honolulu, HI* (pp. 936–944).

Lin, T.-Y., Maire, M., Belongie, S., Hays, J., Perona, P., Ramanan, D., … Zitnick, C.L. (2014). Microsoft COCO: Common objects in context. In D. Fleet, T. Pajdla, B. Schiele, & T. Tuytelaars (Eds.), *Computer vision – ECCV, LNCS, 8693* (pp. 740–755). Cham: Springer.

Lobell, D. B. (2013). The use of satellite data for crop yield gap analysis. *Field Crops Research*, *143*, 56–64.

Marj, A. F., & Meijerink, A. M. J. (2011). Agricultural drought forecasting using satellite images, climate indices and artificial neural network. *International Journal of Remote Sensing*, *32*(24), 9707–9719.

Meedeniya, D. A., Jayanetti, J. A. A. M., Dilini, M. D. N., Wickramapala, M. H., & Madushanka, J. H. (2020). Land-use classification with integrated data. In M. Malarvel, S. R. Nayak, S. N. Panda, P. K. Pattnaik, & N. Muangnak (Eds.), *Machine vision inspection systems: image processing, concepts, methodologies and applications* (pp. 1–38). New York, United States: John Wiley & Sons Inc (chapter 1).

Menike, L. M. C. S., & Arachchi, K. A. G. P. K. (2016). Adaptation to climate change by small-holder farmers in rural communities: Evidence from Sri Lanka. *Procedia Food Science, 6*, 288–292.

Mountrakis, G., Im, J., & Ogole, C. (2011). Support vector machines in remote sensing: A review. *ISPRS Journal of Photogrammetry and Remote Sensing, 66*(3), 247–259.

Nässtrom, R., & Mattsson, E. (2011). *Country report Sri Lanka. Land-use change and forestry at the national and sub-national level. Focali, Sweden.*

Ndikumana, E., Minh, D. H. T., Baghdadi, N., Courault, D., & Hossard, L. (2018). Deep recurrent neural network for agricultural classification using multitemporal SAR Sentinel-1 for Camargue, France. *Remote Sensing, 10*, 1217.

Nguyen, T. T., Thanh, D. H., Minh, T. P., Tuyet, T. V., Thanh, H. N., Quyet-Thang, H., & Jun, J. (2020). Monitoring agriculture areas with satellite images and deep learning. *Applied Soft Computing, 95*, 106565.

Onojeghuo, A. O., Blackburn, G. A., Wang, Q., Atkinson, P. M., Kindred, D., & Miao, Y. (2018). Mapping paddy rice fields by applying machine learning algorithms to multi-temporal Sentinel-1A and Landsat data. *International Journal of Remote Sensing, 39*(4), 1042–1067.

Padmasiri, H., Madurawe, R., Abeysinghe, C., & Meedeniya, D. (2020). Automated vehicle parking occupancy detection in real-time. In *2020 Moratuwa engineering research conference (MER-Con)* (pp. 644–649). IEEE Xplore.

Rahman, M. T. U., Tabassum, F., Rasheduzzaman, M., Saba, H., Sarkar, L., Ferdous, J., ... Islam, A. Z. (2017). Temporal dynamics of land use/land cover change and its prediction using CA-ANN model for southwestern coastal Bangladesh. *Environmental Monitoring and Assessment, 189* (11), 565.

Rathnayake, C. W., Jones, S., & Soto-Berelov, M. (2020). Mapping land cover change over a 25-year period (1993–2018) in Sri Lanka using Landsat time-series. *Land, 9*(1), 27.

Rotairo, L., Durante, A. C., Lapitan, P., & Rao, L. N. (2019). *Use of remote sensing to estimate paddy area and production: A handbook.* Asian Development Bank.

Senanayake, S. M. P., & Premaratne, S. P. (2016). An analysis of the paddy/rice value chains in Sri Lanka. *Asia-Pacific Journal of Rural Development, 26*(1), 105–126.

Sidike, P., Sagan, V., Maimaitijiang, M., Maimaitiyiming, M., Shakoor, N., Burken, J., ... Fritschi, F.B. (2019). dPEN: Deep Progressively Expanded Network for mapping heterogeneous agricultural landscape using WorldView-3 satellite imagery. *Remote Sensing of Environment, 221*, 756–772.

Sirirattanapol, C., Tamkuan, N., Nagai, M., & Ito, M. (2020). Apply deep learning techniques on classification of single-band SAR satellite images. In S. Monprapussorn, Z. Lin, A. Sitthi, & P. Wetchayont (Eds.), *Springer geography: Vol. 2018. Geoinformatics for sustainable development in Asian cities. ICGGS* (pp. 1–11). Cham: Springer.

Song, X., Zhang, G., Liu, F., Li, D., Zhao, Y., & Yang, J. (2016). Modeling spatio-temporal distribution of soil moisture by deep learning-based cellular automata model. *Journal of Arid Land, 8* (5), 734–748.

Steinhausen, M. J., Wagner, P. D., Narasimhan, B., & Waske, B. (2018). Combining Sentinel-1 and Sentinel-2 data for improved land use and land cover mapping of monsoon regions. *International Journal of Applied Earth Observation and Geoinformation, 73*, 595–604.

Subasinghe, S., Estoque, R. C., & Murayama, Y. (2016). Spatiotemporal analysis of urban growth using GIS and remote sensing: A case study of the Colombo Metropolitan Area, Sri Lanka. *ISPRS International Journal of Geo-Information, 5*(11), 197.

Tri, N. C., Duong, H. N., Hoai, T. V., Hoa, T. V., Nguyen, V. H., Toan, N. T., & Snasel, V. (2017). A novel approach based on deep learning techniques and UAVs to yield assessment of paddy fields. In *9th International conference on knowledge and systems engineering (KSE)* (pp. 257–262). IEEE Xplore.

Ustuner, M., Sanli, F. B., & Dixon, B. (2015). Application of support vector machines for landuse classification using high-resolution rapideye images: A sensitivity analysis. *European Journal of Remote Sensing, 48*(1), 403–422.

Vincent, D., Deepa, N., Elavarasan, D., Srinivasan, K., Chauhdary, S. H., & Iwendi, C. (2019). Sensors driven AI-based agriculture recommendation model for assessing land suitability. *Sensors, 19*(17), 3667.

Vogelmann, J. E., Gallant, A. L., Shi, H., & Zhu, Z. (2016). Perspectives on monitoring gradual change across the continuity of Landsat sensors using time-series data. *Remote Sensing of Environment, 185*, 258–270.

Wambua, M. R. (2014). Drought forecasting using indices and artificial neural networks for upper Tana River basin, Kenya—A review concept. *Journal of Civil & Environmental Engineering, 04*(04), 1–12.

Wang, A. X., Tran, C., Desai, N., Lobell, D., & Ermon, S. (2018). Deep transfer learning for crop yield prediction with remote sensing data. In *50. Proceedings of the 1st ACM SIGCAS conference on computing and sustainable societies* (pp. 1–5). ACM.

Weng, Q. (2002). Land use change analysis in the Zhujiang Delta of China using satellite remote sensing, GIS and stochastic modelling. *Journal of Environmental Management, 64*(3), 273–284.

Zhang, M., Lin, H., Wang, G., Sun, H., & Fu, J. (2018). Mapping paddy rice using a convolutional neural network (CNN) with Landsat 8 datasets in the Dongting Lake Area, China. *Remote Sensing, 10*, 1840.

Zhang, Y., Wang, C., Wu, J., Qi, J., & Salas, W. A. (2009). Mapping paddy rice with multi temporal ALOS/PALSAR imagery in southeast China. *International Journal of Remote Sensing, 30*, 6301–6315.

Chapter 14

Artificial intelligence-based detection and counting of olive fruit flies: A comprehensive survey

Nariman Mamdouh, Mohamed Wael, and Ahmed Khattab
Electronics and Electrical Communications Engineering Department, Cairo University, Giza, Egypt

1 Introduction

Olives (*Olea europaea L.*) have been grown for millennia in the Mediterranean basin with great economic impacts. They are also grown in South America, South Africa, Australia, New Zealand, and the United States. Olives have provided livelihood for large communities in rural areas, protected the land from desertification, especially in southern parts of Europe, enriched the soil with organic carbon, and improved its chemical and physical characteristics. During the last 20 years, this extremely important agribusiness has been facing great challenges due to environmental changes, global warming, salinity, diseases, and pests.

Olive fruit fly, also known as *Bactrocera oleae* or *Dacus oleae*, is a monophagous (i.e., it feeds only on one fruit). The olive fruit fly is considered the most damaging pest of olives in southern Europe, North Africa, the Middle East, and recently, California. The olive fruit fly may cause damage to up to 100% of the harvested fruit and cause losses of up to 80% of the oil value because of lower quantity and quality (The Olive Oil Source, 2020). Its population depends on the climate as it flourishes in humid climates, although it may be found also in dry areas. The effect of the microclimate on the olive fruit fly population and its lifecycle in different geographical areas, such as valleys, hills, and beaches, was investigated in one study (Kalamatianos et al., 2019). The most dominant climatic contributors to the increase of olive fruit numbers are temperature and humidity. Temperature degrees between 20°C and 30°C are ideal for the olive

Deep Learning for Sustainable Agriculture. https://doi.org/10.1016/B978-0-323-85214-2.00012-4

fruit fly. The humid environments are more favorable by the olive fruit fly, although they are also found in dry environments. Wind speed and direction sensors are recommended, especially during the spraying process, to minimize the off-targeting. The altitude of the field is also a factor, but it does not need a sensor as it is time invariant (Kalamatianos et al., 2019).

Olive fruit fly control falls under the generic topic of integrated pest management (IPM). IPM is an efficient way of reducing the population of harmful pests under a predefined threshold. IPM covers a wide range of aspects ranging from engineering aspects, such as automated systems for efficient spraying of pesticides, to cultural aspects, such as educating the farmers that overspraying, which means spraying pesticides with a quantity larger than what is needed, harms humans and the environment as traces of the pesticides remain in the fruits, and that may kill other species that feed on the harmful pest. In this chapter, we are interested in the engineering aspects of IPM. The state-of-the-art IPM method is spreading traps in the field according to a density to be calculated based on the field's characteristics. The traps are injected with materials that attract the individual pests. After being trapped, the number of trapped pests is calculated, and if it exceeds a certain threshold, the farmers should spray pesticides over the infected area or take other appropriate countermeasures (e.g., a biological treatment). The spraying process should take the climatic conditions into consideration as some conditions may aid the pests to escape from the sprays leading to a waste of pesticides and harming the fruits, which causes significant economic losses. These phases are all managed by a decision support system (DSS). A DSS is a computer-assisted tool that is used to improve the decision-making processes by including systematic knowledge of the system and by implementing rules to improve and systemize the decision-making. It may be fully automated, that is, it gathers and analyzes the data then takes a decision that is either implemented automatically with zero human intervention or semiautomated, that is, the DSS gathers and analyzes the information and suggests a decision for the farmers to implement on their own (Sciarretta et al., 2019).

Each phase of the aforementioned phases may be implemented in several ways. Regarding setting up the traps, it was suggested that the DSS based on climatic conditions and monitoring the spatial and temporal conditions of the field provides farmers with the optimum locations and the optimum density of the traps (Miranda et al., 2019). This step also may require taking the life cycle of the olive fruit fly into consideration. These traps are parts of location aware systems (LASs) (Pontikakos et al., 2012), that is, the DSS is able to locate precisely each trap such that the pesticides will be sprayed only in the desired region and thus achieves efficient use of resources and prevents harming the fruits. The DSS is thus a geographical information system (GIS). The most common technology to implement GIS is the Global Positioning System (GPS). The field now can be viewed as a grid, and the DSS will help the farmer locate the infected regions precisely leveraging the spatial nonuniformity.

The material injected in the traps may be one of the following substances or a composite of them. Many systems depend on injecting the traps with semiochemicals, which are chemicals that are used by the olive fruit flies to communicate. The most common choice in this context is the sex pheromone known as spiroketal. The sex pheromones attract male adults much more than female adults, if any, and it never attracts larvae. The other substance is the proteins that attract both males and females. The figure of merit here is the duration between reinjecting, the coverage area and the possibility of attracting other species.

In this chapter, we comprehensively survey the literature of olive fruit fly (and related pests, such as the Mediterranean fly and moth) detection and counting. While our main emphasis is on the techniques that exploit artificial intelligence, we also survey other approaches to make the treatment comprehensive. We classify the counting of the trapped pests into either manual, semiautomatic, or automatic. In manual detection and counting systems, the farmers manually count the number of the pests in each trap on a daily basis. In both semiautomatic and automatic systems, the concept of e-trap is introduced. An e-trap is a trap that contains a camera and takes daily images from inside the trap, and a communication module that allows the transmission of the taken images. An intelligent algorithm is then applied first to classify the pests, that is, olive fruit fly from relative species, and then to count the number of trapped pests. Usually the intelligent algorithms cannot distinguish males from females, but the DSS is interested merely in the number of olive fruit flies captured. We categorize the intelligent algorithms that are typically used as either machine learning (ML) based on artificial neural networks (ANNs), deep learning using convolutional neural networks (CNNs), image processing techniques, optoacoustic detection, or hyperspectral imaging using spectroscopy. The intelligent algorithm can be implemented in the trap, or the images can be forwarded to a central node that runs the algorithm. In both cases, the e-trap uses its communication module to send either the images or the number of identified trapped pests such that the network can approximate the spatiotemporal distribution of the pests' population. The usual choices for wireless connectivity are WiFi, Zigbee, and cellular technologies.

The remainder of the chapter is organized as follows. In Section 2, we present our detailed survey of the various detection and counting approaches. These techniques are analyzed and compared alongside our insights in Section 3. Section 4 concludes the chapter and proposes future research directions.

2 Literature survey of recognition systems

Olive fruit fly recognition is considered the bottleneck of the whole pest management system. The system should be able to count the number of pests accurately to guide the farmers about where to spray the pesticides and with what amount, especially in a fully automated DSS. The olive fruit fly recognition depends on the shape of the fly defined in the *Australian Handbook for the Identification of Fruit Flies* V3.1 under the entry "similar species of *Bactrocera oleae*" as: "*Bactrocera oleae* is quite distinct in lacking vittae and having a spot at the apex of the wing. It is superficially similar to *B. tuberculata* and *B. correcta* in having a black scutum and spot at the wing apex instead of a costal band, but lacks lateral vittae. It is superficially similar to *B. melanotus* and *B. passiflorae* in having a black scutum and lacking lateral vittae, but has an orange brown abdomen with lateral coloring on terga II–IV and a spot at the apex of the wing" (Plant Health Australia, 2018). These differentiating traits, shown in Fig. 1, should be taken into consideration while designing a classifier to classify the olive fruit fly pest. Another thing that should be considered is the other pests that attack the olive fruits and whether they are present in the field or not.

In this chapter, we present a comprehensive survey of pest recognition technologies with emphasis on the detection and counting of the olive fruit fly. We broadly classify the existing pest recognition and counting techniques into manual, semiautomatic, and automatic detection and counting techniques, as will be discussed.

2.1 Manual detection and counting

Manual detection and counting are performed by hired personnel who periodically check the traps and classify whether they contain enough numbers of the olive fruit fly or not to spray the pesticide. This method is the conventional one, and it is inefficient for the obvious reasons of inefficiency, expense, and human error. This chapter does not dive deeper into this approach, as it is outdated and behind our scope.

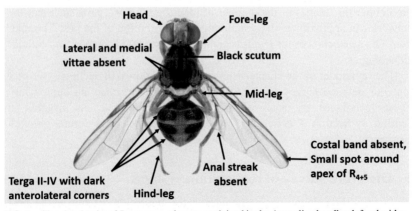

FIG. 1 The visual traits of *Bactrocera oleae* as explained in the Australian handbook for the identification of fruit flies (Plant Health Australia, 2018).

2.2 Semiautomatic detection and counting

Semiautomatic, also referred to as human-assisted, olive fruit fly detection and counting exploits e-traps to help humans in the decision-making process. *E*-traps are modified versions of the conventional traps through adding electronic circuitry to them, such as sensors, cameras, microcontrollers, wireless communication modules, or a composition of all the aforementioned electronic devices. The e-traps in this case use their built-in cameras to capture images of the interior of the trap periodically and send these images via any wireless communication protocol to a user-friendly interface through which the entomologist (expert) decides whether the captured pests are olive fruit flies or not and whether the number of the captured pests demands the spraying of the pesticides or not. Implementations of such identification systems are presented in several studies (Miranda et al., 2019; Sciarretta et al., 2019; Shaked et al., 2018; Wang et al., 2016).

In one study (Shaked et al., 2018), researchers modified the traditional yellow surface trap by augmenting it with Omni Vision OV5647 Noir Raspberry Pi 5 MPXL camera, microcontroller, and wireless communication module. The trap was injected by the female sex pheromone and the ammonium bicarbonate to ensure the attraction of both sexes to the trap in addition to the color of the trap, that is, yellow, which is a well-known attractive color for the olive fruit fly pests. The system experimented both the star topology and the mesh topology. The star topology is simple implementation-wise but is not robust and may not be practical in certain field conditions where a central powerful node is not feasible. The mesh topology is more complex, but it is much more robust and can be resilient to harsh conditions. The authors also experimented with Zigbee and WiFi as the wireless communication protocol. They concluded that Zigbee covers larger areas, but it provides lower data rates. In contrast, the WiFi protocol provides higher data rates, but it is more power hungry. Thus, it was recommended that the image preprocessing, for example, denoising and so on, be locally implemented on each trap. The authors also referred to the climatic effects on the whole system performance. For instance, the rain has a degrading effect on the performance since it helps the pests escape the traps in some cases, and it also increases the error rate of the communication link substantially.

Miranda et al. (2019) developed a DSS based on semiautomatic pest-monitoring systems to monitor olive fruit flies. In LASs, all the trees are georeferenced. The e-traps are distributed in the LAS area and form an ad hoc wireless sensor network (WSN). Each trap is composed of a 15 W solar panel, a 12 V battery, a low-rate and low-power Zigbee RF (xBee S2B) transceiver that can be configured to function as a coordinator or an end device within the WSN, a Raspberry Pi model B + Linux-based platform and controller, a camera (5 MP CMOS sensor Omni Vision 5647), a 32 GB SD card, and a temperature and humidity sensor. The WSN is built using a star topology in which nodes only communicate their information (temperature, humidity, and images) to the coordinator. The coordinator node automatically uploads the collected information to a database sever located at the University of the Balearic Islands (UIB). It was shown that the orchard with LAS reduced the insecticide treated area by 42.85% and the volume of pesticide by 36.84% by comparing with NO-LAS orchards. As a trapping system, only one picture is captured daily by the camera at noon. The developed prototype e-trap costs 750 € for materials and 2100 € for the software. The cost can be reduced in mass production.

Wang et al. (2016) developed a fruit fly image identification system (AFIS1.0), which classifies 74 species that belong to six genera, including the olive fruit fly. AFIS integrates both automatic identification and manual identification to help farmers with less experience to identify the different species of fruit flies. The manual identification component is based on an image retrieval system in which the entomologist sees an image of the whole body, wing, thorax, and abdomen of the pest to be classified and the corresponding images of the possible candidates. The entomologist then compares the images and chooses the best answer. However, it was noticed that due to imperfections in the received images, sometimes the entomologists misclassify the received pest's image with the ground truth being the knowledge gained by a farmer classifying the pest in the physical trap. The automatic component is based on receiving the images and saving them in a relational database. Then, a Gabor surface feature extraction process is performed on the images of the wing, thorax, and abdomen of the pest using a cosine similarity metric, which is the metric of a K-nearest neighbor (K-NN) classifier. The features are based on multiorientation and multiscale techniques. The results of the classifiers were accurate for the wing, thorax, and abdomen with percentages equal to 71%, 69%, and 39%, respectively, and a combined accuracy of 87%.

Sciarretta et al. (2019) developed a DSS to control the Mediterranean fruit fly (medfly). The medfly is a relative species of the olive fruit fly with distinguishable features. The DSS presented by Sciarretta et al. (2019) includes three stages—DSS1, DSS2, and DSS3—as shown in Fig. 2. DSS1 employs an

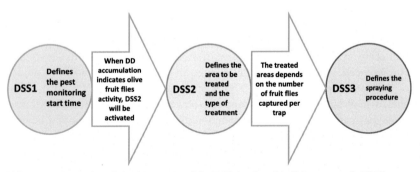

FIG. 2 An illustration of the three stages of the DSS developed in Sciarretta et al. (2019).

algorithm that determines the time at which the traps should be deployed in the field to start monitoring the population of the medfly. Then, DSS1 continuously computes the Degree Days (DD) accumulation based on biofix data (first of January). If the accumulated DD becomes equal to the recommended initial adult activity level, DSS1 issues an alert with instruction to deploy the traps in the orchards and establish the monitoring grids. Hence, the DSS1 algorithm stops and triggers DSS2 to start. The algorithm employed in DSS2 determines the locations to be treated and the best type of treatment depending on the med-fly captures, harvesting times, and phenological stage of cultivars. The kinds of treatments of DSS depends on the phenological stage, either bait spray or cover spray. A bait spray consists of a suitable insecticide mixed with a protein bait. DSS2 also establishes the extension of the area to be treated depending on the ratio between the numbers of traps with the new captures to the number of traps in the plot. If the ratio is less than one-third, pesticide treatments will be conducted only in trap areas where the new captures are recorded. Otherwise, the treatment will be carried out in all cultivars that are within the same phenological stage. The DSS3 algorithm defines the spraying procedure of the individual trees derived from the DSS2 output. The spraying decision depends on the following four factors:

- The active protection time from the previous treatment. No spraying should be applied if the tree is still in the active spraying period from a previous treatment.
- The withholding period, which is the minimum time between the last application and the harvesting time.
- The efficacy duration time, which reflects the insecticide efficacy that is related to the pesticide to be used or previously used.
- The weather conditions such as wind and rain.

The images collected from the e-traps are sent on a daily basis via Wi-Fi and 3G connections to a remote server where an expert inspects the images to detect the fruit flies once a week. The attractive lure is replaced, and the traps are cleaned on a monthly basis. The number of fruit flies is the input to DSS2. The hourly readings of the temperature, wind, and rain sensors from the meteorological stations are the input to DSS3. By comparing the conventional methods against the proposed DSS, it was confirmed that medfly management using the DSS can significantly reduce the number of pesticide applications, the areas of application, and the volume of pesticide utilization without increasing the fruit damage. It was shown that the largest positive effects of the DSS management reduced up to 98.1% in the volume of pesticide applied in contrast to the conventional methods.

2.3 Automatic detection and counting

The automatic systems were proposed as solutions for the problems encountered by semiautomatic systems (Miranda et al., 2019; Sciarretta et al., 2019;

Shaked et al., 2018; Wang et al., 2016). The main idea of automatic detection and counting systems is to exploit the blooming fields of ML and computer vision. Such systems automatically detect the pests in an image without any human intervention thus weaving any effort and the human error factors. After the detection phase, the number of the pests is counted, and spatiotemporal distribution of the sampled pests are provided to the farmers with guides to the hot spots of the olive fruit fly population. This leads to an efficient and wise use of the pesticides while decreasing the pesticides' negative side effects on the olive fruit. The detection and counting process can be done in-network, that is, locally in each trap. In this case, the e-trap only sends its count to the database in which the counts of all other traps are accumulated. The other implementation of the detection and counting process is that each trap sends its periodically captured images to a central node where the detection and counting operation is done. The central node has more powerful computational capabilities and a larger memory, but it is also more power hungry. Special power supplies can be provided for this central node aided by energy scavenging technologies, such as solar panels. A hybrid of both implementations also can be used where the trap is responsible for the preprocessing phase and the central node is responsible for the actual detection process.

Detection is one of the most important problems in computer vision. In olive fruit fly detection, the objectives are to determine whether the image has olive fruit flies and to detect their location. The detection problem differs from the classification problem as classification does not locate the olive fruit fly in the image. Furthermore, detection is an essential step toward automatic counting. Automatic counting systems detect fruit flies using ANN ML, CNNs, deep learning, or image processing techniques. Alternatively, there exist other automatic detection techniques that exploit optoacoustic and spectroscopy data in fruit fly detection. In what follows, we discuss the literature of all automatic detection systems.

2.3.1 Artificial neural networks

ML was defined by Arthur Samuel in 1959 as "Field of study that gives the computer the ability to learn without being explicitly programmed." ANNs are widely used as supervised learning techniques. An ANN mainly consists of neurons (perceptron). Neurons at the same level form a layer. An ANN has an input layer, hidden layers, and an output layer. The neurons in a layer are connected to the neurons in the previous layers through weights. The weights are updated via backpropagation. A neuron computes a linear function (the product sum of inputs and weights), and the output of the linear function is passed to nonlinear activation functions.

An ANN was used as a classifier of 14 butterfly species in one study (Kaya & Kayci, 2014). The butterfly images were captured inside the laboratory, where the butterflies are stored in appropriate conditions and turned into standard museum materials. The image size is 256 × 256 pixels. The total number of images is 140. The texture and color features were extracted for classification. The color features are the mean of red, green, and blue bands. The texture features are extracted using the pixel-based Gray-Level Cooccurrence Matrix (GLCM) image processing technique (Haralick et al., 1973). The texture features extracted from the GLCM are contrast, correlation, energy, and homogeneity. The features are calculated at different orientations (0, 45, 90, and 135 degrees), and the average values of these features are the input to the ANN-based classifier. The used ANN has an input layer with the number of neurons equal to the number of input features. The output layer has 14 neurons, and the single hidden layer has 50 neurons. The learning rate was set to 0.6, and the used learning rule is Levenberg-Marquardt backpropagation. The sigmoid activation function is adopted, and all the weights are randomly initialized. The identification rate was measured to be 92.85%. A comparison between GLCM and local binary pattern (LBP) is carried out in order to prove the effectiveness of GLCM. In the basic version of LBP, each pixel in an image is compared to a threshold of the center pixel to produce a binary code. The authors extended LBP to include all circular neighbors' pixels. The authors extracted four textures from the LBP matrix: average, deviation, energy, and correlation. The identification rate of LBP with ANN was found to be 89.09%.

2.3.2   Deep learning via CNNs

Deep learning is a class of ML. Deep learning has several layers between the input and the output layers that allow for many stages of nonlinear information processing units with hierarchal architectures that are exploited for feature learning and pattern classification (Alom et al., 2019). Deep learning using CNNs seeks hidden relationships in complex data by backpropagation algorithm to adjust the parameters of the neurons in each layer. Unlike ANNs, CNNs do not need the input to be engineered.

CNNs are supervised learning techniques that have been widely used in computer vision. CNNs mainly have a convolution layer, a subsampling (pooling) layer, and a fully connected layer. The convolutional filters extract features from the image. The subsampling layer reduces the spatial resolution of the feature map. The fully connected layer flattens the previous feature map to a single vector. CNNs have been used in olive fruit fly detection in several studies (Ding & Taylor, 2016; Kalamatianos et al., 2018; Xia et al., 2018; Zhong et al., 2018).

Kalamatianos et al. (2018) introduced the Dacus Image Recognition Toolkit (DIRT) that explores deep learning techniques in olive fruit fly identification. DIRT offers a labeled dataset of images collected from McPhail traps and programming code samples in MATLAB. DIRT images were collected from traps from 2015 to 2017. The images were captured by a variety of hardware (smart phones, tablets, photo cameras, etc.), resulting in having different illumination conditions in the images of the DIRT dataset. The dataset size is 542 images, and 486 were randomly selected for training and 56 for evaluation. The dataset is manually labeled by experts using the LabelImg tool. Floating fruit flies in the liquid and the distinguishable submerged fruit flies were annotated. The submerged fruit flies forming clusters make the identification very difficult. Consequently, they were not annotated. The number of annotated fruit flies is 2672. The traps were equipped with a microcomputer, real-time clock, camera, sensors that measure the temperature and humidity, power supply, solar-powered GSM modem, local data storage, and server acting as a processing center. The authors used TensorFlow object detection application programming interface (API) deep learning framework for the identification of olive fruit flies. A pretrained Faster_rcnn_inception_v2 was chosen for DIRT out of six tested CNNs (Kalamatianos et al., 2018). The faster Region-CNN (R-CNN) is composed of two modules (Ren et al., 2017). The first module proposes regions, and the second module is a fast R-CNN. R-CNN is a region CNN that applies convolutional network classification on each region proposed by the first module. The achieved mean Average Precision (mAP) is 91.52%, and it was shown that the RGB and gray scale images have similar performance.

Zhong et al. (2018) designed an automatic pest counting and identification system using the YOLO network architecture in the detection of six species of flying insects. YOLO is an end-to-end CNN for object detection (Redmon et al., 2016). The used dataset has 3000 images, which are manually labeled with the LabelImg tool. The dataset is augmented through rotation, scaling, flipping, translation, contrast adjustment, noise addition, and other operations and transformations to expand the training dataset to 12,000 images. Then, 10,000 images are randomly selected, which include 8000 images for training, 1000 images for validation and 1000 images for testing. YOLO divides the images into 5×5 grids. Each grid predicts N bounding boxes if the object's center falls into the grid. YOLO detection is fast and accurate. The authors of this study (Zhong et al., 2018) added a new convolutional layer to the pretrained YOLO to convert it from classification to detection. The YOLO detection stage of the automatic system depicted in Fig. 3 detects seven classes, including bee, fly, mosquito, moth, chafer fruit fly, and others. The detection stage is followed by a coarse counting stage to obtain the number of flying insects without determining the species. Classification is carried out using a support vector machine (SVM) (Cortes & Vapnik, 1995). Six SVMs were implemented to classify all the species as the model of SVM is "one-versus-rest." Finally, fine counting is

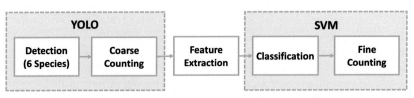

FIG. 3 The YOLO-based automatic counting approach of Zhong et al. (2018).

used to obtain the number of every species of flying insects. The system is tested by comparing the standard expert recognition resulting in counting accuracy 92.5%, counting recall rate 93.99%, counting miss rate 6.01%, classification accuracy of 90.18%, classification recall rate 92.52%, and classification miss rate 7.48%. The test time of 896 × 896 images takes about 5 min on Raspberry Pi.

Ding et al. detect moth from images taken inside field traps (Ding & Taylor, 2016). The traps contain a pheromone lure, an adhesive liner, a digital camera, and a radio transmitter that daily transmits the images to a remote server at fixed time point. The camera captures RGB images to be stored in JPEG format at 640 × 480 resolution. Codling moth are identified and labeled with bounding boxes by technicians trained in entomology. The collected 177 images are randomly split to keep the statistics of each set the same as the entire set into: 110 training images, 27 validation images, and 40 test images. The authors first preprocessed the images with color correction to eliminate the negative effect of illumination variability and canny edge detector on negative patches that do not contain moths to extract patches with textures. A sliding window CNN based on the architecture developed in one study (Lecun et al., 1998) was used to classify moths and detect their locations. The sliding window CNN takes a window of fixed size from the input image at all possible locations and then classifies each patch. The stride, distance between adjacent sliding windows, is set to be a quarter size of the patch. Fig. 4 summarizes the overall detection process. The sliding window CNN is slow and requires high computational resources. The area under precision-recall curve is 0.931, and the log-avg miss rate is 0.099%.

Xia et al. developed an end-to-end automatic system based on a deep neural network—depicted in Fig. 5—that extracts features, detects the locations of the insects from feature maps (localization), and then classifies the insects to 1 out of 24 classes of insects (Xia et al., 2018). The images are preprocessed in order to keep the images at a fixed size of 450 × 750 through a bilinear transformation as the images were adopted from different sources: a prior work (Xie et al., 2015) and the Internet. The first 16 layers of the pretrained VGG19 were adopted to prevent overfitting. VGG19 was designed initially for object classification (Simonyan & Zisserman, 2015). However, VGG19 was used in the study (Xia et al., 2018) for feature extraction. Besides VGG19, a region

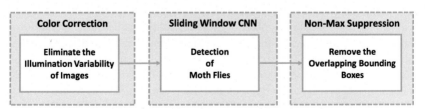

FIG. 4 The automatic moth detection scheme proposed in Ding and Taylor (2016).

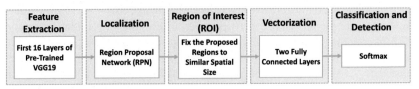

FIG. 5 The deep neural network proposed in Xia et al. (2018).

proposal network (RPN) (Ren et al., 2017; Sommer et al., 2018) is used and trained to detect the locations of the objects. The output of RPN is of variable size. Hence, a region of interest (ROI) pooling layer is used to convert the proposed regions into fixed spatial sizes. Each ROI feature map was input to two fully connected layers that output a 4096-dimension feature vector. The feature vector is input to softmax layer that simultaneously classifies the insects and estimates the insect region. A max pooling layer is added after the second, fourth, seventh, eleventh, and fifteenth convolutional layers. The performance of the whole model was compared to the single-shot detectors and fast R-CNN. The proposed model has the best results with mAP equal to 0.8922, inference (detection) time equal to 0.083 s, and a training time of 11.2 h.

2.3.3 Image processing

The detection of fruit flies based on image processing implements a sequence of image processing algorithms. The algorithms either enhance some features or eliminate negative effects for detection. Image processing does not need much data like the deep learning methods to learn the input features. The collected images are used as a benchmark to tune the thresholds of the algorithms.

Doitsidis et al. (2017) detected olive fruit flies using modified McPhail e-traps distributed in olive groves. The original McPhail traps were modified to increase the distance between the camera lens and the liquid level. The modified McPhail e-traps are injected with a protein instead of a sex pheromone for many reasons, the first being the ability of the protein to attract both sexes. In the sex pheromone case, a male parapheromone should be also injected to assure the attraction of females. The second reason is that the proteins are environment-friendly substances and do not leave any chemical impact on the olive fruit. A 2 MP camera captures the images in JPEG format. The images are sent to a web-based server to perform the image processing tasks shown in Fig. 6. The image processing starts with auto-brightness correction (Vonikakis et al., 2006) to eliminate the effect of different lighting and weather conditions that were reported to reduce the quality and brightness of the image. A coordinate logic filter (CLF) (Tsirikolias, 2015) is then used to enhance edges by magnifying the difference between the dark insect and the bright background. The final stage is applying circle Hough transform (Atherton & Kerbyson, 1999) to determine the bounds of the trap followed by a noise reduction filter. The end result of the image processing is a circular disk of black and white colors where

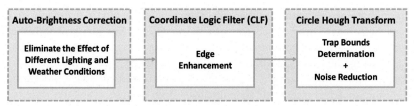

FIG. 6   Block diagram of the image processing technique proposed in Doitsidis et al. (2017).

the black dots represent the insects if their percentage in a cluster falls in a hard-coded range. The benchmarking results of 100 images are used to calculate the thresholds and define the required parameters. The achieved accuracy is 75%.

Tirelli et al. (2011) deployed a WSN system to detect pests in greenhouses automatically. The battery-powered WSN node consists of a Tmote microcontroller, a Zigbee transceiver, and a camera. The network architecture consists of a master node called base station and client nodes. The base station is hosted in a PC. The client nodes capture black and white images with a compressed JPEG resolution of 640 × 480 with 8 bits per pixel. The base station decompresses the images and processes them to detect pests. The adaptive image processing technique shown in Fig. 7 is adopted to cope with the varying luminance conditions inside and outside the traps. The main idea is applying a median filter on the image to remove the pests and dirt particles that appear as dark dots against the bright background of the yellow adhesive traps. After obtaining the background image, it is then subtracted from the original image, thus leaving only the pests and the dirt particles. This technique is called background luminance subtraction. It is resilient to different illumination conditions from the various traps. After obtaining the image that contains only the pests and dirt particles, the size of each cluster of dots is compared to the expected size of the pest, and if it belongs to a specified range, the dot cluster is identified as an olive fruit fly, and the central node increments the count by one. By using unique identifiers, the central node is able to associate each pest count with certain traps, thus it will be able to guide the farmer where to spray the pesticide if the count exceeds certain hardcoded threshold. The nodes acquire two images per day at 7:00 a.m. and 7:00 p.m. for 4 weeks. The system produces an insect population curve that is fairly correlated with the daily counts obtained by visual observation of the trap. It was reported that light conditions variations lead to false positives.

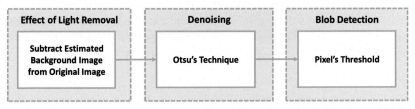

FIG. 7   Illustration of the adaptive image processing technique proposed in Tirelli et al. (2011).

The authors suggest a smart scheduling of the acquisition time to overcome such light variations. The distance between the nodes increase the probability of transmission errors. These errors manifest as image irregularities.

Trapping the insects in a liquid leads to "soup images" where the insects are floating on the liquid surface. Sun et al. (2016) proposed an image processing algorithm to detect insects in "soup images." Both the insects and the scale bar are segmented. Insect segmentation has three processes: preprocessing, region segmentation, and object sorting. Scale bar segmentation decreases the scale bar from 10 to 1 mm. In the preprocessing process, images are converted from RGB space to hue-saturation-lightness (HSL) space (Joblove & Greenberg, 1978). Lightness channel is selected for further processing. HSL space decreases the computational time. Then, the intensities at different image ranges are enhanced by gamma transformation. Finally, small white and dark objects are removed through attribute-based morphologies. In the region segmentation process, the minima of pixels in the image are detected as dark bodies of insects and background as the bright pixels. The combined information of insect bodies and background are treated as seed points. The seeds are expanded to include more pixels to the current region based on the similarity of pixel intensities. In the object sorting process, the insects are sorted (classified) based on size/area, length, width, and color measurements. This scheme was tested using 19 soup images and the algorithm works well in most of the images.

Philimis et al. (2013) developed the e-FlyWatch system, which monitors the medfly and olive fruit flies from the field using McPhail traps. A motion detection module was added along with optical sensors to monitor the entrance of the trap thus making it easier to classify a pest from a dirt in the images. The system architecture consists of traps, local stations, and a central station. The McPhail traps are equipped with cameras. The local station consists of an image processor, sensors, a flash memory, a battery, and the required hardware and software for communicating with traps. Recognition of flies is implemented at the local station based upon image processing algorithms. A template comparison algorithm in which the received image is compared in certain traits against images of the olive fruit fly and images of the medfly is used. The recognition is based on detecting specific anatomy, pattern, and color characteristics. The graphical user interface is divided into four sections: The "Home" section presents the field status over the map. The "Traps" section contains the list of the registered traps with links to each trap details and the geographical position of the field on the map. The "Data" section visualizes statistics on the various data. The "Diary" section allows the user to view and edit the existing entries in the diary or to create new ones. The density maps show the population of flies and other parameters in a certain area. This feature is implemented with a GIS.

2.3.4 Optoacoustic spectral analysis

The optoacoustic spectrum analysis identifies the species of insects from the analysis of their wingbeats. The fluctuations in light intensity caused by flying insect is converted to a signal. The type of the insect can be inferred by processing the resulting signals.

Potamitis et al. (2017) detected the presence of olive fruit flies in McPhail traps by optoacoustic spectrum analysis. The optical sensor consists of a receiver and an emitter placed at opposite sides. The emitter is an array of infrared LEDs with an attached diffuser. The receiver is a light guide with a linear array of photodiodes to collect the fluctuations of the light intensity. A microcontroller sends pulses through the emitter and monitors the light intensity of the receiver to record and deliver data to a server where the processing took place. When the sensor is triggered, fast Fourier transform of the captured data is performed. The detection of fruit fly decision is based on both the time domain and the frequency domain analyses. Time domain analysis checks the amplitude of the recording (signal). Frequency domain analysis examines the frequencies between 170 and 230 Hz where the fundamental frequency of an olive fruit fly's wingbeat lies. The combined features are used by the classifier algorithm. The dataset is split into 80% for training and the remaining 20% as hold out data. The classification is evaluated by precision, recall, and F1 score. The random forest classifier achieves 0.93 precision, 0.93 recall, and F1 equal to 0.93 on all species. This method cannot differentiate between different kinds of fruit flies such as peach and fig. Furthermore, the field measurement differs from the lab measurement. The trap is equipped with infrared blocking film to eliminate autotrigger due to solar radiation. The liquid attractants are replaced with gel-type attractants. The threshold value was adopted to prevent the trap from registering counts due to the shades resulting from moving branches and leaves. The trap is vulnerable to abrupt hits or shocks that registered false alarms on windy days. The single board price is 94.74€ and drops to 62.25€ and 49.15€ for mass production of 100 boards and 1000 boards, respectively.

2.3.5 Spectroscopy hyperspectral imaging

Spectroscopy-based counting systems detect the existence of larvae in the harvested fruit. The fruits are examined by near-infrared radiation (NIR) spectroscopy. Spectroscopy differentiates between the sound fruits and the infested fruits. Infested fruit exportation moves the fruit flies from the infected regions to other places. It is advisable to investigate the exported and imported fruits using spectroscopy. Spectroscopy counting was used in olives (Moscetti et al., 2015), mangoes (Haff et al., 2013), and cherries (Xing et al., 2008; Xing & Guyer, 2008).

Moscetti et al. (2015) showed that an excellent product of olive oil can be achieved if the olives infested by the larvae of the fruit fly could be separated. The damage of fruit flies is not visually detectable on the fruit surface. NIR spectroscopy is used to detect the infested olive fruits. Samples of 896 olives were free from visual external impact damage and decay. Olive spectra were

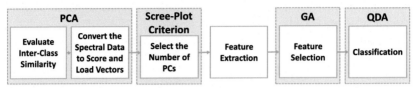

FIG. 8   An illustration of the spectroscopy olive evaluation presented in Moscetti et al. (2015).

acquired using a Luminar 5030 acousto-optic tunable filter near-infrared (AOTF-NIR) Miniature Handheld Analyzer. Fig. 8 illustrates the developed spectroscopy-based detection process. After spectral acquisition, olives were dissected to visually determine the presence of larvae. The samples were split randomly as 50% were assigned to a training set (224 sound and 224 unsound), 25% to a validation set (112 sound and 112 unsound fruits), and 25% to a test set (112 sound and 112 unsound fruits). Each olive is modeled as data vector where the spectral absorbance values were vector components. The authors evaluated the interclass similarity using principal component analysis (PCA) (Jolliffe & Cadima, 2016). The spectral data were converted to score and loading vectors by PCA. The scree-plot criterion (Jolliffe & Cadima, 2016) was used to select the required number of PCs for describing the dimensionality of the data. The authors extracted features from the whole spectra. A set of features selected by the genetic algorithm (GA) (Xing et al., 2008) was input to three different classification algorithms: linear discriminant analysis, quadratic discriminant analysis (QDA), and K-NN. The performance metrics for each classification model are the percentage of false positives (sound fruit classified as unsound), false negative (unsound fruit classified as sound), and total error (incorrectly classified samples). The most accurate representation of 12.50% false positives, 0.00% false negatives, and 6.25% total error, was achieved using QDA.

Haff et al. (2013) exploited hyperspectral imaging for mango crops. The spectrum was acquired by Imspector V10E, spectral imaging. The acquired dataset consisted of 50 mangoes. Twenty-five mangoes were subjected to forced infestation, and the rest acted as control. The hyperspectral imaging followed the processes depicted in Fig. 9. The authors removed the morphological effects by subtracting the background using the "rolling ball" subtracting

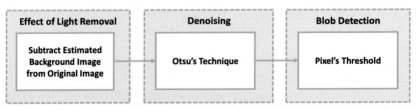

FIG. 9   An illustration of the hyperspectral imaging processing of mango followed in Haff et al. (2013).

routine (Sternberg, 1983). Gaussian blur was then added to reduce noise and detail of the background of the subtracted images. Particle analysis first converts the image into black and white, then separates the overlapping clusters to produce the particle count based on the "water shed" algorithm. The algorithm gives particle size count based on the particle size threshold. The overall ability to detect insects was tested. The samples with high infestation have lower error rates. The overall error rate of higher infestation samples is between 2% and 6%. The samples with lower infestation rates achieved the lowest error of 12.3%.

Hyperspectral imaging is also used in cherries (Xing & Guyer, 2008; Xing et al., 2008). Cherries were divided into six levels according to the level of damage. Level 0 represents sound cherries with no larvae. Levels 1–5 are cherries with different damage levels. The dataset consisted of 242 samples for calibration and 164 samples for external validation. The device used to measure the reflectance and transmittance spectra is spectroradiometer (model: FSFR Field-Spec, Analytical spectral devices, Boulder, CO). The number of variables (wavelengths) between 550 and 950 nm with 10 nm resolution are obtained using average binning 10 neighbor points. The data is preprocessed to enhance the spectral features. The authors classified cherries by canonical discriminant analysis. To improve the classification accuracy, the cherries are modeled as "acceptable" class and "unacceptable" class. The "acceptable" class is a joint of levels 0 and 1 samples, and the remaining four levels belong to the "unacceptable" class. The achieved transmittance classification accuracy is 85%, while the reflectance classification accuracy is 81.7%.

3 Evaluation and discussions

In Section 2, we surveyed the different classes of pest detection schemes with a focus on the detection of the olive fruit fly. In this section, we present our main findings and insights about these classes of pest detection approaches, excluding the manual detection approach as it falls beyond our scope.

3.1 Semiautomatic detection

The idea of the semiautomatic detection and classification combines manual and automatic decisions as seen in a few studies (Miranda et al., 2019; Sciarretta et al., 2019; Shaked et al., 2018; Wang et al., 2016). In the cases where the system is required to classify the olive fruit fly against several relative species, the automatic classifier often has equal similarity metrics for many species given the received image. For instance, consider minimum distance classifiers such as K-NNs. The received image may have equal or very close distances to many species, thus leaving the classifier without a certain decision. In such cases, the automatic detection system chooses arbitrarily among the candidates with a probability of being correct only $1/n$ of the time where n is the number of candidate species that share the same distance to the received image. In the maximum likelihood detector context, such a system is called incomplete maximum likelihood detector rather than the typical complete maximum likelihood detector (CMLD) in which the received image will have minimum distance to only one species. The semiautomatic human-assisted classifiers solve these cases by sending the images that cannot be automatically classified to a user-friendly application with the end user being an expert entomologist or the system can ask an expert farmer to check the trap in person to avoid the cases where images are not clear enough for the entomologists to decide remotely. The classifier may use these decisions as input information and may adapt its decision boundaries to achieve better accuracy with less need for human intervention in an ongoing ML process.

Despite the simple implementation of semiautomatic systems (Miranda et al., 2019; Sciarretta et al., 2019; Shaked et al., 2018; Wang et al., 2016) and the prejudice of the human classification being superior to the computer classification and even considered the ground truth to which the computer results are compared, these systems have serious drawbacks. The first drawback is that they require an entomologist to classify the image, that is, the system addresses experts only as its end-users, while the core of the DSS is to aid the common farmer who usually does not have such expertise. The second issue is that even the entomologists can make mistakes due to the imperfections of the images and the uncanny resemblance between an olive fruit fly and other pests. The third issue is the effort and time consumed in such systems, which make them unsuitable for practical applications. Rather, they should be considered a heuristic or a learning phase for the more advanced, automated systems.

3.2 Image-based automatic detection

Here, we only discuss the image-based automatic detection schemes that are based on either ANN ML (Kaya & Kayci, 2014), CNN deep learning (Ding & Taylor, 2016; Kalamatianos et al., 2018; Xia et al., 2018; Zhong et al., 2018), or image processing (Doitsidis et al., 2017; Philimis et al., 2013; Sun et al., 2016; Tirelli et al., 2011). We defer the discussion of other automatic detection approaches to the following subsection. In image-based detection, the size of the image affects the detection accuracy. On the other hand, it increases the complexity of the system. A bigger image size also increases the power consumption as bigger images require more power to transmit it from the camera to the microcontroller. Power is a scarce resource in WSNs.

3.2.1 Machine and deep learning

Fig. 10 depicts a generic block diagram of machine and deep learning automatic detection that can be summarized as follows. Images are initially preprocessed (if needed) to make all the images similar in light conditions (Ding & Taylor,

FIG. 10   Generic block diagram of image-based automatic detection systems.

2016) by fixing illumination variability or to keep the images at fixed size (Xia et al., 2018) by bilinear transformation. The second step is the detection step in which the objects are detected and separated from the image background, for example, using YOLO as in Zhong et al. (2018). Features are then extracted by a CNN (Xia et al., 2018) or by engineered/tailored image processing techniques (Kaya & Kayci, 2014). A coarse counting step is needed in systems that detect more than one class, where they count all the objects without classification (Zhong et al., 2018). The classifier stage may be implemented using a ML model, such as SVM (Zhong et al., 2018) or ANN (Kaya & Kayci, 2014), or a deep learning model, such as RPN (Xia et al., 2018). Classification using a ML model extracts features to be the input to the classifier (Zhong et al., 2018). A fine counting step is used in systems that are interested in determining the number of insects in the images. Table 1 compares the implementations of the ML-based (Kaya & Kayci, 2014) and deep learning-based (Ding & Taylor, 2016; Kalamatianos et al., 2018; Xia et al., 2018; Zhong et al., 2018) automatic detection approaches.

A major drawback of ANN ML classifiers is the need for engineered features as input (Kaya & Kayci, 2014). The number of trainable parameters (weights) of the ANN is extremely large if the input is the image. Furthermore, ANNs are sensitive to shifting and scaling in the input image. This motivates the use of deep learning using CNNs, which have the advantage of shared weights (Ding & Taylor, 2016; Kalamatianos et al., 2018; Xia et al., 2018; Zhong et al., 2018). Weight sharing in CNNs implies that all the neurons in a feature share the same weight but not the biases. Furthermore, the existing deep CNN-based automatic detection and counting schemes (Ding & Taylor, 2016; Kalamatianos et al., 2018; Xia et al., 2018; Zhong et al., 2018) have used the transfer learning concept in their networks through pretrained networks. In transfer learning, the weights and biases learned from a network can be transferred to other networks. Transfer learning decreases the training time and overfitting.

Automatic systems such as those previously discussed minimize human intervention, and hence, decrease time-, cost-, and effort-consuming activities. However, the accuracy of such systems is never 100%, especially in the cases in which the classifier is required to classify the olive fruit fly against many relative species (Kaya & Kayci, 2014; Xia et al., 2018; Zhong et al., 2018). On the other hand, single class classification (Ding & Taylor, 2016; Kalamatianos et al., 2018) implies less training data that will cause overfitting of the deep

TABLE 1 Comparison of the main image-based automatic detection and counting techniques.

	Kaya and Kayci (2014)	Zhong et al. (2018)	Ding and Taylor (2016)	Kalamatianos et al. (2018)	Xia et al. (2018)
Preprocessing	No	No	Yes	No	Yes
Detection/feature extraction	Features extraction from GLCM + color features	YOLO	Sliding Window CNN	Faster_rcnn_inception_v2	VGG19 + RPN
Coarse counting	No	Yes	No	No	No
Classification	ANN	SVM	Sliding window CNN	Faster_rcnn_inception_v2	Softmax
Fine counting	No	Yes	No	No	No
Accuracy	92.85%	90.34%	Prec-rec AUC = 0.931. Log-avg miss rate = 0.099	mAP = 91.52%	mAP = 89.22%
Complexity	Low	Low	High	Moderate	Moderate
Test time/hardware	–	Five minutes on Raspberry Pi model B	–	–	0.083 s (not on an embedded system)
Resolution of the image	256 × 256	448 × 448	640 × 480	Not standard	450 × 750
Single/multiclass classification	Multiclass classification	Multiclass classification	Single class classification	Single class classification	Multiclass classification
Transfer learning	No	YOLO	No	Faster_rcnn_inception_v2	VGG19

learning model that needs large data size in order to be trained. Some systems have used pretrained models to reduce overfitting (Kalamatianos et al., 2018; Xia et al., 2018; Zhong et al., 2018). There are other techniques to reduce over-fitting as regularization and drop out. Drop out techniques randomly select a subset of activations within a layer to be zero. Regularization techniques regularize the weights from overfitting by including the weights in the cost function.

3.2.2 Image processing

The image processing techniques (Doitsidis et al., 2017; Philimis et al., 2013; Sun et al., 2016; Tirelli et al., 2011) discussed in Section 2 have the virtue of simplicity while not relying on the availability of large datasets for training. However, they suffer from several drawbacks. The first drawback is that their performance is highly correlated with the light conditions of image, the distance between the camera and the trap, and insect population. This leads to less detection accuracies compared to deep learning techniques. Another drawback is the use of a fixed threshold, which triggers the alarm signal. The use of fixed thresholds ignores the evolutional capabilities of the olive fruit fly and the changing statistical metrics associated with its population. The second drawback is the hardcoded range of the pest size against which the image segments is compared to decide whether it is a pest or not. Such hardcoded threshold may be efficient for a short-term IPM while it fails to achieve efficiently for long-term IPM since it neglects the evolution of the pests, which is evident in many papers. The crucial drawback, however, is implicit in the system's simplicity. The idea of comparing the size of a segment in the image against a range actually succeeds in classifying the pest from smaller objects, like dirt particles, or larger objects, however, it is totally blind regarding the classification of the olive fruit fly from other relative species that may have the same sizes range or at least have a range that overlaps with the range of sizes of the olive fruit fly. A field study in such case is a must. If it is noticed that relative species are actually found in the olive field, then this system will be a waste of money and energy and a complete failure; otherwise, it may be implemented with good efficiency.

3.3 Nonimage-based automatic detection

In this chapter, we discussed how automatic detection can be achieved without relying on the images taken for the pests. More specifically, optoacoustic spectrum (Potamitis et al., 2017) and hyperspectral imaging spectroscopy (Haff et al., 2013; Moscetti et al., 2015; Xing & Guyer, 2008; Xing et al., 2008) were used. In what follows, we summarize our main insights about such techniques.

Optoacoustic spectrum detection: Pest detection based on optoacoustic spectrum cannot differentiate between different fruit flies that have the same wingbeat frequency. Moreover, this method is sensitive to external environmental conditions such as sun radiation and wind that cause false detection.

Spectroscopy-based detection: Spectroscopy-based counting may use image processing techniques (Haff et al., 2013) or data analytics based on statistics (Moscetti et al., 2015) and (Xing & Guyer, 2008; Xing et al., 2008) to detect the larvae. Spectroscopy are used to detect the quality of the fruits either for producing high-quality oil (Moscetti et al., 2015) or for exportation (Haff et al., 2013).

4 Conclusions

In this chapter, we presented a detailed survey of the literature of the pest detection technique developed for IPM systems. Even though the main focus was on the detection of the olive fruit fly, we also discussed related detection systems developed for other pests, such as the moth and medfly. We have classified the literature to manual, semiautomatic, and automatic techniques. The semiautomatic approach outperforms the manual detection but still depends on human experts, and hence, is error prone. On the other hand, automatic detection and counting techniques do not incorporate any human intervention. They achieve remarkable accuracies that depend on the computational complexity of the used identification technique. We have classified the techniques used in automatic detection systems into five classes: ML techniques using ANNs; deep learning techniques using CNNs; image processing techniques; optoacoustic detection techniques; and hyperspectral images using spectroscopy. Our analysis of the surveyed literature has indicated that the deep learning identification systems using CNNs are more accurate and immune to environmental variations. However, there is a need for less complex implementations of such systems that can allow the detection algorithm to be implemented locally on the trap rather than communicating the images to a remote location for processing. This prolongs the lifetime of the system. Also, we identified that in all the existing techniques, the classifier did not have the ability to differentiate between the male and the female individuals of the olive fruit fly. While this piece of information might be useful for biological pest management, it was of minimal importance in this surveyed literature.

Acknowledgments

This work is funded by the Egyptian Information Technology Industry Development Agency (ITIDA) through project CFP166: CIPOLIVE Cloud-based Integrated Platform for Monitoring Pests, Salinity and Efficient Irrigation in Olive Precision Farming.

References

Alom, M. Z., Taha, T. M., Yakopcic, C., Westberg, S., Sidike, P., Nasrin, M. S., ... Asari, V.K. (2019). A state-of-the-art survey on deep learning theory and architectures. *Electronics*, *8* (3), 292.

Atherton, T. J., & Kerbyson, D. J. (1999). Size invariant circle detection. *Image and Vision Computing, 17*(11), 795–803.

Cortes, C., & Vapnik, V. (1995). Support-vector networks. *Machine Learning, 20*, 273–297.

Ding, W., & Taylor, G. (2016). Automatic moth detection from trap images for pest management. *Computers and Electronics in Agriculture, 123*, 17–28.

Doitsidis, L., Fouskitakis, G. N., Varikou, K. N., Rigakis, I. I., Chatzichristofis, S. A., Papafilippaki, A. K., & Birouraki, A. E. (2017). Remote monitoring of the Bactrocera oleae (Gmelin) (Diptera: Tephritidae) population using an automated McPhail trap. *Computers and Electronics in Agriculture, 137*, 69–78.

Haff, R. P., Saranwong, S., Thanapase, W., Janhiran, A., Kasemsumran, S., & Kawano, S. (2013). Automatic image analysis and spot classification for detection of fruit fly infestation in hyperspectral images of mangoes. *Postharvest Biology and Technology, 86*, 23–28.

Haralick, R. M., Shanmugam, K., & Dinstein, I. H. (1973). Textural features for image classification. *IEEE Transactions on Systems, Man, and Cybernetics, SMC-3*(6), 610–621.

Joblove, G. H., & Greenberg, D. (1978). Color spaces for computer graphics. In *5th annual conference on computer graphics and interactive techniques.*

Jolliffe, I. T., & Cadima, J. (2016). Principal component analysis: A review and recent developments. *Philosophical Transactions of the Royal Society A: Mathematical, Physical and Engineering Sciences, 374*(2065), 20150202.

Kalamatianos, R., Karydis, I., & Avlonitis, M. (2019). Methods for the identification of microclimates for olive fruit fly. *Agronomy, 9*(6), 337.

Kalamatianos, R., Karydis, I., Doukakis, D., & Avlonitis, M. (2018). DIRT: The Dacus Image Recognition Toolkit. *Journal of Imaging, 4*(11), 129.

Kaya, Y., & Kayci, L. (2014). Application of artificial neural network for automatic detection of butterfly species using color and texture features. *The Visual Computer, 30*(1), 71–79.

Lecun, Y., Bottou, L., Bengio, Y., & Haffner, P. (1998). Gradient-based learning applied to document recognition. *Proceedings of the IEEE, 86*(11), 2278–2324.

Miranda, M.Á., Barceló, C., Valdés, F., Feliu, J. F., Nestel, D., Papadopoulos, N., … Alorda, B. (2019). Developing and implementation of Decision Support System (DSS) for the control of olive fruit fly, Bactrocera Oleae, in Mediterranean olive orchards. *Agronomy, 9*(10), 620.

Moscetti, R., Haff, R. P., Stella, E., Contini, M., Monarca, D., Cecchini, M., & Massantini, R. (2015). Feasibility of NIR spectroscopy to detect olive fruit infested by Bactrocera oleae. *Postharvest Biology and Technology, 99*, 58–62.

Philimis, P., Psimolophitis, E., Hadjiyiannis, S., Giusti, A., Perello, J., Serrat, A., & Avila, P. (2013). A centralised remote data collection system using automated traps for managing and controlling the population of the Mediterranean (*Ceratitis capitata*) and olive (*Dacus oleae*) fruit flies. In *International conference on remote sensing and geoinformation of the environment, Paphos, Cyprus.*

Plant Health Australia. (2018). *Australian handbook for the identification of fruit flies V3.1.* Canberra: Plant Health Australia.

Pontikakos, C. M., Tsiligiridis, T. A., Yialouris, C. P., & Kontodimas, D. C. (2012). Pest management control of olive fruit fly (Bactrocera oleae) based on a location-aware agroenvironmental. *Computers and Electronics in Agriculture, 87*, 39–50.

Potamitis, I., Rigakis, I., & Tatlas, N.-A. (2017). Automated surveillance of fruit flies. *Sensors, 17* (12), 110.

Redmon, J., Divvala, S., Girshick, R., & Farhadi, A. (2016). You only look once: Unified, real-time object detection. In *Proceedings of the IEEE conference on computer vision and pattern recognition, Las Vegas, NV, USA.*

Ren, S., He, K., Girshick, R., & Sun, J. (2017). Faster r-cnn: Towards real-time object detection with region proposal networks. *IEEE Transactions on Pattern Analysis and Machine Intelligence, 39* (6), 1137–1149.

Sciarretta, A., Tabilio, M. R., Amore, A., Colacci, M., Miranda, M.Á., Nestel, D., … Trematerra, P. (2019). Defining and evaluating a Decision Support System (DSS) for the precise pest management of the Mediterranean fruit fly, Ceratitis capitata, at the farm level. *Agronomy, 9* (10), 608.

Shaked, B., Amore, A., Ioannou, C., Valdés, F., Alorda, B., Papanastasiou, S., & Goldshtein, E. (2018). Electronic traps for detection and population monitoring of adult fruit flies (Diptera: Tephritidae). *Journal of Applied Entomology, 142*(1–2), 43–51.

Simonyan, K., & Zisserman, A. (2015). *Very deep convolutional networks for large-scale image recognition.* arXiv preprint arXiv:1409.1556.

Sommer, L., Schumann, A., Schuchert, T., & Beyerer, J. (2018). Multi feature deconvolutional faster r-cnn for precise vehicle detection in aerial imagery. In *IEEE Winter conference on applications of computer vision (WACV).*

Sternberg, S. R. (1983). Biomedical image processing. *Computer, 16*(1), 22–34.

Sun, C., Flemons, P., Gao, Y., Wang, D., Fisher, N., & La Salle, J. (2016). Automated image analysis on insect soups gold coast. In *International conference on digital image computing: Techniques and applications (DICTA), Australia.*

The Olive Oil Source. (2020). *Olive fly control.* https://www.oliveoilsource.com/page/olive-fly-control. (Accessed 10 November 2020).

Tirelli, P., Borghese, N., Pedersini, F., Galassi, G., & Oberti, R. (2011). Automatic monitoring of pest insects traps by Zigbee-based wireless networking of image sensors. In *IEEE international instrumentation and measurement technology conference, Binjiang, Hangzhou, China.*

Tsirikolias, K. D. (2015). Coordinate logic order statistics & applications in image processing. *Circuits, Systems, and Signal Processing, 34*(3), 901–929.

Vonikakis, V., Gasteratos, A., & Andreadis, I. (2006). Enhancement of perceptually salient contours using a parallel artificial cortical network. *Biological Cybernetics, 94*(3), 192–214.

Wang, J.-N., Chen, X.-L., Hou, X.-W., Zhou, L.-B., Zhu, C.-D., & Ji, L.-Q. (2016). Construction, implementation and testing of an image identification system using computer vision methods for fruit flies with economic importance (Diptera: Tephritidae). *Pest Management Science, 73* (7), 1511–1528.

Xia, D., Chen, P., Wang, B., Zhang, J., & Xie, C. (2018). Insect detection and classification based on an improved convolutional neural network. *Sensors, 18*(12), 4169.

Xie, C., Zhang, J., Li, R., Li, J., Hong, P., Xia, J., & Chen, P. (2015). Automatic classification for field crop insects via multiple-task sparse representation and multiple-kernel learning. *Computers and Electronics in Agriculture, 119*, 123–132.

Xing, J., & Guyer, D. (2008). Comparison of transmittance and reflectance to detect insect infestation in Montmorency tart cherry. *Computers and Electronics in Agriculture, 64*(2), 194–201.

Xing, J., Guyer, D., Ariana, D., & Lu, R. (2008). Determining optimal wavebands using genetic algorithm for detection of internal insect infestation in tart cherry. *Sensing and Instrumentation for Food Quality and Safety, 2*, 161–167.

Zhong, Y., Gao, J., Lei, Q., & Zhou, Y. (2018). A vision-based counting and recognition system for flying insects in intelligent agriculture. *Sensors, 18*(5), 1489.

Index

Note: Page numbers followed by *f* indicate figures, *t* indicate tables and *b* indicate boxes.

A

Absolute errors, 122, 123*t*, 124*f*
Acceptable class, 373
Accuracy, 230
  graph, loss *vs.*, 305–306, 306*f*
Activation function, 180, 306–308, 309*f*
Adam configuration parameters, 117
Adam hybrid algorithm, 119–121, 119–120*b*,
    121*f*, 124*t*, 125*f*
Adam optimization algorithm, 97, 110–111,
    116*b*, 117
Adam real dataset, 126*t*
Adaptive Gradient Algorithm (AdaGrad), 117
Adaptive image processing technique,
    369–370, 369*f*
Adaptive moment estimation optimization,
    117–118, 118*f*
Adaptive network-based fuzzy inference system
    (ANFIS), 278–279
Adaptive neuro-fuzzy inference system
    (ANFIS), 147–148, 152–153
Adenine (A), 244
Advanced Scatterometer (ASCAT),
    144–145
Advance nutraceutical production, and
    drug discovery, 240–244
Agent-based GRANITE Network Discovery
    Tool, 267–270
Agent-based modeling (ABM) software, 267
Agricultural automation, 273
Agricultural drone, 32, 33–34*t*
Agricultural production model, 202–203
Agricultural technology, 129
Agriculture, 1–2, 297
  composite band, 336, 336*f*
  geospatial analytics applications for,
    327–334
  mechanization process, 61–62
Agroecological food movement, 204
Agroecological landscapes, 200–201
Agroecological policy, 205–206
Agroecological practices, 201–207, 209
Agroecological research, 206
Agroecological territorial transformation,
    and transition, 207–214
Agroecological transition, 199

Agroecology education, 204
Agro-meteorology, 283
AlexNet, 22–24, 68–69, 301–302
Animal-drawn technology, 61–62
Annual precipitation (AP), 42
AQUACROP model, 157
Aquaculture, 244–255
Area under cultivation, 42
Area under curve (AUC), 230
Area under ROC curve, 125–126*f*
Artificial intelligence (AI) applications, 59–61,
    81–83, 223, 276–277
  in agriculture, 74–75
  domain, 328
  in precision agriculture (PA), 59–61, 74–75
  soil health monitoring using, 73–74
  in soil management, 135–138, 135*f*
    soil fertilizer estimation, 137
    soil mapping, 137–138
    soil temperature (ST) monitoring,
      136–137
    soil water content determination, 136
  in water management, 130–135
    crop water content prediction, 132
    evapotranspiration estimation, 130–131
    groundwater simulation, 132–134
    pan evaporation estimation, 134–135
    water footprint (WF) modeling,
      132, 133*t*
Artificial neural networks (ANNs), 60, 110,
    129–135, 130*f*, 137–138, 147–148, 147*f*,
    152–153, 180, 278, 329, 364–365
  architecture, 179, 180*f*
  parameters, 193*t*
  using conventional objective function, 195*t*
  using objective function, 194*t*
Augmented images, 93, 95*f*
Automated software package, 169–170
Automated testing tools, 169–170
Automatic detection and counting techniques,
    363–373
Automatic moth detection scheme, 367, 367*f*
Autonomous robots, 60, 61*f*
Autonomous weed control systems, 224
Average pooling, 302
Average precision (AP), 341

B

Background luminance subtraction, 369–370
Backpropagation (BP), 278
  neural network, 286–287, 288*t*
Backpropagation algorithm (BPA), 179–181,
  189–192*f*
Back propagation neural network (BPNN),
  130–131
Bactrocera oleae, 357–360, 360*f*
Base station, 369–370
Bayesian model, 238
Belief-desire-intent (BDI) model, 268–269
Big data, 36–39
  analysis, 64
Binary classification, 97–99, 97–99*f*
Biogeography-based optimization (BBO)
  algorithms, 115–116, 115–116*b*, 124*t*,
  125*f*, 126*t*
Boltzmann machine, 330–331
Boosted trees classifiers (BTCs), 39

C

CaffeNet, 16–24
Canny edge detection, 66
Carbon-energy
  cycle, 255–259
  exchange process, 258
Carbon reservoirs, 258
Cattle race classification, 25, 26–29*t*
Cercospora leaf spot, 308–318
CERES-Wheat model, for wheat yield
  prediction, 283, 285*t*
Checkpoints (.ckpt), 304
Chemoautotrophic strategies, 240–241
Chemoheterotrophic strategies, 240–241
Chromatic aberration-based image segment
  method, 5–6
Circular Hough transformation (CHT), 23–24
Classification algorithms, 371–372
Classification and regression tree (CART),
  149–150
Client nodes, 369–370
Climate condition, 30, 36, 42
Climate-smart agroecology, 208–209
Climatic effects, 361
Coal, 171–172
Codon, 244
Colored image processing techniques,
  287–290
Combiner mechanism, 253
Community-supported agroecology, 211
Completely automated testing scheme, 170

Complete manual testing, 170
Complete maximum likelihood detector
  (CMLD), 373–374
Computational intelligence techniques,
  109–110
Computer vision technology, 81–83
Concentration data, 251–252
Confusion matrix, 304–305, 318, 319*t*
ConvNets, 84
Convolutional layer, 84–85, 306, 307*f*
Convolution neural networks (CNNs), 68–69,
  84, 85*f*, 224, 226, 286, 301–302, 326,
  329
  in agricultural applications, 87–88
  architectures of, 86, 86*f*
  deep learning via, 365–368
  layers, 84, 96, 96*f*
  for plant disease classification, 71–72*t*
  training, 87–88
  weight sharing in, 375
Coordinate logic filter (CLF), 368–369
Crop and land assessment, 8
Crop disease, 5, 65
Crop diversification techniques and practices,
  211
Crop management, 275*f*
Crop quality, 15
Crop recommendation system
  feature extraction, 111–113
  optimization layer, 113–121
    adaptive moment estimation optimization,
      117–118, 118*f*
    biogeography-based optimization (BBO)
      algorithms, 115–116, 115–116*b*, 124*t*,
      125*f*, 126*t*
    plate tectonics-based optimization
      (PBO)-Adam hybrid, 119–121,
      119–120*b*, 121*f*, 124*t*, 125*f*
    plate tectonics-based optimization (PBO)
      algorithm, 114–115, 115*b*, 126*t*
    plate tectonics-based optimization
      (PBO)-biogeography-based
      optimization (BBO) hybrid, 118–119,
      119*b*, 120*f*
  preprocessing layer, 111
  rule-based approach, 110
  softmax classification layer, 121–122
Crop selection, 109–110
Crop type classification, 22
Crop water content prediction, 132
Crop yield, 30
  estimation, 23
  prediction, 41–42

Cross-entropy, 250–251
  loss, 122
Cryo-scanning electron microscopy
  (cryo-SEM), 242
Cuban agricultural production, 209
Cyber security, 65
Cytosine (C), 244

D

Dacus Image Recognition Toolkit (DIRT),
  365–366
Dacus oleae, 357–358
Data analysis, 81–83
Data augmentation
  protocol, 94*t*
  strategy, 93
Data download, 111
Data-driven learning process, 103–104
Data mining (DM), in smart agriculture, 36–42
Data set, 231
Decision support system (DSS), 276–277, 358,
  362–363, 362*f*
Deep convolutional neural network
  (DCNN), 16–21
Deep learning (DL), 83–86, 298
  algorithms, 68
  approaches, 329–330
  automatic detection, 374–377, 376*t*
  in image processing, 67–69
  models, 224
  in smart agriculture, 16–25
  via convolutional neural networks
    (CNNs), 365–368
Deep learning (DL)-based geospatial analytics
  model, 325–326
  for agriculture, 327–334
    remote sensing (RS), paddy area
      estimation, 327–328
    internet of things (IoT), 330
    land-use landcover (LULC) map data, 331
    limitations of datasets, 349–350
    material analysis, 334–337
      data source, 334–335
      raster data analysis, 335–337, 336*f*
    satellite imaginary, 328–330
      deep learning approaches, 329–330
      machine learning approaches, 328–329
    system evaluation, 341–348
      contextual analysis, 343–348, 347*t*
      ground truth measurement, 341–343, 342*f*,
        344–345*f*
      model evaluation, 341

system model design and implementation,
  337–341
  data preprocessing and feature selection,
    337–340, 338–339*f*
  process view, 337, 337*f*
  transfer learning process, 340–341
Deep learning regression network (DLRN),
  152–153
Deep neural network (DNN) model, 147–148,
  231–234, 367–368, 368*f*
deep Progressively Expanded Network (dPEN),
  329
DeepWeeds
  dataset, 224, 231
  statistical information of, 232*t*
Defect, 182
Derivative-based optimization algorithms,
  113–114
Detection and identification technology,
  224
Digital agriculture, 1–2, 129, 273
Digital soil mapping (DSM), 74, 137–138
Dimethylsulfonioproprionate (DMSP),
  244–245
Disease detection, 14–15
Disease severity (DS) stages, 286
DL toolbox Ludwig, 244–255
Domain specific language (DSL), 268
double-stranded RNA molecules (dsRNA),
  256–257
Drop out techniques, 375–377

E

Ecosystems, 200–201
Edge-based techniques, 66
e-FlyWatch system, 370
Emiliania huxleyi, 244–245
Empirical rule-based cash rents
  model, 238
End-to-end learning machine, 68
Environmental metabolomics, 239
Environmental sensors, 63
Environmental services, 206–207
Error, 181
European Space Agency Climate Change
  Initiative (ESA CCI), 144–145,
  157–158
Evapotranspiration (ET)
  estimation, 130–131
  for wheat yield prediction, 283–285, 285*t*
E-wastes, 65
Extension neural network (ENN), 13–14

F

Facebook PyTorch framework, 93
Failure, 182
False negative (FN), 187, 304–305
False positive (FP), 187, 304–305
False positive rate (FPR), 230
FAO-56 method, 130–131
Farm management system, 32
Feature extraction, 67, 111–113
Feature maps, 85, 308, 311*f*, 313–314*f*
Feature pyramid networks (FPNs), 340–341
Feed-forward neural network (FFNN),
    132–134
Fertilizer, 40
Fiber Bragg gradient (FBG), 260
Fine-tuning model, 87
Fisher's linear discriminant (FLD) analysis,
    172–173
FITRA, 39
Flux Balance Analysis, 267–268
Fly ash, 171–172
Food, 81–83
    security, 65
    shed strategy, 207–208
    system transformation, 208
Food and Agriculture Organization (FAO), 57,
    297–298
Food Price Index, 42
Forest and Climate Change, 171
Frequency domain analysis, 371
Fruit quality analysis, 8
Fruit sorting and classification, 6–7
Fully connected (FC) layers, 84
Functional genomics, 239–259
Functional link artificial neural networks
    (FLANN), 134–135
Fusarium graminearum, 258–259
Fusarium head blight 7 gene (Fhb7), 259
Fuzzy logic, 60, 135

G

Gabor surface feature extraction process, 362
Gaussian process distribution, 286
Gaussian process regression (GPR), 286
Gene-environment (GE) interactions
    for wheat yield prediction, 276, 277*t*
Genetic algorithms (GAs), 113–114, 134–135,
    371–372
Genetic programming (GP), 130–131
Genetic Regulatory Analysis for Investigational
    Tools Environment (GRANITE),
    267–270

GeoFarmer, 1–2
Geographical information system (GIS)
    data, 7, 81–83, 326–327, 330, 335,
    338, 350, 358
Geospatial analytics, 325
glimpseGRANITE, 268
Global positioning system (GPS), 7, 81–83, 358
Global Positioning System-tagged
    (GPS-tagged) map, 329–330
Google Colab, 93
GoogleNet architecture, 225–226
Gradient boosted regression trees
    (GBRTs), 39
Gradient descent, 113–114
Graph Def (.pb), 304
Graphical user interface (GUI), 268, 370
Graphics processing units (GPUs), 84
Gray-Level Cooccurrence Matrix
    (GLCM) image processing
    technique, 364–365
Greenhouse gas emissions, 182, 184*t*
Grey wolf optimization, 134–135
Ground truth measurement, 341–343, 342*f*,
    344–345*f*
Groundwater levels (GWLs), 132–134
Groundwater simulation, 132–134
Guanine (G), 244
Guidance, 224

H

Habitat suitability index (HSI), 114–116
Hand-tool technology, 61–62
Hardware configuration, 93–97
Hargreaves method, 134–135
Helically wound distributed acoustic sensing
    network, 260–267, 261–266*f*
Helmanthospura leaf spot, 308–318
Heuristic methods, 134–135
Hidden Markov model (HMM), 39–40
Highly productive (HP), 176
Histidine, 243–244
Histogram, 183–185, 186*f*
Histogram of oriented gradients (HoG),
    176, 178
Hits-at-k, 250–251
Homogalacturonan (HG), 242
Horizontal flip processes, 339–340
Horowpothana test data, 343–345, 345*f*
Human geography, 207
Human unemployment Agriculture, 65
HYDRUS-2D model, 152–153
Hyperspectral images (HSIs), 226

I

Image acquisition techniques, 66, 287
Image-based automatic detection systems, 374–377, 375*f*
Image-based methods, 224
Image compression techniques, 290, 291*t*
Image filtering techniques, 287
ImageNet, 84, 96, 96*t*
ImageNet Large Scale Visual Recognition
    Challenge, 69, 86
Image-processing techniques, 90–92, 368–370, 369*f*, 377
    in smart agriculture, 5–9
    for wheat disease detection, 287–290
Image segmentation, 66
Image tiling, 111
Impact on climate change, for agriculture
    backpropagation algorithm (BPA), 179–181, 189–192*f*
    histogram of oriented gradients
        (HoG), 178
    international status, 175
    materials and methods, 178–181
    methodology, 182–183
    national status, 174–175
    principal component analysis (PCA), 179
Inception-ResNets, 301–302
Inception-v1, 301–302
Inception-v3, 233*t*, 234*f*, 301–302
Inception-v4, 301–302
Incomplete maximum likelihood detector, 373–374
Indian agriculture fields, 274*f*
Integrated pest management (IPM), 358
Intelligent agent technology, 276–277
Intelligent algorithm, 359
Intelligent control systems, 252
Intelligent decision support system, 276–277
International Space Station, 259
International status, 175
Internet of Things (IoT), 330
    in smart agriculture, 25–32
Internet of Things-based (IoT-based) smart
    irrigation, 144–145
Intersection over Union (IoU), 341
Irrigation management, 35, 39
Irrigation monitoring system, 31
Isoleucine, 243–244

K

Kernels, 85
Kilinochchi test data, 345–346, 346*f*

k-means, 5–6
    clustering method, 137
K-nearest neighbor (K-NN), 371–372
**kwargs, 252

L

LabelImg tool, 365–366
Lagrange multiplier, 137
Land cover classification, 22
Landsat Data Continuity Mission, 282–283
Landsat images, 111, 112*f*
Landset-8, 282–283
Land-sharing model, 211
Land-use land-cover (LULC) map
    data, 331
Leaf disease detection (LDD) system, 16–21, 298–299
    model architecture, 301–303, 302*f*
    system architecture, 300–301, 301*f*
Leaf location index, 279–282
Leaf water content (LWC), 132
Leaf water potential (LWP), 132
Least squares, 135
Least squares SVM regression (LSSVR), 132, 135
LeNet-5, 301–302
Leucine, 243–244
Levenberg-Marquardt backpropagation, 364–365
Linear discriminant analysis, 371–372
Linearization, 84
Local binary pattern (LBP), 364–365
Location aware systems (LASs), 358, 361–362
Logarithmic softmax function, 97
Low productive (LP), 176
Ludwig
    classical regression in, 254*f*
    code, 250, 250*f*
    combiners, 255–259, 255*f*
    data integration process for, 251*f*
    default model, 252–253
    experiment, 246, 247*f*
    feature encoders for, 246, 248*f*
    hyperparameter visualization in, 247, 249*f*
    image classification in, 253, 253*f*
    machine learning process, 248*f*
    model, 245, 247*f*
    prediction, 246*f*
    training, 246*f*
Lysine, 243–244

M

Machine learning (ML), 84, 97, 99, 273
  algorithms, 67, 275t
    for wheat diseases detection, 286–287
    for wheat yield prediction, 276–279
  approach, 274f, 328–329
  artificial intelligence (AI), 145
  automatic detection, 374–377, 376t
  models, 130–131
  reinforcement learning, 145–146
  in smart agriculture, 9–16
  soil moisture assessment
    artificial neural network/deep neural
      network, 147–148
    classification and regression tree, 149–150
    coarser spatial resolution, 144–145
    conventional approaches, 143–144
    estimation/forecasting, prediction models
      for, 152–153
    extremely randomized trees, 150–151
    irrigation management, 143
    irrigation scheduling, 156–157
    linear regression, 146
    microwave remote sensing, 143–144
    optical remote sensing, 143–144
    pedotransfer functions, 151–152
    random forest, 150
    retrieval, remote sensing, 153–156
    satellite-derived soil moisture products,
      downscaling of, 157–158
    spatial and temporal level, 143–144
    support vector machine, 148–149
    thermal remote sensing, 143–144
  supervised learning, 145
  unsupervised learning, 145
Maize farm, 92f
Manual detection and counting techniques, 360
Map, 279
  image distortions, 350
Mapping
  systems, 63
  technologies, 224
Marine microalgae, 244–255
Mask Region-based CNN (Mask RCNN)
    model, 326–327, 330, 340–343,
    341–342f
MATLAB® software, 183–185
Max pooling, 302
  layer, 308, 316f
Mean squared error (MSE), 180–181
Mechanical-power technology, 61–62
Medium productive (MP), 176
Methionine, 243–244
Metrological simulation model, 283, 284t

Migration, 116
Ministry of Environment, 171
MobileNet, 298–299
Moderate Resolution Imaging
    Spectroradiometer (MODIS), 283
Monaragala test data, 346, 346f
Multiclass classification, 99–101, 100–102f
Multilayer perceptron (MLP), 151, 330
Multilayer perceptron neural network (MLP),
    135f, 278
Multiple linear regression (MLR), 146, 151–152
Multispectral reflectance-based methods, 74
Multistakeholder planning approach, 206
Multivariate adaptive regression splines
    (MARS) model, 130–131
Mutation, 116
Mycobacterium tuberculosis, 267

N

Naïve Bayes algorithm, 39
Nanoimaging sensors, 241–242
National Agricultural Statistics Service
    (NASS), 237
National status, 174–175
Network connectivity, 64
Neural networks (NN), 5–6, 179, 278
Next generation sequencing (NGS) tools, 259
Neyveli, 176
Neyveli Lignite Corporation (NLC), 171
Nonimage-based automatic detection,
    377–378
Normal gradient descent algorithm, 117–118
Normalized Difference Nitrogen Index
    (NDNI), 282
Normalized difference vegetation index
    (NDVI), 87–88, 154, 279–282, 329,
    336, 336f
Normalized Difference Water Index (NDWI),
    282
Numerical weather prediction (NWP), 39

O

Obstacle detection, 24
Olive fruit fly, 357–358
  automatic detection and counting techniques,
    363–373
    artificial neural networks (ANN), 364–365
    deep learning via CNNs, 365–368
    image processing techniques, 368–370,
      369f
    optoacoustic spectral analysis, 370–371
    spectroscopy hyperspectral imaging
      process, 371–373, 372f

image-based automatic detection, 374–377, 375*f*

deep learning automatic detection, 374–377, 376*t*

image processing techniques, 377

machine learning automatic detection, 374–377, 376*t*

manual detection and counting techniques, 360

nonimage-based automatic detection, 377–378

recognition systems, 359–373

semiautomatic detection, 373–374

and counting techniques, 361–363

Operational Land Imager (OLI), 282–283

Optimization layer, 113–121

Optoacoustic spectral analysis, 370–371

Optoacoustic spectrum detection, 377–378

Otsu method, 66

Overlapping process, 339*f*

P

Paddy cultivation, 336–337, 348–349

Paddy fields detection metrics, 345*t*

Pan evaporation estimation, 134–135

Parasitized column, 247–250

Partial least squares (PLS), 132

Partially automated testing, 170

Partially manual testing, 170

Participative management strategy, 214–215

Particle swarm optimization (PSO) algorithm, 113–114, 130–131

Pedotransfer functions (PTFs), 144–145, 151–152

Penman–Monteith (PM) method, 130–131

Performance metrics, 229–230

Permaculture, 213–214

Pesticides, 40

Phenylalanine, 243–244

Photoautotrophic strategies, 240–241

Photoheterotrophic strategies, 240–241

Plantation, 91*f*

Plant disease detection, 21–22, 65–73

challenges, 70–73

image processing in agriculture, 5–6

overview, 65–67

performance analysis, 70

prediction and, 39–40

using image processing and deep learning, 69

Plant disease identification, 5–6

Plant leaves images, 93*t*

Plant life biomass, 279–282

Plant recognition, 22–23

Plant-silicon cycle, agricultural factors in, 259–260

Plant species identification, 7

Plate mobility index (PMI), 114–115

Plate tectonics-based optimization (PBO) algorithm, 114–115, 115*b*, 126*t*

Pollinators, 255–259

Pooling layers, 84, 308, 310*f*

Precision, 230

farming, 7, 35–36, 57–65

farming fields, 129

fertilization, 137

in-row weed control, 224

Precision agriculture (PA), 58, 81–83

artificial intelligence (AI), 59–61

autonomous robots used in, 60, 61*f*

challenges, 63–65

definition, 57–58

foundation of, 59

objectives and design, 61–63

smart farming (SF), 59–60

steps, 60–61

technologies, 58*f*

Preprocessing layer, 111

Principal component analysis (PCA), 5–6, 179, 182, 183*f*, 185–187, 371–372

Protein-protein interactions (PPIs), 239

Python, customized layer in, 97, 97*f*

Q

Quadratic discriminant analysis (QDA), 371–372

Quality assurance, 182

Quality control, 182

R

Radial basis function (RBF), 151

neural network, 132

Radial basis network (RBN), 172–173

Radical urban agroecological politics, 203

Raman spectroscopy, 259

Rand Index, 230

Random forest (RF), 21–22, 150, 277

Raster data analysis, 335–337, 336*f*

Raster models, 335

Recall, 230

Receiver operating curve, 230

Rectified linear unit (ReLU), 85, 306–308, 312*f*

activation function, 308, 312*f*, 315*f*

Red, green, and blue (RGB) images, 13, 87

Region of interest (ROI), 66, 367–368
Region proposal network (RPN), 367–368
Regression method, 277
Regularization techniques, 375–377
Remote sensing (RS), 8, 326–327, 330, 351
  paddy area estimation, 327–328
  technology, 81–83
Residual network (ResNet), 86
ResNet-50, 233t, 234f, 301–302
ResNeXt-50, 301–302
Resolution multiplier, 226
RGB digital images, 132
RNA interference (RNAi), 256–257
Root, segmentation of, 23
Root mean square propagation (RMSprop),
  113–114, 117
Roseobacticide (RSB), 244–245
Rule-based approach, 110

S
SAFAL-FASAL android application, 303–304,
  303f, 318–321, 320–322f
Satellite data classification, 340
Satellite image bands, 334–335, 335f
Satellite imaginary, 328–330
  and deep learning (DL), 331–334, 332–334t
Saved model (.pb), 304
Scalable vector graphics (SVGs), 335f
Self-organizing map (SOM), 279
Semiautomatic detection, 373–374
  and counting techniques, 361–363
Sensitivity, 305
Sensors, 64
  data fusion, 188t
Sex pheromones, 359
Simulation framework, 268
Smart agriculture, 2f
  application, 3f
  data mining (DM) in, 36–42
    climate condition, 42, 43–46t
    crop yield prediction, 41–42
    irrigation management, 39
    optimum management of inputs, 40
    pest monitoring, 40
    prediction and detection of plant diseases,
      39–40
  deep learning (DL) in, 16–25
    cattle race classification, 25, 26–29t
    crop type classification, 22
    crop yield estimation, 23
    fruit counting, 23–24
    land cover classification, 22
    leaf disease detection, 16–21
    obstacle detection, 24

    plant disease detection, 21–22
    plant recognition, 22–23
    prediction of soil moisture, 25
    segmentation of root and soil, 23
    weeds identification, 24–25
  image processing in, 5–9
    crop and land assessment, 8
    fruit quality analysis, 8
    fruit sorting and classification,
      6–7
    plant disease identification, 5–6
    plant species identification, 7
    precision farming, 7
    weed recognition, 8–9, 10–12t
  internet of things (IoT) in, 25–32
    agricultural drone, 32, 33–34t
    climate condition, 30
    crop yield, 30
    farm management system, 32
    irrigation monitoring system, 31
    optimum time for plant and harvesting, 31
    pest and crop disease, 30–31
    soil patter, 30
    tracking and tracing, 31–32
  machine learning (ML) in, 9–16
    crop quality, 15
    disease detection, 14–15
    soil management, 16, 17–20t
    species recognition, 15
    weed recognition, 15
    yield prediction, 13–14
  methodology, 4, 4–5f
  technologies, 2f
  wireless sensor networks (WSNs) in,
    32–36
    climate condition, 36, 37–38t
    irrigation management, 35
    precision farming, 35–36
    soil moisture prediction, 35
Smart farming (SF), 1–2, 59–60, 63, 273
Smart positioning systems, 63
Soft computing approaches, 130–131
Soft-computing methods, 172
Softmax activation function, 303
Softmax classification layer, 121–122
Softmax function, 121–122
Software bug, 181
Software configuration, 93–97
Soil, segmentation of, 23
Soil Adjusted Vegetation Index (SAVI), 282
Soil fertilizer estimation, 137
Soil health management tools, 63
Soil management, 16,
  17–20t

artificial intelligence applications in
(*see* Artificial intelligence (AI)
applications, in soil management)
Soil mapping, 137–138
Soil microbial metabolites, applications of,
239–240
Soil Moisture Active Passive (SMAP),
144–145, 157–158
Soil Moisture and Ocean Salinity (SMOS),
144–145, 157–158
Soil moisture assessment
artificial neural network/deep neural
network, 147–148
classification and regression tree, 149–150
coarser spatial resolution, 144–145
conventional approaches, 143–144
estimation/forecasting, prediction models
for, 152–153
extremely randomized trees, 150–151
irrigation management, 143
irrigation scheduling, 156–157
linear regression, 146
machine learning (ML)
artificial intelligence (AI), 145
reinforcement learning, 145–146
supervised learning, 145
unsupervised learning, 145
microwave remote sensing, 143–144
optical remote sensing, 143–144
pedotransfer functions, 151–152
random forest, 150
retrieval, remote sensing, 153–156
satellite-derived soil moisture products,
downscaling of, 157–158
spatial and temporal level, 143–144
support vector machine, 148–149
thermal remote sensing, 143–144
Soil moisture content, for wheat yield
prediction, 283–285, 285t
Soil moisture
data, 183–185, 185t, 187t
prediction, 25, 35
Soil patter, 30
Soil quality, 112
Soil temperature (ST), 136–137
Soil texture, 73, 111
classification algorithm, 73–74
Soil type, 112–113
Soil water content (SWC), 283–285
determination, 136
Soil water retention curve (SWRC), 151–152
Solar diffuser (SD), 283
Soup images, 370
Spatial-temporal data, 328

Spectral image-based methods, 224
Spectral radiometric calibration meeting
(SRCA), 283
Spectroscopy-based detection, 378
Spectroscopy hyperspectral imaging process,
371–373, 372f
Spectrum-based methods, 224
Spiroketal, 359
Stakeholders, 199, 211–212
Statistical pattern recognition, 252
Stigmergy, 268
Stochastic gradient descent (SGD),
113–114
Sugarcane, 297–298
Sugarcane leaf disease
classes, 300, 300t, 300f
dataset, 299–300
experimentation, 305–308
leaf disease detection (LDD)
classification, 308–318, 317f
model architecture, 301–303, 302f
system architecture, 300–301, 301f
method of evaluation, 304–305
overview, 297–299
performance evaluation, 318, 320t
SAFAL-FASAL android application,
303–304, 303f, 318–321, 320–322f
Suitability index variables (SIVs),
115–116
Sun diffuser stability reveal (SDSM), 283
Supervised Kohonen networks (SKNs), 279,
280–281t
Supervised learning processes, 274, 292f
Support vector machine-firefly approach
(SVM-FFA), 130–131
Support vector machines (SVMs), 5–6,
148–149, 152–153, 226, 278, 328
Support vector regression (SVR), 148,
152, 286
Sustainable agriculture, 351
approach, 223
SVM–wavelet, 130–131
System for Automated Geoscientific Analyses
tool, 337–338

T

Takagi-Sugeno fuzzy inference device,
278–279
TFLite API, 304, 304f
TFLite converter architecture, 304, 305f
TFLite Task Library, 304
Three dimensional direct stochastic optical
reconstruction microscopy
(3DdSTORM), 242

Threonine, 243–244
Threshold-based techniques, 66
Thymine (T), 244
Time domain analysis, 371
Time of use (ToU) model, 39
Tissue chip technology, 243
Transfer learning process, 340–341
Tropodithietic acid (TDA), 244–245
True negative (TN), 187, 304–305
True positive (TP), 187, 304–305
True positive rate (TPR), 187, 230
Tryptophan, 243–244
TSM-Clark algorithm, 174

U

Unacceptable class, 373
U-Net models, 351
Unhealthy leaves, 99
Uninfected column, 247–250
University of the Balearic Islands (UIB), 361–362
Unmanned aerial vehicles (UAVs), 81–83, 88–89, 89f, 153–154
    data collection and processing, 88–89
    specification, 89–90
Unstable climate, 63
Unsupervised learning
    processes, 274
    systems, 252
Urban agroecology, 200–201, 206–207
Urban agroforestry ecology, 212
Urban decentralization, 210
Urban ecology, 210
Urban food forestry, 212
Urban sprawl, 210
Urban sustainable agroecology, 200
Uva province, 343

V

Validation, 182
Valine, 243–244
Vector models, 335
Verification, 182
Vertical flip processes, 339–340
VGG-16, 301–302
V-groove black frame, 283
Visual indicators, 65

W

Water availability, 279–282
Water footprint (WF) modeling, 132, 133t
Water management, artificial intelligence
    applications in. See Artificial
    intelligence (AI), in water management
Water Quality Index (WQI), 174

Water shed algorithm, 372–373
Web-based system, with multiple regression for
    wheat disease detection, 287, 289t
WeedNet, 226–229, 233t, 234f
    architecture, 226–228, 228f
    complexity analysis, 228–229, 229t
    data set, 231
    evaluation, 231
    performance metrics, 229–230
        accuracy, 230
        area under curve (AUC), 230
        precision, 230
        recall, 230
    residual block, 227, 227f
    scaled permuter architecture, 227f, 228
Weed recognition, 8–9, 10–12t, 15
Weeds identification, 24–25, 223
Weight decay, 94
Whale optimization algorithm, 134–135
Wheat diseases detection, 285–290
    image-processing techniques for,
        287–290
    machine learning algorithms for, 286–287
    web-based system with multiple regression
        for, 287, 289t
Wheat yield prediction, 276–285
    CERES-Wheat model for, 283, 285t
    evapotranspiration (ET) for, 283–285, 285t
    gene-environment (GE) interactions, 276,
        277t
    machine learning algorithms for, 276–279
    remote and satellite data for,
        279–283
    soil moisture content for, 283–285, 285t
Widespread urbanization, 210
Width multiplier, 226
WiFi protocol, 361
Wireless sensor networks, 63
    in smart agriculture, 32–36
World Food Studies (WOFOST) crop
        simulation model, 279
WorldView-3 imagery, 329

X

Xception, 301–302

Y

Yield prediction, 13–14
YOLO-based automatic counting approach,
        366–367, 366f
YOLO models, 351

Z

Zigbee, 361
    network, 30–31

Printed in the United States
by Baker & Taylor Publisher Services